THE CHANGING PRACTICES OF INTERNATIONAL LAW

With more than 158 000 treaties and some 125 judicial organizations, international law has become an inescapable factor in world politics since the Second World War. In recent years, however, international law has also been increasingly challenged as states are voicing concerns that it is producing unintended effects and accuse international courts of judicial activism. This book provides an important corrective to existing theories of international law by focusing on how states respond to increased legalization and rely on legal expertise to manoeuvre within and against international law. Through a number of case studies, covering a wide range of topical issues, such as surveillance, environmental regulation, migration and foreign investments, the book argues that the expansion and increased institutionalization of international law itself have created the structural premise for this type of politics of international law. More international law paradoxically increases states' political room of manoeuvre in international society.

TANJA AALBERTS is Professor of Law at the Vrije Universiteit, Amsterdam and Director of the Centre for the Politics of Transnational Law. She has a PhD in International Relations, and her research focuses on the interplay between international law and international politics in practices of governance.

THOMAS GAMMELTOFT-HANSEN is Research Director at the Raoul Wallenberg Institute of Human Rights and Humanitarian Law, Professor II at Oslo University, and Honorary Professor of Law at Aarhus University. He received his PhD in International Law from Aarhus University, his MSc in Refugee Studies from the University of Oxford and his MA in Political Science from the University of Copenhagen.

THE CHANGING PRACTICES OF INTERNATIONAL LAW

Edited by

TANJA AALBERTS

Vrije Universiteit, Amsterdam

THOMAS GAMMELTOFT-HANSEN

Raoul Wallenberg Institute

CAMBRIDGE
UNIVERSITY PRESS

CAMBRIDGE
UNIVERSITY PRESS

University Printing House, Cambridge CB2 8BS, United Kingdom

One Liberty Plaza, 20th Floor, New York, NY 10006, USA

477 Williamstown Road, Port Melbourne, VIC 3207, Australia

314–321, 3rd Floor, Plot 3, Splendor Forum, Jasola District Centre,
New Delhi - 110025, India

79 Anson Road, #06-04/06, Singapore 079906

Cambridge University Press is part of the University of Cambridge.

It furthers the University's mission by disseminating knowledge in the pursuit of education, learning, and research at the highest international levels of excellence.

www.cambridge.org
Information on this title: www.cambridge.org/9781108425971
DOI: 10.1017/9781108349420

First published 2018

Printed in the United Kingdom by Clays, St. Ives plc

A catalogue record for this publication is available from the British Library

Library of Congress Cataloging-in-Publication data
Names: Aalberts, Tanja E., 1976–, editor. | Gammeltoft-Hansen, Thomas, editor.
Title: The changing practices of international law / Edited by Tanja Aalberts, Vrije Universiteit, Amsterdam, Thomas Gammeltoft-Hansen, Raoul Wallenberg Institute.
Description: New York : Cambridge University Press, 2017. | Includes bibliographical references and index.
Identifiers: LCCN 2017042218 | ISBN 9781108425971 (alk. paper)
Subjects: LCSH: International law.
Classification: LCC KZ3410 .C43 2017 | DDC 341 – dc23
LC record available at https://lccn.loc.gov/2017042218

ISBN 978-1-108-42597-1 Hardback

CONTENTS

List of Figures and Tables *page* vii
Notes on Contributors viii
Preface xi
Table of Cases xiii

1 Introduction: The Changing Practices of International Law 1
THOMAS GAMMELTOFT-HANSEN AND TANJA AALBERTS

2 Sovereignty Games, International Law and Politics 26
TANJA AALBERTS AND THOMAS GAMMELTOFT-HANSEN

3 Abandonment, Construction and Denial: The Formation of a Zone 45
MARGARETA BRUMMER

4 Backlash and State Strategies in International Investment Law 70
MALCOLM LANGFORD, DANIEL BEHN AND OLE KRISTIAN FAUCHALD

5 'Part of the Game': Government Strategies against European Litigation Concerning Migrant Rights 103
MORITZ BAUMGÄRTEL

6 The Disaggregated Law of Global Mass Surveillance 129
ITAMAR MANN

7 Legalization in International Environmental Law 158
JAYE ELLIS

8 Search and Rescue as a Geopolitics of International Law 188
THOMAS GAMMELTOFT-HANSEN AND TANJA AALBERTS

9 Conclusion: The Dark Side of Legalization 208
TANJA AALBERTS AND THOMAS GAMMELTOFT-HANSEN

Bibliography 220
Index 240

FIGURES AND TABLES

Figures

4.1 Mapping state tactics *page* 74
4.2 Principal tactics 77
4.3 Claimant–investor success ratios 100

Tables

5.1 Number of Third-Party Interventions by Governments before the CJEU and the ECtHR 120

CONTRIBUTORS

TANJA AALBERTS is Professor in the Department of Transnational Legal Studies, at the Vrije Universiteit, Amsterdam and Director of the Centre for the Politics of Transnational Law (www.ceptl.org). Her research focuses on the interplay between international law and international politics in practices of governance. She is the founder and series editor of the Routledge book series Politics of Transnational Law and editor for the *Leiden Journal of International Law.*

MORITZ BAUMGÄRTEL is Assistant Professor at Utrecht University and University College Roosevelt. He holds a PhD in Law from the Université libre de Bruxelles (2016), an MPhil in International Relations from the University of Cambridge, an LLM in Public International Law from Utrecht University and a BA in Social Sciences from University College Roosevelt. In recent years, he has been a lecturer at Tilburg University and has held visiting positions at University of Michigan Law School, Duke Law School and the University of Copenhagen. His research concerns the rights of vulnerable migrants and is currently focused on the legal obligations and policy initiatives of cities and local governments in this domain.

DANIEL BEHN is a Lecturer in Law at the Unviersity of Liverpool and Postdoctoral Research Fellow in International Investment Law and Arbitration at the PluriCourts Centre for the Study of the Legitimate Roles of the Judiciary in the Global Order, Faculty of Law, University of Oslo. He was previously a visiting professor at Pennsylvania State University, and his research interests relate to theoretical and methodological issues in public international law with a specialized interest in international dispute settlement. His work currently focuses on empirical legal studies relating to international adjudication, specifically investment treaty arbitration.

MARGARETA BRUMMER is currently a PhD candidate in the Faculty of Law, University of Helsinki and Research Fellow at the Erik Castrén

Institute of International Law. Her research interests include questions of sovereign territory and territorial jurisdiction, law of the sea and the history of the privatization of land ownership.

JAYE ELLIS is Associate Professor in the Faculty of Law and School of Environment, McGill University. She teaches public international law, international environmental law and environmental epistemology and ethics. Current research projects focus on transnational law, intersections between law and science, rule of law in transnational and international spheres and risk and uncertainty in public and private law.

OLE KRISTIAN FAUCHALD is Professor at PluriCourts Centre for the Study of the Legitimate Roles of the Judiciary in the Global Order, Faculty of Law, University of Oslo. Fields of research include international investment and trade and environmental law with a main focus on empirically based research on international courts and tribunals. Fauchald coordinates research on investment treaty arbitration at PluriCourts.

THOMAS GAMMELTOFT-HANSEN is Research Director at the Raoul Wallenberg Institute of Human Rights and Humanitarian Law, Professor II at Oslo University, and Honorary Professor of Law at Aarhus University. He received his PhD in International Law from Aarhus University, his MSc in Refugee Studies from the University of Oxford and his MA in Political Science from the University of Copenhagen. In addition to his academic work, Thomas has served as a member of the Danish Refugee Appeals Board and as adviser and consultant to a number of international organizations, governmental institutions and international non-governmental organizations. He is the editor of the series Routledge Studies in Human Rights and is on the editorial board of Cambridge Asylum and Migration Studies.

MALCOLM LANGFORD is Associate Professor, Faculty of Law, University of Oslo and Co-Director of the Centre on Law and Social Transformation, University of Bergen and Chr. Michelsen Institute. He has published widely on human rights, international development, investment arbitration, comparative constitutionalism and the politics of the legal profession. Malcolm Langford is the co-editor of the Cambridge University Press book series Human Rights and Globalization and sits on the editorial board of the *Australian Journal of Human Rights*.

ITAMAR MANN is Senior Lecturer at the University of Haifa Faculty of Law. He works in several areas of international and comparative law, often engaging history and political theory. Particularly, he has focused on human rights, refugee and migration law, international criminal law and national security issues. Itamar Mann also provides legal advice on issues related to his areas of research. He has previously worked as a consultant for Human Rights Watch and the Open Society Foundations on issues related to refugee law. He has also briefly practised human rights and criminal defence law in his home country, Israel. He holds an LLB from Tel Aviv University and LLM and JSD degrees from Yale Law School.

PREFACE

It is with an equal amount of relief and anxiety that we put these last words to paper before submitting the present manuscript to the publisher: relief because we are past the submission deadline and the arduous process of getting this volume to completion has tested the patience of several contributors as well as our families, and anxiety because even in just the last months of editing, several areas of international law have been tested and challenged in ways that few thought possible. What started out as an attempt to provide a small but important corrective to the dominant liberal paradigm in international law has been overtaken by various political head-on confrontations with international law, from the European Union and multilateral trade treaties to refugees, human rights and the Paris Agreement. Who knows what else might happen in the coming months and years?

Watching these events unfold, we, like many of our colleagues, are struck by an eerie feeling that doing away with the so-called progress narrative in international law is not just a matter of intellectual integrity but a lived reality. At the same time, however, it becomes doubly important to recognize just how fundamentally international law has come to shape almost all aspects of human life. The last fifty years have seen a formidable transformation of international affairs, reshaping what it means to be a sovereign state, empowering individuals and corporations and building a whole new cadre of international institutions. That such profound developments prompt resistance is perhaps not surprising; that scholars and practitioners have so long ignored these dynamics is perhaps more so.

The present volume is a truly collective endeavour. The initial idea emerged on a bench in the garden of Villa Schifanoia at the European University Institute and matured during some long walks around Ann Arbor, Michigan. The overall framework was subsequently developed at an unusually stimulating two-day authors' workshop in Reykjavik, Iceland. We would like to recognize the important contribution of each of the participants there to developing the overall argument and framing of the volume, including several who did not contribute a chapter to the final volume: Ciaran Burke, Monika Ambrus, Yohan Ariffin, Claudio Brenni, Anna Dolidze, Erlend Leonhardsen, Isobel Roele, Frederik Rosén and Page Wilson, as well as Dadi Stigmarsson and Eirikur Bergmann from Bifrost University, who hosted the workshop. Funding for this workshop was provided by COST Action 1003: 'International Law between Constitutionalisation and Fragmentation'. For the past four years, this network has served as a sort of extended academic family, and we are deeply indebted to Wouter Werner for his work to create this network and his intellectual and personal generosity to us and others throughout. We would also like to thank Nik Rajkovic for many stimulating interdisciplinary exchanges and his infectious scholarly enthusiasm, even if our collective project with him helped delay the present one.

We are furthermore grateful to Francisca van Schuppen and Sofie Viborg Jensen for their invaluable assistance in preparing the final manuscript. Last, but not least, we would like to thank Finola O'Sullivan and her entire team at Cambridge University Press for their impeccable support.

TABLE OF CASES

International Courts

International Court of Justice

Corfu Case (United Kingdom v. Albania), ICJ Reports 4, 9 April 1949 28, 60–61, 167–68, 174
Fisheries Jurisdiction Case (Spain/Canada), ICJ Reports 432, 4 December 1998 174
Gabčíkovo-Nagymaros Case (Hungary/Slovakia), 25 September 1997 174
MOX Plant Case (*Ireland v. United Kingdom*), no. 10, 3 December 2001 174
Case Concerning Military and Paramilitary Activities In and Against Nicaragua (Nicaragua v. United States of America), 27 June 1986 68, 80–81
Nuclear Test Cases (Australia/France; New Zealand/France), ICJ Reports 253, 20 December 1974 173–79
Pulp on the River Uruguay (Argentina v. Uruguay), 20 April 2010 164, 174
Southern Bluefin Tuna Cases (New Zealand v. Japan; Australia v. Japan), 27 August 1999 174
Whaling in the Antarctic (Australia v. Japan: New Zealand intervening), 31 March 2014 174

Permanent Court of International Justice

Island of Palmas Case (Netherlands v. United States), 2 RIAA 829, 4 April 1928 38–39, 167–68, 174

International Criminal Tribunal for the Former Yugoslavia

Prosecutor v. Duško Tadić, Judgement, Case no. IT-94-1-A, 15 July 1999 68

Human Rights Committee

López Burgos v. Uruguay, UN Doc. A/36/40. 6 June 1979 65

European Court of Human Rights

Abdulaziz, Cabales and Balkandali v. United Kingdom (Application nos. 9214/80, 9473/81, 9474/81), 28 May 1985 105
Abu Zubaydah v. Lithuania (Application no. 46454/11), pending 61–63, 66

Al-Nashiri v. Poland (Application no. 28761/11), 24 July 2014 61–63, 66
Al-Saadoon and Mufdhi v. United Kingdom (Application no. 61498/08), 2 March 2010 65, 199
Al-Skeini and Others v. United Kingdom (Application no. 55721/07), 7 July 2011 64–65, 201
Bahaddar v. the Netherlands (Application no. 25894/94), 19 February 1998 114
Bankovic and Others v. Belgium, Czech Republic, Denmark, France, Germany, Greece, Hungary, Iceland, Italy, Luxemburg, Netherlands, Norway, Poland, Portugal, Spain, Turkey and the UK (Application no. 5207/99), 12 December 2001 201
El-Masri v. the Former Yugoslav Republic of Macedonia (Application no. 39630/09), 13 December 2012 63–64
Gebremedhin [Gaberamadhien] v. France (Application no. 25389/05), 26 April 2007 109, 116
Hirsi Jamaa and Others v. Italy, European Court of Human Rights (Application no. 27765/09), 23 February 2012 108, 110–14, 123–26, 198–200, 202
Husayn (Abu Zubaydah) v. Poland (Application no.7511/13), 24 July 2014 48, 60–64, 66
Hussun and others v. Italy (Application no. 10171/05), 19 January 2010 113–14
Ilascu and Others v. Moldova and Russia (Application no. 48787/99), 8 July 2004 62–63
Issa and Others v. Turkey (Application no. 31821/96), 16 November 2004 65, 68
Jaloud v. The Netherlands (Application no. 47708/08), 20 November 2014 65–66, 68
Jeunesse v. the Netherlands (Application no. 12738/10), 3 October 2014 107
K.R.S. v. the United Kingdom (Application no. 32733/08), 2 December 2008 108
Medvedyed and Others v. France (Application no. 3394/03), 29 March 2010 65, 105
Moustaquim v. Belgium (Application no. 12313/86), 9 February 1991 105
M.S.S. v. Belgium and Greece (Application no. 30696/09), 21 January 2011 108–09, 114, 120, 125
N.A. v. the United Kingdom (Application no. 25904/07), 17 July 2008 107, 112, 114
Pad and Others v. Turkey (Application no. 60167/00), 28 June 2007 201
Paposhvili v. Belgium (Application no. 41738/10), 13 December 2016 115
Ramzy v. the Netherlands (Application no. 25424/05), 27 May 2008 120–22
Rodrigues Da Silva & Hoogkamer v. the Netherlands (Application no. 50435/99), 31 January 2006 107
Salah Sheekh v. the Netherlands (Application no. 1948/04), 11 January 2007 107, 114, 116
Sharifi and others v. Italy and Greece (Application no. 16643/09), 21 October 2014 109
S.J. v. Belgium (Application no. 70055/10), 19 March 2015 109, 114–15, 119
Sufi and Elmi v. the United Kingdom (Application nos. 8319/07 and 11449/07), 28 June 2011 107, 112, 127
T.I. v. the United Kingdom (Application no. 43844/98), 7 March 2000 108

Tarakhel v. Switzerland (Application no. 29217/12), 4 November 2014 109, 121, 123–24
V.M. and others v. Belgium (Application no. 60125/11), 17 November 2016 114
Xhavara and fifteen v. Italy and Albania, European Court of Human Rights (Application no. 39473/98), 11 January 2001 199

Court of Justice of the European Union

Case C-465/07, *Meki Elgafaji, Noor Elgafaji v. Staatssecretaris van Justitie*, [2009] ECR I-921 107
Case C-578/08, *Rhimou Chakroun v. Minister van Buitenlandse Zaken*, [2010] ECR I-1839 108
Case C-34/09, *Gerardo Ruiz Zambrano v. Office national de l'emploi (ONEm)*, [2011] ECR I-1177 111, 113, 116, 120–22
Case C-155/11 PPU, *Bibi Mohammad Imran v. Minister van Buitenlandse Zaken*, [2011] ECR I-5095 117
Case C-434/09, *Shirley McCarthy v. Secretary of State for the Home Department*, [2011] ECR I-3375 111
Case C-153/14, *Minister van Buitenlandse Zaken v. K and A*, ECLI:EU:C:2015:453 117
Case C-362/14, *Maximillian Schrems v. Data Protection Commissioner* [2015] 135
Joined Cases C-411/10 and C-493/10, *N. S. v. Secretary of State for the Home Department* and *M. E. and Others v. Refugee Applications Commissioner and Minister for Justice, Equality and Law Reform*, [2011] ECR I-13905 109
Joined Cases C-71/11 and C-99/11, *Bundesrepublik Deutschland v. Y and Z*, ECLI:EU:C: 2012:518 107
Joined Cases C-199/12 to C-201/12, *Minister voor Immi- gratie en Asiel v. X, Y, and Z*, ECLI:EU:C:2013:720 111, 117–18
Joined Cases C-148/13 to C-150/13, *A, B, and C, v. Staatssecretaris van Veiligheid en Justitie*, EU:C:2014:2406 107

Permanent Court of Arbitration

Aeroport Belbek LLC and Mr. Igor Valerievich Kolomoisky v. The Russian Federation, PCA Case no. 2014-30, pending 87
Bernardus Henricus Funnekotter and others v. Republic of Zimbabwe, ICSID Case No. ARB/05/6, Award, 22 April 2009 96
Chagos Marine Protected Area Arbitration (Mauritius v. United Kingdom), UNCITRAL, PCA Case no. 2011–03, Award, 18 March 2015 45, 58
Chevron Corporation (USA) & Texaco Petroleum Company (USA) v. The Republic of Ecuador (Chevron I), UNCITRAL, PCA Case no. 34877, Award, 31 August 2011 95

Chevron Corporation & Texaco Petroleum Corporation v. The Republic of Ecuador (Chevron II), UNCITRAL, PCA Case no. 2009-23, pending 95
Everest Estate LLC and others v. The Russian Federation, PCA Case no. 2015-36, pending 87
Farouk Bozbey v. Turkmenistan, UNCITRAL, discontinued 16 August 2013 93
Hesham T. M. Al Warraq v. Republic of Indonesia (Al Warraq), UNCITRAL, Award, 15 December 2014 91–92
Hulley Enterprises Limited (Cyprus) v. The Russian Federation, UNCITRAL, PCA Case no. AA 226, Award, 18 July 2014 96
PJSC CB PrivatBank and Finance Company Finilon LLC v. The Russian Federation, PCA Case no. 2015-21, pending 87
Republic of Ecuador v. United States of America, UNCITRAL, PCA Case no. 2012-5, Award, 29 September 2012 95
Sanum Investments Limited v. Lao People's Democratic Republic, UNCITRAL, PCA Case no. 2013-13 94
South China Sea case (Republic of the Philippines v. People's Republic of China), PCA Case no. 2013-19, 12 July 2016 164, 174
Veteran Petroleum Limited (Cyprus) v. The Russian Federation, UNCITRAL, PCA Case no. AA 228, Award, 18 July 2014 96
Walter Bau A.G. v. Kingdom of Thailand, UNCITRAL, Award, 1 July 2009 96
Yukos Universal Limited (Isle of Man) v. The Russian Federation, UNCITRAL, PCA Case no. AA 227, Award, 18 July 2014 96

International Arbitral Tribunal

Trail Smelter Arbitral Decision (United States v. Canada). Trail Smelter Arbitral Tribunal. Reports of International Arbitral Awards 3, 16 April 1938 and 11 March 1941 168

International Centre for Settlement of Investment Disputes (ICSID) Cases

Bernhard von Pezold and Others v. Republic of Zimbabwe (Von Pezold), ICSID Case No. ARB/10/15, Award, 28 July 2015 89–90
Border Timbers Limited, Timber Products International (Private) Limited and Hangani Development Co. (Private) Limited v. Republic of Zimbabwe (Border Timbers), ICSID Case No. ARB/10/25, Award, 28 July 2015 89–90
Caratube International Oil Company LLP v. Republic of Kazakhstan (Caratube I), ICSID Case No. ARB/08/12, Award, 5 June 2012 90–91
Caratube International Oil Company LLP and Devincci Salah Hourani v. Republic of Kazakhstan (Caratube II), ICSID Case No. ARB/13/13, pending 90–91
Cargill Incorporated v. United Mexican States, ICSID Case No. ARB(AF)/05/2, Award, 18 September 2009 97

Churchill Mining and Planet Mining Pty Ltd, formerly ARB/12/40 v. Republic of Indonesia (Churchill), ICSID Case No. ARB/12/40 and 12/14, Award, 6 December 2016 92
Crystallex International Corp. v. Bolivarian Republic of Venezuela, ICSID Case No. ARB(AF)/11/2, Award, 14 April 2016 97
Flughafen Zürich A.G. and Gestión e Ingeniería IDC S.A. v. Bolivarian Republic of Venezuela, ICSID Case No. ARB/10/19, Award, 18 November 2014 97
Gold Reserve Inc. v. Bolivarian Republic of Venezuela, ICSID Case No. ARB(AF)/09/1, Award, 22 September 2014 97
Hydro S.r.L. and others v. Republic of Albania (Hydro), ICSID Case No. ARB/15/28, pending 91
Ioan Micula, Viorel Micula and others v. Romania (Micula), ICSID Case no. ARB/05/20, Award, 11 December 2013 97–98
Italba Corporation v. Oriental Republic of Uruguay, ICSID Case No. ARB/16/9, pending 92
OI European Group B.V. v. Bolivarian Republic of Venezuela, ICSID Case No. ARB/11/25, Award, 10 March 2015 97
Piero Foresti, Laura de Carli & Others v. The Republic of South Africa, ICSID Case No. ARB(AF)/07/01, discontinued 4 August 2010 84
Quiborax S.A. and Non-Metallic Minerals S.A. v. Plurinational State of Bolivia (Quiborax), ICSID Case No. ARB/06/2, Award, 16 September 2015 90
Railroad Development Corporation v. Republic of Guatemala, ICSID Case No. ARB/07/23, Award, 29 June 2012 97
Rumeli Telekom A.S. and Telsim Mobil Telekomunikasyon Hizmetleri A.S. v. Republic of Kazakhstan, ICSID Case No. ARB/05/16, Award, 29 July 2008 97
Rusoro Mining Ltd. v. Bolivarian Republic of Venezuela, ICSID Case No. ARB(AF)/12/5, Award, 22 August 2016 97
Sistem Mühendislik Inşaat Sanayi ve Ticaret A.Ş. v. Kyrgyz Republic, ICSID Case No. ARB(AF)/06/1, Award, 9 September 2009 96
Tenaris S.A. and Talta-Trading e Marketing Sociedade Unipessoal Lda. v. Bolivarian Republic of Venezuela (Tenaris I), ICSID Case No. ARB/11/26, Award, 29 January 2016 97
Tenaris S.A. and Talta-Trading e Marketing Sociedade Unipessoal Lda. v. Bolivarian Republic of Venezuela (Tenaris II), ICSID Case No. ARB/11/26, Award, 12 December 2016 97
Tidewater Investment SRL and Tidewater Caribe C.A. v. Bolivarian Republic of Venezuela, ICSID Case No. ARB/10/5, Award 13 March 2015 97
Venezuela Holdings B.V. v. Bolivarian Republic of Venezuela, ICSID Case No. ARB/07/27, Award, 9 October 2014 97
Vestey Group Ltd. v. Bolivarian Republic of Venezuela, ICSID Case No. ARB/06/4, Award, 15 April 2016 97

Domestic Arbitration Bodies

Arbitration Institute of the Stockholm Chamber of Commerce

Mr. Franz Sedelmayer v. The Russian Federation, SCC, Award, 7 July 1998 96

Petrobart Limited v. Kyrgyz Republic, SCC, Case no. 126/2003, Award, 29 March 2005 96

Renta 4 S.V.S.A, Ahorro Corporación Emergentes F.I., Ahorro Corporación Eurofondo F.I., Rovime Inversiones SICAV S.A., Quasar de Valors SICAV S.A., Orgor de Valores SICAV S.A., GBI 9000 SICAV S.A. v. The Russian Federation, SCC, Case no. 24/2007, Award, 20 July 2012 96

RosInvest Co UK Ltd. v. The Russian Federation, SCC, Case no. V079/2005, Award, 12 September 2010 96

Moscow Chamber of Commerce and Industry

Lee John Beck & Central Asian Development Corporation v. Kyrgyz Republic, MCCI, Award, 13 November 2014 96

OKKV (OKKB) and others v. Kyrgyz Republic, MCCI, Award, 21 November 2013 96

Stans Energy v. Kyrgyz Republic, MCCI, Award, 30 April 2014 96

Cairo Regional Center For International Commercial Arbitration

Mohamed Abdulmohsen Al-Kharafi and Sons Co. v. Libya, CRCICA, Award, 22 March 2013 97

Domestic Courts

Australia

Plaintiffs M70/2011 and M106 of 2011 v. Minister for Immigration and Citizenship ('*the Malaysia-Swap Arrangement case*') [2011] HCA 32 204

Germany

BVerfG, Judgment of the Second Senate of 30 June 2009 ('Lisbon Judgment') 2 BvE 2/08 143

United Kingdom

Abassi v. Secretary of State for Foreign and Commonwealth Affairs, Court of Appeal, (2002) EWCA Civ 1598, CA, 6 November 2002 130

Al-Skeini and others v. Secretary of State for Defence, House of Lords, (2007) UKHL 26, 13 June 2006 64–65, 201

Al-Jedda v. Secretary of State for Defence, House of Lords, (2007) UKHL 58, 12 December 2007 67

Bancoult v. Secretary of State For Foreign and Commonwealth Affairs, House of Lords, (2008) UKHL 61, 22 October 2008 55–58

United States

American Civil Liberties Union v. James R. Clapper, Case 14-42 (2015) 134

Boumediene et al. v. Bush. United States Supreme Court, 06-1195, 553 US, 12 June 2008 51–52

Rasul et al. v. Bush, United States Supreme Court, 03-334, 542 US, 28 June 2004 51

Singapore

Government of the Lao People's Democratic Republic v. Sanum Investments Ltd. [2015] SGHC 15, 20 January 2015 94

Sanum Investments Ltd. v. Government of the Lao People's Democratic Republic [2016] SGCA 57, 29 September 2016 94

1

Introduction

The Changing Practices of International Law

THOMAS GAMMELTOFT-HANSEN AND TANJA AALBERTS

1.1 Introduction

In his seminal work, *The Changing Structure of International Law*, from 1964 Wolfgang Friedmann argued that international law has entered a new phase following the end of the Second World War.[1] In contrast to the formative period of modern international law, where the prime purpose of international law was to ensure co-existence and regulate conflict among sovereign states, contemporary international law has been supplanted by a drive towards deeper transnational cooperation. Next to the classical 'international law of co-existence' a growing 'international law of co-operation' would thus emerge, concerned with topics hitherto considered 'domestic affairs' such as economic development, welfare and good governance.

A cursory view at international law fifty years later largely seems to confirm Friedmann's premonition, and developments in many areas clearly exceed his expectations. The twentieth century has seen an almost exponential growth in multilateral treaties, the multiplication of specialized legal regimes and international institutions taking on a much more pervasive role in international relations.

What is sometimes referred to as the 'legalization of world politics' covers several distinct but related developments at the empirical level. The first is the *multiplication of actors*, or subjects, of international law. By this we mean, first, the increasing number of states participating in the international legal system. The emergence of a range of new states following the end of colonial rule and again following the end of the Cold War has meant

[1] Wolfgang Friedmann, *The Changing Structure of International Law* (London: Stevens & Sons, 1964).

a horizontal or geographical expansion of international law from predominantly Western nations to a host of new states. Secondly, the proliferation of international organizations, transnational corporate entities and other non-state actors has increasingly challenged the notion of sovereign states as the exclusive subjects of international law. We may thus identify a similar vertical or functional expansion of international law as international organizations, corporations and individuals are increasingly recognized as parties to instruments and subjects of international law within such varied areas as international criminal law, trade law and human rights.

The second, parallel, development is the *expansion of treaty law*. Since the end of the Second World War, the world has seen a radical expanse of international legal agreements. The UN Treaty Collection currently counts more than 158 000 treaties and subsequent actions.[2] In some areas, political cooperation has extended a web of bilateral agreements; over the past quarter-century, the number of bilateral investment treaties has thus grown almost ten-fold to almost 3000.[3] Perhaps more significant, more than 6000 multilateral treaties have been signed since the beginning of the twentieth century.[4] Of these 30 per cent are general in nature and thus open for all states to sign.[5] Many of these treaties govern issues qualitatively different from the traditional international law of co-existence, challenging traditional conceptions of state sovereignty based on a separation of internal and external affairs. From trade law, to human rights, to environmental law, the growing international law of cooperation presupposes a fundamentally different commitment of participating states to correspondingly adjust domestic affairs as well as a shift of lawmaking powers towards international organizations and other non-state actors.

Thirdly, international law has been backed by much broader and stronger panoply of *international judicial institutions*, coupled to an

[2] Available online at http://treaties.un.org.

[3] http://investmentpolicyhub.unctad.org/IIA. As of 25 May 2017, there are 2960 bilateral investment treaties. In addition, there are 303 other treaties with investment provisions (e.g. free trade agreements). See www.unctad.org.

[4] A development that seems to have slowed down somewhat the last two decades.

[5] ILC Analytical Study 2006, ILC Study Group on the Fragmentation of International Law. Fragmentation of International Law: Difficulties Arising from the Diversification and Expansion of International Law; Report of the Study Group of the International Law Commission, Finalized by Martti Koskenniemi. UN Doc. A/CN.4/L.682 and Add.1 and Corr. 1. New York: International Law Commission, 2006; Christopher J. Borgen, 'Resolving Treaty Conflicts' (2005) 37 *George Washington International Law Review* 57–80; Charlotte Ku, *Global Governance and the Changing Face of International Law*, ACUNS Keynote Paper (2001–2).

expansion and increasing overlap of their respective jurisdictions. With some 125 international judiciary institutions,[6] international law today is no longer the 'law without courts' as Hugo Grotius once described it.[7] Moreover, over the last decades the International Court of Justice has found violations in a number of controversial and security and human rights related cases.[8] The reach and case load of regional courts, such the European Court of Justice, and the regional human rights courts have similarly expanded; the European Court of Human Rights alone receives around 50 000 applications and issues some 1500 substantive judgments annually.[9] This growing adjudication is partly a result of the two trends above. The ratification of UNCLOS, WTO, NAFTA and the Energy Charter Treaty has each brought with them specialized adjudicatory and dispute resolution mechanisms, many of them encompassing powerful states that have traditionally avoided submitting to international jurisdiction.[10] The expansion in treaty law, such as bilateral investment treaties, has also led to a slew of interstate arbitrations before the Permanent Court of Arbitration (PCA). Yet, today the PCA also provides dispute resolution services in cases involving claims involving non-state actors such as transnational corporations. Similarly, new protocols have expanded the right to individual petition under a number of human rights treaties. Perhaps most noteworthy a host of new adjudicatory mechanisms has emerged since the 1990s. The two ad hoc International Criminal Tribunals for Rwanda and the former Yugoslavia were succeeded by the establishment of the International Criminal Court.

In addition to these trends of expansion, the different components of international law arguably display a higher degree of both political and judicial *interdependence* than Friedmann foresaw. In the context of the proliferation of specialized regimes, it is noteworthy that both legal instruments themselves and international legal institutions often make cross-references to other treaties and institutions. This is visible at the judicial level as well. Not only do different regional human rights courts cite each

6 Calculation from the Project on International Courts and Tribunals, available at www.pict-pcti.org.

7 Benedict Kingsbury, 'International Courts: Uneven Judicialisation in Global Order', in James Crawford and Martti Koskenniemi (eds), *The Cambridge Companion to Interntional Law* (Cambridge: Cambridge University Press, 2012), 203–27.

8 Malcolm Langford, 'The New Apologists: The International Court of Justice and Human Rights' (2015) 48(1) *Retfærd* 49–78.

9 Kingsbury, 'International Courts', 208.

10 J. H. H. Weiler et al., 'Special Issue: Changing Paradigms in International Law' (2009) 20 *European Journal of International Law* 21–109.

other, the appointment of prominent human rights lawyers to the International Court of Justice has arguably lend a stronger human rights profile to this institution as well.[11] Inter-operation equally works to break down the national-international divide.[12] Legislation allowing for universal jurisdiction in criminal cases and domestic incorporation of e.g. human rights instruments have allowed national institutions to play a much more decisive role in enforcing international law, and many national courts have become more confident to interpret and refer to international legal instruments.[13]

At the political level, different bodies of international law today interact to an extent where it becomes difficult to disentangle formally separate legal commitments. Recent suggestions have been made by some countries to renegotiate the 1951 Refugee Convention, yet the corner-stone of that instrument – the principle of non-refoulement – is enshrined in, or follows from, numerous other international and regional human rights treaties. Among EU Member States, any move to step down from the European Convention on Human Rights would further have political repercussions within the EU system, and informally the Strasbourg and Brussels Courts are clearly doing much to coordinate and avoid adjudicative conflicts. Interdependence is also evident at the level of treaty law, where cross-referencing multilateral obligations is becoming increasingly commonplace as part of bilateral agreements. Thus, foreign investment treaties may require the signing state to legally and politically commit to international standards in a wide range of other areas in order to secure a stable investment environment. States choosing to completely ignore property rights, labour laws and good governance principles thus ultimately risk financial isolation.[14]

Last, but not least, this changing landscape of international law clearly impacts its subjects. A number of scholars have pointed to the fact that the international law of cooperation and increasing powers granted to

[11] Rosalyn Higgins, 'Human Rights in the International Court of Justice' (2007) 20 *Leiden Journal of International Law* 745–751, at 746.

[12] André Nollkaemper, 'Inside or Out: Two Types of International Legal Pluralism', in Jan Klabbers and Touko Piiparinen (eds), *Normative Pluralism and International Law: Exploring Global Governance* (Cambridge: Cambridge University Press, 2014), 94–142.

[13] Kingsbury, 'International Courts', 222; B. S. Chimni, 'Legitimating the International Rule of Law', in James Crawford and Martti Koskenniemi (eds), *The Cambridge Companion to Interntional Law* (Cambridge: Cambridge University Press, 2012), 290–308, at 296.

[14] H. R. Fabri, 'Regulating Trade, Investments and Money', in J. Crawford and M. Koskenniemi (eds), *The Cambridge Companion to International Law* (Cambridge: Cambridge University Press, 2012), 352–372, at 359.

international legal institutions are undercutting national sovereignty and marginalizing the role of states as singular actors in the international legal field. In today's world, trans-governmental regulatory organizations,[15] transnational corporations[16] and NGOs[17] are becoming increasingly important actors in the development and governing of international law.

This normative thickening and expansion of law at all levels of international life has led some scholars to suggest that we live in an unprecedented era of 'legalization'.[18] This concept was originally forwarded as part of a particular theoretical framework, carrying with it a number of both analytical and normative assumptions with which we do not necessarily agree.[19] We use it here as a purely descriptive term. Legalization, in other words, is employed as a short-hand for the different developments in regard to international law described above. That across issue areas, resort to international law and institutions has become an 'ubiquitous presence' in political, academic and public discourse.[20] This empirical observation is shared by international lawyers across a wide range of theoretical positions. As David Kennedy observes:

> Although it is easy to think of international affairs as a rolling sea of politics over which we have managed to throw but a thin net of legal rules, in truth the situation today is more the reverse. There is law at every turn – and only the most marginal opportunities for engaged political contestation.[21]

15 Anne-Marie Slaughter, 'Governing the Global Economy through Government Networks', in Michael Byers (ed.), *The Role of Law in International Politics: Essays in International Relations and International Law* (Oxford: Oxford University Press, 2000), 177–205, at 204.

16 Jonathan I. Charney, 'Transnational Corporations and Developing Public International Law' (1983) 4 *Duke Law Journal* 748–88.

17 Christine Chinkin, 'Human Rights and the Politics of Representation: Is There a Role for International Law', in Michael Byers (ed.), *The Role of Law in International Politics* (Oxford: Oxford University Press, 2000), 131–48.

18 Judith Goldstein et al., 'Introduction: Legalization and World Politics' (2000) 54 *International Organization* 385–99.

19 For an engagement with and critique of this theoretical framework, see Chapter 7 in this volume; André Nollkaemper, 'The Process of Legalisation after 1989 and Its Contribution to the International Rule of Law', in James Crawford and Sarah Nouwen (eds), *Select Proceedings of the European Society of International Law* (Oxford: Hart, 2012) 89–102; Friedrich Kratochwil, *The Status of Law in World Society: Meditations on the Role and Rule of Law* (Cambridge: Cambridge University Press, 2014).

20 James Crawford and Martti Koskenniemi, 'Introduction', in James Crawford and Martti Koskenniemi (eds), *The Cambridge Companion to International Law* (Cambridge: Cambridge University Press, 2012), 1–21, at 1.

21 David Kennedy, 'Challenging Expert Rule: The Politics of Global Governance' (2005) 27 *Sydney Law Review* 5–28, at 5.

In short, international law has moved from being the *Buchrecht* of esoteric academics, to occupying a central position in diplomacy and public discourse. The question remains, however, what implications the legalization of world politics has for political life. For the original proponents of the legalization argument, the assumption was that the room for politics consequently narrowed and that conflicts would increasingly be resolved by or through legal means. As we shall see, however, not only has international law come to face substantial challenges, the very conception of international law and politics as a zero-sum game underlying such claims is fundamentally flawed.[22]

1.2 The Challenges to International Law

The 'legalization of world politics' is only part of the story. As part of its expansion and deepening, international law has also been confronted with certain structural and political challenges. First, the picture of legal codification has been questioned by those emphasizing the continued blind spots, gaps and inefficiencies. Critics have correctly pointed out that international law has yet to find satisfactory solutions to some of the world's most pressing problems. Globalization has brought with it a range of issues that do not easily fit the ordering categories of international law as traditionally defined. International law has thus struggled to respond to challenges brought on by e.g. climate change, global economic flows, corporate power and new forms of governance, each of which remain caught between the need for dynamic regulation and the traditional principles of sovereignty still underpinning international law. Moreover, breaches of international law continue to flourish in many areas. This is particularly evident in the area of international humanitarian law and human rights, where an obvious gap exists between rights and realities. Despite important developments, some human rights treaties are still associated with weak or selective monitoring and enforcement mechanisms, making the effect of ratifying human rights treaties no guarantee for actual implementation.[23] Despite the flurry of litigation, economists similarly disagree whether investment treaties actually deliver foreign investments. If we do live an era of legalization, this is still very much work in progress.

Secondly, the expansion of international law has also created concerns that international law may be losing internal coherence. The decentralized

[22] See further Chapter 2, this volume.

[23] Kingsbury, 'International Courts', pp. 203–27; Oona Hathaway, 'Between Power and Principle: An Integrated Theory of International Law' (2005) 71 *University of Chicago Law Review* 469–536.

structure of international law means that the proliferation of treaty law and international judicial institutions have not developed in the systematic fashion imagined by the international law's founding fathers. Rather, specialized regimes, functional differentiation and multiple fora for adjudication have emerged in a non-hierarchical setting, carrying with them an increased potential for conflicts between different bodies of law and centres of legal authority.[24] Conflicts may be sought resolved through tribunals, committees and commissions, but international law itself far from always provide clear solutions.[25] Concerns have been raised that growing fragmentation of international law will create normative incoherence.[26] While such concerns are hardly new,[27] international law has arguably become a much more messy place, harder for lawyers and judges to systematize and more demanding for states to navigate. For some this is both a natural and preferable outcome of an inherently pluralist international legal order.[28] For others this has led to calls for constitutionalism and the establishment of clearer hierarchies and enforcement mechanisms as known from national legal systems.[29]

Third, and perhaps most important, the political backlash to the increased influence of international law has become undeniable. States have voiced repeated concerns that international law is imposing unrealistic burdens and that international legal institutions are undermining democratic decision making and national sovereignty.[30] In Europe, several states have criticized its two regional courts, The Court of Justice of the European Union (CJEU) and the European Court of Human

24 Karin J. Alter and Sophie Meunier, 'The Politics of International Regime Complexity' (2009) 7(1) *Perspectives on Politics* 13–24; Fischer-Lescano, Andreas and Gunther Teubner, 'Regime-Collisions: The Vain Search for Legal Unity in the Fragmentation of Global Law' (2004) 25 *Michigan Journal of International Law* 999–1046; Margaret A. Young (ed.), *Regime Interaction in International Law. Facing Fragmentation* (Cambridge: Cambridge University Press, 2012); Joost Pauwelyn, 'The Rule of Law without the Rule of Lawyers? Why Investment Arbitrators Are from Mars, Trade Panelists Are from Venus' (2015) 109 *American Journal of International Law* 761–805.

25 J. Klabbers and T. Piiparinen (eds), *Normative Pluralism and International Law: Exploring Global Governance* (Cambridge: Cambridge University Press, 2013), 7.

26 Martti Koskenniemi and Päivi Leino, 'Fragmentation of International Law? Postmodern Anxieties' (2002) 15 *Leiden Journal of International Law* 553–79.

27 W. Jenks, 'The Conflict of Law-Making Treaties' (1953) 30 *British Yearbook of International Law* 401–453.

28 Nico Krisch, *Beyond Constitutionalism: The Pluralist Structure of Postnational Law* (Oxford: Oxford University Press, 2010).

29 Jan Klabbers, Anne Peters and Geir Ulfstein, *The Constitutionalization of International Law* (Oxford: Oxford University Press, 2009).

30 Ivan Anthony Shearer, 'In Fear of International Law' (2005) 12 *Indiana Journal of Global Legal Studies* 345–78.

Rights (ECtHR), for 'judicial activism' and overly dynamic interpretation, not least in regard to sensitive political issues such as welfare distribution, immigration and minority rights.[31] In 2016, the Danish Supreme Court, in clear defiance of the interpretation of the CJEU, reasserted the pre-eminence of Danish domestic law in a case concerning employment rights.[32] Resistance to the jurisdiction of the CJEU similarly played a prominent role in the UK campaign to leave the European Union, just as it has in the ensuring negotiations of the Brexit process.[33] In the US, the Trump administration announced withdrawals from both the Trans-Pacific Partnership Agreement (TPPA) on trade and the Paris Agreement on climate change, in addition to introducing a moratorium on new multilateral treaties.[34]

In sum, while we have seen an expansion and deepening of international codification and judicial institutions that place international law at the heart of international politics, any 'liberal progressive narrative'[35] must also take account of the mounting challenges to international law. International law far from always deliver on its promises. It does not necessarily resolve internal or external conflicts. Last, but not least, in a number of areas the international law has developed to a point where states feel threatened by their own creation. Never before has international law been so important, and never before subject to such intense political contestation.

[31] Mark Dawson, B. De Witte and Elise Muir (eds), *Judicial Activism at the European Court of Justice* (Cheltenham, UK: Edward Elgar, 2013); Mikael Rask Madsen, 'The Challenging Authority of the European Court of Human Rights' (2016) 79 *Law and Contemporary Problems* 141–78.

[32] Mikael Rask Madsen, Henrik Palmer Olsen and Urska Sadl, 'Competing Supremacies and Clashing Institutional Rationalities: The Danish Supreme Court's Decision in the Ajos Case and the National Limits of Judicial Cooperation' 23 *European Law Journal*, Issue 1–2, pp. 140–150.

[33] As noted by Theresa May in her speech at Lancaster House on 17 January 2017, 'We will take back control of our laws and bring an end to the jurisdiction of the European Court of Justice in Britain. Leaving the European Union will mean that our laws will be made in Westminster, Edinburgh, Cardiff and Belfast. And those laws will be interpreted by judges not in Luxembourg but in courts across this country'. Available at www.gov.uk/government/speeches/the-governments-negotiating-objectives-for-exiting-the-eu-pm-speech.

[34] Jack L. Goldsmith, 'The Trump Onslaught on International Law and Institutions', Lawfare Blog, 17 March 2017. Available at www.lawfareblog.com/trump-onslaught-international-law-and-institutions; Monica Hakimi, 'International Law in the Age of Trump', EJIL:Talk!, 28 February 2017. Available at www.ejiltalk.org/international-law-in-the-age-of-trump.

[35] Tilmann Altwicker and Oliver Diggelmann, 'How Is Progress Constructed in International Legal Scholarship?' (2014) 25 *European Journal of International Law* 425–44.

1.3 Changing Politico-Legal Practices

The above characterization of simultaneous proliferation and growing challenges to international law are often presented as separate narratives or world views on the status of international law in contemporary society, and dealt with in isolation by legal and political scholars alike. In contrast, this volume aims to explore the interplay between these two dynamics and its implications for the development of international law. While other works have focused on what these developments mean for the role of international courts,[36] international organizations[37] or private actors,[38] such as transnational corporations or individuals, our focus is on how states as the original masters navigate the increasingly complex international legal order in which they find themselves embedded.

The starting premise for our analysis is that in this expanded web of bilateral and multilateral treaties, internationally empowered institutions and arbitrational bodies, the room for politics *outside* international law has arguably diminished. For the vast majority of states today, global governance means that international law has increasingly become a *sine qua non* for doing politics. At the same time, the shackles of international law have left many states eager to recoup sovereign power in areas of particular political importance. In extreme cases, this may lead states to resign from existing multilateral agreements. Yet, although the UK leaving the European Union, or the US abandoning the TPPA may well have deep-seated implications for the development of international law also beyond these specific regimes, it is far from clear that they spell a diminished role for international law as such. In their wake, different forms of international law are likely to emerge, spinning a web of bilateral and intergovernmental agreements. As several of the chapters point to, we may be seeing a qualitative transformation of international law towards different and more 'disaggregated' forms of international cooperation.[39]

At the same time, however, the multiplication of legal regimes, overlapping jurisdictions and shifting centres of authority seems to have opened up an increased playing field for political contestation *within* international

[36] See e.g. Karen Alter, *The New Terrain of International Law: Courts, Politics, Rights* (Cambridge: Cambridge University Press, 2014).

[37] See e.g. Jan Klabbers, 'Two Concepts of International Organization' (2005) 2 *International Organizations Law Review* 277–94.

[38] See e.g. Andrew Clapham, *Human Rights Obligations of Non-State Actors* (Oxford: Oxford University Press, 2006).

[39] This terminology comes from Chapter 6, this volume.

law. As states are increasingly required to translate and justify their actions in legal terms,[40] governments have become much more adept at navigating and manoeuvring legal structures. When governments rely more heavily on their legal advisors,[41] it is not just to ensure compliance with international law or to successfully stake their claims as part of legal challenges, but also to resort to what might be called 'creative legal thinking'.[42]

As H. L. A. Hart famously noted, international obligations are by definition 'open-textured', and interpretation thus often depends on general principles, transnational adjudication and state practice.[43] Normative developments in the form of further codification, adjudication and soft law are often assumed to remedy this problem by further clarifying interpretation. As international law has developed, however, it could well be argued that this may also work in reverse. The multiplication of legal regimes, overlapping jurisdictions and diffusion of authority also provides for more conflicts within and between international law. This in turn opens up an increased room for political manoeuvring in relation to international law, where governments are able to apply a pick-and-choose approach across different legal regimes, standards and adjudicatory venues. International law in this sense is not only regulating and constraining but also enabling, legitimizing and constituting certain politics, often unforeseen and far removed from the original intentions behind the particular legal regimes and instruments in question. From migration control, to surveillance and trading of emission and fishing quotas, states are increasingly designing policies and actions to work at the fringes or in between the mazes of international law, exploiting interpretative uncertainties, reverting on soft law standards, or establishing novel categories and concepts on the basis of domestic or other parts of international law.

The range of these practices is broad, not only in terms of the different issue areas where they can be observed, but also in terms of the kind of strategies that may be identified. At the more general level at least six

[40] Ian Johnstone, *The Power of Deliberation: International Law, Politics and Organizations* (Oxford: Oxford University Press, 2011).

[41] Kennedy, 'Challenging Expert Rule', 5; see also Anna Leander and Tanja Aalberts, 'Introduction: The Co-Constitution of Legal Expertise and International Security (Symposium)' (2013) 26 *Leiden Journal of International Law* 783–92.

[42] Thomas Gammeltoft-Hansen, 'The Role of International Refugee Law in Refugee Policy' (2014) 27 *Journal of Refugee Studies* 574–95.

[43] H. L. A. Hart, *The Concept of Law* (Oxford: Clarendon Press, 1961), 121–44; Brian Bix, 'H.L.A. Hart and the "Open Texture" of Language' (1991) 10 *Law and Philosophy* 51–72.

different types of strategies may be identified, which are used across different issues areas.

A first set of practices relates to the strategic use of extra-territorial venues – often termed *jurisdiction shopping* – in the attempt to shift or avoid legal liability under either domestic or international law. For example, since the 1990s states have interdicted migrants on the high seas, arguing that this nullified any right to claim asylum as a matter of international refugee or human rights law, as the asylum seekers would never reach their territories.[44] It can also involve deals to make use of another state's territory. Transnational law enforcement and detention has similarly been used to disclaim sovereign obligations in relation to domestic due process guarantees or international human rights.[45] This may involve the concomitant commercialization of sovereignty by the territorial state, as in the case of Guantanamo Bay, where a bilateral agreement is drawn up 'renting' parts of Cuban territory to the US.[46] Or it may involve more complex arrangements between multiple states, as in the case of the CIA rendition programme. Jurisdiction shopping may also be pursued in relation to commercial interests. States may thus be seen to negotiate agreements to allow industrial manufacturing in third countries with fewer or lower environmental and labour rights restrictions. The effort to establish national fishing quotas as a matter of international law has thus equally seen a number of southern European states negotiate agreements with its African neighbours to allow European trawlers to fish within their territorial waters and exclusive economic zones.[47]

Closely related to jurisdiction shopping, states may also be seen to engage in *international cooperation* for the purpose of circumventing or shifting particular legal obligations. As in the above case, the argument is that the active, or even nominal, involvement of another state's authorities can be used to either avoid legal liability on behalf of the sponsoring state, or to circumvent constraints otherwise posed by international law. Examples of such outsourcing between states are rife across various issues

44 A practice subsequently accepted to entail jurisdiction as a matter of international human rights. Thomas Gammeltoft-Hansen, 'Sale's Legacy – "Creative Legal Thinking" and Dynamic Interpretation of Refugee Law', Opinio Juris, 15 March 2014. Available from www.opiniojuris.org. See further Chapter 8, this volume.

45 See more generally, Thomas Gammeltoft-Hansen and Jens Vedsted-Hansen (eds), *Human Rights and the Dark Side of Globalization: Transnational law enforcement and migration control* (Abingdon: Routledge, 2016).

46 See Chapter 3, this volume.

47 Francisco Orrego Vicuna, *The Changing International Law of High Seas Fisheries* (Cambridge: Cambridge University Press, 1999).

of law enforcement. Some states have thus been known to send terrorist suspects to partner states in order to effect interrogations with techniques that would not be allowed in the sponsoring state under either domestic or international law. In both the Pacific and the Americas deals have similarly been struck to involve third state authorities in efforts to combat international crime, and in particular drug smuggling, thereby circumventing the obvious constraints otherwise posed by international law when intercepting suspected smuggling vessels on the high seas or carrying out raids inside the territory of another state. It may equally involve joint or concerted actions.[48] The use of ship-riders – authorities of a territorial or neighbouring state – has thus become increasingly popular in the area of both migration control and efforts to stop drug smuggling.[49] Similarly, countries such as Denmark have routinely involved British soldiers when undertaking military patrols in Iraq in the attempt to avoid triggering any direct human rights obligations when taking persons into custody.[50]

The expansion of international law has also encountered a transformation of international politics through the process of new governance patterns, including the *outsourcing of governmental functions to private actors*. Hence another set of political-legal strategies makes use of (and contributes to) the shifting boundaries between public and private authorities. The practice of states to contract private military companies has been an increasingly common practice, raising a number of different issues in terms of state responsibility and accountability under both domestic and international law.[51] Private security companies have similarly been employed by maritime companies and in the context of anti-piracy operations.[52] Privatization has similarly become popular in the area of

[48] Douglas Guilfoyle, *Shipping Interdiction and the Law of the Sea*(Cambridge: Cambridge University Press, 2009).

[49] Ibid., p. 72ff.

[50] Anders Henriksen, 'Fanger, folkeret og "brite-finter"' [Detainees, international law and 'the British Trick'] (2014) 87 *Økonomi & Politik* 6–15.

[51] Anna Leander, 'The Paradoxical Impunity of Private Military Companies: Authority and the Limits to Legal Accountability' (2010) 41 *Security Dialogue* 467–90; A. Claire Cutler, 'The Legitimacy of Private Transnational Governance: Experts and the Transnational Market for Force' (2010) 8 *Socio-Economic Review* 157–85; Carsten Hoppe, 'Passing the Buck: State Responsibility for Private Military Companies' (2008) 19 *European Journal of International Law* 989–1014.

[52] John J. Pitney Jr and John-Clark Levin, *Private Anti-Piracy Navies: Warships for Hire Are Changing Maritime Security* (Plymouth, UK: Lexington Books, 2013); Jill Harrelson, 'Blackbeard Meets Blackwater: An Analysis of International Conventions That Address

migration, where private actors have taken on a broad range of migration management functions, from visa issuance and migration control, to the operation of detention facilities and carrying out deportations.[53] The widespread use of carrier sanctions legislation – fining airlines and other transportation companies for bringing in unauthorized passengers – is perhaps the clearest example of how private actors are routinely taking on migration control functions through a legal construction that effectively distances the state from any associated human rights responsibility. Often these arrangements involve several layers of subcontracting, or take place as part of extra-territorial operations, thereby further complicating questions of accountability and the possibility to 'pass the buck' for any subsequent wrongdoing.[54]

A third strategy involves what might be called *regime or treaty shopping*. Whereas the strategies above both seek to exploit jurisdictional differences in terms of regulation, regime shopping is premised on a functional logic and the co-existence of multiple, partly overlapping and non-hierarchical treaty regimes. International regime complexity[55] means that issues can be dealt with via multiple regimes, nested in different institutional arrangements, and with different responsibilities towards different parties. For instance, the issue of intellectual property rights is regulated via the WTO's trade regime through the Agreement on Trade-Related Aspects of Intellectual Property Rights (TRIPS), but is also addressed by the World Health Organisation (for instance in case of patented pharmaceuticals in the fight against HIV/Aids in developing countries), and the Convention on Biological Diversity. The latter enables the subordination of intellectual property rights to environmental protection and development goals, which goes against the TRIPS arrangements.[56] The

Piracy and the Use of Private Security Companies to Protect the Shipping Industry' (2010) 25 *American University International Law Review* 283.

53 Thomas Gammeltoft-Hansen, 'Private Security and the Migration Control Industry', in Rita Abrahamsen and Anna Leander (eds), *Routledge Handbook on Private Security* (New York: Routledge, 2015), 207–217.

54 Carsten Hoppe, 'Passing the Buck: State Responsibility for Private Military Companies' (2008) 19 *European Journal of International Law* 989–1014.

55 Alter and Meunier, 'The Politics of International Regime Complexity'; cf. Kal Raustiala and David Victor, 'The Regime Complex for Plant Genetic Resources' (2004) 85 *International Organization* 277–309.

56 Raustiala and Victor, 'The Regime Complex'; Laurence R. Helfer, 'Regime Shifting; the Trips Agreement and the New Dynamics of International Intellectual Property Making' (2004) 29 *Yale Journal of Intenational Law* 1–81. Raustiala and Victor push the argument even further and identify this as a practice of 'strategic inconsistency', which is the creation

dynamics of regime complexity are further enhanced by the expansion of 'soft law' instruments, such as declarations, guidelines, standard-setting and recommendations.[57]

Following on from this, states may fourthly seek to resolve legal conflicts at the judicial venues where they expect the most favourable view on the legal case, or where the underlying legal regime at both primary and secondary level may work most to their benefit – what might be called *judicial forum shopping*. Again, the room for such practices has increased as a result of the proliferation of international arbitration bodies with partly overlapping mandates. For instance, North American trade disputes can be brought to either the WTO or to NAFTA, which will then have a different effect of precedence, and be binding upon different partners. Judicial forum shopping, hence, is not only about winning a particular case, but can also be about discriminating among overlapping memberships[58] in light of a legal 'shadow of the future logic'. Judicial forum shopping is not only a matter of strategic choice at the moment of decision where to file your case, but can also involve the simultaneous or successive litigation of claims.[59]

A fifth aspect of political manoeuvring relates to *interpretive framing* more generally. As noted above, international law, in particular, tends to be 'open-textured', and interpretation thus often depends on general principles, soft law, transnational adjudication and state practice. As such, interpretation and framing is inherent in the operation of law. In the expansive developments of international law, the potential for conflicts further multiply, and international law itself far from always provides clear-cut or singular solutions to solve them. Yet, interpretative framing is not only a matter of stating your case before the court or in international diplomacy. Madeleine Albright's famous suggestion to Robin Cook 'to get new lawyers' in order to justify the unilateral intervention in Kosovo illustrates the partisan function of advocacy and apology that legal advisors often

of contradictory rules in parallel regimes in order to undermine existing rules in other agreements.

57 Cf. mapping of the regime complex for climate change in Robert O. Keohane and David G. Victor, 'The Regime Complex for Climate Change' (2011) 9 *Perspectives on Politics* 7–23.

58 Mark L. Busch, 'Overlapping Institutions, Forum Shopping, and Dispute Settlement in International Trade' (2007) 61 *International Organization* 735–61.

59 Laurence R. Helfer, 'Forum Shopping for Human Rights' (1999) 148 *University of Pennsylvania Law Review* 285–400. He does not see this as a threat to the unity of the legal system but rather emphasizes the aforementioned practice of interdecision making which makes international human rights litigation a 'shared and ongoing enterprise' producing 'harmonious, though not necessarily uniform, set of human rights standards' (ibid., at 400).

occupy.[60] Indeed, it is a hallmark of a good lawyer that s/he can provide a valid legal argumentation for either position in a dispute, which is sometimes what governmental legal advisors are expected to do.[61] At its most extreme, this practice of lawyering as part of high politics is sometimes referred to as 'lawfare'.[62] It illustrates that the formalist and categorical distinction between lawmaking and its subsequent application ignores the interpretive aspect of any linguistic activity, and naively assumes that law can speak for itself. At the same time, it is precisely international law's appearance of objectivity that makes it such a powerful tool for the pursuit and legitimation of political objectives.[63]

Last, but not least, deference to other forms of non-legal expertise may be considered a distinct political-legal strategy in this connection. Although not directly a practice of creatively manoeuvring international law itself, the role of technical and scientific expertise has become an ingrained aspect of much legal discourse today.[64] In order to settle disputes in international environmental law or various jurisdictional and exploitation claims under the Law of the Sea, specialized technical knowledge concerning respectively emissions or the determination of e.g. equidistance principles and underwater geology is required. Rather than only lawyers, it is more and more scientists that are called into the courtroom to provide scientific evidence to support a given case. This technicalization has in some instances led to the privatization of legal rulemaking and dispute settlement, for instance in the case of internet domains to the International Corporation for Assigned Names and Numbers.[65] This 'politics of (legal) expertise'[66] is thus another interesting example

60 James Rubin, 'Countdown to a Very Personal War', Financial Times, 30 September 2000.

61 Shirley V. Scott, *International Law in World Politics: An Introduction* (Boulder, CO: Lynne Rienner, 2010), 138n9. See also the special issue on the role of legal advisers in foreign policy making in (1991) 2 *European Journal of International Law*.

62 David Kennedy, *Of War and Law* (Oxford: Oxford University Press, 2006); Wouter G. Werner, 'The Curious Career of Lawfare' (2010) 43 *Case Western Reserve Journal of International Law* 61–72; Pascal Vennesson and Nikolas M. Rajkovic, 'The Transnational Politics of Warfare Accountability: Human Rights Watch versus the Israel Defense Forces' (2012) 26 *International Relations* 409–29.

63 Scott, *International Law in World Politics*, Chapter 7.

64 Chapter 7, this volume.

65 Gillian K. Hadfield, 'Privatizing Commercial Law: Lessons from ICANN' (2002) 6 *Journal of Small and Emerging Business Law*, 257–288; A. Claire Cutler, 'The Legitimacy of Private Transnational Governance: Experts and the Transnational Market for Force' (2010) 8 *Socio-Economic Review* 157–85.

66 Leander and Aalberts, 'The Co-Constitution of Legal Expertise and International Security'; Wouter G. Werner, 'The Politics of Expertise: Applying Paradoxes of Scientific Expertise to International Law', in Monika Ambrus et al. (eds), *The Role of Experts in International*

of manoeuvring in which legal objectivity is boosted with supposed-scientific objectivity.

These forms of *extralegal deferral* are of interest here because they implicitly define the boundaries between what fall under the remits of international law.[67] Whereas this entails a formal authority question (cf. the US Act of State doctrine),[68] it is also linked to questions of different kinds of expertise. For instance, in the *Targeted Killings* case, the US District Court of Columbia dismissed the case on the basis of the constitutional division of power and because the issue required 'expertise beyond the capacity of the Judiciary'.[69] Whereas in the case of such high security issues this is in turn often linked to the availability of classified evidence,[70] international legal questions today are increasingly subject to a variety of extra-legal expertise, each with their own standards of what is 'proportionate', 'optimal' or 'reasonable' for the issue at hand.[71]

These political-legal strategies form the starting point for exploring the paradox of increasing legalization increasing the room for politicization within/of international law through empirical case studies. This typology should not be considered an exhaustive nor a conclusive list. Focusing on different legal regimes and issue areas, the various chapters to the volume each analyze examples of politico-legal manoeuvring enabled by these regimes. As the case studies show, different strategies are often employed in combination in relation to a given policy issue.

Decision-Making: Advisors, Decision-Makers or Irrelevant? (Cambridge: Cambridge University Press, 2014).

67 Leander and Aalberts, 'The Co-Constitution of Legal Expertise and International Security'; Werner, 'The Politics of Expertise'.

68 The US Act of State doctrine seeks to exclude matters of foreign policy from judicial overview by domestic courts. As an avoidance doctrine, under the Act of State judges can decide to refrain from adjudication to determine the (il)legality of a state's action, and thus de facto defer to politics. It runs parallel to the 'political question' doctrine, also known as the non-justiciability principle from the *Buttes Gas and Oil* case.

69 Cf. Al-Aulaqi v. Obama, 727 F. Supp. 2d 1 (D.D.C. 2010), 77. Available at www.ccrjustice.org/files/2010.12.07_Al-Aulaqi%20Decision_0.pdf.

70 Erna Rijsdijk, 'The Politics of Hard Knowledge: Uncertainty, Intelligence Failures, and the "Last Minute Genocide" of Srebrenica' (2011) 37 *Review of International Studies* 2221–35; Gavin Sullivan and Marieke De Goede, 'Between Law and the Exception: The Un 1267 Ombudsperson as a Hybrid Model of Expertise' (2013) 26 *Leiden Journal of International Law* 833–54.

71 Martti Koskenniemi, 'The Fate of Public International Law: Between Technique and Politics' (2007) 70 *Modern Law Review* 1–30. Cf example of software engineers who develop algorythms for drones, Louise Amoore, *The Politics of Possibility* (Durham, NC: Duke University Press, 2013).

1.4 Implications for International Law

It is important to note that the kind of practices examined in the present volume are hardly representative of states' commitment to all aspects of international law. Henkin's famous observation that '[a]lmost all nations observe almost all principles of international law and almost all their obligations almost all of the time' arguably still holds true today, despite recent challenges to core parts of the international legal corpus.[72] The practices explored in the following chapters rather represent a particular kind of political response in areas where states feel unduly constrained by international law in light of important political priorities, and where the two obvious alternatives – openly disregarding legal obligations or seeking to renegotiate or step down from international legal instruments – are considered unfeasible or too costly. What these practices represent is a different way for states to broker the *pouvoirs constitué-pouvoirs constituant* dilemma of international law.

Two further points follow from this. The emergence of these practices is not tantamount to a rejection of international law as such – far from it. In most cases, policies to e.g. offshore or outsource certain law enforcement functions in order to avoid incurring correlate legal obligations inter alia presume that such norms do actually matter and, under ordinary circumstances, affect state action. If governments felt they could simply disrespect international law 'at home', then there would be little need to engage in cumbersome and often costly schemes to engage in extra-territorial law enforcement or cooperation with third state authorities. These governance strategies are exactly what makes it possible for states to apply a more managerial approach to international law, but nonetheless still formally present themselves as countries abiding by their international law commitments.

In much of the existing literature, the different policies listed above are treated as exceptions or aberrations to the ordinary *modus operandi* of international law; something taking place 'beyond the rule of law', in a 'rights vacuum' or creating a 'legal black hole', where international politics trumps international law.[73] Such dismissals, however fail to acknowledge how these practices are in fact enabled by international law

[72] Louis Henkin, *How Nations Behave* (New York: Columbia University Press, 1979), 47.

[73] See e.g. Johan Steyn, 'Guantanamo Bay: The Legal Black Hole' (2004) 53 *International and Comparative Law Quarterly* 1–15; Ralph Wilde, 'Legal "Black Hole"? Extraterritorial State Action and International Treaty Law on Civil and Political Rights' (2005) 26 *Michigan Journal of International Law* 739–806.

itself.[74] Moreover, most, if not all, of these practices are coached and framed through bilateral or multilateral international legal agreements. The international law of cooperation, in other words, is the very vessel through which they are implemented.

More fundamentally, it is important to recognize that these practices are not merely temporal aberration or exceptions to an idealized idea of the standard *modus operandi* of international law, but rather a pervasive and systematic trait of the international legal system today.[75] That is not say that they are necessarily a new phenomenon. The modern-day contracts with private security and military companies have their historical precursors in the use of mercenaries and privateers. In the US, carrier sanctions was first introduced in the 1902 Passenger Act, requiring shipmasters to sign an affidavit to verify that all passengers were in good physical and mental health,[76] and as early as 1751 Denmark levied fines from shipmasters bringing in Jewish passengers.[77] More generally, strategies of interpretative framing and forum shopping have always been part of international law, just as several historical cases before the International Court of Justice have hinged on the production of relevant scientific data.[78]

It is, however, during the most recent decades that such practices have become more prevalent and more visible, facilitated by the aforementioned development in international law. Developments in international law provide both cause and solution. As international legal commitments expand and deepen, states are actively looking for ways to recoup sovereign manoeuvrability in other ways. At the same time, this very expansion simultaneously create more opportunities for states to strategically engage with and seek to navigate international law. International law has similarly paved the way for changing patterns of governance. Many of these practices rely on transnational arrangements, allowing states to

[74] See e.g. Chapter 3, this volume. See further Fleur Johns, 'Guantánamo Bay and the Annihilition of the Exception' (2005) 16 *European Journal of International Law* 613–35; Fleur Johns, *Non-Legality in International Law: Unruly Law* (Cambridge: Cambridge University Press, 2013).

[75] Scott Veitch, *Law and Irresponsibility: On the Legitimation of Human Suffering* (Abingdon: Routledge, 2007).

[76] Aristide Zolberg, 'Matters of State', in Charles Hirschman, Philip Kasinitz and Josh DeWind (eds), *The Handbook on International Immigration* (New York: Russell Sage Foundation, 1999), 71–93, at 75.

[77] Martin Schwartz Lausten, *Jøder og kristne i Danmark: Fra middelalderen til nyere tid* (Copenhagen: Anis, 2012).

[78] See e.g. *North Sea Continental Shelf, Germany v. Denmark*, International Court of Justice, ICJ Rep 3, ICGJ 150, 20 February 1969.

exercise sovereign functions in concert, extra-territorially, through private parties or as part of international organizations.

Moreover, it should be underscored that states may well feel politically justified in this approach. While some of the above examples may seem to suggest a 'bad state' theory akin to Oliver Wendell Holmes's famous jurisprudential doctrine,[79] in some instances states may have a legitimate interest in regaining political control against international law. For many developing countries, creative legal thinking might be a necessary precondition to re-establish public control vis-à-vis international investors, regardless of how one views such practices.[80] Indeed, this and other volumes have shown that developing countries are significantly more likely to lose or have less influence in adjudication even after one controls for various factors.[81] At a more general level, some might argue that the practices described in this volume ultimately serve a constructive purpose, functioning as a political pressure valve and avoiding more direct confrontations leading to disrespect for or regressive revisions of important areas of international law.

It should also be remembered that state strategies to avoid or eclipse legal responsibility are of course far from always successful. While Madeline Albright's new lawyers may be argued to have tipped the balance in the Kosovo war to 'illegal but legitimate' in the eyes of the international community, creative legal thinking did not do the trick for the US, the UK and their allies in the 2003 Iraq war. While they argued a revival of the 1990s resolutions as the legal basis for an intervention, the overall opinion of the international community and legal scholars was that Resolution 1441 indicated that a second resolution was necessary to authorize the use of force. However, our focus here is not necessarily on the success of a particular legal argument, but on which arguments can be made in the first

79 Oliver Wendell Holmes Jr, 'The Path of the Law' (1897) 10 *Harvard Law Review* 457–61; see further Thomas Gammeltoft-Hansen and Jens Vedsted-Hansen, eds, *Human Rights and the Dark Side of Globalisation; Transnational Law Enforcement and Migration Control* (London: Routledge, 2016).

80 See Chapter 4, this volume.

81 See Daniel Behn, Tarald Berge and Malcolm Langford, 'Poor States or Poor Governance? Testing Claims of Systemic Bias in Investment Treaty Arbitration' (forthcoming) *Northwestern Journal of International Law & Business*; Cosette Creamer, 'Between the Letter of the Law and the Demands of Politics: The Judicial Balancing of Trade Authority within the WTO' *Working Paper* (2015). Note though that Cesare Romano claims that the situation has as least improved for developing countries compared to the post-war years: Cesare Romano, 'International Justice and Developing Countries' (2002) 1 *The Law and Practice of International Courts and Tribunals* 539–611.

place. Thus we are interested in the boundaries for validity, more than success, truth or legality as such.[82]

Moreover, it should not be forgotten that the expansion of international law has also enhanced the ability of courts and other legal institutions to reign in such practices. Although the establishment of state responsibility in such cases are, by design, a far from straightforward matter, those who proclaim that these practices take place in a legal black hole tend to overlook the substantial developments in the interpretation of, for example, international human rights, international humanitarian law and international environmental law. In many areas, normative developments and jurisprudence have managed to respond to new policy developments. Several policies regarding jurisdiction shopping have thus been successfully challenged by domestic or international courts, forcing governments to abandon or substantially adjust their practice. At the same time, however, this jurisprudence is often politically contested, and itself subject to a host of different politico-legal strategies.[83] What emerges is a dialectic between normative and policy developments, each driving the other.

By focusing on the above practices of international law, the present volume seeks to develop two arguments simultaneously: one about international law as increasingly regulating and constraining international relations by defining or reconfiguring the parameters of international political action; the other, about international law as enabling certain policies that exploit the particularities of international law to recoup and legitimize political power. In other words, governments appear to have become both more norm-savvy and more strategic in their relationship to international law. This is a distinctive form of politics, both constrained *and* facilitated by a plethora of international rules and legal institutions.[84] It

[82] This shifts the inquiry away from the pitfalls of policy-oriented jurisprudence and instrumental understandings of international law in its wake, on one side, and of a formalism that blends out the creativity and the politics of the legal practice, on the other. Tanja E. Aalberts and Ingo Venzke, 'Moving Beyond Interdisciplinary Turfwars: Toward an Understanding of International Law as Practice', in André Nollkaemper et al. (eds), *International Law as Profession* (Cambridge: Cambridge University Press, 2017), 287–310, at 305. On legality as a form of practice, see Nikolas M. Rajkovic, Tanja E. Aalberts and Thomas Gammeltoft-Hansen (eds), *The Power of Legality: Practices of International Law and Their Politics* (Cambridge: Cambridge University Press, 2016).

[83] See e.g. Chapter 5, this volume.

[84] Kenneth W. Abbott and Duncan Snidal, 'Law, Legalization, and Politics: An Agenda for the Next Generation of IL/IR Scholars', in Jeffrey L. Dunoff and Mark A. Pollack (eds), *Interdisciplinary Perspectives on International Law and International Relations: The State of the Art* (Cambridge: Cambridge University Press, 2013), 33–56, at 35.

is this dual dynamic between politics and international law that accounts for both the success of and challenges to international law in our current age. These practices are thus not a sign of eroding respect for international law and cooperation. On the contrary, they should be seen as a systemic feature of the international legal landscape today, and a logical countermove to the growing power of international law and its political and judicial institutions.[85]

This in turn means that international law itself cannot provide the solution to its shortcomings and challenges through more rules and better institutions, nor can social science models that only seek to determine international law's effectiveness through analysis and prediction of state behaviour. Rather, the very paradox of international law is like grannie's crochet blanket: the more layers you add, the more holes or gaps emerge.

The last decades have seen a tremendous growth in scholarly literature seeking to theorize the politics of international law from different perspectives. While this body of literature carries many important insights as reflected above and in the following chapters, the starting point for the present volume is deliberately inductive. Each chapter is based on an empirical mapping and overview of contrasting developments in international law, from which we build our analytical framework. Such an approach may be seen to share certain affinities with other recent scholarship, including the call for 'empirical' and 'anti-formalist' approaches to international law forwarded by e.g. new legal realism,[86] as well as the turn to 'practice theory'[87] as a counter-strategy to the a priori theorizing that has characterized much of the literature at the intersection between international law and International Relations. The contributors to this volume, however, represent scholars from a broad church of international legal theory. For the present project, we have thus adopted a more pluralistic approach with the hope of opening up space for more fruitful academic exchange in light of recent developments in international law.

1.5 Structure of the Volume

The ensuing chapters to this volume are all empirically grounded; each chapter seeking to analyze the various ways in which states have made

[85] See further Chapter 2, this volume.

[86] See e.g. Jakob Holtermann and Mikael Rask Madsen, 'European New Legal Realism and International Law: How to Make International Law Intelligible' (2015) 28 *Leiden Journal of International Law* 211–30, as well as other articles in this special issue on new legal realism.

[87] Rajkovic, Aalberts and Gammeltoft-Hansen, *The Power of Legality*.

creative use of developments of international law and globalization. To demonstrate the breath and pervasiveness of these practices, we have included chapters that span a range of different topics, from migration and surveillance to foreign investment arbitration and environmental policy, and a number of different legal regimes, from EU and international human rights law to the law of the sea.

As the conceptual backdrop to the empirical observations in this chapter and the case studies, Chapter 2, by Tanja Aalberts and Thomas Gammeltoft-Hansen, locates the approach of the present volume amidst different conceptions of the relationship between politics and international law within International Law and International Relations. In line with the empirical and problem-driven approach presented here, the ambition is not to dictate one particular theoretical framework upon the case studies, but rather to open up dialogue across theoretical orientations and academic disciplines about the role of international law in contemporary world politics. To this end, the chapter employs the notion of sovereignty games as a heuristic to unpack the relationship between sovereignty, international law and politics.

The following chapter, by Margareta Brummer, aims to expose the structure of the formation process of the extra-territorial location. It retraces how three particular geographical zones – the Guantanamo Bay detention centre, the military base of the US in Diego Garcia and the CIA-led prison in Poland – are rendered extra-territorial by a tripartite process of *abandonment*, *construction* and *denial* in form of creative legal argumentation. Her chapter argues that the formation of a zone can always be articulated with the territorial-legal vocabulary that serves the actors in the fulfilment of their aims and preferences, while discarding those arguments that do not fit their aims. International law should thus be seen as complicit in creating regular instances of territorialization.

The development of the modern investment treaty regime represents a remarkable extension of international law in the post-war period. However, the development of this regime has precipitated a backlash from various states, civil society actors and scholars over the past decade, particularly on account of the explosion of litigation by foreign investors against host states. Many of these investment treaty arbitrations have resulted in sizeable compensation awards for actions that many states believe are both legitimate and within their exclusive purview as sovereigns. This tension between the rights afforded to private foreign investors under international treaties and the legitimate rights of sovereign states to regulate in the public interest of their domestic citizenry has culminated in efforts by states to weaken the regime. In Chapter 4, Malcolm Langford, Daniel Behn and Ole Kristian Fauchald analyze the strategies and tactics, particularly those of a more questionable nature, that states are employing to scale back the unintended consequences of the international investment regime while simultaneously claiming adherence to its international legal obligations.

Chapter 5, by Moritz Baumgärtel, examines state strategies in relation to the European Court of Human Rights and the Court of Justice of the EU in regard to cases concerning migrants and asylum seekers. This represent one of, if not the, most difficult and pressing issues before the two courts. The current refugee crisis and the ascendance of a right-wing political climate have created a volatile situation in which European governments increasingly enact legally questionable policies, which in turn are being challenged before the two European courts. Looking at recent cases, this chapter explores how governments maximize their 'sovereign manoeuvrability' when confronted with European-level litigation. It describes four different strategies of 'managing' and containing the impact of such rulings: legal argumentation about the scope of the relevant instruments, policy implications and procedural requirements; 'anticipatory measures' aiming to strike out cases or to contain public reactions to adverse rulings; 'peer mobilization' exerting collective pressure on the courts; and post-judgment positioning vis-à-vis the judgment or the court in question. The chapter thereby highlights how changing practices of international law require more differentiated evaluations even of the influence of strong and assertive international judicial bodies such as the two European courts.

In the following chapter, Itamar Mann takes on the equally thorny issue of surveillance and examines bilateral and multilateral arrangements for the collection of signals intelligence between the US's National Security Agency and its partner organizations in other countries. He argues that these arrangements, which at face value appear far removed from the domain of public international law, in fact embody a particular genre of transnational lawmaking. They involve the work of lawyers, and include various soft law instruments that have partaken in a radical disaggregation of the national security state. While the chapter's main objectives are descriptive and analytic, Mann also signals a normative insight: rather than focusing exclusively on individual rights to privacy, lawyers seeking to intervene in the emerging transnational law of mass surveillance ought to focus more on the structural aspects of the agreements that facilitate it.

Jaye Ellis focuses on international environmental protection in Chapter 7. While this is often considered be a highly legalized field, a closer look reveals a good deal of ambiguity regarding law's role. Legal instruments and regimes to address various aspects of environmental protection have proliferated, but at the same time states have managed to maintain a reasonably high degree of control over their legal obligations pertaining to environmental protection. Strategies to manage legal obligations include deference to experts, opportunities for forum shopping by virtue of a multiplication of self-contained regimes, and inefficiency. This is in sharp contrast to the functioning of trade disciplines that states have imposed on their environmental and health standards. As environmental regimes become more complex and highly specialized, the role of law loses ground to other forms of expertise, notably scientific and economic. Legalization turns out to be a thinly disguised managerialism.

Chapter 8, by Thomas Gammeltoft-Hansen and Tanja Aalberts, analyzes the interplay between politics and law in the recent attempts to strengthen the humanitarian commitment to saving lives of migrants in the Mediterranean. Despite a long-standing obligation to aid people in distress at sea, the search and rescue regime has been marred by conflicts and political stand-offs as states were faced with a growing number of capsizing boat migrants potentially claiming international protection once on dry land. Attempts to provide a legal solution to these problems have resulted in a re-spatialization of the high seas, extending the states' obligations in the international public domain based on geography rather than traditional functionalist principles that operated in the open seas. However, inadvertently, this attempt towards further regulation has simultaneously enabled states to instrumentalize international law to barter off and deconstruct responsibility by reference to traditional norms of sovereignty and the law of the sea. In other words, states may be seen to skilfully navigate the different waters of international law themselves in order to recoup sovereign power.

The final chapter recapitulates the main findings of the substantive chapters and their relationship to the overall argument of the volume. One argument going through all chapters is that in order to understand the seemingly contradictory developments of international law today, we need to take a step back and pay more attention to how strategic navigation of rules is facilitated by international law itself. The second section of the chapter sets out to outline a possible research agenda on this basis. At the most immediate level, this relates to nuancing and expanding the attempted typology set out in this chapter, as well as expanding the empirical gaze to include other pertinent issues, such as international tax regulation, the law of armed conflict and the current claims for resources and navigation rights in the Arctic. More generally, such an agenda emphasizes more empirical approaches to the study of international law as a strategy to accommodate different theoretical orientations and explanatory frameworks.

2

Sovereignty Games, International Law and Politics

TANJA AALBERTS AND THOMAS GAMMELTOFT-HANSEN

2.1 Introduction

Our starting point for this volume is the interplay of different empirical developments: the expansion and transformation of international law, on the one hand, and the response of states in terms of their engagement with and contestation of international law, on the other. More specifically, we investigate how the proliferation, fragmentation, constitutionalization and deformalization of international law impact how states engage with and resist the rule of law. As the conceptual backdrop to the empirical starting point and analytical framework set out in Chapter 1, this chapter outlines the conceptual issues behind these observations and addresses some of the theoretical questions they raise about our understanding of the relationship between international law and politics, between rules and strategy and between legalization and sovereignty.

As alluded to in the previous chapter, the increasing legalization of the international realm entails not only the quantitative expansion of international law into ever more legal regimes but also a qualitative transformation of international law towards regulating issues like economic development, human rights and welfare, and thus increasingly undercutting the traditional separation of domestic and international affairs.[1] This separation is the backbone of how sovereignty, as a claim to supreme authority over a territory, traditionally operates. Domestic supremacy (internal sovereignty) is linked to a lack of such overarching authority in the international realm, where external sovereignty manifests itself in the principles of sovereign equality and non-intervention and the ability to regulate

[1] Other qualitative transformations of international law entail increasing resort to soft law, managerialism and risk management. See further below and Chapters 6 and 7, this volume.

and order international relations.[2] Insofar as these regulative principles are based on respecting every state's freedom and autonomy, the expansion of international law and in particular the shift to more substantive regulation and the international law of cooperation are often seen as an intrusion of states' sovereignty and political freedom. As Langford et al. suggest in Chapter 4, sovereignty appears to be giving way to governance, and politics to law. Yet, such an analysis, they point out, is built on a teleological perspective on the evolution of international society, which simply assumes that more international law (i.e. legalization) automatically constrains state behaviour and reduces power politics. Equally unsatisfying is the opposite view forwarded by, for example, International Relations (IR) realists and certain legal scholars that international law has little or no impact on sovereignty or politics. Neither perspective seems to capture the dynamics between international law and politics that we observe, as both these optics share a zero-sum conception of their relationship: either international law trumps politics (and curtails sovereignty) or politics trumps international law.

This presentation of international law and politics as mutually exclusive has a long-standing history and lies at the root of the disciplinary separation of IR from IL. As noted by one of IR's founding fathers, Hans Morgenthau, 'the political realist maintains the autonomy of the political sphere [and] thinks in terms of interest defined as power . . . the lawyer, of conformity of action with legal rules'.[3] In other words, politics is about power and strategy, law about rules and norms – and never the twain shall meet. While various approaches in both IL and IR have sought to analyze the relationship between politics and law since the 1970s, Morgenthau's division of labour has proven to be very tenacious. It has continued to inform subsequent attempts to bring IL and IR into contact again. A popular identification of the parameters of interdisciplinary cooperation sees it as a research agenda based on two fundamentally different 'optics' to studying international society – 'instrumentalist' versus 'rule governed' – within IR and IL, respectively.[4]

2 F. H. Hinsley, *Sovereignty*, 2nd edn (Cambridge: Cambridge University Press, 1986).

3 Hans J. Morgenthau, *Politics among Nations: The Struggle for Power and Peace*, 3rd edn (New York: Knoff, 1966), 13.

4 Robert O. Keohane, 'International Relations and International Law: Two Optics' (1997) 38 *Harvard International Law Journal* 487–502. See also Jeffrey L. Dunoff and Mark A. Pollack (eds), *Interdisciplinary Perspectives on International Law and International Relations: The State of the Art* (Cambridge: Cambridge University Press, 2013).

Such a strict juxtaposition between strategy and rules, however, turns a blind eye to the dynamics that form the starting point of our current analysis: that the expansion and transformation of international law may enable states to recoup sovereign manoeuvrability. Not by rejecting or disregarding international law, but through active and strategic engagement with the structures and substance of international law. The basic observation that, in contemporary international society, politics is concerned with international law just as much as international law must be understood in relation to the society it seeks to regulate (rather than as a self-contained normative order) is hardly new. As highlighted by Judge Alvarez in the 1949 *Corfu Channel* case:

> Jurists, imbued with traditional law, have regarded international law as being of a strictly juridical character; they only consider what they describe as pure law, to the entire exclusion of politics as something alien to law. But pure law does not exist: law is the result of social life and evolves with it; in other words, it is, to a large extent, the effect of politics – especially of a collective kind – as practised by the States. We must therefore beware of considering law and politics as mutually antagonistic.[5]

Judge Alvarez essentially points to the need to move beyond a conceptualization of politics and law as mutually exclusive optics and instead appreciate how international law and politics constantly inform and transform each other.[6] Several scholars have followed this lead, eager to push on from Morgenthau's legacy. Distinctly different approaches to analyzing the relationship between politics and law in the international realm have thus emerged:[7] within IL, for instance, the New Haven school,[8]

[5] *Corfu Channel Case (United Kingdom of Great Britain and Northern Ireland v. People's Republic of Albania)*, judgment of 9 April 1949, ICJ Rep, Individual Opinion Judge Alvarez, pp. 41–2.

[6] Friedrich Kratochwil, *The Status of Law in World Society: Meditations on the Role and Rule of Law* (Cambridge: Cambridge University Press, 2014); Nikolas M. Rajkovic, Tanja E. Aalberts and Thomas Gammeltoft-Hansen (eds), *The Power of Legality: Practices of International Law and Their Politics* (Cambridge: Cambridge University Press, 2016).

[7] For an (interdisciplinary) overview of different approaches, see Robert J. Beck, Anthony Clark Arend and Robert D. Vander Lugt (eds), *International Rules: Approaches from International Law and International Relations* (Oxford: Oxford University Press, 1996); Michael Byers (ed.), *The Role of Law in International Politics: Essays in International Relations and International Law* (Oxford: Oxford University Press, 2000); Robert J. Beck, 'International Law and International Relations Scholarship', in David Armstrong (ed.), *Routledge Handbook of International Law* (Abingdon, UK: Routledge, 2009).

[8] See e.g. Myres S. McDougal, *Studies in World Public Order* (New Haven, CT: Yale University Press, 1960).

international legal process scholarship[9] and critical legal studies;[10] and within IR, for example, the English school,[11] regime theory,[12] the 'legalization debate'[13] and different branches of constructivism.[14] In addition, specific research agendas have emerged seeking to theorize the politics *of* international law.[15] While this diverse theoretical landscape within both disciplines carries many important insights, as reflected throughout the different chapters of this volume, it has also created somewhat of a turf war between different theoretical approaches and disciplines.[15] This in turn has hampered (inter)disciplinary dialogue and risks producing theory-promoting or theory-testing rather than problem-driven research.

To avoid this pitfall, the present chapter thus proposes a different avenue. In line with the above, the practices described in this volume may be seen to represent a particular kind of 'sovereignty game', where states respond to the developing rules and jurisprudence of international law. As a heuristic device, the sovereignty game metaphor serves to bring

[9] See e.g. Harold H. Koh, 'Why Do Nations Obey International Law' (1996) 106 *Yale Law Journal* 2599–659.

[10] See e.g. Nigel Purvis, 'Critical Legal Studies in Public International Law' (1991) 32 *Harvard International Law Journal* 80–127.

[11] See e.g. Hedley Bull, *The Anarchical Society: A Study of Order in World Politics*, 2nd edn (London: Macmillan, 1995 [1977]).

[12] See e.g. Stephen D. Krasner (ed.), *International Regimes* (Ithaca, NY: Cornell University Press, 1983).

[13] See e.g. Judith Goldstein et al., 'Introduction: Legalization and World Politics' (2000) 54 *International Organization* 385–99.

[14] See e.g. Jutta Brunnée and Stephen J. Toope, 'International Law and Constructivism: Elements of an Interactional Theory of International Law' (2000) 39 *Columbia Journal of Transnational Law* 19–74; Friedrich Kratochwil, *Rules, Norms and Decisions: On the Conditions of Practical and Legal Reasoning in International Relations and Domestic Affairs* (Cambridge: Cambridge University Press, 1991).

[15] Key contributions to the development of the 'politics of law' agenda are Martti Koskenniemi, 'The Politics of International Law' (1990) 1 *European Journal of International Law* 4–33; Christian Reus-Smit (ed.), *The Politics of International Law* (Cambridge: Cambridge University Press, 2004); Martti Koskenniemi, 'The Politics of International Law – 20 Years Later' (2009) 20 *European Journal of International Law* 7–19.

[16] In some cases this has led to outright rejections of interdisciplinary approaches altogether: Jan Klabbers, 'The Bridge Crack'd: A Critical Look at Interdisciplinary Relations' (2009) 23 *International Relations* 119–25; Jan Klabbers, 'Counterdisciplinarity' (2010) 4 *International Political Sociology*; Martti Koskenniemi, 'Law, Teleology and International Relations: An Essay in Counterdisciplinarity' (2012) 26 *International Relations* 3–34. See also Jeffrey L. Dunoff, 'From Interdisicplinarity to Counterdisciplinarity: Is There Madness in Martti's Method?' (2013) 27 *Temple International and Comparative Law Journal* 309–37; Tanja Aalberts, 'IR and the Challenges of Interdisciplinarity', in Andreas Gofas, Inanna Hamati-Ataya and Nicholas Onuf (eds), *The Sage Handbook of the History, Philosophy and Sociology of International Relations* (Thousand Oaks, CA: Sage, 2018).

attention to the interrelationship between players, rules and strategy. Employing this metaphor, the present chapter thus seeks to unpack the fundamental paradox of this volume: how the changing landscape of international law enables states to maximize their room for manoeuvre *within* the legal field, and both reclaim or disclaim sovereign authority. More specifically, the sovereignty game is a useful heuristic to explore the interrelationship between strategy and rules and move beyond their juxtaposition as different optics.

As is elaborated below, the notion of '(sovereignty) games' has further been employed by a range of different theoretical perspectives. Rather than staking out a particular position within this field or trying to resolve the different controversies among different theoretical approaches, the present chapter seeks to maintain a pluralist stance that – while obviously drawing on different scholarship within both IL and IR – does not self-identify with any specific position within the current field of IL-IR studies. Such a pluralist approach not only fits the empirical and problem-driven starting point of this volume as well as the diverse theoretical orientations of its contributors but also, we hope, opens up a space for fruitful academic exchange across theoretical perspectives in light of recent developments in international law.

2.2 Sovereignty Games

The notion of sovereignty games is a popular metaphor through which to analyze world politics.[17] As heuristic tools, metaphors help us to distil the key traits of a concept or activity and are particularly helpful when it comes to an elusive concept like sovereignty.[18] Interestingly, the game metaphor has been adopted by very distinct approaches, illuminating different aspects of the relationship between law and politics, as we discuss below. At a more general level, a focus on sovereignty games, or

[17] For analytical usages of the metaphor, see Robert H. Jackson, *Quasi-States: Sovereignty, International Relations and the Third World* (Cambridge: Cambridge University Press, 1990); Georg Sørensen, *Changes in Statehood: The Transformation of International Relations* (Houndmills, UK: Palgrave, 2001); Tanja E. Aalberts, 'The Sovereignty Game States Play: (Quasi-)States in the International Order' (2004) 17 *International Journal for the Semiotics of Law* 245–57; Rebecca Adler-Nissen and Thomas Gammeltoft-Hansen (eds), *Sovereignty Games: Instrumentalising State Sovereignty in Europe and Beyond* (Houndmills, UK: Palgrave, 2008); Tanja E. Aalberts, 'Playing the Game of Sovereign States: Charles Manning's Constructivism *Avant-La-Lettre*' (2010) 16 *European Journal of International Relations* 247–68.

[18] See George Lakoff and Mark Johnson (eds), *Metaphors We Live By*, 2nd edn (Chicago: University of Chicago Press, 2003).

sovereignty as a game, is a useful metaphor by drawing our attention to three necessary elements of any game: players, rules and moves.[19]

First, who are the players involved? Who are the subjects of the sovereignty game? From a legal perspective, this seems a rather straightforward question, as within international law only states have a sovereign status, even if other subjects have gained some form of international legal personality. In practice, however, we witness other actors taking over sovereign prerogatives. This includes most palpably the European Union but also less obvious candidates like private security agencies, foreign investors and airflight carriers, who are now exercising powers that used to be firmly and exclusively in state hands.[20] Moreover, there has been increasing attention for the disaggregation of sovereignty, and the need to move beyond the focus on the state as a single actor, to the various government agencies that act in its name.[21]

The prism of this volume remains with states as the key players of the sovereignty game, but with a specific focus on how processes of legalization have changed the sovereign playing field as well as the state as actor and what it can do. This relates to the second element of the game metaphor: its characteristic as an activity defined by rules. Crucially, these rules do not merely regulate moves in the game but also constitute the game at a more fundamental level.[22] Without rules, there is no game. In terms of the sovereignty game, it is the rules of non-use of force and non-intervention (Articles 2(4) and 2(7) of the UN Charter) that are usually highlighted as the defining rules for the international society of sovereign states. But as already suggested by Friedmann, and elaborated below, these negative duties of co-existence have expanded into more positive and substantive duties. Rather than identifying this as the beginning of the end of sovereignty, the game metaphor directs us to a more nuanced position, distinguishing between the status as a sovereign player and the changing content of what it means to be a member of international society, based on the fundamental rules and principles that govern that society and the interaction between its members.[23] This in turn relates to making moves

19 Thomas Gammeltoft-Hansen and Rebecca Adler-Nissen, 'An Introduction to Sovereignty Games', in Adler-Nissen and Gammeltoft-Hansen, *Sovereignty Games*, pp. 1–17.

20 See Chapters 4, 6, and 8, this volume.

21 Anne-Marie Slaughter, *A New World Order* (Princeton, NJ: Princeton University Press, 2004); see also Chapter 6, this volume, which contrasts Anne-Marie Slaughter's positive presentation of disaggregated sovereignty with its dark sides.

22 John R. Searle, *The Construction of Social Reality* (New York: Free Press, 1995).

23 Martti Koskenniemi, 'The Future of Statehood', 32 *Harvard International Law Journal* (1991), 397–410. Wouter G. Werner, 'State Sovereignty and International Legal Discourse',

in a game, as the third component of the game metaphor. The possible moves are defined by the rules of the game. This category also includes (but is not limited to) strategic play. Strategy can be defined as the skilled use of rules for specific purposes.[24]

This general heuristic of the sovereignty game, calling attention to players, rules and moves and strategies, enables us to move beyond the juxtaposition of law and politics and instead examine them as interwoven practices. Before we do so, the next section engages with different ways in which the game metaphor has been applied in analyses of world politics and international law, as the background theoretical discussion for our more specific analytical focus on sovereignty games to analyse the changing practices of international law.

2.3 Metaphors of Games

Casual references to the metaphor aside, the game metaphor is rooted in two different traditions within international studies and legal theory: rationalist game theory, which has inspired contemporary legal research through, notably, the work of Jack Goldsmith and Eric Posner,[25] on the one hand, and the Wittgensteinian notion of language games, which has inspired critical approaches in both IL and IR (notably through the work of Martti Koskenniemi and Friedrich Kratochwil, respectively),[26] on the other.[27] As is elaborated below, these traditions highlight different aspects of the politicization and instrumentalization of law that are the focus of this volume.

in Ige F. Dekker and Wouter G Werner (ed) *Governance and International Legal Theory* (Leiden: Martinus Nijhoff, 2004), 125–157. See also Abram Chayes and Antonia Handler Chayes, *The New Sovereignty: Compliance with International Regulatory Agreements* (Cambridge, MA: Harvard University Press, 1995).

24 Gammeltoft-Hansen and Adler-Nissen, Introduction.

25 Jack Goldsmith and Eric A. Posner, *The Limits of International Law* (Oxford: Oxford University Press, 2005).

26 The classical works are Martti Koskenniemi, *From Apology to Utopia: The Structure of International Legal Argument* (Cambridge: Cambridge University Press, 2005 [1989]), and Friedrich Kratochwil, *Rules, Norms and Decisions: On the Conditions of Practical and Legal Reasoning in International Relations and Domestic Affairs* (Cambridge: Cambridge University Press, 1991); see also Anthony Carty, 'Language Games of International Law: Koskenniemi as the Discipline's Wittgenstein' (2012) 13 *Melbourne Journal of International Law* 1–20. The game metaphor has recently been used in a volume on interpretation in international law: Andrea Bianchi, Daniel Peat and Matthew Windsor (eds), *Interpretation in International Law* (Oxford: Oxford University Press, 2015).

27 See Tanja E. Aalberts, *Constructing Sovereignty between Politics and Law* (London: Routledge, 2012), Chapter 5, for a more elaborate discussion of these different traditions.

Probably the most well-known application of the game metaphor is so-called rational choice game theory. Originating in Economics, game theory has gained popularity within Political Science. The focus here is on different strategies that actors may pursue and different game scenarios, such as the Prisoner's Dilemma, Chicken Game and Battle of the Sexes. The imaginative starting point is that of states playing a game, adopting different strategic behaviour, occasional cheating practices and free interpretation or breaking of the rules in order to win the game or protect one's interests as best possible. With the emergence of Law and Economics as a separate field, as well as the interdisciplinary agenda with IR, this mode of analysis has also found its way into IL, notably through the work of Jack Goldsmith and Eric Posner.[28] In the elaboration of Goldsmith and Posner, economic models help to determine the power of law by measuring compliance based on state behaviour driven by state interests.

According to this approach, states only comply with international law to the extent that rules align with their political interests.[29] In their influential volume, Goldsmith and Posner argue that international law lacks (causal) force or effectiveness because it has no independent moral force. International law is thus epiphenomenal to power politics. Indeed, international law itself is the product of state interests: 'international law emerges from states acting rationally to maximize their interests, given their perceptions of the interests of other states and the distribution of power'.[30] Accordingly, a game theoretical approach to international law addresses the politics of international law by focusing on the 'why' question: why, and under what circumstance, do states comply with international law?[31] Located within rational choice thinking, the focus is usually on (given) material interests of states, although particular strands of constructivist research

[28] Douglas G. Baird, Robert H. Gertner and Randal C. Picker, *Game Theory and the Law* (Cambridge, MA: Harvard University Press, 1998); Goldsmith and Posner, *The Limits of International Law*; Andrew T. Guzman, *How International Law Works: A Rational Choice Theory* (New York: Oxford University Press, 2008). To be sure, law and economics is a broader school, and not all approaches are similarly focused on realist premises about individual state interest but rather foreground economic utility as a systemic or collective good and telos of international law. Goldsmith and Posner's volume, however, has gained most traction in the interdisciplinary debate with International Relations, precisely because of their affinity with realism.

[29] Stephen D. Krasner, *Sovereignty: Organized Hypocrisy* (Princeton, NJ: Princeton University Press, 1999).

[30] Goldsmith and Posner, *The Limits of International Law*, p. 3.

[31] Critics conversely argue that such a framework has a built-in assumption of interest-driven behaviour (whatever a state does, it proves what state interest are as only interests drive state behaviour). Moreover, it assumes that rules speak for themselves. See e.g. Koskenniemi, 'Law, Teleology and International Relations'; Kratochwil, *Rules, Norms and Decisions*.

have broadened the agenda to also include the social context in which norms and interests operate.[32] In such a view, states may change their conception of their interests owing to, for instance, processes of socialization between members of international society.

A rather different approach to games emerges from critical approaches within both IL and IR, inspired by philosophy of language.[33] These scholars suggest that we should not only broaden our focus to look at different mechanisms for compliance, but ask *how* it is possible for states to comply with international law and *what* compliance means in the first place. For Koskenniemi, a crucial question for understanding the operation of international law is to ask 'what there is to comply with in the first place, what, of the many possibilities, is the preferable meaning of the rule, and should the rule be applied, or the exception?'[34] Such a perspective draws attention to the important role of contestation as part of increasing legalization and that such contestation as well as seemingly aberrant behaviour may serve a productive role vis-à-vis the validity and moral force of international law.[35] For instance, non-compliant behaviour may be justified by reference to rules themselves – e.g. by appealing to exceptional circumstances, hence confirming that in normal situations the rules do indeed apply.

The emphasis on justification and on viewing international law as an argumentative practice are characteristic of another application of the game metaphor,[36] drawing on Ludwig Wittgenstein's philosophy of

[32] E.g. Chayes and Chayes, *The New Sovereignty*; James Fearon and Alexander Wendt, 'Rationalism v. Constructivism: A Skeptical View', in Walter Carlsnaes, Thomas Risse and Beth A. Simmons (eds), *Handbook of International Relations* (London: Sage, 2002), 52–72; Martha Finnemore and Stephen J. Toope, 'Alternatives to "Legalization": Richer Views of Law and Politics' (2001) 55 *International Organization* 743–58, at 745. This rationalist-constructivist debate or even synthesis has been an important driver of the mainstream IL/IR agenda. See Dunoff and Pollack, *Interdisciplinary Perspectives*.

[33] See e.g. Kratochwil, *Rules, Norms and Decisions*; Kratochwil, *Status of Law;* Koskenniemi, *From Apology to Utopia*.

[34] Koskenniemi, 'Law, Teleology and International Relations', p. 17, italics ommitted; Kratochwil, *Rules, Norms and Decisions*; Kratochwil, *Status of Law*.

[35] Kratochwil, *Status of Law*.

[36] Koskenniemi, *From Apology to Utopia*, and Kratochwil, *Rules, Norms and Decisions*. Goldsmith and Posner discuss the communicative utility of law, whose formal and abstract language enables states to explain their policies and clarify their interests to an audience that does not share the same community (*The Limits of International Law*, pp. 182–84). As elaborated by linguistic approaches, language has a more constitutive function than being merely a communicative device.

language.[37] Wittgenstein compares language to making moves in a game to explicate that language is itself a form of action, a form of life, governed by rules.[38] In other words, he uses the game metaphor to illuminate the productivity of language, i.e. the role of language in constructing reality. Whereas this was an important and controversial insight for IR theory and its 'linguistic turn',[39] the power of language is common knowledge for both legal scholars and practising lawyers. Language and words, such as 'war' or 'genocide', produce distinct legal categories and effects. By labelling particular actions as (part of) an armed conflict, we enter into a different legal game, with specific rules of legal and illegal conduct.[40] In Wittgensteinian terms, the language and categories of international law are a form of action, they *do* something to reality. Moreover, like a language game, practices of international law are based on rules and conventions, which on the one hand describe possible moves and prohibit others, and on the other hand are flexible in that they do not dictate which specific course of action is taken.

Another element follows from this. To identify language as action means that words are not self-contained, but gain their meaning in practice: 'the meaning of a word is its use in the language'.[41] As H. L. A. Hart argues, rules do not speak for themselves, but can only be interpreted and applied in relation to concrete cases, and the open texture of general terms in language render international rules and obligations indeterminate.[42] In contrast to a positivist conception, critical approaches within both IL and

[37] Ludwig J. J. Wittgenstein, *Philosophical Investigations*, 3rd edn (London: Prentice Hall, 1958). Both Koskenniemi and Kratochwil rely on Wittgensteinian philosophy of language. See also Carty, 'Language Games of International Law'.

[38] Wittgenstein, *Philosophical Investigations*, para. 7.

[39] This linguistic turn was instigated in IR by Nicholas G. Onuf, *World of Our Making: Rules and Rule in Social Theory and International Relations* (Columbia: University of South Carolina Press, 1989); Kratochwil, *Rules, Norms and Decisions*; and a special issue in (1990) 34 *International Studies Quarterly* 259–416.

[40] Tanja E. Aalberts and Wouter G. Werner, 'International Law and International Political Sociology', in Xavier Guillaume and Pınar Bilgin (eds), *The Routledge Handbook of International Political Sociology* (New York: Routledge, 2017), 40–41. See also David Kennedy, *Of War and Law* (Oxford: Oxford University Press, 2006).

[41] Wittgenstein, *Philosophical Investigations*, para. 43, see also paras 23, 83.

[42] H. L. A. Hart, *The Concept of Law* (Oxford: Clarendon Press, 1961), 121–44. In his later writings, Hart distances himself from this linguistic argumentation of indeterminacy and suggests that 'a legal system often has other resources besides the words used in the formulations of its rules which serve to determine their content or meaning in particular cases' (Hart, *Essays in Jurisprudence and Philosophy* [Oxford: Oxford University Press, 1993], pp. 7–8).

IR similarly reject the existence of a rule outside or beyond its interpretation. In other words, interpretation creates meaning, rather than discovers it.[43] If law is a linguistic activity and argumentative practice, the language game metaphor highlights that the meaning of international law – and hence international law itself – is produced through its usage. This becomes even more complex when the legal landscape is composed of a patchwork of overlapping regimes and transnational networks, operating in deformalized, highly pluralistic contexts where 'international norms [are] enforced through decentralized processes [by the] "international community"',[44] as the background of this volume's analysis.

A further point follows from this, namely that legal arguments are always made from particular subject positions with various interests and preferences at play.[45] Recall again Madeleine Albright's request for new lawyers in the Kosovo war.[46] This opens up a whole different venue to analyze the 'politics of international law'. As one of its significant contributions to international legal theory, critical legal studies lays bare how the inherent indeterminacy of the law gives a prominent place to political choices that not only drive legal practice, but constitute its meaning.[47] This also means that the juxtaposition of rules versus strategy is too crude to capture the interplay between politics and law. The success story of international law and the legalization of world politics does not rule out strategic engagement – states not only playing *by* but also *with* the rules and their international normative commitments.[48] However, as mentioned in

[43] Koskenniemi, *From Apology to Utopia*, p. 531. See also Ingo Venzke, *How Interpretation Makes International Law: On Semantic Change and Normative Twists* (Oxford: Oxford University Press, 2013). This also means that the distinction between rule creation and rule application collapses. In addition, in *From Apology*, Koskenniemi further elaborates the power of discourse and the structure of legal argumentation in terms of a specific post-structuralist tradition of deconstruction. In Derridian fashion, he deconstructs the structure of legal argumentation as a system of conceptual differentiations that manifestly produces internal contradictions (see also Chapter 3, this volume). Koskenniemi, however, distances himself from the idea of radical indeterminacy based on semantic openness (Koskenniemi, *From Apology to Utopia*, p. 595). See also Iain Scobbie, 'Towards the Elimination of International Law: Some Radical Scepticism about Sceptical Radicalism' (1991) 61 *British Yearbook of International Law* 339–62.

[44] Kennedy, *Of War and Law*, p. 91. See also Rajkovic et al., *Power of Legality*.

[45] See e.g. Chapters 3, 4 and 8, this volume. This focus on (state) preferences and interests is akin to rational choice theorists, even if the conceptualization of what these interests are differs. See Alexander Wendt, *A Social Theory of International Politics* (Cambridge: Cambridge University Press, 1999), 113–38.

[46] Chapter 1, this volume. [47] See Chapter 3, this volume.

[48] In this context, critical legal studies identifies law as an instrument of hegemony and power. Martti Koskenniemi, 'International Law and Hegemony: A Reconfiguration' (2004) 17 *Cambridge Review of International Affairs* 197–218; Eyal Benvenisti and George W. Downs,

Chapter 1, identifying the role of strategy is not the same as reducing international law to a tool for power politics and introducing realism through the backdoor. Indeed, the language game metaphor draws attention to the fact that 'rationality' involves a (dynamic) interpretation of one's situation, the normative context (what game are we playing, which rules apply?), and one's identity (what is my position within this game, what role do I play?).[49] In other (more abstract) words, actors, actions and objects obtain their meaning and identity in the context of a set of rules and practices that defines their interrelationships. The linguistic turn hence highlights the productive function of language by focusing on what it *does* – how interpretations shape (our knowledge of) the world, and how they render particular actions possible, obvious or legitimate, but also leave room for contestation of rules, their interpretation and applicability.

Together, this means that the usual juxtaposition of politics and law as a zero-sum game is too simplistic to capture the role of international law, its simultaneous expansion and contestation within contemporary global governance. Analyzing these dynamics requires a move beyond the focus on law as (not) constraining the behaviour of key actors, to analyzing its role as facilitating, enabling *and* disciplining politics.[50] Moreover, the (sovereignty) game metaphor invokes the idea of law as a practice, 'an activity, whose "being" is in the "doing" of the participants within the practice' (rather than a 'thing' as a given and self-evident body of rules), as will be elaborated in the next section.[51] This includes, but is not limited to argumentative practices or legal discourse. The current volume analyzes politico-legal practices more broadly, to identify specific strategies of political contestation *through* international law, to carve out the space of sovereignty politics in relation to the changing parameters of international law. Based on their different theoretical affiliations, the various chapters will provide different answers as to why and how states are doing this.

2.4 The Game of Sovereigns and International Law

Bringing these insights to bear on our discussion on changing practices of international law, we suggest that the notion of sovereignty games is a

'The Empire's New Clothes: Political Economy and the Fragmentation of International Law' (2007) 60 *Stanford Law Review* 595–631.

49 See also Kratochwil, *Rules, Norms and Decisions*; Kratochwil, *Status of Law*.

50 Michel Foucault, 'Truth and Power', in Colin Gordon (ed.), *Power/Knowledge: Selected Interviews and Other Writings 1972–1977* (Brighton, UK: Harvester Press, 1980), 109–33.

51 Dennis M. Patterson, 'Law's Pragmatism: Law as Practice and Narrative', in Dennis M. Patterson (ed.), *Wittgenstein and Legal Theory* (Boulder, CO: Westview Press, 1992), 87.

helpful tool to analyze the relationship between sovereignty, politics and law as mutually constitutive practices of international society. Building on our initial identification of the different elements of the sovereignty game, it highlights that sovereignty is not just about winning a game, and pursuing foreign policy goals and state interests, but also how to play, identifying which manoeuvres are possible or prohibited, and who gets to play, in the first place (i.e. moves, rules and players). In other words, apart from instrumental rules and tactics (i.e. the instructions given by a coach), games also entail constitutive rules which define which game we are playing, and who are the designated players (rules of recognition) and what moves can be made by different pieces/actors.[52] This also means that world politics can only be understood by taking the normative framework within which sovereign actors emerge and act into account.[53] Even if sovereignty is commonly identified with autonomy and freedom, this independence is not separate from the development of an international legal order, but produced in tandem. Not only is sovereign statehood inherently linked to changing membership rules of international society, its features of independence, autonomy and freedom are also themselves products of international law; they are a condition of specific political communities *according to* international law, to paraphrase Judge Anzilotti in the *Customs Union case*.[54] In other words, in international legal discourse, sovereignty is used to identify the legal status of a political community as an independent state.

In terms of our game metaphor, this also means that the role of international law within the sovereignty game entails more than just the regulation of international affairs between pre-existing state entities; it constitutes the very players of the game in the first place by legitimating their participation and empowering their international capacity, and by defining the parameters within which they can exercise their independence and sovereignty. These parameters include, but are not limited to, the basic rules of conduct for international

[52] Jackson, *Quasi-States*, pp. 34–5.

[53] Christian Reus-Smit, 'Introduction', in Christian Reus-Smit (ed.), *The Politics of International Law* (Cambridge: Cambridge University Press, 2004), p. 3.

[54] Separate Opinion of Judge Anzilotti to the *Austro-German Customs Union Case* (*Austria v. Germany*), Advisory Opinion, Permanent Court of Justice, PCIJ Series A/B, no. 41, 1931 (emphasis added). See also *Island of Palmas Case* (*Netherlands v. United States*), Permanent Court of Arbitration, 2 RIAA 829, 1928, p. 838.

intercourse, which entails both their freedom and rights, and their duties and obligations.[55] In other words, sovereignty can be conceived of as a specific way of ordering international life by linking freedom and responsibility.[56]

At the same time, the rules of the game are not carved in stone: the meaning of sovereignty, its legal scope and content, are produced in practice, i.e. in their usage. As pointed out by the Permanent Court in the *Nationality Decrees* case: 'The question whether a certain matter is or is not solely within the jurisdiction of a State is an essentially relative question; it depends upon the development of international relations'.[57] The development of international law means that such sovereign obligations or responsibilities have significantly expanded to include international obligations towards the state's own citizens, humans everywhere (as claimed by e.g. the Responsibility to Protect paradigm) and even towards non-personal entities such as the environment.[58] It is through the conceptual shift from sovereignty as autonomy and freedom to sovereignty as responsibility that we can understand state strategies that sometimes involve attempts to eschew their sovereign prerogatives, shift sovereign responsibility elsewhere or recoup sovereign freedom by engaging with the rules. This in turn means that the paradoxical outcome of the success of international law (in terms of its multiplication and expansion) can be law's complicity in organizing and creating irresponsibility.[59]

55 'This right [to exercise sovereignty and the functions of a State] has as corollary a duty: the obligation to protect within the territory the rights of other States, in particular their right to integrity and inviolability in peace and in war, together with the rights which each State may claim for its nations in foreign territory'. *Island of Palmas Case (Netherlands v. United States)*, Permanent Court of Arbitration, 2 RIAA 829, 1928, p. 839.

56 Tanja E. Aalberts and Wouter G. Werner, 'Sovereignty beyond Borders: Sovereignty, Self-Defense and the Disciplining of States', in Adler-Nissen and Gammeltoft-Hansen, *Sovereignty Games*, pp. 129–50.

57 *Nationality Decrees in Tunis and Morocco (Britain v. France)*, PCIJ, Series B, no. 4, 1923, p. 24. For a historical analysis, see Christian Reus-Smit, *The Moral Purpose of the State: Culture, Social Identity, and Institutional Rationality in International Relations* (Princeton, NJ: Princeton University Press, 1999).

58 Tanja E. Aalberts and Wouter G. Werner, 'Mastering the Globe: Law, Sovereignty and the Commons of Mankind', in Rens van Munster and Casper Sylvest (eds), *Assembling the Planet: Post-War Politics of Globality* (New York: Routledge, 2016).

59 Scott Veitch, *Law and Irresponsibility: On the Legitimation of Human Suffering* (Abingdon, UK: Routledge, 2007). See also discussion in Chapter 3, this volume.

But the 'meaning in use' also plays at the level of interpretative struggles about the application of international law. This struggle does not take place in normative isolation, but among players that need to defend and justify their positions, whether during judicial proceedings before a court[60] or as part of everyday political practice, both within national parliaments and international diplomatic fora. Like any game, playing by the rules does not rule out strategizing.[61] As mentioned above, importantly, this focus on meaning-in-use and strategy should not be seen to introduce radical indeterminacy or instrumentalization-all-the-way-down through the back door. In fact, what counts as a strategic move is to a great extent determined (although not dictated) by the rules of the game. What is a strategic move depends on which game is being played and from which position. There is no rule in soccer that forbids a goalkeeper from moving at the frontlines; nevertheless, given the aim and rules of the game, s/he would be a fool to do so under normal circumstances. In Chapter 4, Langford et al. in this context distinguish between strategies that states engage with as the principal of international investment regimes and their tactics as litigant in front of an arbitration body.

Moreover, as a practice, strategizing in regard to policies and interpretation has to take account of the wider field of possible interpretations of a given issue. Consequently, by entering into the juridical field, governments have to accept 'the specific requirements of the juridical construction of the issue'.[62] Yet within this framework it is entirely possible to affect both the legal interpretation and framing of a particular issue as well as to organize political practices so as to avoid liability. Here too, strategy as such is not opposite to rule-play, but indeed dependent on knowledge of the rules (*know-what*) as well as the skills for engaging in legal argumentation (*know-how*). In Chapter 6, Mann refers to legal practice as lawyerly craft, to encompass both the element of skilled use, the art or professional practice of doing law, *and* the element of cunning and strategizing. Government legal advisors become the crucial intermediaries in this interplay between politics and international law – at once deciphering the boundaries of legitimate political action and actively engaging in

60 See Chapters 4 and 5, this volume.

61 Cf. Wittgenstein, *Philosophical Investigations*, para. 85.

62 Pierre Bourdieu, 'The Force of Law: Toward a Sociology of the Juridical Field' (1987) 38 *Hastings Law Journal* 805–53, at 831.

devising creative solutions to ensure that these boundaries are not static but negotiable.

2.5 The Legal Room for Manoeuvre

The overall argument of this volume is that the expansion of international law into a complex web of overlapping legal regimes provides further leverage for playing the sovereignty game, regaining sovereign power while at the same time disclaiming sovereign responsibility. As Baumgärtel shows in Chapter 5, this 'legislative patchwork' can be used creatively not only prior to legal procedures (in the case of judicial forum shopping), but also during court proceedings, as well as in post-judgment positioning. Moreover, as the chapters in this volume collectively show, the combined quantitative and qualitative transformation of international law – from positivist rules to a wider variety of legal instruments, including soft law such as codes of conduct and Memoranda of Understanding – further facilitate strategic engagement, or navigating the room for semi-compliance, as Langford et al. formulate it with regard to international investment regimes in Chapter 4. The varied patchwork of legal regimes, institutions and instruments enables the invocation of one register of international law against another, not to disregard or violate legal norms, but to avoid it by 'comply[ing] with other law – while at the same time thwarting law's stated normative commitments'.[63] The result, as Brummer provocatively suggests in Chapter 3, is law's complicity in organizing and creating irresponsibility. Together the case studies show how the expansion of international law has not eliminated politics, but transformed its operation as states are now pursuing their foreign policy goals through a variety of legalized strategies that mobilize international law in sophisticated ways in order to mitigate its constraining effects while legitimizing international politics.

Thus, we have moved from the identification of rules and strategy as two separate optics on the workings of international politics and law,[64] to their workings as intertwined aspects of international law as an argumentative practice in international society. And crucially, as this volume shows, the politics of international law works both ways.[65] The

[63] Chapter 6, this volume, p. 131. [64] Keohane, 'Two Optics'.
[65] Reus-Smit, 'The Politics of International Law', p. 14.

recent discussion on lawfare is only the most outspoken illustration of how law has become an integrated part of world politics, a *sine qua non* for doing and justifying foreign policies and politics.[66] Indeed, in Chapter 5, Baumgärtel suggests that finding ways to manage the courts has now become part of the game of policy making. The case studies in this volume demonstrate that despite their desire to ensure greater political manoeuvrability in regard to international law, states nonetheless go to great lengths to find solutions that maintain a certain degree of legal legitimacy.

A key question in examining the current range of practices in regard to international law is thus what makes certain policy options appear unviable from the perspective of governments? The very resort to 'exceptionalism' and creative policy measures suggest that at least under some circumstances international law sets certain boundaries that states accept as being beyond dispute. Indeed, as aforementioned, calling upon an exception reinforces the discursive power of international law as the framework and vocabulary for international intercourse. At other occasions, states can try and push the legal boundaries through creative legal argumentation – such as the revival or corpus theory developed by the US allies to try and justify the Iraq intervention by relying on the body of resolutions issued by the UN Security Council in the 1990s, or the infamous torture memos by the Bush administration. Rather than calling upon the exception as a way to suspend international law in the face of vital threats to global security, these are practices of legal representation, trying to embed security practices within the law.[67] The shift to risk management, and the transferral of the 'precautionary principle' from international environmental law to the field of security in the war on terror, further stretches the legal register, as does the international law's move towards managerialism, incorporating non-legal experts' vocabulary of 'reasonableness', 'ethics', or 'efficiency' as part of legal reasoning.[68] As Ellis argues in Chapter 7, this is at least partly the effect of making the crafting and application of its

66 Kennedy, *Of War and Law*; Wouter G. Werner, 'The Curious Career of Lawfare' (2010) 43 *Case Western Reserve Journal of International Law* 61–72.

67 Fleur Johns, *Non-Legality in International Law: Unruly Law* (Cambridge: Cambridge University Press, 2013). See also Chapter 3 (on the legal creation of extraterritorial zones) and Chapter 6 (on the legal design of global mass surveillance), this volume.

68 Kennedy, *Of War and Law*; Martti Koskenniemi, 'The Fate of Public International Law: Between Technique and Politics' (2007) 70 *Modern Law Review* 1–30. See also the symposium on 'The Risks of International Law' (2008) *Leiden Journal of International Law*

specialized norms heavily dependent upon scientific expertise, or what in our typology is referred to as 'extralegal deferral'.[69]

2.6 Conclusion

Rather than assuming that power politics always trumps international law, or vice versa, assuming that the expansion of international law constrains and disciplines the operation of sovereign power unidirectionally, this chapter argues that we need to understand how international law, sovereignty and the operation of power are intimately intertwined and that, accordingly, we need to engage in empirical investigations of how players, notably states, proceed when they encounter the expansion of international law into diverse areas and different modalities, how states put the rules to practices and relate them to their actions.[70] In this chapter, the sovereignty game serves as a heuristic starting point for more generally examining how the expansion of international law goes hand in hand with changing state practices and increasing – rather than diminishing – politico-legal manoeuvrability.

The game metaphor also highlights that sovereignty cannot be reduced to freedom and autonomy, rights and duties alone, as it is about status (being a player in the game) as much as it is about competences. From the above discussion, it is clear that we see neither sovereignty nor international law as something given. This includes not only the volume's focus on the quantitative and qualitative transformations of international law, but also a move beyond international law as only a body of rules, to a focus on how these rules come to life through sovereign practices (and vice versa). As outlined in the preceding chapter, different developments of international law have indeed changed the playing field for members of the international society, leading many states to engage more profoundly and creatively with this normative corpus in order to retain or recoup room

21(4), 783–884. Chayes and Chayes, *The New Sovereignty* proposes a managerial approach to increase state compliance with international law.

69 See also the symposium on 'Expertise, Uncertainty, and International Law' in (2013) *Leiden Journal of International Law* 26(4), 783–854, and Wouter G. Werner, 'The Politics of Expertise: Applying Paradoxes of Scientific Expertise to International Law', in Monika Ambrus et al. (eds), *The Role of Experts in International and European Decision-Making Processes. Advisors, Decision Makers or Irrelevant Actors?* (Cambridge: Cambridge University Press, 2014), 44–62.

70 Kratochwil, *Status of Law*, p. 54.

for sovereign manoeuvre. The following chapters analyze these politico-legal practices in the field of human rights litigation, international investment regimes, environmental law, global mass surveillance, irregular boat migration and extra-territorial detention.

3

Abandonment, Construction and Denial

The Formation of a Zone

MARGARETA BRUMMER

3.1 Introduction

Guantanamo Bay in Cuba, the island of Diego Garcia in the British Indian Ocean Territory, and the village of Stare Kiejkuty in Poland may well be separated by thousands of miles on the map. However, they are united in their extra-territorial character. Situated outside the sovereign territory of the US, these zones host military facilities located on Cuban, British[1] and Polish territory, yet controlled by the US. Aimed to be hidden from the public eye, these zones are considered to have witnessed human rights violations on a major scale conducted in the name of the war on terror. The mere existence of these zones, let alone what action takes place there, is justified by a complex division of sovereign rights and responsibilities on the one hand and of jurisdictional authorities on the other, over the formation and maintenance of such extra-territorial locations. These are not legal black holes; instead, they are created through and by law: law is operating here, as Johns put it, 'in excess'.[2]

Reports analyzing the CIA's secret detention and extraordinary rendition programme have later characterized that detaining terrorist suspects outside US territory aimed to keep them 'beyond the reach of the law'.[3]

[1] Diego Garcia is one of the Chagos Islands, which in turn is a unit of British Indian Ocean Territory (BIOT), administered by the UK. However, Mauritius has claimed that the Chagos Islands should be considered as Mauritian sovereign territory. On the positions of the two governments, see e.g. S. Allen, *The Chagos Islanders and International Law* (Hart 2014), 213–15. Also Chagos Marine Protected Area Arbitration *(Mauritius v. the United Kingdom)*, Arbitration, award of 19 March 2015.

[2] F. Johns, *Non-legality in International Law – Unruly Law* (Cambridge: Cambridge University Press, 2013), 70.

[3] For instance the report of Open Society Justice Initiative, *Globalizing Torture – CIA Secret Detention and Extraordinary Rendition* (Open Society Foundations 2013), 5.

Where could that be? And why would the interrogations then be held on the territories of Poland, the UK and Cuba; in other words in states hardly beyond the reach of international law or human rights regulations?[4] In this chapter, I suggest that much has to do with procedures of extra-territorialization and with commitments to certain political-legal vocabularies of international law. I propose that in order to get a better understanding of the activities that take place in a special extra-territorial zone, one should analyze the *formation processes of territorial zones*, and especially how international legal language is creatively used in those processes. Thus, this chapter will contribute to existing discussions on the phenomenon of extra-territorialization by looking at how particular territorial zones are created and maintained through commitments to certain legal vocabularies that, I claim, will *actively render* a territorial place 'beyond the reach of the law'.[5]

3.2 'Beyond the Reach of the Law?'

In order to place a terrorist detainee 'beyond the reach of the law', one needs to find a territorial location where legal means of human rights protection would not provide obstacles for the using of questionable interrogation techniques. International spaces, such as the high seas could, in general, be spaces beyond the reach of national regulations – after all, they formally extend beyond sovereign claims and national jurisdiction of states and are not regulated by human rights treaties in the same way as areas of sovereignty or of sovereign rights.[6] That said, the detention centres were nevertheless ran, amongst others, on territories of EU states that are committed to human rights obligations and procedures aiming to control the legality of activities taking place on their territories. As a result, the procedures of 'zoning' do not seem to rely on any lack of legal regulation. Instead, the crisscrossing legal commitments and entitlements are

4 Some other states, such as Romania and Lithuania have been widely mentioned as sites of the CIA rendition programme.

5 Certainly, 'zoning' may occur for other reasons than extrajudicial interrogations and military operations. See e.g. J. Urry, *Offshoring* (Oxford: Polity, 2014) (on the offshoring of e.g. waste management, taxation, and energy production); R. Palan, R. Murphy and C. Chavagneux, *Tax Havens – How Globalization Really Works* (Ithaca, NY: Cornell University Press, 2010).

6 Although the principle of the flagship jurisdiction applies in the high seas with vessels, *as a space*, the high seas is considered to be beyond sovereign or jurisdictional claims.

expected to produce such a complicated web of legal relationships that, in the end, the location resembles something beyond the reach of *any* law.[7]

In this chapter, I aim to expose the structure of the formation process of an extra-territorial location. I will do this by retracing how three particular territorial locations – the Guantanamo Bay detention centre, the military base of the US in Diego Garcia, and the CIA-led prison in Poland – are rendered extra-territorial by a tripartite process of *abandonment*, *construction* and *denial*. This tripartite process makes use of creative legal arguments. Since states may favour one political-legal vocabulary over other vocabularies – for instance that of sovereignty leading to responsibility – the claim that exercising jurisdiction should lead to responsibility may be discarded as non-applicable or legally irrelevant. Each time, the chosen commitment to a political goal gets articulated by the strategic use of formal legal terms and claims that finds counterparts in the political goal – here Milanovic refers to 'formal categories' of sovereignty or territory, behind which states may hide when convenient.[8]

Although the formation process of a zone is often referred to as extra-territorialization, the definition is not fully satisfying. True enough, the strategic use of extra-territorial locations – also termed jurisdiction shopping – is commonly taken to mean that states argue for certain international or national legal commitments not to bind them outside their territorial borders.[9] However, the strategic use of extra-territorial locations may also indicate that *some*, but not all, international or national legal commitments are extended beyond that state's territorial borders, while others are discarded. Moreover, the strategic use of locations does not necessarily need to be *extra*-territorial in nature. Thus, when the reach of domestic law (or of domestically adopted international obligations) is restricted to only some parts of the national territory, this

[7] The 'problem of many hands' is analyzed in the context of space by K. Easterling, who refers to the 'global architecture and its political masquerades' with modification of spaces for political and legal needs. The result of the modification processes resembles Agamben's concept of 'camp' (dislocating localization and aterritoriality) and Latour's vision of space where 'everything happens in the middle, everything passes between the two, everything happens by way of mediation, translation and networks' while the space 'does not exist, it has no place'. See K. Easterling, *Enduring Innocence – Global Architecture and its Political Masquerades* (Cambridge, MA: MIT Press, 2005), especially 13–14.

[8] M. Milanovic, *Extraterritorial Application of Human Right Treaties – Law, Principles, and Policy* (Cambridge: Cambridge Univerity Press, 2011), 58–61.

[9] See Chapter 1, this volume.

practice may be called *intra*-territoriality.[10] Examples may include the excision of territory for purposes of refugee applications, special economic zones or zones where national minorities reside. Like extra-territoriality, intra-territoriality can result from strategic considerations, and moreover, one state's extra-territoriality may be accompanied by another state's intra-territoriality, as will be later demonstrated in this chapter.

Practices of intra- and extra-terrioriality enjoy a peculiar mutual dependency. If *some* legal commitments are to be denied *within* the borders of the state, it might be easier for the state to maintain that *no* legal commitments should apply *outside* those borders, even when the state concerned exercises jurisdiction and control beyond its territorial borders.[11] Conversely then, the ability to reach outside the territorial borders through extra-territorial activities may diminish the need to restrict the reach of laws and obligations within the territory. Thus, states may continue to flag that on their sovereign territories they are constantly fully committed to their sovereign laws and obligations.

The result is that a state exercising control over a zone outside its sovereign borders may argue for the legal liability or responsibility of that state on whose territory it operates, in order to circumvent legal obligations that could arise from the exercise of jurisdiction or control.[12] The situation, however, might also be reversed. On those accounts, claims in favour of the responsibility or liability of that or those who are exercising jurisdiction or authority over the zone are raised, thus possibly undermining the role that the holder of the sovereign territorial rights would have in the zone.[13]

This chapter illustrates that strategic moves involving extra-territoriality may often follow a general model consisting of three elements: abandonment, construction and denial. When states intentionally

[10] For the concept of intra-territoriality, see K. Raustiala, *Does the Constitution Follow the Flag? The Evolution of Territoriality in American Law* (Oxford: Oxford University Press, 2009), 5.

[11] For the mutual dependency, see more ibid., 7, 233.

[12] The CIA 2004 Report ('Torture Report') mentions that the interrogation of Al-Qaeda members was seen not to violate the Fifth and Fourteenth Amendments of the US Constitution for the reason that those provisions '*do not apply extraterritorially*'. See ECtHR *Husayn (Abu Zubaydah) v. Poland* (Application no. 7511/13), 24 July 2014, para. 57 (on the presumption against extraterritorial obligations).

[13] Continuing with the same example of the CIA 'black site prisons', Poland has been advocating for the US's responsibility over the detention facility located on Polish territory. See ECtHR *Husayn (Abu Zubaydah) v. Poland* (Application no.7511/13), 24 July 2014, para. 234. See also the case of Guantanamo Bay and Cuba later in this chapter.

locate some action outside their sovereign territory, they often later maintain that responsibility over the action can no longer be maintained. In the first place, sovereign territory may be abandoned for the reason that it might prove to be too inflexible and legally restrictive for the fulfilment of the preferences of the state. Ironically enough, this abandonment illustrates that the legal system is working – now the state may again be praised for its commitment to enforce laws and international obligations on its *own* sovereign territory. Leaving the sovereign territory behind is *extra*-territorialization, followed by the state's confirmation that sovereignty, and only sovereignty, leads to responsibility.

Accompanying the abandonment of sovereign territory, a zone is constructed somewhere outside that sovereign territory. This construction involves several legal procedures in the transformation of the sovereign-jurisdictional status of the location. Some may even include the re-naming of the location – the colonial unit of Chagos Archipelago, e.g., was rechristened a separate unit of British Indian Ocean Territory in the 1960s that could then be leased to the US.[14] Indeed, through bilateral or multilateral treaties, leases and concession agreements, states may divide and re-divide the juridical status of the zone. Simultaneously, private agreements between states and other legal actors concerning the legal status of the ownership of the land or of the resources on the location are negotiated.

Once the territorial zone has been constructed, the existence of the zone, the acts in the zone, or the responsibility over the acts in the zone is often denied by all actors involved, with legally the latter being the most noticeable. The existence of zones and acts taking place can often (though not exclusively) be seen as matters of fact; responsibility, however, is a legal category. The one whose territory is being instrumentalized, may argue for the loss of control over the zone and actions committed therein. Here, a sort of *intra*-territorial claim is maintained by the host state's confirmation that jurisdiction (or effective control over the zone) – and not sovereignty – leads to responsibility. Subsequently, the one exercising jurisdiction and control over the zone may claim that asserting jurisdiction without any sovereign control cannot result in responsibility over the acts in the zone.

In Sections 3.3, 3.4 and 3.5 of this chapter, I will systematically address abandonment, construction and denial through three exemplary cases. I will illustrate the first phase of extra-territoralization (abandonment) through the example of Guantanamo Bay, the second (construction)

[14] See Section 3.4.

through the situation in Diego Garcia and the final (denial) on the basis of happenings in Poland – however, all three strategic moves are present in all examples. These sections will be followed by Section 3.6 sketching briefly some of the legal-theoretical background against which this strategic manoeuvring takes place, continued by a discussion on courts and their institutional bias as actors within the inevitable political setting of international law. The point to make is that strategic concerns need not be all-decisive in and of themselves. The law offers so much discretion and leeway that situations and actions can always be re-described in different vocabularies leading to different conclusions.

3.3 The Formation of the Zone: Abandonment

To 'find the legal equivalent of outer space': this was the task given to a handful of lawyers in the US in order to figure out where the captured foreign fighters and terrorist suspects could be placed. As later restated by D Bowker, one of the lawyers in the Bush administration, the aim of a governmental working group after 9/11 was to find a 'suitable location' for prisoners.[15] By 'suitable' the government meant that only few legal restraints would apply: the place would preferably be outside the reach of both national laws and international obligations. Arguably, the most imaginative option was international territory such as outer space, where constitutional courts or provisions of human rights treaties would not reach. At some point, so it was reported, the plan was to keep all the terrorist suspects on ships in international waters.[16] Despite being discarded for security, logistical, and perhaps legal reasons too[17], the spirit remained: a suitable place to hold the terrorist suspects was to be found outside US sovereign soil, on which too many constitutional rights and human rights obligations would otherwise apply.[18]

[15] See M. Isikoff and S. Taylor Jr, 'The Gitmo Fallout', *Newsweek*, 17 July 2006 (available at www.truth-out.org/archive/component/k2/item/64022:the-gitmo-fallout, last visited 14 February 2015).

[16] D. Priest, 'CIA Holds Terror Suspects in Secret Prisons', *Washington Post*, 2 November 2005 (available at www.washingtonpost.com, last visited 14 February 2015). For a report on prison ships holding terrorist suspects, see M. Porges, 'America's Floating Prisons – The U.S. Navy Has Taken on a Curious New Counterterrorism Role', *The Atlantic*, 27 June 2014 (available at www.theatlantic.com, last visited 15 August 2015).

[17] The principle of the exclusive jurisdiction of the flag State stipulates that on the high seas, the flag State exercises both legislative and enforcement jurisdiction over all individuals within the ship. See e.g. Y. Tanaka, *The International Law of the Sea* (Cambridge: Cambridge University Press, 2012), 152.

[18] On offshoring the war on terror, see Raustiala, 187–223.

The option chosen for the storage of the prisoners was the naval base of Guantanamo Bay on Cuban soil – its tumultuous history is well known. After the Spanish-American War of 1898 followed by Cuban independence, the US and Cuban governments negotiated a lease that provided the US with the right to use Guantanamo Bay for coaling and naval purposes. The original lease of 1903 was reconfirmed by a bilateral treaty in 1934, which stipulated that the lease was to be terminated only by agreement between both states or by the US abandoning the base.[19] Most importantly, the lease assigned 'complete jurisdiction and control' over Guantanamo Bay to the US, while Cuba would hold 'ultimate sovereignty'.[20] Thus, the same piece of territory was to have two identities: it was simultaneously the sovereign territory of Cuba and the jurisdictional territory of the US. Nevertheless, over the years, the US enjoyed its territorial presence in Cuba to the fullest. Under strict supervision, the coaling and naval station in Guantanamo Bay evolved gradually into a fully functional naval and military base, first detaining Haitian refugee claimants fleeing for the US in the 1980s and 1990s[21] and later the suspected terrorists of 9/11.

The base seemed to represent an optimal legal solution: someone else's sovereign soil under US control would at its best guarantee the government maximum liberty, together with minimum legal responsibility.[22] At the time it made sense to maintain this belief, since court decisions such as *Rasul v. Bush* and *Boumediene v. Bush* were yet to come.[23] Thus, the

[19] Agreement of 16/23 February 1903, Lease to the United States by Cuba of Land and Water for Naval or Coaling Stations in Guantanamo and Bahia Honda, 2 July 1903; 1934 Treaty of Relations with Cuba (with Platt Amendment).

[20] On the Guantanamo Bay Naval Base lease, see M. Strauss, *The Leasing of Guantanamo Bay* (Westport, CT: Praeger, 2009). Strauss mentions that the perpetual lease introduced 'the concept of a state having 'ultimate sovereignty' or 'definitive sovereignty' over a territory where it does not have, and may never have, any jurisdiction or control', 187.

[21] See e.g. H. Koh, 'America's Offshore Refugee Camps', 29 *University of Richmond Law Review* (1995), 139–73, especially 143–4 ('Had they been brought to the United States, they would have been entitled by statute to asylum interviews with lawyers present').

[22] P. Sands, *Lawless World: America and the Making and Breaking of Global Rules* (Allen Lane, 2005), 144 ('They were being held at Guantanamo because it was outside the sovereign territory of the United States and the Administration believed that this geographic fact would remove all legal protections – both of American constitutional law and international law').

[23] See Raustiala (2009), 200–3, 214–15. In *Rasul v. Bush* (2004), the US Supreme Court argued that there was no question of extraterritoriality, since the lease with Cuba established that Guantanamo was within territorial jurisdiction of the US. Thus the federal habeas corpus statute did permit even foreign detainees in Guantanamo to contest the detention in US Courts. After *Rasul* the statute was amended. In *Boumediene v. Bush* (2008), the Supreme

US government could well hope that by leaving its own territory behind, it would also discard questions of responsibility and of possible habeas corpus. Although not completely certain about its finding, the US Justice Department had thought it through in the following way: 'We conclude that the great weight of legal authority indicates that a federal district court could not properly exercise habeas jurisdiction over an alien detained at GBC'.[24] This view originated from the legal tradition which cherishes a rather strong presumption against extra-territorial application of constitutional rights.[25] Additionally, the Bush administration could hope that the complete jurisdiction and control exercised by the Americans in Guantanamo Bay would only operate on the level of international relations and keep silent about the extension of domestic legal responsibilities of the US on foreign soil.[26]

It should be noted that the US was fulfilling both a familiar and a novel mission when contemplating the ideas of leaving its soil in order to manage a detention centre on Cuban territory beyond the possible reach of the constitutional rights. The familiarity was evident in that imperial locations under US control had already been part of the political-legal aspirations for some time. The mission was to spread and plant the idea of the US as a global power, although only some selected parts of that idea were actually imported to the newly established territories.[27] Thus, if a legal case would arise in one of these colonial locations, the US could quickly limit the reach of the constitutional rights.[28] The novelty in the establishment of imperial extensions lay perhaps in the evolving and

Court ruled again for 'de facto sovereignty' of the territory in Guantanamo Bay and on the constitutional rights of the detainees to challenge their detention in Guantanamo before a federal court.

24 'Possible Habeas Jurisdiction over Aliens Held in Guantanamo Bay, Cuba', in Memorandum to William J. Haynes II from Patrick Philpin and John Yoo, 28 December 2001 (also called the Torture Memos) (Justice Department, 28 December 2001). The writers continue: 'Nonetheless, we cannot say with absolute certainty that any such petition would be dismissed for lack of jurisdiction' (GBC stands for Guantanamo Bay).

25 On the American legal tradition on the presumption against extraterritoriality, see C. Ryngaert, *Jurisdiction in International Law* (Oxford: Oxford University Press, 2008), 59–74.

26 M. Strauss, 'Cuba and State Responsibility for Human Rights at Guantanamo' (2013) *Southern Illinois University Law Journal* 27, 533–50, 543.

27 On the American imperial aspirations, see F. Ninkovich, *The United States and Imperialism* (Malden, MA: Blackwell, 2001), confirming that '... imperialism was not an aberration, but a logical outgrowth of a growing conviction that the nation had a global future in a rapidly modernizing world', 249; and W. Zimmermann, *First Great Triumph: How Five Americans Made Their Country a World Power* (New York: Farrar, Straus and Giroux, 2002) ('Americans like to pretend that they have no imperial past'), 17.

28 For examples, see Raustiala, 59–92.

more strategic thinking related to the use of the extra-territorial location. Arguably there was quite a political and legal jump from a mere naval station evolving into a detention centre for asylum seekers and for terrorism suspects, aimed to be kept outside US territory.

Thus, it can be suggested that the point in having imperial locations was to render them as ordinary as possible in order to strengthen the US's identity as an imperial power in the world, while they would fulfil an exceptional agenda related to their uses. If the leasing of the naval station of Guantanamo Bay was originally not done in order to create a completely exceptional place for the storage of people (but rather to secure naval and coaling interests)[29], Guantanamo Bay gradually became a suitable location for human rights omissions. At some point, it was realized that the mere transportation of people to non-US soil could be argued to have rendered them unreachable to US courts and unreachable by its laws, whether international or domestic in origin. Nothing else was needed than to abandon the sovereign soil, since US soil could promise rule of law and legal remedies.[30] Simple and efficient, one could have thought.

A dual abandonment is thus taking place. While the US is leaving its territory to escape its (constitutional) obligations, Cuba abandons territorial jurisdiction and possible obligations stemming from that principle. Cuba has repeatedly claimed that the presence of the US on Cuban sovereign soil is illegal as the use of territory in the form of a detention centre is against the wording of the lease,[31] while simultaneously the Cuban government has stated that it would not place 'any obstacles to the development of the operation' of bringing the terrorist detainees to its territory.[32] Some have argued that not just the US but also the government of Cuba should thus be

[29] The wording of Platt Amendment requires: 'That to enable the United States to maintain the independence of Cuba, and to protect the people thereof, as well as for its own defence, the government of Cuba will sell or lease to the United States lands *necessary for coaling or naval stations* at certain specified points to be agreed upon with the President of the United States' (italics added).

[30] Ironically, this provides a rather tragic counterpoint to the moments when individuals aim to reach US soil in hope of legal protection: as used to be embodied in the 'wet-foot/dry-foot' policy of the immigration laws of the US. See T. Gammeltoft-Hansen, *Access to Asylum: International Refugee Law and the Globalisation of Migration Control* (Cambridge: Cambridge University Press, 2011), 115–16.

[31] Platt Amendment stipulates that only land necessary for coaling and naval stations is being leased or sold; no other use of land is mentioned. On the evolvement of the practice of the use of the Guantanamo Naval Base in relation to the lease, see M. Strauss, *The Leasing of Guantanamo Bay* (Westport, CT: Praeger, 2009), especially 67–70.

[32] Press Release, Statement of the Ministry of Foreign Affairs of Cuba, 11 January 2002 (available at www.cuba.cu/gobierno/documentos/2002/ing/d110102i.html, last visited 14 January 2015).

seen responsible for hosting the detention centres in Guantanamo Bay.[33] In any case, the story of the Guantanamo Bay detention facility constitutes an example of creative legal reasoning. In abandoning sovereign territory, the rationale is to juxtapose concepts such as sovereign territory with jurisdictional territory, or constitutional territory with extra-territorial territory, in such a way that invoking one can always exclude the other.

3.4 The Formation of the Zone: Construction

In 2005, the foreign secretary of the UK Jack Straw gave the following statement. For some time, several reporters of the British press went on to cite it word for word:

> Unless we all start to believe in conspiracy theories and that the officials are lying, that I am lying, that behind this there is some kind of secret state which is in league with some dark forces in the United States, and also let me say, we believe that Secretary Rice is lying, there simply is no truth in the claims that the United Kingdom has been involved in rendition full stop.[34]

This defensive statement was an answer to a series of allegations claiming that the UK had a role in the extraordinary rendition programme led by the US. Almost a decade later, however, the allegations were in no way dismissed. On the contrary, it was suggested that the UK together with the US had instrumentalized the overseas British territorial location of Diego Garcia to function as a secret rendition prison where captives of the war on terror could be held 'outside' all legal regimes and obligations.[35]

Constructing the sovereign-jurisdictional legal status of Diego Garcia in such a way that the island would be suitable to host an extra-territorial prison has been a complex process. The rather tragic story of the construction of a US military base on one of the Chagos Islands originates

33 For instance M. Strauss, 'Cuba and State Responsibility for Human Rights at Guantanamo', 37 *Southern Illinois University Law Journal* (2013), 533–50.

34 P. Oborne, 'Torture Casts a Ghastly Shadow over Our Country's reputation', *The Telegraph*, 11 April 2012 (available at www.telegraph.co.uk/news/uknews/law-and-order/9197844/Torture-casts-a-ghastly-shadow-over-our-countrys-reputation.html, last visited 15 August 2015).

35 J. Leopold, 'Revealed: Senate Report Contains New Details on CIA Black Sites', *Al-Jazeera America*, 9 April 2014 (available at http://america.aljazeera.com/articles/2014/4/9/senate-cia-torture.html, last visited 14 February 2015). This article reported that the uncensored 2014 US Senate Intelligence report would have included information on the US detaining terrorist suspects in Diego Garcia.

from the 1960s, but has a much longer trajectory going back to British colonization. The process has included several beneficiaries related to territorial rule and private land ownership. The process is best divided into six crucial events: Britain colonizing the islands in the early 1800s; Britain separating the islands from their previous colonial unit with Mauritius to form the new colonial unit of British Indian Ocean Territory (BIOT) in the 1960s; Britain granting the US jurisdictional rights over the island of Diego Garcia in 1966; the British Crown acquiring all land rights from private plantation companies in 1967; the US building a military base on the island in cooperation with the British government starting in the 1970s; and finally in 2010 Britain announcing that the area was part of a new marine protected area (MPA) where the evicted Chagos Islanders could never return.

In 1814, the islands of the Chagos Archipelago, together with the island of Mauritius, were ceded by France to Great Britain. The French had governed the islands since the early 1700s. Most importantly, the French had initiated large coconut plantations on the islands by means of allowing private companies to claim title over the land.[36] Subsequently, the title to the land was carried on by private plantation companies under British colonial rule. Thus for over a century, the Chagos Archipelago and the Island of Mauritius formed one colonial territory, governed by the British Crown while the land was owned by private agricultural companies.

This all changed in the 1960s. In the aftermath of the Cuban missile crisis, the US was looking for suitable territorial locations for its military bases and the strategic location of Diego Garcia in the Indian Ocean seemed ideal.[37] Followed by some governmental exchanges of notes between the US and the UK, the UK promulgated the British Indian Ocean Territory Order of 1965. With the Order, the Chagos Islands were administratively separated from the colonial territorial unit that they used to form together with the island of Mauritius.[38] The Chagos Archipelago, together with some other islands, was thus re-organized under the British Crown to form a separate colonial unit of British Indian Ocean Territory. Here, the British Crown relied on powers contained in the Colonial Boundaries Act 1895. Chapter 34(1) of the Act stipulated that the Crown may by Order alter the boundaries of the colony and 'the boundaries as

36 *Bancoult* [2008 UKHL 61], at 4.

37 About establishing Diego Garcia, see V. Bandjunis, *Diego Garcia: Creation of the Indian Base* (San Jose, CA: Writer's Showcase, 2001). Also Bancoult [2008 UKHL 61] at 6.

38 *Bancoult* [2008 UKHL 61], at 6–7.

so altered shall be [. . .] the boundaries of the colony'.[39] The newly established colonial unit was now ruled by a separate office of the Commissioner of BIOT, ultimately in charge of the laws and the governance of the territory.

By establishing a separate territorial unit, the British Crown made sure that the planned independence of Mauritius would not affect the colonial status of the Chagos Islands. Moreover, the UK maintained the power to conclude an agreement with the US concerning the BIOT.[40] With the agreement, the ultimate sovereignty over the territory remained with the UK, while the jurisdiction over the territories would be jointly organized.[41] The proposition included a long timeframe, since the joint UK-US defence base envisaged in the wake of the Cuban crisis would remain available to meet the needs of both governments for an indefinite period.[42] It was proposed that after the first fifty years, the agreement would continue to be in force for another twenty years, 'unless, not more than two years before the end of the initial period, either Government shall give notice of termination to the other, in which case this Agreement shall terminate two years from the date of such notice'.[43] On 30 December 1966, the BIOT was designated a colonial unit under British sovereignty, but governed by both the UK and the US.[44]

Once the jurisdictional status of the BIOT was settled, the ownership of the land came into question. The land of the BIOT was under the ownership of a Seychelles plantation company *Chagos Agalega Ltd*, for the indigenous population of the island had never enjoyed any official land

[39] Colonial Boundaries Act of 1895 (available at www.legislation.gov.uk/ukpga/1895/34/pdfs/ukpga_18950034_en.pdf, last visited 14 February 2015).

[40] On the strategic relationship between the UK and US, see D. Vine, *Island of Shame: The Secret History of the U.S. Military Base on Diego Garcia* (Princeton, NJ: Princeton University Press, 2009), especially 70–1.

[41] *Bancoult* [2008 UKHL 61], at 7.

[42] Exchange of Notes between the Government of the United Kingdom of Great Britain and Northern Ireland and the Government of the United States of America concerning the Availability for Defence Purposes of the British Indian Ocean Territory, 30 December 1966.

[43] Exchange of Notes between the Government of the United Kingdom of Great Britain and Northern Ireland and the Government of the United States of America concerning the Availability for Defence Purposes of the British Indian Ocean Territory, 30 December 1966, at 11.

[44] It has been reported that the right to use British territory as a US military base was done in exchange for cancelling 14 million dollar debt owed by the UK to the US. See S. Ross, 'Diego Garcia Military Base: Islanders Forcibly Deported', 27 October 2009, available at www.globalresearch.ca/diego-garcia-military-base-islanders-forcibly-deported/15840 (last visited 14 February 2015).

rights.[45] In 1967, the British Crown purchased the land rights held by the company, and subsequently leased the land back to the company. The company was re-organized under the name *Moulinie & Co Ltd*, and it continued to manage the land under contract with the Crown.[46] The land lease between *Moulinie & Co Ltd* and the British Crown was made conditional and it was agreed that the lease would be terminated once the US would start the establishment of the military base.[47] When in 1970 the US announced that the territory should be vacated the following year, the plantation company lost what was still left of its land rights, and the company's employees were evicted from the islands. In December 1970, the construction of the military base initiated on the island of Diego Garcia[48] and agreements between the US and the UK provided for the establishment of military facilities pursuant to the 1966 BIOT agreement.[49] The presence of any other persons than the military forces of the US and UK on the island was denied, but ironically the flora and fauna of the island was to be left as far as possible untouched.[50]

No competing claims of sovereignty over the islands were raised at the time, since the BIOT was separated from Mauritius prior to the independence of the latter.[51] The private plantation companies could no longer present any claims for the ownership of the land, since the Crown had bought them years before the construction of the military facilities were to start. The process was later reported by one British governmental document in the following terms:

> The primary objective in acquiring these islands from Mauritius and the Seychelles to form the new 'British Indian Ocean Territory' was to ensure that Her Majesty's Government had full title to, and control over, these islands so that they could be used for the construction of defence facilities without hindrance or political agitation and so that when a particular

45 *Bancoult* [2008 UKHL 61] at 4.
46 *Bancoult* [2001 QB 1067] at 7.
47 *Bancoult* [2008 UKHL 61] at 7.
48 Bandjunis (2001), 45.
49 Diego Garcia Agreements of 1972 & 1976, available at https://treaties.un.org/doc/.
50 Diego Garcia Agreement of 1972, at 4 and 8. As a similar anecdote, officials on the US–Mexico border may allow cross-border corridors for wildlife animals, while fences will still be blocking illegal immigration. See for instance https://news.utexas.edu/2011/07/12/border_wildlife.
51 However, Mauritius has later claimed that the BIOT was in breach of a 1960 United Nations General Assembly resolution, which stipulates that colonial units may not be divided prior to independence. According to Mauritius, the UK is not in a position to exercise any sovereign territorial powers over the Chagos Islands. Supporting Mauritius's claim, see GA Resolution 1514 (1960) and GA Resolution 2066 (1965). Also Allen (2014), 198–207.

> island would be needed for the construction of British or United States defence facilities Britain or the United States should be able to clear it of its current population.[52]

The strategic legal planning involved in the 'smooth transformation of the territory into its intended role as a defence establishment'[53] could be admired for its creativity, if it would not have had such tragic consequences. The tragedy is not merely related to the alleged use of the island as a black site prison. More generally, the territorial-legal strategy adopted by both the UK and the US eventually lead to the eviction of the indigenous population of the islands. Together with the disappearance of the plantation company, the company's employees – consisting mostly of Chagos Islanders – were evicted from the islands.[54] With the eviction of the workers of the plantation company, the non-existence of a permanent population on the island could be demonstrated, and no private persons or companies could claim ownership of the land.[55]

In 2010, the UK announced that it would create a marine protected area (MPA) around the islands of BIOT. While officially this change is purely for environmental and conservation purposes, the MPA would 'in effect, put paid to resettlement claims of the archipelago's former residents', shielding the place from residential use, and in favour of military activities.[56] The legality of the MPA in relation to the return of the Chagossians has been challenged in the British courts. On appeal, the Court concluded that the MPA was not actuated by the improper motive of intending to create an effective long-term way to prevent Chagossians from resettling the BIOT and that the MPA was compatible with EU law.[57] How a marine protected area would fit together with a military base was not discussed.

52 *Bancoult* [2008 UKHL 61] at 10, (emphasis omitted by the author).

53 *Bancoult* [2008 UKHL 61] at 12.

54 *Bancoult* [2013 EWHC 1502] at 4. By 1973, the indigenous population had been evicted.

55 *Bancoult* [2001 QB 1067], at 7. The fate of the Chagos Islanders has been discussed in the British courts several times, as well as in international arbitration before the Permanent Court of Arbitration. In 2008 the House of Lords ruled in favour of the UK government (Bancoult [2008 UKHL 61]. The order abrogating the Chagossian right to return in the BIOT was thus upheld. For a detailed discussion on the cases, see S. Allen, *The Chagos Islanders and International Law* (Hart, 2014). See also Chagos Marine Protected Area Arbitration (*Mauritius v. The United Kingdom*), arbitration, award of 19 March 2015.

56 Officials of the United Kingdom commenting on the creation of the MPA. WikiLeaks, Cable 09London1156, 15 May 2009, available at https://wikileaks.org/cable/2009/05/09LONDON1156.html (last visited 14 February 2015).

57 The legality of the MPA in relation to the return of the Chagossians has been challenged in the British courts (*Bancoult* [2013 EWHC 1502 Admin] & *Bancoult* [2014 EWCA Civ 708]).

It might prove difficult to challenge the legality of the way that states have behaved when constructing the extra-territorial zone of Diego Garcia. That said even if rendering the Chagos Islands 'a zone beyond the reach of the law', seems like a well-planned historical project with several political-legal turns that could legitimate the result. If the UK is to be answering in Europe to accusations of having hosted a CIA prison on the island of Diego Garcia, the legal reasoning could make use of the 'wriggle space' provided by the law. For instance, according to some human rights experts, the detention and interrogation of prisoners has been taking place on warships of the US anchored in the Diego Garcia lagoon, and not on the military base.[58] The difference between allowing a warship to be anchored and hosting a prison might just be what the UK needs in order to maintain that it has not been involved in possible human rights violations in the interrogation of the detainees.[59] This position would reflect an earlier statement of the Foreign and Commonwealth Office of the UK regarding the storage of anti-personnel mines in Diego Garcia, as reported by Sand. Since it was claimed that the mines were not located on the UK's territory but on the warships of the US in the Diego Garcia lagoon, the implication was that Britain had not violated any of its international obligations.[60]

3.5 The Formation of the Zone: Denial

The year 2014 saw multiple state officials around the world denying that they had hosted secret CIA prisons. The same year, the US Senate Intelligence Committee had released the infamous 'torture report' on the practices of the US in the war against terror. The report, while not mentioning Diego Garcia as a location of a black site prison, did mention several other places where some of the detainees had been kept, interrogated and allegedly tortured. One of such places was the 'Cat's Eye' or the 'Detention Site Green' (a prison in Thailand).[61] The press reported on Thai officials commenting on the allegations:

58 I. Cobain, 'CIA Interrogated Suspects on Diego Garcia, Says Colin Powell Aide', *The Guardian*, 30 January 2015, available at www.theguardian.com/world/2015/jan/30/cia-interrogation-diego-garcia-lawrence-wilkerson (last visited 15 August 2015).

59 On the differences between general territorial locations and buildings, ships and aircrafts in relation to jurisdiction and the extension of treaties, see M. Milanovic (2011), 151–70.

60 P. Sand, 'Diego Garcia: British-American Legal Black Hole in the Indian Ocean?', 21 *Journal of Environmental Law* (2009), 115.

61 See Senate Select Committee on Intelligence, *Committee Study of the Central Intelligence Agency's Detention and Interrogation Program*, Executive Summary, approved 13 December 2012, updated for release 3 April 2014, declassification revisions 3 December 2014, e.g. at

> A secret prison has not existed here and there are no [documented] reports of torture in Thailand [. . .] We have never conducted any illegal activities with the US.[62]

A few days later, the press reported a slightly altered comment by the Thai government, now acknowledging the existence of the American-led prison on Thai territory, but denying any responsibility over the facility:

> The U.S. did not tell us anything. We didn't know where it was hidden. We didn't have to take responsibility because they were already handed over.[63]

With respect to Poland, the explanations offered by Polish officials followed a similar line. First, the entire existence of a CIA detention centre was denied – later, Poland admitted that the CIA had been running a secret prison on Polish territory without Poland knowing any details of the acts committed on the territory.[64] The former president of Poland Aleksander Kwasniewski explained the lack of control by Poland over the detention centre in the following manner: 'But if a CIA agent brutally treated a prisoner in the Warsaw Marriott Hotel, would you charge the management of that hotel for the actions of the agent?'[65]

These comments raise questions about the sort of knowledge that a sovereign state is expected to have over actions taking place on its sovereign territory. Some international courts have assessed this question in the past. In the well-known *Corfu Channel* case, the International Court of Justice (ICJ) was called upon to decide whether Albania was responsible for mines that had damaged British ships in the Corfu Channel.[66] During

24. Although the country name is erased from the study, it has been publicly confirmed that Detention Site Green is located in Thailand.

62 K. Hodal','Thailand Denies It Ran Secret Prison for CIA or Allowed Torture on Its Territory', *Guardian*, 12 December 2014, available at www.theguardian.com/us-news/2014/dec/12/thailand-denies-secret-prison-torture-senate-cia (last visited 15 February 2015).

63 S. Neuman, 'Thailand Says It Was Unaware of CIA "Black Site" on Its Soil', 19 December 2014, available at www.npr.org/blogs/thetwo-way/2014/12/19/371865080/thailand-says-it-was-unaware-of-cia-black-site-on-its-soil (last visited 15 February 2015).

64 See e.g. A. H., 'Poland's Secret CIA Prisons', *The Economist*, 28 August 2012 (available at www.economist.com/blogs/easternapproaches/2012/08/poland-and-america (last visited 14 February 2015); D. Ernst, 'Ex-president Kwasniewski Admits Poland Hosted CIA "Black Sites"', *Washington Times*, 10 December 2014, available at www.washingtontimes.com/news/2014/dec/10/aleksander-kwasniewski-admits-poland-hosted-cia-bl/ (last visited 14 February 2015). C. Lowe and P. Sobczak, 'Polish Ex-leader Acknowledges CIA Site but Denies Knowing about Torture', 10 December 2014, available at http://uk.reuters.com/article/2014/12/10/uk-usa-cia-torture-poland-idUKKBN0JO1GB20141210 (last visited 14 February 2015). Also *Husayn* at 167, 234, 246.

65 *Husayn* at 234.

66 ICJ *Corfu Channel*, merits (1949) ICJ Reports 4.

the proceedings, Albania claimed that although the mines were located on Albania's territory, it was not proven that Albania had anything to do with the mines in its territorial waters. Actually, Albania continued, it was not even proven that Albania knew of the existence of the mines until the explosions occurred. As a consequence, Albania concluded, it could not be held responsible for events that had taken place in its territorial waters.[67] The ICJ, eventually, did not agree with Albania. It first proclaimed that '(I)t cannot be concluded from the mere fact of the control exercised by a State over its territory and waters that that State necessarily knew, or ought to have known, of any unlawful act perpetrated therein, nor yet that it necessarily knew, or should have known, the authors'.[68] However, the Court presented some geographical facts that defied Albania's arguments:

> The Bay of Saranda and the channel used by shipping through the Strait are, from their geographical configuration, easily watched; the entrance of the bay is dominated by heights offering excellent observation points, both over the bay and over the Strait; whilst the channel throughout is close to the Albanian coast. The laying of a minefield in these waters could hardly fail to have been observed by the Albanian coastal defences. [...] the Court draws the conclusion that the laying of the minefield which caused the explosions on October 22nd, 1946, could not have been accomplished without the knowledge of the Albanian Government.[69]

Thus, the ICJ concluded that a denial of knowledge over the existence of acts on sovereign territory should not be treated as liberating a state from responsibility. Albania should have known what activities were conducted on its territory, for the reason that the bay was not hidden from any governmental supervision. Although the case leaves open on what basis the opposite argument – denying Albania's knowledge over the acts – could have been made, it was clear that this time the Court took a restrictive view concerning the state not knowing its territory.

In 2014, it was the European Court of Human Rights's turn to assess whether Poland had knowledge over the events that took place in the CIA-led prison on Polish sovereign territory.[70] In *Husayn (Abu Zubaydah) v. Poland* and *Al-Nashiri v. Poland*, the applicants claimed that they had been transferred to Poland from another secret prison located in Thailand. Subsequently, they were held and tortured in the Stare Kiejkuty military

[67] *Corfu Channel*, 11. [68] *Corfu Channel*, 18. [69] *Corfu Channel*, 20 and 22.

[70] ECtHR *Husayn (Abu Zubaydah) v. Poland* (Application no. 7511/13) and ECtHR *Al-Nashiri v. Poland* (Application no. 28761/11), 24 July 2014. References are made only to *Husayn* since the cases are similar in relevant respects.

base in north-eastern Poland. The Court ended up ruling that Poland had violated several articles of the European Convention of Human Rights by hosting a secret CIA prison on its territory.[71] Both rulings were unanimous and maintained that Poland cooperated with the CIA rendition programme on its own territory; given the widespread public information about the ill-treatment and abuse of detained terrorist suspects in the custody of the US officials, Poland was considered to have violated several articles of the Human Rights Convention.

Although not fully expressed in the cases,[72] it seems that Poland and the Court disagreed on what Poland knew, or should have known, about the mistreatment of prisoners, and how that information would have affected the enactment of responsibility.[73] In some respects, the Court had to accept that Poland might not have known about the ill-treatment conducted during the interrogations. The Court expressed that

> This [the experts stating that Poland had had, or should have had, general knowledge of the CIA rendition operations] did not mean, in the experts' view, that the Polish authorities had known the details of what went on inside the black site, since the interrogations had been the exclusive responsibility of the CIA, or that they had witnessed treatment to which High-Value Detainees had been subjected in Poland [...] The Court, being confronted with no evidence to the contrary, accepts the experts' abovementioned assessment.[74]

However, after taking the elements 'as a whole', the Court declared that Poland was enabling the US authorities to subject Zubaydah and Nashiri to torture and ill-treatment on its territory. The Court reached this assessment via a two-part argument.[75] First, the Court maintained that Poland cooperated in the preparation and execution of the CIA rendition, secret detention and interrogation operations on its territory. Second, Poland ought to have known that, by enabling the CIA to detain such persons on its territory, it was exposing them to a serious risk of treatment contrary to the Convention. Consequently, Poland was responsible for the treatment of the detainees on its territory.[76] On one's sovereign territory, the Court

[71] Also in ECtHR Abu Zubaydah against Lithuania (Application 46454/11), 14 December 2012, pending. Similar investigations with Romania have taken place.

[72] *Husayn* at 125 (Poland disclosed only limited information of the investigation, allegedly since its own national investigations were still going on). Poland has requested for referral to the Grand Chamber in the ECtHR.

[73] A similar assessment was made in another ECtHR case, see *Ilascu and Others v. Moldova and Russia*, Application no. 48787/99, 8 July 2004.

[74] *Husayn* at 443. [75] *Husayn* at 444. [76] *Husayn* at 445.

deduced, a state simply needs to know what acts take place, or might take place. Thus, an ignorant attitude of looking-the-other-way was not to be accepted.

The Court was disappointingly brief when addressing the responsibility of the host state for the treatment of terrorist suspects by foreign officials. In one sentence, the Court held that 'in accordance with its settled case law, the respondent State must be regarded as responsible under the Convention for acts performed by foreign officials on its territory with the acquiescence or connivance of its authorities' and referred to some paragraphs in its previous decisions in *Ilascu* and *El-Masri*.[77] However, the relevant paragraphs of *Ilascu* and *El-Masri* do not suggest that a state *must* be held responsible for acts committed by another *state* on its territory. Paragraph 318 of *Ilascu* maintains that the acquiescence or connivance of the authorities in the acts of *private individuals* which violate the Convention rights of other individuals within the jurisdiction of the state *may* engage the state's responsibility under the Convention. The paragraph continues: 'That is particularly true in the case of recognition by the State *in question of the acts of self-proclaimed authorities which are not recognized by the international community*'.[78] Hence, *Ilascu* can hardly be invoked as relevant precedent describing acts of a sovereign state on another state's territory. Moreover, the Court only mentions the possibility of state responsibility being activated instead of any automatic activation of responsibility.

The case of *El-Masri* is arguably more closely related to the subject-matter of the Polish prison cases. In *El-Masri*, the Court had to assess whether the treatment of a person in an airport by the CIA rendition team lead to the responsibility of the state on whose territory the airport was located. Paragraph 206 of *El-Masri*, however, emphasizes that 'the acts complained of were carried out *in the presence* of officials of the respondent State and within its jurisdiction'.[79] Consequently, the Court concluded, the state must be regarded as responsible under the Convention for acts by foreign officials on its territory. Again, then, the Court relied on a precedent that establishes state responsibility over acts witnessed by the state authorities in question. Contrary to this, the Court admitted in *Husayn* that

77 *Husayn* at 449.

78 ECtHR *Ilascu and Others v. Moldova and Russia* (Application no. 48787/99) 8 July 2004, at 318 (emphasis added by the author).

79 ECtHR *El-Masri v. the Former Yugoslav Republic of Macedonia* (Application no. 39630/09) 13 December 2012, at 206 (emphasis added by the author).

Poland had not been present in the detention facility where the acts were committed, and that the US was completely in charge of the detentions.[80]

To sum up, the ECtHR concluded that although '(t)he secret detention facilities in Europe were run directly and exclusively by the CIA',[81] Poland had cooperated in the establishment of one of these prisons on its own territory. And while the Court could not demonstrate any involvement of Poland in the torturing of the prisoners, Poland should have known that it was exposing the detainees to such a risk by letting the US use its territory for the rendition. The fact that Poland had not exercised any authority over the detention centre at the time of the torture was not enough for the Court to determine that Poland was not responsible for the treatment of the detainees. Neither was the fact that the US, another sovereign state, was undeniably responsible for the acts, but unreachable in terms of the Court's jurisdiction. For a human rights court, the risk of eventually nobody being held responsible for such atrocities taking place on European territory was perhaps too much to accept.

The Polish prison cases never touched in any substantial manner on the possible existence of an agreement between the US and Poland over the jurisdiction over the prison. A bilateral agreement made within the broader NATO framework seems to exist, but the details of such an agreement are not made public.[82] The Court concluded that it did not need to establish whether a 'special' bilateral agreement between the CIA and the Polish officials existed or what kind of jurisdictional divisions that agreement would have contained – it explained that the intrusion by the US in Poland's jurisdiction would have been 'inconceivable' without prior agreement between the two states concerned.[83] In the future, Poland might maintain that there exists a separate 'layer' of lawful territorial leasing including cooperation in the establishment of an extra-territorial site, and a separate 'layer' of torture and illegal detention – and that those layers are in no way indistinguishable. A state might excise territorial locations from the extent of its international and national legal obligations, and still not be held responsible under international law.[84] Similarly, as Cuba argues in

80 *Husayn* at 443. 81 Ibid. at 246. 82 Ibid. at 248–9.

83 Ibid. at 425–30. Bilateral agreement may obviously impact the jurisdiction assessment; see for instance *Al-Skeini and others v. Secretary of State for Defence*, House of Lords, (2007) UKHL 26, 13 June 2006, at 135. On the division of jurisdiction and territorial control, see J. Hathaway and T. Gammeltoft-Hansen, 'Non-Refoulement in a World of Cooperative Deterrence', *Law & Economics Working Papers*, paper 106 (2014). http://repository.law.umich.edu/law_econ_current/106.

84 Some years ago, Australia aimed at excising territories from the reach of its migration laws. See e.g. in M. Foster and J. Pobjoy, 'A Failed Case of Legal Exceptionalism? Refugee Status

relation to Guantanamo, Poland could argue that since jurisdiction and authority over the location had been transferred to the US, Poland had no way of controlling that part of its sovereign territory.

3.6 Inviting the Inevitable

In the Polish prison case, the European Court of Human Rights took a strong position in order to confirm the responsibility of a Member State for atrocities taking place in a prison ran by another, non-member, state partner. Should international courts and tribunals control states in their attempts to evade responsibility when invoking multiple legal grounds, and if so, how? Whether it concerns the International Court of Justice, the European Court of Human Rights, or any other international court addressing the activities of states, a court may be able to stress the importance of the multiple legal character of the (extra)territorial location; the location can be seen as one state's sovereign land, another state's jurisdictional territory, *and* as a place where a third state commits acts when questions of responsibility arise. In order to do so, courts often choose the argumentative avenue that will avoid a responsibility vacuum.[85] In another recent case, namely *Jaloud v. Netherlands*, the ECtHR – under reference to several of its previous cases[86] – maintained that jurisdiction (and

Determination in Australia's "Excised" Territory', 23 *International Journal of Refugee Law* (2011), 1–49.

85 See ECtHR *Issa and Others v. Turkey* (Application no 31821/96), 16 November 2004, para. 71. Similarly, in *López Burgos v. Uruguay*, the Human Rights Committee has maintained that 'it would be unconscionable to so interpret the responsibility under Art. 2 of the Covenant as to permit a State party to perpetrate violations of the Covenant on the territory of another State, which violations it could not perpetrate on its own territory'. UN Doc. A/36/40, 6 June 1979, para. 12.3.

86 In ECtHR *Jaloud v. The Netherlands* (Application no. 47708/08), 20 November 2014, the Court referred via ECtHR *Al-Skeini and Others v. United Kingdom* (Application no. 55721/07) 7 July 2011 to ECtHR *Al-Saadoon and Mufdhi v. United Kingdom* (Application no. 61498/08) 2 March 2010 by saying that 'Iraqi nationals detained in British-controlled military prisons in Iraq fell within the jurisdiction of the United Kingdom, since the United Kingdom exercised total and exclusive control over the prisons and the individuals detained in them', and to ECtHR *Medvedyed and Others v. France* (Application 3394/03), 29 March 2010, by saying that 'the Court held the applicants were within French jurisdiction by virtue of the exercise by French agents of full and exclusive control over a ship and its crew from the time of its interception in international waters'. Both cases cited in *Jaloud* para. 136. In Jaloud, the Court acknowledged that the Netherlands relied heavily on the argument that it could not be blamed for the events complained of since authority lay elsewhere (either within the US or the UK). The Court found that Jaloud's death occurred within the jurisdiction of the Netherlands. However, the alleged acts and omissions of Netherlands military personnel and investigative and judicial authorities would

subsequently accountability or responsibility) would not arise solely from the control exercised by the state over locations in which the individuals are held. Instead, the *decisive* element was the exercise of physical power and *control over the person* in question.[87] Yet in the Polish CIA prison cases, the Court held that decisive was *not* who controlled the detainees in question, but instead *on whose territory* the events took place.[88] The argumentative practices related to sovereignty and the exercising of effective control thus seem to vary depending on the situation in order for *someone* to be found accountable.

When adopting multiple approaches to accountability regimes, a court may be said to demonstrate a more wholesome understanding of the legal character of a territorial location. In doing so, the court, like all actors in the international legal arena, will commit to one specific legal language. For the ECtHR, this language is often that of law as accountability and responsibility. This choice leads it to commit to those territorial-legal argumentations that eventually result in the fulfilment of that aim in each case, while possibly discarding some others avenues of argumentation. The task of a European human rights court, it might be argued, is to protect human rights in Europe; consequently, such a court should not argue for the responsibility of the actor exercising power over the acts in a case where this state would turn out to be a non-European state and outside the Court's jurisdiction.[89] To avoid a vacuum, it should attribute behaviour as much as possible to those with its jurisdiction.

Doing so, however, suggests that structural biases in legal reasoning are in place. Koskenniemi has approached the structural biases of courts in the context of the choice of arguments they maintain. For instance, when a matter can be examined from the perspectives of both 'security' as well as 'human rights', a court may choose to frame the issue through the perspective that it feels more related to. Some courts are biased to favour human

on their own give rise to the responsibility of the Netherlands, regardless if a link could be found between exercising jurisdiction and being responsible. See *Jaloud*, at 140, 150, 151–5.

87 *Jaloud* at 136 (emphasis added), also 155.

88 ECtHR *Husayn (Abu Zubaydah) v. Poland* (Application no. 7511/13) and ECtHR *Al-Nashiri v. Poland* (Application no. 28761/11) 24 July 2014. See Husayn, para. 443.

89 In relation to its case *Behrami*, the ECtHR has been strongly criticized for not holding accountable those states in its reach, but instead addressed the responsibility of the United Nations. Thus, having determined that the acts and omissions were attributable to the UN, the Court concluded that it did not have jurisdiction to evaluate the actions of the UN. See G. Verdirame, *The UN and Human Rights – Who Guards the Guardians*? (Cambridge: Cambridge University Press, 2011), 112.

rights; others are biased to favour security.[90] Discussing the 2005 *Al-Jedda* case before the UK High Court, Koskenniemi concludes:

> There was no doubt that the matter could be examined from the perspective of 'security' as well as 'human rights'. The choice of the frame determined the decision. But for determining the frame, there was no meta-regime, directive or rule. The Court's reading of the applicant's rights from the perspective of considerations of security may or may not be approved. However, it can only be understood once it is viewed in terms of the Court's bias towards security.[91]

Thus, courts may indeed uphold the complex legal character of the cases on extra-territorial locations – sometimes in favour of the ones exercising power over persons, and in other situations for the exercise of sovereignty over the location. In the end, a court enjoys the power to frame the issue so that someone can be held responsible, although finding someone responsible is not necessarily a 'meta-directive' of international law.[92] In framing the question, a court articulates its own preferences and reflects its own self-image, instead of applying a meta-regime, directive or rule. When for instance addressing the issue of the CIA prisons on the Polish territory, the ECtHR had to highlight the importance of effective enforcement of European human rights standards over events taking place on the European territory. This bias could be articulated through paraphrasing Koskenniemi's reasoning mentioned above: *The Court's reading of the Polish responsibility from the perspective of considerations of territorial obligations may or may not be approved; however, it can only be understood once it is viewed in terms of the Court's bias towards upholding the effective enforcement of European human rights obligations.*

3.7 In the End: Irresponsible Law?

The formation processes of extra-territorial locations, and the legal manoeuvring related to them, cannot be rejected or approved *per se*.

[90] See the *Al-Jedda* case in the High Court of Justice in Britain (*The Queen (on the application of Hilal Abdul-Razzaq Ali Al-Jedda) v. Secretary of State for Defence*, Judgment of 12 August 2005, Case no. CO/3673/2005, [2005] EWHC1809 (Admin)). In M. Koskenniemi, 'The Fate of Public International Law – Between Technique and Politics', 70 *Modern Law Review* (2007), 1–30.

[91] Ibid. Koskenniemi, 6.

[92] See S. Veitch, *Law and Irresponsibility: On the Legitimation of Human Suffering* (New York: Routledge, 2007).

Instead they are examples of the 'machinery' of international legal argument, familiar from the 'cool structuralism' of Koskenniemi.[93] The language of law based on understandings of what the international legal rules should aim to do, will always find different expressions in territorial-legal argumentation and state practices, leading to a Ping-Pong game between confirmations and denials stemming from different legal positions. Thus, the legal character of one specific piece of territory *can be* constructed through the concept of sovereign territory, but also through ideas of jurisdictional powers on the territory, or through the different ways of exercising territorial control, all simultaneously but also exclusively presented.

Every actor chooses the territorial-legal vocabulary that fits her interests and preferences the best. In the end, the processes through which responsibilities and liabilities are either attributed or not, are products of re-definition projects articulated in the language of territoriality and law. For this reason, those advocating that it is precisely *sovereignty* that leads to responsibility, are to be disappointed. Equally, jurisdiction and control might, but equally might not, be the basis for finding a state responsible.[94] This view pays homage not just to the indeterminacy of the legal argument, but to the idea of law actively creating irresponsibility instead of responsibility.[95] Eventually, the question of responsibility need not be discussed at all, since the frame of the legal discourse can be re-described over and over so that *no one* is held responsible. Responsibility is left hanging between arguments of non-applicability of sovereign responsibility on the one hand, and non-applicability of jurisdictional responsibility on the other, since both views can be equally defended or ignored.[96] Here, to quote Veitch in the context of the British sanctions regime in Iraq:

> Irresponsibility, in this sense, would essentially mean a disregard for consequences in the name of upholding the law. But it might also mean something else. It might mean that these officials were able to rely on their legal obligations as a way of *evading* the very question of responsibility for their

93 M. Koskenniemi, *From Apology to Utopia: The Structure of International Legal Argument* (Cambridge: Cambridge University Press, 2005), 617.

94 The discussion on whether responsibility and accountability should follow from 'effective control' (ICJ *Nicaragua* 1986), 'overall control' (ICTY *Tadić* 1999) or 'effective overall control' (ECtHR *Issa* 2004) exercised over the territory, or from control over persons (ECtHR Jaloud 2014), or from all of the above, shows the complexity of the matter.

95 Veitch, *Law and Irresponsibility*. See also F. Johns, *Non-legality in International Law – Unruly Law* (Cambridge: Cambridge University Press, 2013).

96 On diffused responsibility leading to by-standing even when atrocities are committed, see J. Conroy, *Unspeakable Acts, Ordinary People – The Dynamics of Torture* (Berkeley: University of California Press, 2000), especially at 249.

> decisions and their consequences. The officials could, in effect, put themselves in a zone of *non*-responsibility, within which the matter of their responsibility did not arise at all.[97]

Treating that which actually is a manifestation of organized irresponsibility as something purely exceptional in fact thus ignores the tremendous amount of legal organization required in its maintenance.[98] With this chapter, I hope to have contributed to the discussion on how legal arguments may work in normalizing and legitimizing – instead of rendering exceptional – the zoning of territory on a global scale.[99] The chapter has described some territorial-legal argumentation surrounding the construction of three particular extra-territorial locations, namely the Guantanamo Bay detention centre, the military base of Diego Garcia and the CIA-led prison in Poland. These locations are seen as the outcome of three intertwined elements, crucial for their formation: the abandoning of sovereign territory in order to escape from possible sovereign responsibilities, the construction of a particular zone through legal and political instruments, and finally the denial by the parties of any knowledge or responsibility over such location.

The main argument of this article has been that the formation of a zone can always be articulated with the territorial-legal vocabulary that serves the actors in the fulfilment of their aims and preferences, while discarding those arguments that do not fit their aims. International law should thus be seen as complicit in creating regular instances of legally regulated territorial zone-making. Any normative concerns should stem not so much from the very exercise of territorial-legal argumentation, but instead from the ways in which these arguments may be embedded in some specific political-legal projects that we might have good reasons to reject.

97 Veitch, 21.

98 *Ibid.*, 23. See also F. Johns, 'Guantanamo Bay and the Annihilation of the Exception' (2005) 16 *European Journal of International Law* 613–635, at 615.

99 Of law normalizing and legitimizing processes that might first seem exceptional and mere failures of the system, see Veitch, 19: '(F)ailure is *not* in fact failure; rather it is, almost incomprehensibly, a success – because this is a political system *working*'.

4

Backlash and State Strategies in International Investment Law

MALCOLM LANGFORD,* DANIEL BEHN** AND OLE KRISTIAN FAUCHALD***

4.1 Introduction

The development of the modern investment treaty regime is emblematic of the post–Second World War period in international law. With the increasing 'legalization of world politics', international legal institutions have shifted structurally from a classic model of co-existence to an international law of cooperation.[1] This structural shift is exemplified by a number of key features such as the expansion of treaty law, the multiplication of actors subject to international law and the emergence of novel adjudicatory mechanisms for resolving international legal disputes. Such legalization of global affairs has also precipitated a backlash from some states claiming that the proliferation of international law is undercutting national sovereignty and marginalizing the political manoeuvrability of states at the international level.

All of these features are apparent in the international treaty regulation of foreign investment. Largely built on a network of more than 3500 bilateral investment treaties (BITs) and regional free trade agreements (FTAs),[2] a handful of plurilateral investment treaties,[3] as well as customary

* Professor, Faculty of Law, University of Oslo. Special thanks to research assistant, Maxim Usynin, for his valuable assistance with the research for Section 4.4. The analysis is current at July 2017.

** Postdoctoral researcher, PluriCourts, Faculty of Law, University of Oslo.

*** Professor, PluriCourts, Faculty of Law, University of Oslo.

[1] Chapter 1, this volume.

[2] UNCTAD provides an extensive database on international investment agreements, http://investmentpolicyhub.unctad.org/IIA (accessed 16 May 2017).

[3] Such treaties include the *Energy Charter Treaty* (ECT), Chapter 11 of the *North American Free Trade Agreement* (NAFTA) and the *Association of South-East Asian Nations Comprehensive Investment Agreement*.

international law,[4] foreign investors are granted beneficiary rights aimed at the post-establishment protection of their investments. It has been claimed that 'no other category of private individuals' is 'given such expansive rights in international law as are private actors investing across borders'.[5]

These developments, like other areas of international law, were viewed in teleological terms: an ever-expanding pattern of treaties and custom that, even if fragmented, would increasingly constrain domestic sovereignty for the greater good of global governance. Success was thus defined as the 'victory of the supra- or multi-national over the parochial national'.[6] Yet, this assumption of path dependency and evolutionary progress is risky. While the rules and institutions determined by politics are 'stickier' than those determined in economic markets,[7] they can shift decidedly over time in the reverse direction. If political contestation was present during the formation of any institution or rule, it is not axiomatic that it will disappear afterwards. Moreover, even when such seminal political contestation was not present, a regime's trajectory or external developments may engender new forms of political contestation.

In this respect, we should not be surprised that some states have reasserted themselves in their role as treaty-makers and overall regime shapers. Commonly referred to as a legitimacy crisis,[8] the international investment regime is under attack, with even some prominent 'insiders' expressing disquiet.[9] Primarily, however, this phenomenon is not solely about the expansiveness of the substantive rights granted to foreign investors under international investment agreements (IIAs), but rather the combination of such rights with the robustness of their investor–state

[4] Patrick Dumberry, 'Are BITs Representing the "New" Customary International Law in International Investment Law?' (2010) 28(4) *Penn State International Law Review* 675–701.

[5] Beth Simmons, 'Bargaining over BITS, Arbitrating Awards: The Regime for Protection and Promotion of International Investment' (2014) 66 *World Politics* 12–46, at 42.

[6] Jose Alvarez, 'The Return of the State' (2011) 20 *Minnesota Journal of International Law* 223–64, at 223.

[7] Paul Pierson, 'Increasing Returns, Path Dependence, and the Study of Politics' (2000) 94 *American Political Science Review* 251–67.

[8] Michael Waibel, Asha Kaushal, Kyo-Hwa Chung and Claire Balchin (eds), *The Backlash against Investment Arbitration: Perceptions and Reality* (The Hague: Kluwer Law, 2010); for an overview, see Malcolm Langford, 'Cosmopolitan Competition: The Case of International Investment' in Cecilia Bailliet and Katja Aas (eds), *Cosmpolitanism Justice and Its Discontents* (New York: Routledge, 2011), 178–204.

[9] See, inter alia, contributions in Jean Kalicki and Anna Joubin-Bret (eds), *Reshaping the Investor-State Dispute Settlement System: Journeys for the 21st Century* (The Hague: Brill, 2015); and Roberto Echandi and Pierre Sauvé (eds), *Prospects in International Investment Law and Policy* (Cambridge: Cambridge University Press, 2013).

dispute settlement (ISDS) provisions and the increasing number and range of states subject to disputes. With over 850 known investment treaty arbitrations (ITAs) initiated to date,[10] as well as an unknown number of instances in which the threat of ITA has been used as a bargaining tool, states hosting foreign investors are increasingly finding themselves having to defend their domestic laws and policies before and in the shadow of international arbitral tribunals.

Such a backlash would not have occurred without the existence of the remedial right granted to foreign investors (a private individual or corporation). Claims can be directly brought by them against the state hosting their investment. The litigation has resulted in sizeable compensation awards for actions that many states believe are both legitimate and within their exclusive purview as sovereigns.[11] This tension between the rights afforded to foreign investors under IIAs and the legitimate rights of sovereign states to regulate in the public interest of their domestic citizenry has arguably resulted in a single overarching strategy being employed by certain states dissatisfied with the international investment regime. It is the reassertion of sovereign control by limiting legally or effectively the international legal rights granted to foreign investors. As we shall see, this strategy is almost always employed by states that have been subject to at least one dispute;[12] and has been labelled the 'return of the state' by one investment law scholar.[13]

For those states dissatisfied with the practice of the international investment regime, the strategic importance in reasserting sovereign control

[10] PluriCourts Investment Treaty Arbitration Database (PITAD), https://jus-pitad01.uio.no/ (accessed 16 May 2017). Not all ITAs are public, and many awards remain confidential. Awards that are public are made available at www.italaw.com/ (accessed 16 May 2017). Our estimate is that less than 20 per cent of ITA awards are not in the public domain.

[11] See, inter alia, David Collins, 'Loss Aversion Bias or Fear of Missing Out: A Behavioural Economics Analysis of Compensation in Investor–State Dispute Settlement' (2016) 8(3) *Journal of International Dispute Settlement* 460–82. See also Daniel Behn, 'Legitimacy, Evolution, and Growth in Investment Treaty Arbitration: An Empirical Evaluation of Recent Decisions' (2015) 46(2) *Georgetown Journal of International Law* 363–415 at 373–75.

[12] Lauge Poulsen and Emma Aisbett, 'When the Claim Hits: Bilateral Investment Treaties and Bounded Rational Learning' (2013) 65(2) *World Politics* 273–313; but compare with Wolfgang Alschner, 'The Impact of Investment Arbitration on Investment Treaty Design: Myth versus Reality' (2017) 42(1) *Yale Journal of International Law* 1–66, where the author finds that the incidence of ITA claims do not in and of themselves trigger changes in IIA design.

[13] Alvarez, note 6 above.

over this area of international law is justified by claims that ITA over the last decade has been lop-sided, biased against states and constitutes an unacceptable delegation of sovereign authority and control to international adjudicators.[14] However, the precise reasons for the backlash vary amongst states and there are competing explanations. There is arguably a complex set of instrumental calculations, intrinsic beliefs and background factors that drive state behaviour in this field. While there are no states that have achieved a complete exit from the international investment regime, there are a number that have sought to make significant changes to their practice in order to address perceived or real gaps and imbalances. However, only a minority have launched a vocal and existential attack on the investment regime. The majority have sought to implement changes in order to maximize sovereign manoeuvrability while simultaneously adhering to international law, mirroring the form of state behaviour under study in this book. As the editors state, the 'multiplication of legal regimes, overlapping jurisdictions, and diffusion of authority', of which the international investment is emblematic, 'opens up an increased room for political manoeuvring in relation to international law'.[15]

This chapter examines how states are shaping their critical responses to an international legal order. For most states, the challenge is to choose tactics that enable the reassertion of control while permitting ongoing participation in the international investment regime and enjoyment of its potential economic benefits. The chapter proceeds as follows. Section 4.2 sets out an analytical framework in order to categorize distinct strategic and tactical choices made by states in reaction to the current regime. Section 4.3 examines what tactics states as *principals* are using to scale back the rights granted to foreign investors in IIAs; and Section 4.4 analyzes tactics states are using as *litigants* when defending and justifying their actions in ITA.

4.2 Strategic and Tactical Choices

Many states share an overarching goal of reasserting sovereign control by maximizing sovereign manoeuvrability, increasing the policy space of states to regulate in the public interest without running afoul of IIA

14 Daniel Behn, Tarald Berge and Malcolm Langford, 'Poor States or Poor Governance: Explaining Outcomes in Investment Treaty Arbitration' (forthcoming) *Northwestern Journal of International Law & Business*.

15 Chapter 1, this volume, p. 10.

		Principal tactics	
		Strong	Weak or none
Litigation tactics	Strong	I. Absolute opponents	III. Reluctant compliers
	Weak or none	II. Principled opponents	IV. Compliers

Figure 4.1 Mapping state tactics

obligations, and reducing potential liability in ITAs brought by aggrieved foreign investors. However, it is important to distinguish between the scope and intensity of this objective along a spectrum and one can identify two distinct strategies. Some states have sought a radical reshaping of the regime in law or practice while the majority have opted to remain but sought to reduce the breadth of their international legal obligations. Thus, tactics employed by some states to achieve the more modest strategy may be somewhat *weak*, involving subtle and discrete acts that amount to a tweaking of, or partial expression of discontent with, the regime. However, tactics oriented towards radical reform will be *strong*. The state may take a systemic approach (e.g. seek to terminate some treaties or engage in constant non-compliance) or make radical departures from the spirit of the regime (e.g. drastically curtailing foreign investor protections or harassing foreign investors with domestic criminal proceedings). We have therefore sought to distinguish along a horitonal axis the strength of the tactics (Figure 4.1).

Moreover, we can distinguish between two roles that states perform in the regime: (1) the state *as principal* – i.e. treaty-maker and international regime shaper; and (2) the state *as litigant* in ITA.[16] The relevant tactics that states have as *principals* include, inter alia: imposing moratoriums on the signing of new IIAs; refraining from ratifying signed IIAs; publicly critiquing the regime; adjusting negotiating strategies over new IIAs

[16] Anthea Roberts also discusses the dual role as treaty parties and respondents in 'Power and Persuasion in Investment Treaty Interpretation: The Dual Role of States' (2010) 104(2) *American Journal of International Law* 179–205, 180.

(including development of model IIAs and increased use of impact assessments and policy coordination during negotiations); excluding ISDS from some IIAs; calling for the renegotiation of IIAs already in force; terminating of IIAs; and withdrawing from arbitration institutions (in particular, ICSID[17]).

The tactics used by states as litigants in disputes include, inter alia: attempting to bind adjudicators to sovereignty protecting interpretations of certain treaty provisions; commencing domestic criminal proceedings against foreign investor claimants after a dispute arises; refusing to comply with awards; engaging in delay tactics; increasing the use of procedural motions for challenging arbitrators; requesting security for costs and other forms of injunctive relief; and making novel challenges to the jurisdiction of tribunals.

Figure 4.1 melds this principal/litigant and strong/weak strategic dichotomy in order to group the relationships of states to the *current* regime (i.e. that which has emerged since the early 2000s).[18] States that deploy strong tactics as both principals and litigants can be characterized as *absolute opponents* as reflecting their total opposition to the regime (group I). States that strongly seek reform but largely play by the rules of fair litigation can be labelled *principled opponents*: they wish to change the framework but largely abide by previous commitments (group II). States that largely support the regime but seek to obstruct proceedings when subject to ITA through strong-form litigation tactics can be labelled *reluctant compliers* (group III). Finally, there is a diverse group of states that adopt neither set of tactics, which we will call *compliers* (group IV). By *compliers* we mean states that actively or passively evince a formal commitment to the idea and practice of the regime. However, this group may contain false positives (states that move easily into another group once the costs of compliance become too high).

The functions of these tactics differ. Their activation may carry different material or symbolic effects for the international investment regime, with some tactics potentially precipitating both types of effects.[19] Primarily, tactics with material effects will aim at revising, restricting, reforming

[17] International Centre for Settlement of Investment Disputes.

[18] Modern IIAs emerged from Europe in the years following the Second World War. However, it was not until the 1990s that the majority of the 3000 plus IIAs were signed. We delimit the current regime from the early 2000s for the reason that this is when ITAs (as based on IIAs) began to be filed with increasing frequency.

[19] On this general distinction, see César Rodriguez-Garavito, 'Beyond the Courtroom: The Impact of Judicial Activism on Socioeconomic Rights in Latin America' (2011) 89 *Texas*

or terminating the IIAs that grant arbitrators the direct legal authority to effectively adjudicate claims. Such material effects may be systemic if the space in which arbitrators operate in future disputes is significantly curtailed or states regularly obstruct or block individual arbitral disputes to which they are a party.

Tactics employed by states and other stakeholders may have *symbolic* effects if they send a signal to arbitrators about state displeasure with the operation of the regime, which might result in arbitrators being more cautious or deferential in ruling against states.[20] These symbolic effects might result from state criticism of the regime or partial exit but also indirectly through the use of various litigation tactics, which collectively might shift arbitrator behaviour towards a more deferential mode of adjudication. Such behaviour may also indirectly influence the behaviour of other states. As a response to reduced legitimacy of the investment regime, states may be more cautious in their treaty-making and bolder in their litigation tactics.

In the next two sections, we explore the emergence of different state tactics in their roles as principals and litigators.

4.3 States as Principals

In the literature on the international investment regime, state tactics as 'principals' have been divided categorically into exit and voice.[21] Exit involves a break with the regime while the use of voice seeks regime reform. These tactics can vary significantly in nature and strength. As foreshadowed above and illustrated in moe detail in Figure 4.2, they range from full system exit (i.e. systemic termination of all treaties with no intent to renegotiate) through to minor modifications to treaty texts.

Law Review 1669–98 at 1679–81; on the symbolic and communicative effect of law generally, see Thomas Meisenhelder, 'Law as Symbolic Action: Kenneth Burke's Sociology of Law' (1981) 4 *Symbolic Interaction* 43–57.

20 However, if these tactics by states are seen as overtly abusive or in violation of general principles of law, arbitrators may actually become less deferential. For a theory and test of arbitrator reflexivity, see Malcolm Langford and Daniel Behn, 'Managing Backlash: The Evolving Investment Treaty Arbitrator' (forthcoming) *European Journal of International Law*.

21 Roberts, note 16 above; Alvarez, note 6 above; Nancy Welsh, Andrea Kupfer Schneider and Kathryn Rimpfel, 'Using the Theories of Exit Voice, Loyalty, and Procedural Justice to Reconceptualize Brazil's Rejection of Bilateral Investment Treaties' (2014) 45 *Washington Universtity Journal of Law and Policy* 105–43; on the general distinction between exit and voice, see Albert Hirschman, *Exit, Voice, and Loyalty: Responses to Decline in Firms, Organizations, and States* (Cambridge, MA: Harvard University Press, 1970), 4.

	Strong (absolute or principled opponents)	**Weak** (reluctant compliers or compliers)
Exit	Systemic termination of treaties Termination of ISDS provisions Refraining from ratifying signed treaties	Sporadic termination of treaties Sporadic termination of ISDS provisions Sporadic refusal to ratify signed treaties
Voice	Withdrawal from ICSID Attempting forced treaty renegotiation Systemic political delegitimisation New model treaties	Sporadic treaty renegotiation Sporadic clarifications of treaties Sporadic adoption of new models

Figure 4.2 Principal tactics

From the perspective of this volume, full exit is not a tactic of particular interest. In such a scenario, states would transparently relinquish their commitment to the regime and could not be accused of seeking to reform or undermine their existing commitments. However, while announced exits have grabbed headlines, there is no example to date of any states conducting a full exit from the international investment regime.[22] The reasons for this will be explored below. Moreover, a number of states have employed a combination of partial exit and partial voice tactics simultaneously, although their intentions for such a combination are not always clear. We can therefore classify tentatively three types of strong tactics by states which have been used and are likely to impact the regime: (1) partial exit; (2) hybrid tactics; and (3) systemic voice.

However, it is worth noting that not all states share the overarching strategy of limiting the protections granted to foreign investors under existing and future treaties. The tactics are not unidirectional. A few states, such as China and Germany, have sought to *expand* the rights of foreign investors under future IIAs.[23] Moreover, most states continue to sign new

[22] However, a few Latin American states are getting close. Both Ecuador and Bolivia have terminated a number of their IIAs with no intent to renegotiate them; and both of these states have denounced the ICSID Convention.

[23] Kate Hadley, 'Do China's BITS matter? Assessing the Effect of China's Investment Agreements on Foreign Direct Investment Flows, Investor's Rights, and the Rule of Law' (2013) 45 *Georgetown Journal of International Law* 255–321, at 275–309; Chester Brown,

IIAs (particularly through FTAs) although their support may be for a less potent regime.

4.3.1 Partial Exit

The first category is partial exit and is exemplified by announced attempts by a cluster of Latin American states to leave the regime. Yet, these strident proclamations of exit provide a certain puzzle. States such as Bolivia, Venezuela, Ecuador and Argentina have terminated some of their BITs and/or exited or announced an exit from the ICSID Convention (also known as the Washington Convention);[24] but they are far from executing a full exit from the international investment regime.[25] It might be thought that these states are being duplicitous – seeking to remain within the international investment regime (in order to capture its benefits) while weakening their own obligations. However, it seems that the partial exit of these states might be better characterized as unintended. They genuinely thought they could fully exit. Instead, they discovered that the legal infrastructure of the regime makes the regime sticky.[26] In the Argentinean

Commentaries on Selected Model Investment Treaties (Oxford: Oxford University Press, 2013), 7.

24 Bolivia, Ecuador and Venezuela withdrew from the ICSID Convention in 2007, 2010 and 2012, respectively. At one point, Argentina also signalled its intention to follow suit, and the government introduced a bill in its parliament in March 2012 to this effect. Federico Lavopa, Lucas Barreiros and Victoria Bruno, 'How to Kill a BIT and Not Die Trying: Legal and Political Challenges of Denouncing or Renegotiating Bilateral Investmewnt Treaties' (2013) 17 *Journal of International Economic Law* 869–91, at 871.

25 Clint Peinhardt and Rachel Wellhausen, 'Withdrawing from Investment Treaties but Protecting Investment' (2016) 7(2) *Global Policy* 571–76, 'documents the group of states that have taken advantage of unilateral withdrawal, and demonstrate that states can recalibrate their international legal commitments without eschewing contemporary international investment law'. While this might be correct at the aggregate level, our updated numbers show that a small but growing number of states might be classified as absolute opponents to the regime.

26 One challenging issue that arises when the parties to an IIA mutually agree to terminate the treaty arises in relation to foreign investors' interests. To what extent are their rights protected in such situations? This remains a largely unresolved issue in international law. On the one hand, it can be argued that states are free to eliminate the effects of a treaty if they are in mutual agreement. On the other hand, it can possibly be argued that states are not free to do so if it would detrimentally affect essential rights and expectations of third parties. Whether it could be argued that IIAs provide rights to investors that would be protected according to this latter argument is debatable. Tania Voon, Andrew Mitchell and James Munro, 'Parting Ways: The Impact of Investor Rights on Mutual Termination of Investment Treaties' (2014) 29(2) *ICSID Review – Foreign Investment Law Journal* 451–73.

case, however, a shift in political leadership (the election of the Macri Government in 2015) seems also to have been a major contributing factor.

The two principal forms of exit are *termination* of IIAs and *withdrawal* from procedural commitments to particular arbitration fora, e.g. through denunciation of the ICSID Convention. The first wave of states initially embraced the latter approach.[27] This 'Latin American' strategy was precipitated by investment-related disputes that culminated in ITAs – mostly through the ICSID procedure.[28] However, the effectiveness of this ICSID Convention exit strategy has been questioned. The ICSID Convention is procedural and not substantive in orientation.[29] Frequently, an ISDS provision in an IIA will include a number of institutional and non-institutional options for claim initiation (of which ICSID arbitration is just one option). Obviously, withdrawal from the ICSID Convention does not imply withdrawal from other venues for ITA. Moreover, withdrawal from the ICSID Convention would not prevent foreign investors from bringing cases under the ISCID Additional Facility rules.[30] Thus, to date, the impact of ICSID Convention withdrawal has been more symbolic than material.

Where there is lack of mutual agreement among states as to termination, the stickiness of the international investment regime depends on the challenges of unilaterally terminating the individual IIA. Various lock-in provisions extend the horizon of investment protections well into the future. First, most treaties include 'tacit' renewal clauses, a feature somewhat peculiar to IIAs. These clauses usually provide for automatic renewal of the IIA for a new fixed period (frequently for a subsequent period of ten years). Any unilateral termination of these agreements would have no effect on foreign investors' rights unless the IIA includes a separate

[27] Our PITAD database (note 10 above) reveals the following number of disputes filed per state: Bolivia (fifteen), Venezuela (forty-three) and Ecuador (twenty-four). The majority are ICSID arbitrations (62 per cent or fifty-one out of eighty-two ITAs).

[28] See Malcolm Langford and Daniel Behn, 'Managing Backlash: The Evolving Investment Treaty Arbitrator' (forthcoming) *European Journal of International Law*.

[29] See Lavopa, Barreiros and Bruno, note 24 above, at 874–78.

[30] An effective unilateral withdrawal from the ISDS provisions of IIAs would require termination of the IIA or renegotiation of the IIA with ISDS provisions excluded. Moreover, it is not clear when, and sometimes even if, the denunciation of ICSID takes effect. There is dispute in the literature over whether consent is required from parties to different bilateral treaties (since it affects the possibility of access to dispute resolution) and whether ICSID continues to apply to 'survival' clauses in treaties. See discussion in Lavopa, Barreiros and Bruno, note 24 above, at 877–78.

termination clause. Second, even once termination is achieved, states may face 'survival clauses'. Most IIAs include a 'tail' that provides treaty protections for foreign investors (who made their investment prior to the termination of the treaty) for an extended period after the treaty terminates. One study found that such provisions prolong investor protections for an average of twelve and a half years after treaty termination in order to provide a predictable legal environment.[31] The stickiness of IIAs is further enhanced by the bilateral character of most of these treaties. Such IIAs are frequently signed as a token of friendly relations. It is likely that a decision to unilaterally terminate an IIA with all or particular states could be perceived as unnecessarily unfriendly. Nevertheless, many states, including those that have withdrawn from the ICSID Convention, have also unilaterally or through mutual consent terminated some of their IIAs. Most IIAs have termination clauses allowing for one state party to the treaty to unilaterally give notice of the intent to not renew a treaty for an extended period as stipulated in the treaty. This automatic renewal is typically subject to provisions that allow for either state party to unilaterally terminate the treaty by giving notice prior to the treaties' expiration (often requiring such notice one year ahead of the renewal).

An emerging tactic is to request termination of the treaty with the intention of renegotiating a new treaty with the same state party. The approach is staggered so that it takes account of the various lock-in provisions. If we look closer at the states that have withdrawn from ICSID, we find that two of them have terminated or are in the process of terminating a very significant number of their BITs; Bolivia has terminated eleven and eleven remain in force,[32] and Ecuador has terminated or decided to terminate twenty-two and four will remain in force.[33] Arguably, these two

[31] Kathryn Gordon and Joachim Pohl, 'Investment Treaties over Time: Treaty Practice and Interpretation in a Changing World', *OECD Working Papers on International Investment* (Paris: OECD Publishing, 2015), at 19.

[32] Bolivia has unilaterally terminated its BITs with Argentina (2014), Austria (2013), the Belgium-Luxembourg Economic Union (2014), Denmark (2014), France (2013), Germany (2013), the Netherlands (2009), Spain (2012), Sweden (2013) and the United States (US) (2012). It has not signed any new BITs or other IIAs since 2004. UNCTAD, note 2 above, as of 16 May 2017.

[33] Ecuador has terminated its BITs with Cuba (2008), Dominican Republic (2008), El Salvador (2008), Finland (2010), Guatemala (2008), Honduras (2008), Nicaragua (2008), Paraguay (2008), Romania (2008) and Uruguay (2008). It has not signed any new BITs or other IIAs with ISDS clauses since 2002. UNCTAD, note 2 above, as of 16 May 2017. Parliamentary decisions of 3 May 2017 decided that Ecuador shall denounce its BITs with Argentina, Bolivia, Canada, Chile, China, Italy, the Netherlands, Peru, Spain,

states might qualify as 'absolute opponents' to the regime. The same could be the case for Brazil, which has signed twenty BITs of which none have entered into force.[34] Brazil published a model BIT in 2015 and signed six new BITs the same year, none of which include ISDS. Hence, Brazil could be classified as an absolute opponent to ISDS, but not to IIAs in general. Venezuela has not pursued any policy of denouncing its BITs (except its BIT with the Netherlands), and while it seems to have wished to pursue a strategy of material exit, the result has been a tactic of voice, an expression of displeasure.[35]

4.3.2 *Hybrid Tactics*

A second group of states have adopted an approach that clearly combines different exit and voice tactics, which may be effective in balancing enhanced sovereignty with the need to maintain a reputation for a positive investment climate. Such initiatives could include termination of BITs combined with the aim of renegotiating ISDS provisions or substantive clauses that are regarded as particularly controversial. Whether other states are always likely to be more sympathetic to such approaches than to unilateral termination is hard to say. States belonging to the group of compliers could in some cases prefer that other states remain within the regime, and accept the renegotiation of the IIA. However, other compliers may oppose renegotiation because it could set a precedent and lead to further calls for systemic reform.

Based on a review of states that have terminated a significant number of their treaties, either unilaterally or by mutual consent, we may possibly consider the Czech Republic, India, Indonesia, Italy and South Africa in this category.[36] In addition, it is important to consider a wider group of

Switzerland, the US and Venezuela. See 'La Asamblea Denuncia 12 Tratados Bilaterales de Inversión', *El Telégrafo*, 3 May 2017. This decision follows decisions by the Constitutional Court regarding the constitutionality of ISDS clauses in BITs, see Alexander Avtgis, 'Rethinking Article 422: A Retrospective on Ecuador's 2008 Constitutional ISDS Recalibration' (2016) 2(2) *Indiana Journal of Constitutional Design*, 1–21, at 8–11.

[34] The new BITs were signed with Angola, Chile, Colombia, Malawi, Mexico and Mozambique. UNCTAD, note 2 above, as of 16 May 2017. An explanation could be that these BITs were signed by Brazil as an emerging capital exporter. See also Welsh et al., note 21 above; Yoram Haftel and Alexander Thompson, 'Delayed Ratification: The Domestic Fate of Bilateral Investment Treaties' (2013) 67 *International Organization* 355–87.

[35] Venezuela terminated its BIT with the Netherlands in 2008. Twenty-seven BITs remain in force. UNCTAD, note 2 above, as of 16 May 2017.

[36] The Czech Republic has by mutual consent terminated its BITs with Denmark (2009), Estonia (2011), Ireland (2011), Italy (2009), Malta (2010), Slovakia (2004) and

states that have engaged in systematic renegotiation of their IIAs. Based on theoretical considerations and anecdotal evidence, Haftel and Thompson hypothesize that 'states renegotiate when they acquire new information about the legal and political consequences of their treaty commitments, and that this learning occurs especially when states are involved in investment arbitration'.[37] Thus, based on their findings, the following can be regarded as significant renegotiators, as each has renegotiated ten or more BITs: Romania, the Czech Republic, Germany, China, Egypt, Bulgaria, Morocco, Slovakia and Finland. The only overlap with our preliminary list is the Czech Republic.[38] However, given that there are many alternative reasons why states may choose to renegotiate, we should exclude states that only or essentially have renegotiated old BITs that are ripe for renegotiation due to their limited investment protections (Bulgaria,[39] Egypt,[40]

Slovenia (2009) – seventy-seven BITs remain in force. India has unilaterally terminated its BITs with Argentina (2013), Australia (2017), Austria (2017), Hungary (2017), Indonesia (2016), Italy (2017), the Netherlands (2016) and Oman (2017) – sixty-six BITs remain in force. Indonesia has unilaterally (except for Argentina) terminated its BITs with Argentina (2016), Bulgaria (2015), Cambodia (2016), China (2015), Egypt (2014), France (2015), Hungary (2016), India (2016), Italy (2015), Lao PDR (2015), Malaysia (2015), the Netherlands (2015), Norway (2004), Pakistan (2016), Romania (2016), Singapore (2016), Slovakia (2015), Spain (2016), Switzerland (2016), Turkey (2016) and Viet Nam (2016) – twenty-seven BITs remain in force. Italy has terminated its BITs with Bulgaria (2010, by consent), Croatia (2013), Czech Republic (2009, by consent), Estonia (2009, by consent), Hungary (2008, by consent), India (2017), Indonesia (2015), Latvia (2009, by consent), Poland (2013, by consent), Romania (2010, by consent), Slovakia (2012, by consent), Slovenia (2009, by consent), Uganda (2014) and Ukraine (2012, by consent) – seventy-six BITs remain in force. Italy also withdrew from the Energy Charter Treaty (2014, effective 2016). South Africa has unilaterally terminated its BITs with Austria (2014), the Belgium-Luxembourg Economic Union (2013), Denmark (2014), France (2014), Germany (2014), the Netherlands (2014), Spain (2013), Switzerland (2014) and the UK (2014) – fourteen BITs remain in force. Moreover, a significant number of treaties that these states have signed have not entered into force (Czech Republic, four; India, ten; Italy, twelve; South Africa, twenty-six), UNCTAD, note 2 above, as of 16 May 2017. See also Haftel and Thompson, note 31 above.

[37] Yoram Haftel and Alexander Thompson, 'When Do States Renegotiate Investment Agreements? The Impact of Arbitration' (forthcoming) *The Review of International Organizations* 1–24, at 20 (pre-published version).

[38] Ibid., at 10.

[39] According to our findings based on BITs that have been replaced by newer version BITs (a narrower definition of renegotiation than that of Haftel and Thompson, ibid.), we find that Bulgaria has only renegotiated two BITs which first were signed during the period of 1984–88 and renegotiated versions were signed in 1997–99. UNCTAD supra note 2 as of 16 May 2017.

[40] Egypt's thirteen renegotiated BITs were first signed during period of 1966–88 and renegotiated versions were signed between 1994 and 2010. UNCTAD, note 2 above, as of 16 May 2017.

Germany[41] and Morocco,[42] as well as China[43] and Finland[44]). This means that we only add Romania and Slovakia to our list of states following a hybrid approach.[45] What is common to all states in this hybrid category is that they have also been subject to ITA.[46] This fits with the aggregative pattern of renegotiation tactics. According to Haftel and Thompson, there is only a 15 per cent likelihood of renegotiation amongst states who have never experienced ITA; a figure that rises to 25 per cent for states that have experienced three or more disputes.[47]

This hybrid approach is likely to become frequently adopted amongst those states who believe that IIAs are one-sided agreements that protect investors at the expense of a state's legitimate policy goals and its ability to regulate in the public interest. Prominent examples include Indonesia's notification that it intends to terminate all of its existing BITs with the goal of renegotiating new BITs with many (if not all) of its previous treaty

[41] Germany's eighteen renegotiated BITs were first signed during the period of 1959–83 and renegotiated versions were signed between1996 and 2010. UNCTAD, note 2 above, as of May 2017.

[42] Morocco's twelve renegotiated BITs were first signed during the period of 1961–89 and renegotiated versions were signed in the period of 1996–2007. The status of the two remaining BITs is unclear as neither the original versions (signed in 1997 and 2001) nor the renegotiated versions (signed in 2001 and 2006) have entered into force. UNCTAD, note 2 above, as of 16 May 2017.

[43] We find a somewhat mixed picture for China concerning renegotiation: 13 of 15 renegotiated BITs were signed during the period of 1984–92, a period during which China included very limited ISDS clauses in its BITs. However, we do not have access to the treaty texts of all these treaties. The remaining two treaties were first signed with African states in 1997. UNCTAD, note 2 above, as of 16 May 2017.

[44] We find a somewhat mixed picture for Finland concerning renegotiation: only four of nine renegotiated BITs were signed during the period of 1980–90 (three of which did not include ISDS clauses) and new versions were signed in the period of 1996–2004. The remaining five BITs were first signed between 1992–96 and renegotiated versions were signed between 2004 and 2008, UNCTAD, note 2 above, as of 16 May 2017.

[45] We find a mixed picture for Romania; seven out of twelve renegotiated BITs originated in the period of 1976–82 and renegotiated versions of these were signed between 1994 and 1996. Two of the remaining BITs also seem to have been renegotiated at least partly due to weak protection of investors' rights (BITs with Korea and Turkey). The remaining three seem to have been renegotiated for other reasons (BITs with Canada, Greece and Kazakhstan). All the four renegotiated treaties of Slovakia were originally signed between1990 and 2000 and renegotiated versions were signed between 2002 and 2010. UNCTAD, note 2 above, as of 16 May 2017.

[46] Our PITAD database (note 10 above) reveals the following number of disputes filed per state: Czech Republic (35), India (21), Indonesia (8), Italy (8), Romania (13), Slovakia (14) and South Africa (1). Only a minority of these disputes are ICSID arbitrations (32 per cent or thirty-two out of one hundred disputes).

[47] Haftel and Thompson, note 37 above, at 17.

partners,[48] the Czech Republic which has actively terminated and renegotiated a high number of treaties out of public policy and other concerns,[49] and South Africa whose new policy towards IIAs was triggered by the case of *Foresti v. South Africa*, which challenged its affirmative action legislation.[50] In 2007, South Africa placed a moratorium on the negotiation of any new IIAs and conducted a full and comprehensive review of its IIA policy. Following the conclusion of the review in 2010, South Africa announced that it would refrain from entering into BITs unless there were compelling reasons for such a course of action and terminate existing BITs and offer renegotiation on the basis of a new model agreement.[51]

A materially different but symbolically similar strategy was pursued by Australia. The Gillard government announced in 2011 that no future IIA with Australia would include ISDS provisions.[52] Subsequently, ITA provisions in IIAs have generally had a limited scope.[53] However, after a change of government, Australia did sign and ratify an FTA with Korea that included strong ISDS provisions in 2014. It is therefore not clear that Australia could be added to our list of states with hybrid tactics.

4.3.3 *Systemic Voice*

A final approach is a more indirect or step-by-step move towards 'balanced' IIAs. As noted above, there is a recent emergence of initiatives to renegotiate IIAs. These tactics generally form part of a hybrid strategy and thus it is rare to find states outside this category pursuing this goal. Moreover, clear instances of systemic political delegitimization of IIAs

[48] Leon Trakman and Kunal Sharma, 'Indonesia's Termination of the Nethelrands-Indonesia BIT: Broader Implications in the Asia-Pacific' (Kluwer Arbitration Blog, 1 September 2014).

[49] Tomáš Fecák, 'Czech Experience with Bilateral Investment Treaties: Somewhat Bitter Taste of Investment Protection' (2011) 2 *Czech Yearbook of Public & Private International Law* 233–67.

[50] *Piero Foresti, Laura de Carli & Others v. The Republic of South Africa*, ICSID Case No. ARB(AF)/07/01, discontinued 4 August 2010.

[51] The Cabinet based their decision on the DTI, *Bilateral Investment Treaty Policy Framework Review*, Pretoria, South Africa, June 2009.

[52] Jürgen Kurtz, 'Australia's Rejection of Investor–State Arbitration: Causation, Omission and Implication' (2012) 27(1) *ICSID Review* 65–86.

[53] See the investment chapter in the *Australia – China Free Trade Agreement* (2015), the *Agreement between Australia and Japan for an Economic Partnership* (2014), the *Malaysia – Australia Free Trade Agreement* (2012) and the *Protocol on Investment to the New Zealand – Australia Closer Economic Relations Trade Agreement* (2011). UNCTAD, note 2 above, as of 16 May 2017.

are hard to identify beyond states' attempts at termination of the ICSID Convention.

However, the adoption of a 'new generation' of model treaties over the past ten years is a signal from some key states that IIAs are in need of reform. These states form a category that seeks to use systemic voice tactics.[54] In the early 2000s, the US sought to develop a third-generation model BIT that reflected the fact that it had been the subject of a number of suits by Canadian corporations under the NAFTA. The 2004 model US BIT scaled back a number of foreign investor protections in favour of protecting the sovereign prerogatives of the state hosting the foreign investment. While the 2004 model and more recent 2012 model include robust ISDS provisions, these provisions have been more thoroughly refined and many of the substantive provisions have been revised (with the level of foreign investor protection reduced). Overall, the models seek to recalibrate the balance between the rights accorded investors and a nation's right to regulate in the public interest.[55]

It has been contended that the new restrictive US model treaty has been as influential as the earlier expansive version:

> If the United States led the charge in favour of investor protections, it now appears to be leading the drive in the opposite direction. The 2004 U.S. Model BIT is at least twice as long as it once was – and as every lawyer knows, the length of a treaty is often inversely related to the rights that it accords. The 2004 U.S. Model BIT has now shrunk, sometimes dramatically, virtually every right originally accorded to foreign investors while at the same time increasing, sometimes vastly, the discretion accorded host states.[56]

The changes were noticed and are reflected in treaties negotiated by states as diverse as Canada, Mexico, India and China.[57] The recently concluded Comprehensive Economic and Trade Agreement between Canada and the EU (CETA, 2014) is particularly important in this regard, as it signals the future direction of the EU and consequently of its Member States with regard to IIAs. The CETA follows the approach of the US and Canada in most respects. Gordon and Pohl find that while significant differences remain, there is a convergence towards the US and Canadian model

54 See Tarald Laudal Berge and Øyvind Stiansen, 'Negotiating BITs with Models: The Power of Expertise' (2016) *PluriCourts Research Paper* No. 16–13.

55 Jose Alvarez, 'Contemporary International Law: An "Empire of Law" or the "Law of Empire"' (2009) 24(5) *American University International Law Review* 811–42 at 834.

56 Alvarez, note 6 above, at 235.

57 Ibid., at 237.

treaties.[58] We know of fifty-three states that have drafted model treaties, of which forty-eight have made them publicly available potentially with a view to influencing the drafting policy of other states. The most active producer of such models has been the US which published its fifth model in 2012. Thereafter follow Germany, Guatemala and Turkey which have drafted three editions, as well as Colombia, India, the Netherlands, Norway and the UK which have drafted second editions. Moreover, some states of particular interest have joined in recent years, including Brazil (2015), the Czech Republic (2016) and Slovakia (2016).[59]

4.3.4 *Concluding Remarks*

The above discussion reveals that a number of states have made some significant changes in their approach to IIAs which intentionally or otherwise have sought to weaken their commitments as principals. While the number is small and may seem geographically limited, there are signs that more and more states are revising their approach to IIAs. However, the reforms vary in their intention, strength and significance. So far, there are only two states (Ecuador and Bolivia) that are seeking a full and clean exit from the international investment regime. Other states have displayed a willingness to rebuild the ship while it sails at sea: some strengthening foreign investor rights, including ISDS (e.g. China and Germany), while the majority of others are weakening foreign investor rights while still remaining part of the regime. These states have sought to renegotiate treaties directly or exclude or limit ISDS clauses in treaties (e.g. Indonesia, India, Poland, Romania, the Czech Republic, Slovakia, Morocco, Italy, Bulgaria, Egypt, and South Africa) or changed the terms of their model treaties or their future negotiating strategy (e.g. the US, the EU, Canada, Norway, Russia and Australia). Interestingly, the latter may exert the strongest material and symbolic effects on the overall international investment regime, although it is dependent on how arbitrators respond to the new provisions and signals.

4.4 States as Litigants in Investment Treaty Arbitration

The role of the state as a litigant in international legal disputes is quite different from its role as principal. It is different because when a state is a

[58] Gordon and Pohl, note 31 above, at 37–38.

[59] UNCTAD, note 2 above, as of 16 May 2017. We have included the Norwegian model treaties even if none of the two versions have been formally adopted. The most recent version of the Turkish model (2016) is not (yet) publicly available.

litigant in an international dispute, much of its authority as a sovereign is limited. Once a state has consented to a treaty that includes ISDS, control is largely deferred to a third-party adjudicator. This is a reversal of the classical model of international arbitration in which jurisdiction for a dispute was negotiated on a case-by-case basis. In the case of ISDS, the state has a reduced ability to ex post modify the terms upon which it had previously agreed to be bound. Once a dispute has been initiated, the state is limited in the types of tactics it can employ to influence the proceedings. We will therefore examine the particular tactics that states do (and can) wield in defending against private parties' investment treaty claims.

States are always on the respondent side of the dispute in ITA. With counter-claims being infrequently invoked, state respondents in ITA are primarily concerned with avoiding liability that could result in large damage awards. In the early days of ITA claims, the infrequency of disputes meant that states likely responded and participated in defending investment treaty claims with few specific tactics in mind. However, as the regime has grown, states have developed a variety of tactics in defending claims; especially those states that have had to defend against multiple claims (e.g. Argentina and Venezuela).

While there is little evidence that states are taking extreme measures such as refusing to participate in arbitral proceedings[60] or directly influencing arbitrators,[61] there is evidence that states are employing increasingly aggressive tactics in defending ITA claims. These include a number of procedural and legal tactics, such as: utilizing the domestic criminal system of the respondent state; claimant and witness intimidation; reinterpreting treaties after a dispute is filed; refusing or delaying enforcement of awards (including excessive use of the ICSID annulment

[60] Some of the early (mid-twentieth-century) investment arbitrations involving contract-based claims were adjudicated without participation of the respondent state (see e.g. the Libyan hydrocarbon concession arbitrations of the 1970s). However, there is a recent example, whereby the Russian Federation is refusing to participate in ITA proceedings brought by Ukrainian investors in Crimea under the Russia-Ukraine BIT. See *Aeroport Belbek LLC and Mr. Igor Valerievich Kolomoisky v. The Russian Federation*, PCA Case No. 2014–30, pending; *PJSC CB PrivatBank and Finance Company Finilon LLC v. The Russian Federation*, PCA Case No. 2015–21, pending; *Everest Estate LLC and others v. The Russian Federation*, PCA Case No. 2015–36, pending.

[61] There is an infamous (and fairly unique) example where Indonesian officials abducted an arbitrator upon arrival at Schiphol airport in the Netherlands in order to prevent him from attending hearings in the Hague to which he was a member of the tribunal. See 'Himpurna v. Indonesia' (2000) 15 *Mealey's Int'l Arb. Rep.* (February); see also Stephen Schwebel, 'Injunction of Arbitral Proceedings and Truncation of the Tribunal' (2003) 18(4) *Int'l Arb. Rep.* 33.

process); using novel jurisdictional challenges; and employing various tactics for delaying proceedings or making them excessively costly (such as refusing claim consolidation, claim bifurcation, challenging arbitrators and partial, delayed or no compliance with procedural and substantive orders).

But states are not alone. The high-stakes and serious nature of many ITA claims can lead to the employment of aggressive litigation tactics on both sides. In this chapter, however, we focus exclusively on shifting trends in litigation tactics employed by respondent states. In some cases, these essentially mirror tactics equally available to foreign investor claimants. Yet, the state's sovereign authority may be used to obstruct or unbalance arbitral proceedings initiated by private parties. We will therefore draw on particular examples where the tactics employed by respondent states in ITA can be *only* pursued by a state (i.e. where the state uses both its sovereign status and/or the apparatus of the state itself to gain a tactical advantage in a proceeding against a private litigant).

Extensive resort to 'strong' litigation tactics by (ab)using the state's sovereign position would place states as either 'absolute opponents' of or 'reluctant compliers' to the international investment regime. However, an excessive use of other obstructionist tactics *may* also, in some circumstances, place a state in these categories. (Ab)use of such tactics may easily breach the 'equality of arms' principle. We are particularly concerned with litigation tactics that can be seen to deviate from this principle. Waelde states the issue as:

> 'Equality of arms' is a foundation principle of investment arbitration procedure. A government sued on the basis of an investment treaty, signed to encourage foreign and private investment by promising effective protection, should prosecute its case vigorously but within the framework of the principles of 'good faith' arbitration, the applicable arbitration rules, and with respect to 'equality of arms'.[62]

As the ITA caseload grows, we are increasingly able to identify litigation trends where sovereign deference to the 'equality of arms' principle is waning. We will look at three recent trends that represent strong litigation tactics in which the state (perhaps) most clearly abuses its role as sovereign: (1) criminal proceedings during disputes; (2) (ab)using the dual role of states in ITA; and (3) refusing to enforce or satisfy arbitral awards.

[62] Thomas Waelde, '"Equality of Arms" in Investment Arbitration: Procedural Challenges', in Katia Yannaca-Small (ed.) *Arbitration Under International Investment Agreements: A Guide to the Key Issues* (Oxford: Oxford University Press, 2008), 167.

4.4.1 *Criminal Proceedings during Disputes*

The most significant and recent tactical shift in the way that respondent states are defending ITA claims is in the area of domestic judicial proceedings. It is of course reasonable and not unusual for respondent states to use their judiciary to enforce domestic law against foreign investors operating within their borders. What is relatively new is a tactic whereby the domestic judicial machinery is activated as a response to an ITA claim. This tactic is arguably (ab)used for three purposes: (1) to obstruct, delay or interfere with the proceedings of the ITA; (2) to (ab)use the domestic legal system to obtain evidence and information that can be used against the claimant in the arbitration proceedings; and (3) to intimidate, scare or coerce the claimant and its witnesses after the ITA is initiated. All three of these tactics are within the purview of the respondent host state to initiate, but can be seen as troubling where they have disguised objectives or can be seen as bad faith manoeuvres in order to gain tactical advantage in a pending arbitration.

To highlight how states have used this tactic in recent cases, a number of pertinent examples are provided. In *Border Timbers v. Zimbabwe* and *Von Pezold v. Zimbabwe*,[63] a group of Dutch and Swiss farm owners in Zimbabwe claimed that their farms were unlawfully expropriated. During the course of the proceedings, the claimants received a letter from Zimbabwe's attorney general demanding that they disclose certain documents in connection with the arbitration; and that if they refused, Zimbabwe would institute domestic criminal proceedings.[64] In a procedural order dated 13 June 2012, the president of the tribunal directed Zimbabwe to cease pursuit of the demands.[65] A year later the claimants requested urgent injunctive relief in relation to a number of threatening altercations on the claimant's farm to which the local police refused to provide assistance. In a procedural order refusing to grant the claimant's relief, the tribunal noted 'that the Claimants continue to "feel intimidated" by the

[63] *Border Timbers Limited, Timber Products International (Private) Limited and Hangani Development Co. (Private) Limited v. Republic of Zimbabwe (Border Timbers)*, ICSID Case No. ARB/10/25, Award, 28 July 2015; *Bernhard von Pezold and Others v. Republic of Zimbabwe (Von Pezold)*, ICSID Case No. ARB/10/15, Award, 28 July 2015.

[64] *Border Timbers*, Directions Concerning Claimants' Application for Provisional Measures of 12 June 2012, 13 June 2012; *Von Pezold*, Directions Concerning Claimants' Application for Provisional Measures of 12 June 2012, 13 June 2012.

[65] *Border Timbers*, Directions Concerning Claimants' Application for Provisional Measures, 12 June 2012; *Von Pezold*, Directions Concerning Claimants' Application for Provisional Measures, 12 June 2012.

threats made against their staff and that this intimidation is "heightened by the fact that the Police will not act"'.[66]

In *Quiborax v. Bolivia*,[67] the claimant brought a claim for compensation against Bolivia for unilaterally revoking several mining concessions. Almost three years into the arbitration, Bolivia initiated criminal proceedings against the main shareholder of Quiborax for allegedly forging documents.[68] The effect was to limit the claimant's ability to access important documents relevant to the arbitration (they were seized by the state in relation to the domestic criminal proceedings); and the investors claimed that 'the criminal proceedings are aggravating the dispute because they put intolerable pressure on them to abandon their claim and are thus aimed at avoiding the resolution of the dispute'.[69] Interestingly, there is evidence that the initiation of the criminal proceedings was designed as part of a larger defence strategy Bolivia developed specifically for this arbitration.[70]

The tribunal ultimately ordered Bolivia to suspend all pending criminal proceedings against the claimants and their witnesses pending the outcome of the arbitration.[71] Given the close connection of these criminal proceedings with the arbitration, the tribunal was concerned that the respondent state's domestic actions could 'jeopardize the procedural integrity of this arbitration'.[72] The claimant alleged that these criminal proceedings also served to reduce the willingness of witnesses to participate in the arbitration for fear of reprisals.[73]

In *Caratube v. Kazakhstan (Caratube II)*,[74] the claimants initiated new proceedings relating to a previous award, *Caratube v. Kazakhstan*

66 *Border Timbers*, Procedural Order No. 4, 16 March 2013; *Von Pezold*, Procedural Order No. 4, 16 March 2013.

67 *Quiborax S.A. and Non-Metallic Minerals S.A. v. Plurinational State of Bolivia (Quiborax)*, ICSID Case No. ARB/06/2, Award, 16 September 2015.

68 Luke Peterson, 'Arbitrators order that (Bolivian) criminal proceedings be suspended' (Investment Arbitration Reporter, 9 April 2010).

69 *Quiborax*, Decision on Provisional Measures 1 February 2010, para. III.132.

70 Ibid., para. III.122. '[T]hat it cannot fail to note that these [criminal proceeding] actions were taken after an inter-ministerial committee specifically recommended in the 2004 Memo that Bolivia should try to find flaws in Claimants' mining concessions as a defense strategy for the ICSID arbitration. Seen jointly with the 2004 Memo, the corporate audit and the criminal proceedings appear to be part of a defense strategy adopted by Bolivia with respect to the ICSID arbitration'.

71 Ibid., para. V.2. 72 Ibid., para. V.1. 73 Peterson supra note 68.

74 *Caratube International Oil Company LLP and Devincci Salah Hourani v. Republic of Kazakhstan (Caratube II)*, ICSID Case No. ARB/13/13, pending.

(Caratube I),[75] which concerned the unilateral termination of a hydrocarbon concession. In what appears to be an increasingly personal and highly charged dispute, the claimants sought injunctive relief in order to protect Devincci Hourani (one of the primary claimants in the case), his relatives and associates from investigations and harassment relating to their alleged involvement in a 2004 murder in Lebanon. According to the request, Kazakhstan had enjoined as a *partie civile* in criminal proceedings against Hourani in Lebanon for an alleged murder.[76] While the tribunal denied the claimants' request for provisional measures, it 'found that the Claimants have shown a certain need for protection in this Arbitration' and that the request was not 'unreasonable under the circumstances'.[77]

In *Hydro v. Albania*,[78] a group of Italian investors and their companies brought a claim alleging that the Albanian authorities had failed to honour prior commitments in relation to their electricity generation enterprises in Albania. After the arbitration was initiated, Albania sought to have two of the claimants (Francesco Becchetti and Mauro De Renzis) extradited from the UK on allegations of money laundering and fraud. The claimants sought interim relief from the tribunal, requesting that the tribunal order Albania to desist from seeking the extradition of these two individuals from the UK. In its decision on provisional measures, the tribunal ordered Albania to cease the criminal and extradition proceedings pending the outcome of the arbitration.[79]

In *Al Warraq v. Indonesia*,[80] a Saudi banker brought a claim that the nationalization of a bank to which he was a shareholder amounted to an unlawful expropriation. Indonesia defended the nationalization as an appropriate response to a foundering institution, and argued that the claimant was actually responsible for why the bank needed to be bailed out in the first place. In a domestic criminal proceeding that pre-dated the initiation of the arbitration, an Indonesian court found Al Warraq guilty in absentia of numerous financial crimes relating to his involvement in

75 *Caratube International Oil Company LLP v. Republic of Kazakhstan (Caratube I)*, ICSID Case No. ARB/08/12, Award, 5 June 2012.

76 *Caratube II*, Decision on the Claimants' Request for Provisional Measures, 4 December 2014, para. 135.

77 Ibid., para. 155.

78 *Hydro S.r.l. and others v. Republic of Albania (Hydro)*, ICSID Case No. ARB/15/28, pending.

79 *Hydro*, Order on Provisional Measures, 3 March 2016.

80 *Hesham T. M. Al Warraq v. Republic of Indonesia (Al Warraq)*, UNCITRAL, Award, 15 December 2014.

Bank Century.[81] After the initiation of the arbitration, Al Warraq claimed that Indonesia attempted to derail the arbitration by freezing his assets and obtaining an Interpol Red Notice against him.[82]

Churchill v. Indonesia,[83] concerns a claim that Indonesia had unilaterally, and without cause, terminated mining licences in East Kalimantan. After the claim was brought, Indonesia initiated criminal proceedings against the claimants alleging that the mining licences were procured through forged documents.[84] The claimants contend that these criminal proceedings were initiated by Indonesia to '"cause maximum surprise and disruption", and was a "tactical move" directly connected to the arbitration'.[85] In carrying out their criminal prosecution against the claimants domestically, Indonesia raided the offices of the claimants and confiscated numerous documents and computer hard drives that (as claimants allege) could be used as evidence against them in the pending ITA.[86] While it is possible that the raid and the forgery proceedings were not being pursued in order to gain tactical advantage in the arbitration, there may be an good argument that Indonesia is using its sovereign authority in contravention of the 'equality of arms' principle or that its level of obstructionism places its actions in a more questionable category.

In a decision dated 15 February 2017, a tribunal in the case of *Italba v. Uruguay*[87] refused to enjoin Uruguay from pursuing a criminal investigation against two of the claimant's witnesses in the case.[88] Uruguay initiated the investigation on the basis that certain documents submitted to the tribunal by these witnesses were not authentic. Claimants in the case alleged that Uruguay was abusing its position as a sovereign in the case for the sole purpose of frustrating the arbitral proceedings.

The final example is slightly different from the previous. It deals with threats related to the potential initiation of an investment treaty claim. In

[81] Luke Peterson, 'In Al Warraq v. Indonesia award, arbitrators devote bulk of their analysis to assessing investor's treatment in light of UN human rights treaty norms' (Investment Arbitration Reporter, 19 December 2014).

[82] Ibid.

[83] *Churchill Mining and Planet Mining Pty Ltd, formerly ARB/12/40 v. Republic of Indonesia (Churchill)*, ICSID Case No. ARB/12/40 and 12/14, Award 6 December 2016.

[84] Jarrod Hepburn, 'Arbitrators Again Decline to Order Indonesia to Desist with Criminal Investigation into Alleged Forgery of Mining License in Churchill & Planet Mining Case' (Investment Arbitration Reporter, 30 December 2014).

[85] Ibid. [86] Ibid.

[87] *Italba Corporation v. Oriental Republic of Uruguay*, ICSID Case No. ARB/16/9, pending.

[88] *Italba*, Decision on Claimant's Application for Provisional Measures and Temporary Relief, 15 February 2017.

Bozbey v. Turkmenistan,[89] a Turkish businessman brought a claim relating to investments made in the agricultural sector in the 1990s. Bozbey alleged that 'he was caught up in a wave of anti-Turkish sentiment in Turkmenistan, culminating in his imprisonment and mistreatment after he refused to comply with a request for a bribe issued by a local tax official'.[90] After eighteen months in prison, he returned to Turkey and initiated a claim with the United Nations Human Rights Committee (UNHRC). In that claim, he alleged that he was tortured while in prison and most importantly, he claimed that while in prison, officials 'wanted him to sign legal documents... to undertake that he would not make any complaints and apply to any international arbitration institution regarding his investments in the country'.[91] The UNHRC concluded that his conditions of detention constituted 'a violation of his right to be treated with humanity and with respect for the inherent dignity of the human person under article 10, paragraph 1, of the Covenant'.[92] While Bozbey did ultimately bring an investment treaty claim, he had to abandon it before its conclusion because he could not meet the tribunal's request for an advance on costs.

As these cases demonstrate, it may be difficult to trace whether and how states use criminal proceedings in the context of ITAs. Moreover, we are frequently faced with situations where it is impossible or very difficult to determine who is at fault – the foreign investor, the state or both. The cases we have identified indicate varying types of domestic proceedings that states have brought against claimants after the initiation of the claim as well as the general reluctance of tribunals to order injunctive relief against such domestic proceedings. Tactically speaking, it appears that respondent states have a general degree of latitude in pursuing domestic criminal proceedings and that these proceedings may be effective in gaining an advantage over claimants. We may fear that as a consequence of such proceedings, states that suffer from corruption or lag behind in their implementation of 'rule of law' standards could be more successful than other states in ISDS. It is therefore essential that tribunals find ways to deal with such cases that do not place an excessive burden of proof on the claimant.

89 *Farouk Bozbey v. Turkmenistan*, UNCITRAL, discontinued 16 August 2013.

90 Jarrod Hepburn and Luke Peterson, 'After Claims of Human Rights Violation Are Borne Out, Businessman Pursues Ad-Hoc Investment Treaty Arbitration against Turkmenistan' (Investment Arbitration Reporter, 3 April 2013).

91 *Omar Faruk Bozbey v. Turkmenistan*, Communication No. 1530/2006, UN Doc. CCPR/C/100/D/1530/2006 (2010), para. 5.6.

92 Ibid., para. 7.3.

4.4.2 (Ab)using the Dual Role of States

The second category of litigation tactics pursued with increasing frequency by respondent states relate to a state's dual role as both party to the dispute with a foreign investor and party to the treaty upon which the dispute is based. This dynamic can create a scenario where the respondent state attempts to modify the provisions of a treaty in order to gain advantage in a dispute to which it is a party. Timing is crucial. As a party to a treaty, a state can always request the renegotiation (or interpretation of particular provisions) of the treaty with a treaty partner or partners. In a variety of ways, these new or subsequent treaties or agreements will bind adjudicators in future disputes.[93] Renegotiation or modification becomes problematic when conducted *after* a particular dispute has been initiated. Below we provide a few examples where respondent states have sought the assistance of the investor home state for the purpose of weakening the investor's position in the arbitration.

In *Sanum v. Lao PDR*,[94] an investor from Macau brought a claim based on the China-Lao BIT. At issue in the case was whether the BIT was intended to include protections for investors from Macau (the location of the foreign investor claimant). In its award on jurisdiction, the tribunal held that the BIT does cover the investor from Macau and that the tribunal does have jurisdiction over the claim. Despite agreement to settle the case in mid 2014,[95] the respondent state continued to pursue set-aside proceedings against the award on jurisdiction in Singapore (the seat of the arbitration); and in January 2015, the Singapore High Court issued a decision setting aside the jurisdictional award;[96] but was ultimately overturned on Appeal.[97] Nonetheless, the respondent state sought to set aside the award

[93] The classic example is the interpretive statement issued by the Free Trade Commission (FTC) under the North American Free Trade Agreement (NAFTA). After arbitrations brought under NAFTA Chapter 11 where treaty parties were dissatisfied with interpretations of the FET standard in the treaty, the FTC (comprising the US, Canada and Mexico) issued a binding interpretive statement restricting the interpretation of the FET standard to the customary international law minimum standard of treatment. This statement has had the effect of constituting a subsequent agreement under international law and has bound future NAFTA tribunals.

[94] *Sanum Investments Limited v. Lao People's Democratic Republic*, UNCITRAL, PCA Case No. 2013–13, Award on Jurisdiction, 13 December 2013.

[95] *Sanum Investments Limited v. Lao People's Democratic Republic*, UNCITRAL, PCA Case No. 2013–13, Settlement Award, 15 June 2014.

[96] *Government of the Lao People's Democratic Republic v. Sanum Investments Ltd.* [2015] SGHC 15, 20 January 2015.

[97] *Sanum Investments Ltd. v. Government of the Lao People's Democratic Republic* [2016] SGCA 57, 29 September 2016.

on the basis of two letters from the Chinese government (which were a response to a request from Lao) stating that the China-Lao PDR BIT does not apply to Macau. What is striking, and troubling, in this case is that the respondent state used its position as a treaty party to alter the outcome of the dispute by changing the meaning of a treaty after a dispute (to which it was a party) had already been decided by an international tribunal.

In *Ecuador v. US*,[98] one of very few state to state disputes based on a BIT, Ecuador argued that US refusal to issue an interpretive note or amendment to the US-Ecuador BIT on the scope of the 'access to justice' provision in that treaty was unlawful. This dispute arose out of an earlier investment treaty claim, *Chevron v. Ecuador (Chevron I)*,[99] where Ecuador was dissatisfied with the tribunal's interpretation of the 'access to justice' provision. Ecuador brought the case with the aim of binding tribunals, including the tribunal in the ongoing dispute of *Chevron v. Ecuador (Chevron II)*.[100] While the state-to-state dispute was dismissed by the tribunal for lack of jurisdiction, if it had been successful it would have bound a tribunal to a restrictive interpretation of a treaty provision that would favour Ecuador in an ongoing case.

These cases indicate that states may find difficulty in making unilateral modification to its commitments under IIAs after a dispute has arisen. However, the first case referenced above does provide anecdotal evidence that some post-dispute interpretations of IIAs may be possible. Generally speaking though, rules of international law, according to which disputes shall be determined on the basis of the law applicable at the time of the event that triggered the disputes, would in most cases prevent abuse. In situations where one could argue for flexibility in the application of the general rules, it is likely that tribunals will require strong arguments for exemptions to be accepted.

4.4.3 *Refusing to Enforce or Satisfy Arbitral Awards*

The difficulty in compelling a state to satisfy an international arbitral award against it is a long-standing problem.[101] What might be new or

[98] *Republic of Ecuador v. United States of America*, UNCITRAL, PCA Case No. 2012–5, Award, 29 September 2012.

[99] *Chevron Corporation (USA) & Texaco Petroleum Company (USA) v. The Republic of Ecuador (Chevron I)*, UNCITRAL, PCA Case No. 34877, Award, 31 August 2011.

[100] *Chevron Corporation & Texaco Petroleum Corporation v. The Republic of Ecuador (Chevron II)*, UNCITRAL, PCA Case No. 2009–23, pending.

[101] See 1958 Convention on the Recognition and Enforcement of Foreign Arbitral Awards (New York Convention), 330 UNTS 38; 21 UST 2517; 7 ILM 1046 (1968).

shifting is the means by which states are avoiding enforcement. One of the central reasons driving the negotiation of the ICSID Convention in the 1960s was precisely related to the problem of enforcement. Article 53 of the ICSID Convention attempted to resolve this problem by making ICSID arbitration awards directly enforceable against the state.

The direct enforceability of awards under the ICSID Convention was systemically challenged for the first time following Argentina's financial collapse in 2001. Argentina has been steadfast in refusing to enforce ICSID awards. The argument has been that despite reference to the direct enforceability of awards in the ICSID Convention, the Argentinian constitution requires that all payments out of the state treasury must first be authorized through a domestic court judgment. Given the high number of ICSID awards against Argentina in the past ten years, this non-compliance has put considerable strain on the long-term viability of the regime overall. While Argentina has recently satisfied five of its outstanding awards through a negotiated settlement, a number of final awards remain unsatisfied.[102]

In addition to the Argentinian cases, Zimbabwe,[103] Russia,[104] Kyrgyzstan,[105] Venezuela[106] and Thailand[107] have all refused to comply

[102] Luke Peterson, 'After Settling Some Awards, Argentina Takes More Fractious Path in Bond-holders Case, with New Bid to Disqualify Arbitrators' (Investment Arbitration Reporter, 20 December 2013); Luke Peterson, 'Argentina Announces Another Settlement of Unpaid BIT Awards, Once Again at a Discount' (Investment Arbitration Reporter, 15 May 2016).

[103] *Bernardus Henricus Funnekotter and others v. Republic of Zimbabwe*, ICSID Case No. ARB/05/6, Award, 22 April 2009.

[104] *Hulley Enterprises Limited (Cyprus) v. The Russian Federation*, UNCITRAL, PCA Case No. AA 226, Award, 18 July 2014; *Yukos Universal Limited (Isle of Man) v. The Russian Federation*, UNCITRAL, PCA Case No. AA 227, Award, 18 July 2014; *Veteran Petroleum Limited (Cyprus) v. The Russian Federation*, UNCITRAL, PCA Case No. AA 228, Award, 18 July 2014; *Renta 4 S.V.S.A, Ahorro Corporación Emergentes F.I., Ahorro Corporación Eurofondo F.I., Rovime Inversiones SICAV S.A., Quasar de Valors SICAV S.A., Orgor de Valores SICAV S.A., GBI 9000 SICAV S.A. v. The Russian Federation*, SCC, Case No. 24/2007, Award, 20 July 2012; *RosInvest Co UK Ltd. v. The Russian Federation*, SCC, Case No. V079/2005, Award, 12 September 2010; *Mr. Franz Sedelmayer v. The Russian Federation*, SCC, Award, 7 July 1998.

[105] *Stans Energy v. Kyrgyz Republic*, Moscow Chamber of Commerce and Industry (MCCI), Award, 30 April 2014; *OKKV (OKKB) and others v. Kyrgyz Republic*, MCCI, Award, 21 November 2013; *Lee John Beck & Central Asian Development Corporation v. Kyrgyz Republic*, MCCI, Award, 13 November 2014; *Sistem Mühendislik Inşaat Sanayi ve Ticaret A.Ş. v. Kyrgyz Republic*, ICSID Case No. ARB(AF)/06/1, Award, 9 September 2009; *Petrobart Limited v. Kyrgyz Republic*, SCC, Case No. 126/2003, Award, 29 March 2005.

[106] All treaty-based arbitration awards based on Chavez-era nationalizations have not been honoured to date. See *Tenaris S.A. and Talta-Trading e Marketing Sociedade Unipessoal Lda. v. Bolivarian Republic of Venezuela (Tenaris II)*, ICSID Case No. ARB/11/26, Award, 12 December 2016; *Rusoro Mining Ltd. v. Bolivarian Republic*

with any awards rendered against them.[108] In addition, there are a number of respondent states that have sought to delay or refuse enforcement in individual cases: Guatemala,[109] Libya,[110] Kazakhstan,[111] Mexico[112] and Romania.[113] These states have a record of complying with some awards and rigorously fighting enforcement in others.

The above list of states includes none from North America and Western Europe. However, there is one case that illustrates that refusal to enforce awards may be relevant for such states – at least EU states. In *Micula v. Romania*,[114] a group of foreign investors initiated a claim under the Sweden-Romania BIT alleging that Romania withdrew a number of incentives in breach of the BIT. The European Commission (EC) intervened as *amicus curiae* expressing doubts as to whether an ICSID award against Romania would be enforceable. Nonetheless, on 11 December 2013, the tribunal issued a final award against Romania in the amount of US$250 million. In April 2014, Romania initiated annulment proceedings, but ultimately failed in annulling the result.[115] In May 2014,

of Venezuela, ICSID Case No. ARB(AF)/12/5, Award, 22 August 2016; *Vestey Group Ltd. v. Bolivarian Republic of Venezuela*, ICSID Case No. ARB/06/4, Award, 15 April 2016; *Crystallex International Corp. v. Bolivarian Republic of Venezuela*, ICSID Case No. ARB(AF)/11/2, Award, 14 April 2016; *Tenaris S.A. and Talta-Trading e Marketing Sociedade Unipessoal Lda. v. Bolivarian Republic of Venezuela (Tenaris I)*, ICSID Case No. ARB/11/26, Award 29 January 2016; *Tidewater Investment SRL and Tidewater Caribe C.A. v. Bolivarian Republic of Venezuela*, ICSID Case No. ARB/10/5, Award 13 March 2015; *OI European Group B.V. v. Bolivarian Republic of Venezuela*, ICSID Case No. ARB/11/25, Award, 10 March 2015; *Flughafen Zürich A.G. and Gestión e Ingeniería IDC S.A. v. Bolivarian Republic of Venezuela*, ICSID Case No. ARB/10/19, Award, 18 November 2014; *Venezuela Holdings B.V. v. Bolivarian Republic of Venezuela*, ICSID Case No. ARB/07/27, Award, 9 October 2014; *Gold Reserve Inc. v. Bolivarian Republic of Venezuela*, ICSID Case No. ARB(AF)/09/1, Award, 22 September 2014.

107 *Walter Bau A.G. v. Kingdom of Thailand*, UNCITRAL, Award, 1 July 2009.

108 The cases listed in this section are limited to treaty-based investment claims (and may not be exhaustive). In addition to the states listed, there are a few states that have not enforced contract-based investment claims or have not complied with settlement agreements. Primarily, these include Lao PDR, the Dominican Republic, the Democratic Republic of Congo, Ukraine and Turkmenistan.

109 *Railroad Development Corporation v. Republic of Guatemala*, ICSID Case No. ARB/07/23, Award, 29 June 2012.

110 *Mohamed Abdulmohsen Al-Kharafi and Sons Co. v. Libya*, CRCICA, Award, 22 March 2013.

111 *Rumeli Telekom A.S. and Telsim Mobil Telekomunikasyon Hizmetleri A.S. v. Republic of Kazakhstan*, ICSID Case No. ARB/05/16, Award, 29 July 2008.

112 *Cargill Incorporated v. United Mexican States*, ICSID Case No. ARB(AF)/05/2, Award, 18 September 2009.

113 *Ioan Micula, Viorel Micula and others v. Romania (Micula)*, ICSID Case No. ARB/05/20, Award, 11 December 2013.

114 Ibid. 115 *Micula*, Decision on Annulment, 26 February 2016.

the EC formally enjoined Romania from satisfying the ICSID award.[116] The EC claims that the ICSID award is compensation for incentives that Romania had to remove in order to join the EU. These incentives constituted illegal state aid under the EU; and therefore, as the EC argues, any payment of compensation for the withdrawal of such illegal state aid (i.e. the ICSID award) would be considered illegal state aid itself and therefore unenforceable.[117]

4.4.5 *Concluding Remarks*

While some tactics used by respondent states can be highly obstructionist in effect, many simply mirror those adopted by foreign investors. However, more recently, and directly related to the expansion of ITA, respondent states are also using their sovereign position to fight claims. It is also becoming apparent that the more experienced a state is in defending against investment treaty claims, the more sophisticated (and less deferential to its power as a state) it becomes in its litigation tactics. While some of these tactics will have both material and symbolic effects, it is the latter that are likely to have the most influence on the system. Certain tactics may not have many material consequences beyond the specific dispute; but collectively, the various tactics we have explored may have significant effect on the way that investment treaty arbitration is perceived. Potential litigants may think twice before bringing a case. And states may have a strong interest in making system watchers aware of the burden that these cases place on them.

Even more profound, however, is the increasing acceptability of respondent state litigation tactics that can be classified as abusing their position as sovereign. For a few states, such tactics are part of their overall strategy to oppose the international investment regime, perhaps qualifying as 'absolute opponents' who aim at exiting the regime. However, most states applying such tactics do so in an ad hoc manner, and should rather be classified as 'reluctant compliers'. Moreover, it remains unclear how the tribunals will respond to the increasingly strong litigation tactics employed by some states. Therefore, it is still too early to tell what impact litigation tactics will have on the international investment regime as such.

[116] Letter from the European Commission 26 May 2014, as confirmed in: European Commission State Aid Investigation, State aid SA.38517(2014/C) (ex 2014/NN) – Romania Implementation of Arbitral award *Micula v. Romania* of 11 December 2013, 1 October 2014.

[117] Ibid.

4.5 Conclusion

Considering the current field of international investment law, it is easy to forget the fact that states have voluntarily consented to being bound by the provisions of the IIAs and that they have voluntarily accepted that such obligations can be adjudicated and enforced through mandatory ISDS provisions. In that sense, all participating states start out as compliers to the IIAs to which they are parties.

This chapter has suggested that when states become dissatisfied with aspects of their IIAs, they may become 'reluctant compliers',[118] 'principled opponents',[119] and occasionally 'absolute opponents';[120] and it is these distinct choices that frame the type of tactics that a state chooses to pursue its aims. It should be noted however, that while there is a significant shift in the tactics that states are pursing to increase sovereign manoeuvrability, no state to date has completely exited from the international investment regime. As such, this means that the strategy employed to date fits within the general thesis of this volume: states continue to engage with – and be a participant in – an increasingly legalized international landscape – while at the same time making adjustments that attempt to minimize the effects on their on sovereign discretion. However, we have shown that the existing web of IIAs has a high degree of 'stickiness' and that some states have faced significant delays in their efforts to exit or change their obligations. The regime is thus designed in a manner to constrain such state strategies. We have also suggested that certain tactics may be pursued through two principal avenues: states acting 'as principals' and states acting 'as litigants', and it is clear that states have the ability to modify and influence the international regimes to which they have consented.

It is possible also that these strategies have had some success. Elsewhere, Langford and Behn have analyzed whether the backlash has affected outcomes in investment arbitration.[121] There was a clear and early drop in success ratios after the emergence of the legitimacy crisis discourse and success in jurisdictional claims has declined over time. The multivariate

118 Arguably, the following states could be considered to be in the process of becoming 'reluctant compliers', based on our findings above: Argentina, Bolivia, Indonesia, Kazakhstan, Kyrgyzstan, Russia, Thailand and Zimbabwe.

119 Arguably, the following states could be considered to be in the process of becoming 'principled opponents', based on our findings above: Argentina, Australia, Bolivia, the Czech Republic, Ecuador, Indonesia, South Africa and Zimbabwe.

120 States qualifying as both 'reluctant compliers' and 'principled opponents' may be classified as 'absolute opponents'. This could apply to Argentina, Bolivia, Indonesia and Zimbabwe.

121 Malcolm Langford and Daniel Behn, 'Managing Backlash: The Evolving Investment Treaty Arbitrator' (forthcoming) *European Journal of International Law*.

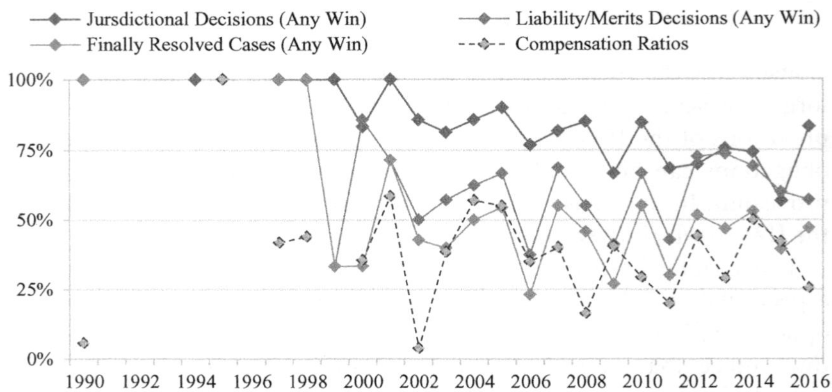

Figure 4.3 Claimant–investor success ratios (by year)
Extracted from Malcolm Langford and Daniel Behn, 'Managing Backlash: The Evolving Investment Treaty Arbitrator' (forthcoming) *European Journal of International Law*.

analysis finds that some of this drop could be attributed to the backlash. However, the recalibration in outcomes for investors should not necessarily be viewed with great alarm. Success rates are much higher for investor claimants than human rights claimants in international and regional adjudicative bodies (Figure 4.3).

Why are states employing these strategies? Their invocation of legitimacy concerns with IIAs and ISDS arguably has some basis and their tactics cannot be reduced to a kneejerk sovereignty or *realist* reflex: that states never intended to cede sovereignty and that treaty commitment constitutes a false positive. It is true that one of the main concerns that states express about IIAs is their potential to interfere with domestic policy and the ability of the state to regulate in the public interest,[122] even if the IIAs manifest the states' sovereign ability to advance another public interest: the long-term policy goal of economic development through the promotion of foreign direct investment.

A more nuanced approach comes from *rational choice* theories which highlight the incentives and constraints for states in entering the regime. In the case of the international investment regime, states may balance: (1) making credible commitments in order to gain investment versus ensuring sufficient legal certainty over the potential costs of commitment; and (2) the likelihood that they will be predominantly capital exporters or importers in the future. The existence of these two uncertainties means

[122] David Schneiderman, *Constitutionalizing Economic Globalization: Investment Rules and Democracy's Promise* (Cambridge: Cambridge University Press, 2008).

that states may need to ensure sufficient flexibility in regime design (or impose it later) to be able to respond if the basis for these trade-offs changes.

Arguably, these calculations were also affected by certain background institutional, legal and political conditions that fostered ready commitment yet turned out to be highly fragile in practice. First, IIAs were an easy and attractive to sign. Only two states were required for an agreement, parliamentary assent was often not required, and the whole event provided a perfect media event for visiting heads of state. Secondly, the pedigree of many of these treaties can be traced to a small number of model BITs developed by a few capital-exporting states in the 1980s and 1990s. Therefore, while each BIT should be viewed as a distinct and negotiated document between two states, the reality is that many BITs are very similar in the rights granted and – until the mid 1990s – do not appear to be the result of hard fought negotiation, but rather were often signed with little or no change from the capital-exporting states' model. Thirdly, the ideological climate at the domestic and international level has also shifted with a partial pushback in the last decade against the march of global neoliberalism. In the 1990s, UNCTAD recorded that 90 per cent of regulatory reforms concerning investment inflows were pro-liberalization while that figure fell to less than 70 per cent in 2009 – one-third were restrictive.

Thus, one way of understanding the current backlash is that states are reassessing the actual and perceived utility of the treaties.[123] As the practice of investment treaty arbitration develops, originally unanticipated consequences have become clearer. The importance of mandatory ISDS provisions in IIAs as a means to challenge policies that foreign investors view as detrimental to their interests has become clearer to many states. Moreover, there have been significant shifts in stocks and flows of foreign direct investment in recent decades changing the nature of capital exporter and importer states.[124] The state – as the primary mover in consenting to international treaties – can assert its sovereign authority by modifying or exiting regimes that are no longer perceived to be in that state's interests. Provided sufficient knowledge, whether IIAs remain a benefit to the state can be subjected to a cost-benefit analysis. For some states, it is clear that the costs do outweigh the benefits; and in coming to this realization they are likely to design strategies and tactics to remedy the imbalance.[125] In

[123] See e.g. Lavopa, Barreiros and Bruno, note 24 above.

[124] See *World Investment Report 2015: Reforming International Investment Governance* (Geneva: UNCTAD, 2015).

[125] At the time the vast majority of these treaties were signed, there was very little precedent on how the ISDS provisions would operate in practice: through the 1980s, there were only

this respect, we should be cautious about treating all international treaties as comparable, as is partly done in this volume. The logic of an investment treaty is partly different than a human rights treaty. The former is partly about fundamental protections but it is also deeply grounded in reciprocity and strategic economic policy choices.

In short, there are many reasons why we are seeing a backlash against the extensive web of IIAs that were signed during the last decades of the twentieth century. Commentators and negotiators talk about new 'generations' of treaties that seek to redefine the balance between rights of investors and policy freedom of states, as well as the role of ISDS. However, in this chapter, we do not comment on whether states are morally right in engaging in this strategic behaviour as principals or litigants. The legitimacy or justice of such state action is the subject of a burgeoning and heated literature. Nonetheless, we could find broader agreement that litigation tactics that involve states abusing their sovereign position are particularly problematic. The use of domestic criminal proceedings during disputes, refusals to comply with awards, and attempts to change treaties after a dispute is filed reveal not only an infidelity by states to their treaty commitments but a failure to respect the international rule of law.

Postscript

In mid-2017, Ecuador announced that it would be withdrawing from all of its remaining IIAs in force. While there is no indication that this withdrawal has formally taken place yet, but when and if Ecuador follows through with its intention to do so, it will be the first and only state to have fully exited from the international investment regime. We also draw attention to the new reform process facilitated by UNCITRAL, which is to address concerns with ISDS and propose possible reforms. The working group sessions in late 2017 revealed many of the splits amongst states identified in this chapter but also create the possibility for a multi-state response to legitimacy crisis.*

a handful of ITAs that had been initiated. While the modern investment treaty regime has its roots in the customary international law on the treatment of aliens, its specific development as a means of protecting and promoting foreign investment is a relatively new phenomenon that is frequently said to date from the signing of the first BIT between Pakistan and Germany in 1959. However, this BIT did not include any dispute settlement mechanism and instead could be viewed as a largely aspirational statement about the future cooperation between states on the promotion of foreign investment. It was not until 10 years later, in 1969, that the first BIT with ISDS was signed.

* See Anthea Roberts, 'UNCITRAL and ISDS Reform: Not Business as Usual', *EJIL:Talk!*, 11 December 2017.

5

'Part of the Game'

Government Strategies against European Litigation Concerning Migrant Rights

MORITZ BAUMGÄRTEL*

5.1 Introduction

Even in times of changing legal practices, the courtroom remains symbolically the ultimate place for states to 'encounter' international law. The rise of 'new-style' international courts with expanded and compulsory jurisdictions has been one of the driving forces behind the legalization of world politics.[1] Rather than simply offering venues for the peaceful settlement of disputes, they are increasingly becoming the assertive guardians of their respective legal instruments. The European Court of Human Rights (ECtHR) in Strasbourg for instance continuously develops the 1951 European Convention on Human Rights (ECHR),[2] to which it famously referred to as 'an instrument of European public order'.[3] From a traditional legal-theoretical viewpoint, such confidence is not necessarily to be expected. States as the original 'masters of the treaty' were long assumed to hold sufficient power to override and even dismantle international courts

* This research has been funded by the Interuniversity Attraction Poles Programme initiated by the Belgian Science Policy Office, more specifically the IAP 'The Global Challenge of Human Rights Integration: Towards a Users' Perspective'. I am greatly indebted to Tanja Aalberts and Thomas Gammeltoft-Hansen for their thorough editorial input and to Shai Dothan, Sarah Ganty and the anonymous reviewers for very helpful comments on an earlier version of this chapter.

1 Karen J. Alter, *The New Terrain of International Law: Courts, Politics, Rights* (Princeton, NJ: Princeton University Press, 2014).

2 European Convention for the Protection of Human Rights and Fundamental Freedoms, 4 November 1950, 213 UNTS 222.

3 *Loizidou v. Turkey*, European Court of Human Rights, Application no. 15318/89, 23 March 1995, para. 93.

if they deemed so necessary.[4] As so often the case, reality turns out to be more complicated. Although more frequently lacking direct control over courts, states and their governments are developing ways to manage the influence of even the most independent ones like the Court of Justice of the EU (CJEU).[5] Achieving greater 'sovereign manoeuvrability' in the European legal order(s) is hereby particularly important where politically sensitive questions such as migration are concerned. As one government official has stated, international courts are now simply 'part of the game' in the intricate process of policymaking in such domains.[6]

This chapter explores the strategies that governments have used to contain the influence of fundamental rights jurisprudence of the two aforementioned European courts in cases concerning migrants and asylum seekers. Over the last two decades, growing migration flows and right-wing political climates in many European countries have created a difficult situation in which governments have enacted legally questionable policies. This, in turn, has led to a rise in litigation before European courts. But despite this increased 'legalization' as reflected in an expanded jurisdiction of the CJEU and the strong involvement of the ECtHR, the degree and the type of their influence remains unclear. This chapter argues that government strategies play an essential factor in this context, as they influence the effectiveness with which the European courts can protect migrant rights. In the domain of migration, four such strategies appear to be particularly prominent: *legal argumentation* concerning the scope of the relevant instruments, policy implications and procedural requirements; *anticipatory measures* aiming to strike out cases or to dampen public reactions to adverse rulings; *peer mobilization* exerting collective pressure on the courts; and *post-judgment positioning* vis-à-vis the judgment or the court in question. To prove the existence and relevance of these practices, this chapter relies amongst others on original research in the form of interviews that were conducted with persons involved in litigation before the European courts, including lawyers, NGO representatives and government officials.[7] The primary focus will be on those politically charged

[4] Eric A. Posner and John C. Yoo, 'Judicial Independence in International Tribunals' (2005) 93 *California Law Review* 1–74.

[5] See Lisa J. Conant, *Justice Contained: Law and Politics in the European Union* (Ithaca, NY: Cornell University Press, 2002) and Andreas J. Obermaier, *The End of Territoriality? The Impact of ECJ Rulings on British, German and French Social Policy* (Aldershot, UK: Ashgate, 2009).

[6] Interview with government official, August 2014.

[7] Twenty-two semi-structured interviews were conducted in Belgium, Luxembourg, the Netherlands, Spain and the UK in the period of August 2014 to May 2015.

migration cases in which governments had a heightened interest in acting strategically.

The chapter is divided into five parts. The first section describes the judicialization of migration policy in Europe and summarizes the most important legal interventions of the two European courts. The following four sections each address in greater detail one strategy in the following order: legal argumentation, anticipatory measures, peer mobilization and post-judgment positioning. The conclusion sums up the findings and places them into the general context of the changing practices in international law.

5.2 The European Courts and the Question of Migrant Rights

While both the ECtHR and CJEU have recently become more involved in matters relating to the human rights of migrants and asylum seekers,[8] their interventions remain firmly based on distinct legal frameworks. On the one hand, the ECtHR relies on human rights law in the form of the ECHR, and especially on article 3 (prohibition of torture and inhumane and degrading treatment) and article 8 (right to family life). The CJEU, on the other hand, in applying EU law, deals with questions of both asylum and immigration law and the EU Charter of Fundamental Rights.[9] One important similarity shared by both legal frameworks is, however, that they impose clear limits on the judicial control of migration policy. The ECtHR has thus continuously recognized 'the Contracting States' concern to maintain public order, in particular in exercising their right, as a matter of well-established international law [. . .] to control the entry, residence and expulsion of aliens', although 'subject to their treaty obligations'.[10] And while the CJEU now has jurisdiction over EU asylum and immigration law,[11] it does not have the competence to regulate the central aspect of immigration of workers which, according to article 79(5) of the 2007

[8] In this chapter, the expression 'migrants' does not refer to citizens of other EU Member States who under EU law, and especially due to the principle of the freedom of movement, enjoy far greater protection than so-called 'third-country nationals'.

[9] Charter of Fundamental Rights of the European Union (OJ 2012 no. C 326/391, 26 October 2012).

[10] *Moustaquim v. Belgium*, European Court of Human Rights, Application no. 12313/86, 9 February 1991, para. 43. See also *Abdulaziz, Cabales and Balkandali v. United Kingdom*, European Court of Human Rights, Application nos 9214/80, 9473/81, 9474/81, 28 May 1985, para. 67.

[11] States expanded the jurisdiction of the CJEU to also cover asylum and migration law with the signing of the Treaty of Amsterdam in October 1997.

Treaty on the Functioning of the EU,[12] remains a competence of the Member States.[13] Some authors thus conclude provocatively that in the EU legal framework, 'the flow and volume of migration is left to the autonomy and control of Member States, but once the migrants are within EU borders, EU law regulates residence and expulsion'.[14]

The mandate limitations set on both courts have significant repercussions. Saroléa claims that the departing principle of the ECtHR functions as 'a limit of the judicial control that will be exercised and a standard presented as higher than the human rights whose protection is required'.[15] What is more, the situation highlights that migration policy is usually regarded as a *domaine réservé* area which states do not want to concede to international courts.[16] Still, both European courts have witnessed a notable rise in their caseloads relating to migrants and their rights, with a small but growing number of NGOs and specialized lawyers even engaging in strategic litigation.[17] One of the reasons for this expansion has been the reinforcement of the already strong institutional positions of the European courts in recent decades. On the one hand, Protocol 11

[12] Consolidated version of the Treaty on the Functioning of the European Union (OJ 2012 no. C 326/391, 26 October 2012.

[13] Art. 79(5) reads: 'This Article shall not affect the right of Member States to determine volumes of admission of third-country nationals coming from third countries to their territory in order to seek work, whether employed or self-employed'.

[14] Sonia Morano-Foadi and Stelios Andreadakis, 'The Convergence of the European Legal System in the Treatment of Third Country Nationals in Europe: The ECJ and ECtHR Jurisprudence' (2011) 22 *European Journal of International Law* 1071–88, at 1084. Evidently, the latter will have a substantive impact on the former, rendering the conclusion somewhat simplistic. The authors are still correct in highlighting the problem that fundamental aspects of migration policy remain outside the scope of EU law.

[15] Sylvie Saroléa, 'From Protection of the Migrant to the Rights of the Migrant Person: Free the Migrant from His Legal Exile . . .', in Jean-Christophe Merle (ed.), *Spheres of Global Justice* (Dordrecht: Springer, 2013), 357. A similar argument is presented and elaborated upon in Marie-Bénédicte Dembour, *When Humans Become Migrants: Study of the European Court of Human Rights with an Inter-American Counterpoint* (Oxford: Oxford University Press, 2015).

[16] Whether or not the unwillingness of states effectively prevents legalization has been questioned in research focusing on the influence of EU law on social and taxation policy, especially with a view to ensuring long-term compliance. See Diana Panke, 'Socil and Taxation Policies – Domaine Réservé Fields? Member States Non-Compliance with Sensitive European Secondary Law' (2009) 31 *European Integration* 489–509.

[17] Interviews with several lawyers and NGO representatives, November 2014 to February 2015. For a more detailed discussion, see Moritz Baumgärtel, 'From Deficit to Dilemma: An Evaluation of the Contribution of Europe's Supranational Courts to the Promotion of the Rights of Vulnerable Migrants', unpublished PhD thesis, Université libre de Bruxelles (2016), 84–89.

to the ECHR of 1994 facilitated direct individual access to the ECtHR. The resulting high number of petitions even threatened, at some point, to make the Court the 'victim of its own success'. On the other hand, states have expanded the jurisdiction of the CJEU to cover asylum and migration law with the signing of the Treaty of Amsterdam in October 1997. Taken together, these institutional and political developments have brought the European courts to the very heart of migration controversies in Europe.

At this point, several important legal interventions can be highlighted without covering all the details of this sometimes technical jurisprudence. Firstly, the European courts have, on several occasions, expanded the conditions under which groups of persons are eligible for residency. Especially significant are the decisions regarding the scope of the *non-refoulement* principle, which the European courts found to be applicable when asylum seekers are not personally targeted, but threatened by generally or cumulatively high risks of mistreatment upon return.[18] Moreover, the CJEU has held that persons could not be expected to hide or restrain their religious convictions or their sexual orientation to 'avoid' persecution.[19] In the latter case, states are also barred from subjecting asylum seekers to certain types of credibility assessments such as a detailed questioning of sexual practices.[20] A quite different but also expanding ground for residency is derived from the right to a family life.[21] The ECtHR ruled in this context that even persons who had lived in a country without a valid permit for a long time could have their presence regularized if this was in the best interest of their children.[22] The CJEU went even further in

[18] The Strasbourg Court in particular has gradually extended the scope of the principle under Art. 3 of the ECHR. See most notably *Salah Sheekh v. the Netherlands*, European Court of Human Rights, Application no. 1948/04, 11 January 2007, para. 148, *N.A. v. the United Kingdom*, European Court of Human Rights, Application no. 25904/07, 17 July 2008, para. 147 and *Sufi and Elmi v. the United Kingdom*, European Court of Human Rights, Application nos 8319/07 and 11449/07, 28 June 2011, para. 293. The CJEU has come to a similar conclusion in looking at the scope of subsidiary protection as established in the Qualification Directive 2004/83/EC, and more specifically Art. 15(c). See Case C-465/07, *Meki Elgafaji, Noor Elgafaji v. Staatssecretaris van Justitie*, [2009] ECR I-921, para. 35.

[19] Joined Cases C-71/11 and C-99/11, *Bundesrepublik Deutschland v. Y and Z*, ECLI:EU:C:2012:518, paras 78–79, and Joined Cases C-199/12 to C-201/12, *Minister voor Immigratie en Asiel v. X, Y, and Z*, ECLI:EU:C:2013:720, para. 71.

[20] Joined Cases C-148/13 to C-150/13, *A, B, and C, v. Staatssecretaris van Veiligheid en Justitie*, EU:C:2014:2406.

[21] See Daniel Thym, 'Respect for Private and Family Fife under Art. 8 ECHR in Immigration Cases: a Human Right to Regularize Illegal Stay?' (2008) 57 *International and Comparative Law Quarterly* 87–112.

[22] *Rodrigues Da Silva & Hoogkamer v. the Netherlands* European Court of Human Rights, Application no. 50435/99, 31 January 2006, para. 44, and more recently *Jeunesse v. the*

stating that non-EU parents could remain in Europe solely by virtue of their dependent child holding European citizenship.[23] On another occasion it held that EU law did not permit decisions about family reunification to be determined based on the point in time (that is, before or after immigration of the 'sponsor') when the relationship was formed.[24]

Some of the most crucial judgments concern the question of state responsibility. Indeed, extra-territorialization and 'outsourcing' of migration control to private actors are two principal methods by which states try to circumvent international obligations in human rights and refugee law.[25] The ECtHR in particular has addressed these practices with some force. In *Hirsi*, the Court decided that Italy had violated several human rights obligations by intercepting and 'pushing back' a vessel with around 200 migrants on board on the high seas.[26] It has also handed down a number of decisions that deal with the EU's Dublin Regulation,[27] which establishes the principle that asylum seekers have to submit their application in the country in which they first entered the Union. Reversing its initially cautious approach towards this principle,[28] the Court held in *M.S.S. v. Belgium and Greece* that Belgium had violated the Convention by returning an asylum seeker to Greece because it 'knew or ought to have known that he had no guarantee that his asylum application would be seriously examined by the Greek authorities'.[29] States cannot therefore deny legal

Netherlands, European Court of Human Rights, Application no. 12738/10, 3 October 2014, paras 120–122.

23 Case C-34/09, *Gerardo Ruiz Zambrano v. Office national de l'emploi (ONEm)*, [2011] ECR I-1177, para. 45. The fact that this judgment is primarily based on the rights derived from EU citizenship arguably constitutes a decisive difference in comparison to other 'pure' immigration cases related to the right to family life.

24 Case C-578/08, *Rhimou Chakroun v. Minister van Buitenlandse Zaken*, [2010] ECR I-1839, paras 59–66.

25 See Thomas Gammeltoft-Hansen, *Access to Asylum: International Refugee Law and the Globalisation of Migration Control* (Cambridge: Cambridge University Press, 2011).

26 *Hirsi Jamaa and Others v. Italy*, European Court of Human Rights, Application no. 27765/09, 23 February 2012.

27 The most recent version ('Dublin III') of which is Regulation (EU) No 604/2013 of the European Parliament and of the Council of 26 June 2013 establishing the criteria and mechanisms for determining the Member State responsible for examining an application for international protection lodged in one of the Member States by a third-country national or a stateless person (recast) (OJ 2013 no. L 180/30, 29 June 2013).

28 See *T.I. v. the United Kingdom*, European Court of Human Rights, Application no. 43844/98 (admissibility), and *K.R.S. v. the United Kingdom*, European Court of Human Rights, Application no. 32733/08 (admissibility), 2 December 2008.

29 *M.S.S. v. Belgium and Greece*, European Court of Human Rights, Application no. 30696/09, 21 January 2011, para. 385.

responsibility solely on the grounds that they were implementing the Dublin regulation. Subsequent rulings further lowered the threshold for rebutting the presumption that another EU Member State was complying with its obligations under the ECHR.[30] The CJEU has by and large followed this approach,[31] though not using the opportunity to clarify whether EU Member States had further obligations under the EU Charter of Fundamental Rights.[32]

Finally, the ECtHR has, on several occasions, found that asylum seekers had been deprived of their right to an effective remedy – a recurrent problem in some countries, such as, for example, Belgium.[33] In *M.S.S.*, the Court concluded that Belgium and Greece had violated the right to an effective remedy under the ECHR. To qualify as effective under Article 13, a remedy has to be accessible 'in practice', as ensured, amongst others, by a timely and functioning system of communication of decisions and a realistic prospect of obtaining legal aid.[34] It also has to consider the vulnerability of certain groups of asylum seekers such as mothers with underage children.[35] In the context of asylum procedures, an effective remedy is also required to have suspensive effect, which would preclude a measure of return to be executed during appeal.[36] In contrast to this, the CJEU has been somewhat more cautious on this specific aspect.[37]

[30] *Tarakhel v. Switzerland*, European Court of Human Rights, Application no. 29217/12, 4 November 2014, and *Sharifi and others v. Italy and Greece*, European Court of Human Rights, Application no. 16643/09, 21 October 2014.

[31] Joined Cases C-411/10 and C-493/10, *N. S. v. Secretary of State for the Home Department and M. E. and Others v. Refugee Applications Commissioner and Minister for Justice, Equality and Law Reform*, [2011] ECR I-13905.

[32] More specifically, the CJEU could have addressed the obligations under Arts 1 (human dignity) and 18 (right to asylum) of the Charter. The decision not to do so was received critically by those involved in the case, as several lawyers and NGO representatives stated during the interviews (November 2014 to February 2015).

[33] Sarah Ganty and Moritz Baumgärtel, 'Effective Remedies as Capabilities: Towards a User Perspective to Human Rights of Migrants in Belgium' (2014) 8 *Human Rights & International Legal Discourse* 215–34.

[34] *M.S.S.*, paras 318–19.

[35] *S.J. v. Belgium*, European Court of Human Rights, Application no. 70055/10, 27 February 2014, paras 103–4.

[36] *Gebremedhin [Gaberamadhien] v. France*, European Court of Human Rights, Application no. 25389/05, 26 April 2007, para. 66.

[37] According to Basilien-Gainche, the CJEU apparently considers restrictions of 'the right to be heard' a legitimate policy tool in the fight against illegal migration. See Marie-Laure Basilien-Gainche, 'Immigration Detention under the Return Directive: The CJEU Shadowed Lights' (2015) 17 *European Journal of Migration and Law* 104–26, at 122.

The growing involvement of the two European courts has been generally welcomed. In some cases, it has even been hailed as 'a beacon for protecting the rights of migrants'.[38] Yet, considering the hypothesis of this volume, the courts' practical influence may well be influenced (that is, diminished) by the changing and increasingly strategic approach of states in dealing with international law. In this context, obligations concerning the human rights of migrants are no exception.[39] The following sections describe and analyze some of the strategies that governments have used to manage and contain the impact of some of the most important judgments. To perform this analysis, this work relies on first-hand accounts of individuals who were directly involved in the litigation process before the European courts.

5.3 Legal Arguments and Strategies in Court

The first aspect that needs to be considered is the strategies employed by governments *in* the European courts as opposed to in the domestic sphere or vis-à-vis the claimant. Most obviously, in-court strategies include attempts of 'interpretive framing' of rules which, as Gammeltoft-Hansen and Aalberts point out, are widespread and even 'inherent in the operation of (international) law'.[40] While courts are generally the forum *par excellence* for the deployment of such practices, interpretative framing can be particularly effective when new or unclear provisions offer the litigating parties the chance to advance their own readings. This, in fact, is frequently the case regarding the human rights of migrants and asylum seekers. EU law on migration and asylum remains arguably 'a legislative patchwork'[41] and a 'bric-à-brac' system,[42] in which the relationship between various parts is often unclear. Moreover, international obligations regarding, for example, the prohibition of *refoulement* are at the same time

[38] Maarten Den Heijer, 'Reflections on Refoulement and Collective Expulsion in the Hirsi Case' (2013) 25 *International Journal of Refugee Law* 265–90, at 265.

[39] Gammeltoft-Hansen, *Access to Asylum*, and Itamar Mann, 'Dialectic of Transnationalism: Unauthorized Migration and Human Rights, 1993–2013' (2013) 54 *Harvard International Law Journal* 315–523.

[40] See Chapter 1, this volume, p. 14.

[41] Kees Groenendijk, 'Recent Developments in EU Law on Migration: The Legislative Patchwork and the Court's Approach' (2014) 16 *European Journal of Migration and Law* 313–35.

[42] Vincent Chetail, 'The Common European Asylum System: Bric-à-Brac or System?', in Vincent Chetail, Philippe De Bruycker and Francesco Maiani (eds), *Reforming the Common European Asylum System: The New European Refugee Law* (Leiden: Martinus Nijhoff, 2016).

subject to constant reinterpretation due to evolving state practice such as the establishment of external border controls.[43] Another example, which is discussed in greater detail in this section, are governments' frequent contestations of the scope of various relevant legal instruments. Yet, in-court strategies can go beyond the interpretive framing of obligations and into the terrain of 'regime and treaty shopping'. This is most notably the case when governments propose arguments regarding policy implications or procedural requirements, which will be discussed thereafter.

Considering the aforementioned state of the law in the migration domain, it is unsurprising that governments frequently try to put their stamp on the interpretation of the scope of protective provisions. Especially the CJEU has dealt with many questions regarding the application of certain provisions and the scope of EU law. In *N.S./M.E.*, the respondent and intervening governments argued that they were not bound by European law in exercising their discretionary right to assume responsibility for an asylum seeker as established in the Dublin regulation.[44] Being outside this scope would also have implied the non-applicability of the EU Charter of Fundamental Rights – a view that the CJEU rejected. In *Zambrano*, a total of seven governments contested the application of EU law, arguing that European citizens, including minor children, would have to have crossed EU internal borders for their non-EU family members to be able to claim residency on the grounds of their European citizenship.[45] The CJEU did not share this view to the strong dismay of the involved governments.[46] However, in some cases governments have successfully impacted the development of EU law, for example in *X, Y and Z* where they opposed the applicants' claim that criminalizing homosexual activities alone constituted an act of persecution according to the EU Qualifications Directive.[47]

[43] Gammeltoft-Hansen, *Access to Asylum*, 94–96.

[44] *N.S./M.E.*, para. 61. [45] *Zambrano*, para. 37.

[46] Interviews with lawyers, NGO representatives and government officials, August to December 2014. It is however worth noting that the argument was accepted by the Court in later cases, which did not include minor children. See for instance Case C-434/09, *Shirley McCarthy v. Secretary of State for the Home Department*, [2011] ECR I-3375. In fact, the Court 'fine-tuned' its decision in *Zambrano*, which therefore represents somewhat of an exception. See Susanne K. Schmidt, 'Judicial Europeanisation: The Case of Zambrano in Ireland' (2014) 37 *West European Politics* 769–85, at 774–6.

[47] See *X, Y and Z*, as well as the opinion of Advocate-General Eleanor Sharpston, delivered on 11 July 2013, paras 40–45. The most recent version of the instrument is Directive 2011/95/EU of the European Parliament and of the Council of 13 December 2011 on standards for the qualification of third-country nationals or stateless persons as beneficiaries

While narrowing interpretations about the scope of protection are routinely proposed, in-court strategies take a more creative shape when they feature a reference to the jurisdiction of the other European court. In this context, governments seek to engage in 'regime or treaty shopping', highlighting its close link to legal argumentation and the fact that the latter may be attempted not only prior but also during judicial proceedings.[48] For instance, the UK government, when appearing before the European courts, has repeatedly sought to benefit from the co-existence of the two European legal frameworks dealing with the human rights of migrants. In *N.S./M.E.*, it suggested that a restrictive interpretation of the scope of EU law did not mean that there would be no human rights protection because the ECHR and the 1951 UN Refugee Convention would still have to be considered.[49] The non-application of EU law was thus presented as unproblematic in human rights terms. At the same time, in some ECtHR cases the UK used precisely the reverse argument. Regarding the scope of the *non-refoulement* principle under the ECHR, the UK argued that the EU Qualifications Directive offered 'a higher level of protection than that provided for by the Convention'.[50] In *Sufi and Elmi*, it stated even more explicitly that the adoption of the Directive 'clearly chose a wider scope than that of the Convention', thus warning the ECtHR not to equate the protection frameworks 'in the absence of the express agreement of the Contracting States'.[51] The flexible and strategic way of construing the relationship between the two legal regimes is further illustrated by the fact that the UK government claimed before the CJEU in *Elgafaji* that the EU legislature 'did not intend to burden the Member States with new obligations . . . concerning the right to asylum'.[52] The arguments in these cases did not persuade either European court, both of which retained a focus on their own instruments.

of international protection, for a uniform status for refugees or for persons eligible for subsidiary protection, and for the content of the protection granted (OJ 2011 no. L 337/9, 20 December 2011).

48 Chapter 1, this volume. In relation to immigration, treaty shopping may similarly be observed in relation to public international law, notably the law of the sea, see Chapter 8, this volume.

49 *N.S./M.E.*, para. 61.

50 *N.A.*, para. 105.

51 *Sufi and Elmi*, para. 223.

52 See *Elgafaji*, Opinion of Advocate-General Poiares Maduro, delivered on 9 September 2008, para. 27. The Advocate-General was highly critical of this stance, claiming that the position of the UK (and the Netherlands) 'play down, if not evade, the reference made by recital 25 to other international and European instruments for protection of human rights and practices existing in Member States'.

A less frequent and arguably more surprising strategy used during proceedings has been to appeal to the possible policy consequences of an expansive judgment. In *Zambrano*, for example, several governments drew attention to the consequences of granting non-EU parents a right to remain on Union territory on the basis of the EU citizenship of their children. According to Advocate-General Sharpston, the Irish authorities, in particular, proposed a 'floodgates' argument, drawing 'a dramatic picture of the wave of immigration by third country nationals' that would lead to '"unmanageable" results'.[53] An interview with two persons present at the hearing suggests that the governments of Germany and the UK made equally strong appeals on the same basis.[54] A different type of claim concerning possible policy consequences was advanced by Belgium, Italy and Poland in *N.S./M.E.* regarding the lack of 'instruments necessary to assess compliance with fundamental rights by the Member State responsible and, therefore, the risks to which the asylum seeker would be exposed were he to be transferred to that Member State'.[55] Although the arguments did not succeed in these specific cases, these propositions are generally not unrealistic regarding the CJEU's modes of interpretation. In fact, the Court itself has frequently relied on consequentialist arguments, though normally with precisely the opposite intention, namely trying to expand the scope and application of EU law and to further European integration.[56]

Finally, in the case of the ECtHR, another very common and effective practice for governments has been to challenge applications regarding the rights of asylum seekers on procedural grounds. Legal arguments about procedure are in fact only seemingly formal and often turn out to imply important substantive questions for the Court, particularly where they can influence decisions about returns of asylum seekers.[57] This pertains for example to Article 35 of the ECHR about the necessity to exhaust

[53] *Zambrano*, Opinion of Advocate-General Eleanor Sharpston, delivered on 30 September 2010, paras 112 and 114. Interestingly, Schmidt finds the reaction of the Irish government to *Zambrano* ruling to be more proactive than would have been strictly necessary since the CJEU subsequently 'fine-tuned' (that is, qualified) its stance. One of the explanations provided for such unexpected behaviour is the change in government, which occurred around the time. See Schmidt 2014.

[54] Interview with lawyers, December 2014.

[55] *N.S./M.E.*, para. 91.

[56] Gerard Conway, *The Limits of Legal Reasoning and the European Court of Justice* (Cambridge: Cambridge University Press, 2012).

[57] Thomas Spijkerboer, 'Subsidiarity and "Arguability": The European Court of Human Rights' Case Law on Judicial Review in Asylum Cases' (2009) 21 *International Journal of Refugee Law* 48–74, at 57–58.

domestic remedies at the time of application, which is in practical terms a submission that 'responding governments will frequently raise, wherever possible'.[58] A cursory look at some of the migration-related cases before Strasbourg confirms the general trend.[59] More recent and forceful, however, are attempts of governments to rely on Article 37 of the ECHR according to which the Court may strike out an application when 'the matter has been resolved' or when 'for any other reason … it is no longer justified to continue the examination of the application', for example when defending lawyer have difficulties to maintain regular contact with their migrant clients.[60] In practice, the ECtHR has used this and other reasons to invoke this article and to thereby reduce its caseload, also encouraging friendly settlements and (more problematically) unilateral declarations of governments accepting allegations of violations together with commitments to provide adequate redress.[61] In *Salah Sheekh*, the Dutch government invoked the article, claiming that the applicant had already obtained protection covering a certain category of people (namely Somalis).[62] The Court disagreed.[63] The Dutch government was consequently taken by surprise, having considered the matter to be settled.[64] The Belgian authorities were luckier in the Grand Chamber case of *S.J.*, where they reached a friendly settlement with an HIV-positive applicant with children who demanded a leave to remain on medical grounds.[65] In a burning

[58] Philip Leach, *Taking a Case to the European Court of Human Rights* (Oxford: Oxford University Press, 2011), 126.

[59] One of the earliest occasions at which the Court was confronted with the argument in this context was *Bahaddar v. the Netherlands*, European Court of Human Rights, Application no. 25894/94, 19 February 1998, para. 38. But see also, amongst others, *Salah Sheekh*, para. 119, *N.A.*, para. 86, *M.S.S.*, para. 283, and *Hirsi*, paras 60–61.

[60] This can be the case when vulnerable migrant clients are in hiding, difficult to trace, or when they have lost confidence in the legal system, including in their own lawyers. Two high-profile cases that problematically were struck down for this reason are *Hussun and others v. Italy*, European Court of Human Rights, Application no. 10171/05, 19 January 2010, and more recently *V.M. and others v. Belgium*, European Court of Human Rights, Application no. 60125/11, 17 November 2016.

[61] For a more detailed analysis of the effects of this provision, see Lize R. Glas, 'Changes in the Procedural Practice of the European Court of Human Rights: Consequences for the Convention System and Lessons to Be Drawn' (2014) 14 *Human Rights Law Review* 671–99, at 677–78.

[62] *Salah Sheekh*, para. 115.

[63] More specifically, it held that it could not see the matter as settled since the reconsideration of this temporary protection policy had explicitly been related to the Court making a decision on the merits of a case regarding a Somali national. Ibid., para. 117.

[64] Interview with government official, February 2015.

[65] *S.J. v. Belgium*, European Court of Human Rights, Application no. 70055/10, 19 March 2015 (striking out).

dissenting opinion, Judge Pinto de Albuquerque stressed that in this case a substantive decision would have been 'necessary for the sake of decent protection of the human rights of seriously ill persons in Europe'.[66] In his opinion, reliance on Article 37 enabled the government to 'resolv[e] the situation of the present applicant in order to remain free 'to do business as usual' with all other foreign nationals in a similar situation'.

5.4 Anticipatory Measures

The dissenting opinion of Judge Pinto de Albuquerque in *S.J.* draws attention to a wider governmental 'cost-benefit strategy consisting in "buying" a strike-out decision'.[67] In his view, governments seek friendly settlements in order to limit the impact of the Strasbourg Court in particular cases. However, such a strategy requires the taking of steps outside the (European) courtrooms. In the case of *S.J.*, the Belgian government proposed to grant the applicant a residence permit on the basis of 'strong humanitarian considerations'.[68] The applicant posed additional conditions, including unconditional and indefinite leave for her and her children to remain in Belgium and compensation of 7000 euros for 'the suffering undergone . . . as a result of the Belgian State's decision'.[69] The government accepted, thereby avoiding further proceedings and even the hearing before the Grand Chamber, which would, however, come to pronounce itself on the issue in *Paposhvili* two years later.[70]

Empirical evidence shows that the strategy in *S.J.*, although heavily criticized by one of the Court's own judges, is by no means atypical. In fact, governments frequently adopt what one could call anticipatory measures, which pursue the goal of limiting the influence of European courts as much as possible, mostly in cases where the factual situation is about to lead to an undesirable judgment such as the finding of a violation. From a governmental viewpoint, the complete strike-out of a case will represent the optimal result. More specifically, preventing a decision on the principles will allow governments to maintain interpretative flexibility in the future, thereby maximizing 'sovereign manoeuvrability'. To achieve this goal before the Strasbourg Court, they must, in principle, acknowledge the violation and offer some redress, meaning that it is insufficient simply

[66] *S.J.*, 19 March 2015, Dissenting Opinion of Judge Pinto de Albuquerque, para. 1.
[67] Ibid., para. 1, note 3. [68] *S.J.*, 19 March 2015, para. 56. [69] Ibid., para. 57.
[70] *Paposhvili v. Belgium*, European Court of Human Rights, Application no. 41738/10, 13 December 2016.

to prove that the situation of the applicant now complies with the Convention's provisions, as for instance argued by France in *Gebremedhin*.[71] In practice, however, states manage to strike off a substantive number of cases, at times even without an explicit acknowledgment of a violation.[72] In fact, the latter is frequently not 'worth its price', which is why governments will try to avoid it wherever possible. Anticipatory measures thus take different forms, depending on the 'stakes in the case'[73] and the procedural possibilities in the proceedings before the two European courts.

In proceedings before the CJEU, national courts have the right to withdraw the reference for a preliminary ruling that they have submitted earlier.[74] Governments can consequently try to reach a settlement and prevent the CJEU from handing down a ruling.[75] This has been tried in some important instances, although the generally lower number of cases before the CJEU also translates into fewer such attempts when compared to the ECtHR.[76] For example, the Belgian government granted a temporary residence permit for the duration of the national proceedings in *Zambrano*, most likely in the hope that the Court would not hand down a judgment regarding the right to stay.[77] According to one of the involved lawyers, the Court decided to address the question only because the applicant's claim to unemployment benefits concerned the period not covered by this permit. In another instance, the strategy proved at least temporarily

71 *Gebremedhin*, para. 56.

72 Dembour, for example, mentions that there were around fifteen 'Dutch hidden cases' with similar facts to *Salah Sheekh*, where the granting of residence permits led to the cases being struck off. Dembour, *When Humans Become Migrants*, 324.

73 As Galanter pointed out in a seminal article, repeat players (such as European governments in the present context) will 'trade off' tangible gains in a single case to 'rule gains' that may lead to favourable outcomes in future proceedings. See Marc Galanter, 'Why the 'Haves' Come Out Ahead: Speculations on the Limits of Legal Change' (1974) 9 *Law and Society Review* 95–160, at 100–101.

74 Rules of Procedure of the Court of Justice of 25 September 2012 (OJ 2012 no. L265, 29 September 2012), as amended on 18 June 2013 (OJ 2013 no. L173, 26 June 2013).

75 However, Art. 100(1) also states that '[t]he withdrawal of a request may be taken into account until notice of the date of delivery of the judgment', which has been interpreted as meaning that the Court may after this date hand down a decision even if a case has been withdrawn. See Morten Broberg and Niels Fenger, *Preliminary References to the European Court of Justice* (Oxford: Oxford University Press, 2014), 324.

76 One can also assume that given there is still a significant backlog of cases, the ECtHR will still be open to accepting a wide variety of settlements in order to reduce its caseload. This assessment is also in line with the conclusions drawn in Helen Keller, Magdalena Forowicz and Lorenz Engi, *Friendly Settlements before the European Court of Human Rights: Theory and Practice* (Oxford: Oxford University Press, 2010).

77 Interviews with various lawyers, November and December 2014.

successful. In the *Imran* case, the Court found that a ruling was 'not necessary' after the Dutch government had granted a provisional visa to the spouse of the applicant.[78] The case concerned the highly pertinent question of whether the application for family reunification could be rejected solely on the grounds that a spouse had not passed a civic integration examination. A similar case in Germany was not even referred to the CJEU for the same reason, leading Block and Bonjour to state defiantly that the 'covert strategy of selective lenience [. . .] may postpone an EU Court decision, but it cannot permanently diffuse the "liberal constraint" emanating from the EU judiciary'.[79] The fact that the question finally re-emerged in the case of *K and A* confirms their assessment.[80] Seeking a 'removal' of cases appears thus to be a less profitable strategy before the CJEU as compared to the ECtHR, although it has been tried there with some limited success.

Besides offering individual remedies, another way for governments to anticipate a ruling of the CJEU has been to enact partial legislative changes. This practice is reflected in a number of recent Dutch cases, in which asylum was claimed on the grounds of persecution due to sexual orientation. In *X, Y and Z*, the question referred to the Court was whether foreign nationals could be expected to conceal their orientation after returning to their country in order to avoid persecution.[81] As argued not only by the Court, but before the judgment also by Advocate-General Sharpston and scholars,[82] this view was not compatible with legal obligations. According to Sharpston, 'a requirement that applicants should conceal their sexual orientation might be regarded as constituting an act of persecution in itself'.[83] However, interviews with members of NGOs

[78] Case C-155/11 PPU, *Bibi Mohammad Imran v. Minister van Buitenlandse Zaken*, [2011] ECR I-5095, para. 22.

[79] Laura Block and Saskia Bonjour, 'Fortress Europe or Europe of Rights? The Europeanisation of Family Migration Policies in France, Germany and the Netherlands' (2013) 15 *European Journal of Migration and Law* 203–224, at 221.

[80] The CJEU held in this case that civic integration exams should not make it excessively difficult or impossible for families to reunite, for instance regarding the fees required to prepare and participate in such an examination. See Case C-153/14, *Minister van Buitenlandse Zaken v. K and A*, ECLI:EU:C:2015:453.

[81] *X, Y and Z*, para. 37.

[82] See e.g. Sabine Jansen, 'Introduction: Fleeing Homophobia, Asylum Claims Related to Sexual Orientation and Gender Identity in Europe', in Thomas Spijkerboer (ed.), *Fleeing Homophobia: Sexual Orientation, Gender Identity and Asylum* (London: Routledge, 2013), 1–31.

[83] *X, Y and Z*, Opinion of Advocate-General Eleanor Sharpston, delivered on 11 July 2013, para 64.

revealed that the Dutch government had been quite aware of this fact. It responded quickly to the reference and adjusted its practices already prior to the judgment by shifting towards a stricter assessment of the credibility of the applicants. Since these aspects were not covered in the questions posed in *X, Y and Z*, they had to be addressed in the subsequent case of *A, B and C*, where the CJEU held that assessments could not be based on stereotyped questions, detailed questions about sexual practices or the performance (or offering evidence thereof) of homosexual acts.[84] Again, interviewees suggested that the government took action already prior to the delivery of the judgment after having seen the questions that were referred to the Court.[85] While these quick reactions were beneficial for the asylum seekers making such claims, they also had downsides. As one NGO representative points out, the problem is that the resulting judgments represent 'a more difficult story to spin'. Governments are able to downplay the failings of their former restrictive policies and agendas:

> *[T]hey will say, 'Well... that's what they said and that's what we're doing! What do they want us to change?', which makes the position of those criticizing the government beforehand a little bit difficult, because then we have to say, 'Well, they already adjusted their behaviour'.*[86]

The interviewee stressed with some frustration the practical problems that this strategy causes for post-judgment mobilization and lobbying as the story becomes 'not that sexy to sell for papers, for news, and then it doesn't get the attention it should because there was a big issue about the Netherlands'.[87] A similar effect was also achieved in the *Elgafaji* case, where the government had introduced a temporary policy of protecting certain categories of persons (*categoriaal beschermingsbeleid*), namely those originating from central Iraq. This measure, which was granted by the State Secretary for Justice on a discretionary basis 'protected' the applicant at least for a temporary period during the proceedings and – according to the Dutch government – regardless of the protection eventually offered under EU law.[88]

[84] *A, B and C*, para. 72. [85] Interview with civil society representative, February 2015.
[86] Ibid. [87] Ibid.
[88] The national and discretionary nature of this kind of protection (former art. 29(1)(d) of the Dutch Aliens Law of 2000, which no longer exists in this form) was of paramount legal importance to this case. More specifically, the applicant was covered by this measure at the time of the hearing before the Court on 8 July 2008, though it was officially abolished for migrants from Central Iraq already on 22 November 2008 (thus before the final judgment of 17 February 2009). Having granted this kind of protection, the government argued that it did not amount to a type of 'subsidiary protection' in the meaning of the EU Qualifications

While anticipatory measures against European court judgments can be employed in different domains, they are particularly effective in cases dealing with migration and asylum. Especially asylum seekers are satisfied when litigation achieves 'concrete, particular, individual immigration measures, such as the revocation of a deportation order or the granting of a residence permit'[89] due to their vulnerable position and a fear of being returned. The interviews revealed that lawyers and civil society organizations across countries face a difficult dilemma between accepting settlements beneficial for their clients and pursuing promising cases with a potential strategic value for persons with similar interests.[90] Where it is not possible to pursue both goals, interviewees stated a strong preference for the former. However, the examples of *Imran* and *S.J.* both show that it is unclear whether the strategy can indeed secure 'sovereign manoeuvrability' in the long term. Where large numbers of persons are affected, it is likely that legal challenges will continue to be filed, especially as lawyers and civil society organizations are also increasingly driven by a strategic approach to litigation. Hypothetically, the launching of subsequent cases could even lead to a 'complete surrender' by a government on a certain point if only enough applications are filed – a question that needs to be addressed in future research.[91]

5.5 International Cooperation: Peer Mobilization

In the past, International Relations scholars claimed that the power of international courts was strongly constrained by their mandate providers, especially states.[92] However, by the end of the Cold War, this view had been heavily challenged and qualified in mainstream theory: rather than

Directive (and more specifically Art. 15(c)). This would leave the discretionary nature of the provision intact while possibly convincing the Court that persons in a similar situation like the applicant were in principle protected under Dutch law. The final ruling in *Elgafaji* thus represents a success for the Dutch government since it did not address the question of whether national legislation offered sufficient protection for such persons under EU law, providing instead a general interpretation and status of Art. 15(c) of the Directive.

89 Dembour, *When Humans Become Migrants*, 324.

90 Even strategically oriented lawyers and organizations are therefore forced to act like 'one shotters', while the governments enjoy the position of 'repeat players' before the European courts. The asymmetry of these two positions is well known in scholarship, having been elaborated upon in Galanter, 'Why the "Haves" Come Out Ahead'.

91 I thank Shai Dothan for drawing my attention to this point.

92 See most notably Geoffrey Garrett and Barry Weingast, 'Ideas, Interests, and Institutions: Constructing the EC's Internal Market', in Judith Goldstein and Robert Keohane (eds), *Ideas and Foreign Policy* (Ithaca, NY: Cornell University Press, 1993), 173–206.

Table 5.1 *Number of Third-Party Interventions by Governments before the CJEU and the ECtHR*

CJEU			ECtHR		
Name	Case no.	Appl. no.	Name	Case no.	Appl. no.
N.S. and M.E.	C-411/10	13	*Tarakhel*	29217/12	5
Elgafaji	C-465/07	7	*Ramzy*	25424/05	4
Zambrano	C-34/09	7	*M.S.S.*	30696/09	2
O and B	C-456/12	7	*Saadi*	37201/06	1
Abdullahi	C-394/12	6	*Slivenko*	48321/99	1

Note: As can be found in EUR-Lex (available at http://eur-lex.europa.eu) and HUDOC (available at http://hudoc.echr.coe.int) databases.

being mere 'agents' of state power, international courts were argued to represent 'trustees'. As a consequence, states would rarely find themselves in a position of using heavy-handed 'recontracting powers' and institutional sanctions to influence international courts.[93] While this observation holds particularly true for the relatively independent European courts, it would be a mistake to ignore the persistent desire of states to defend their legal and political status as 'principals' vis-à-vis the European courts.[94] One effective way of doing this is through peer mobilization. The concept refers to the collective intervention of a multitude of contracting states before European courts (or any other international court for that matter) in order to demarcate a *domaine réservé* and to stress the high political stakes of a case. As such, it can be classified as a special type of 'international cooperation' through which governments attempt to shape (rather than circumvent) the 'constraints' imposed by international legal obligations.[95] While it is difficult to gather reliable data about this practice, a few observations can still be made.

Firstly, one has to consider the frequency of its usage. Table 5.1 illustrates the five 'most popular' migration-related cases before each

[93] Karen J. Alter, 'Agents or Trustees? International Courts in Their Political Context' (2008) 14 *European Journal of International Relations* 33–63.

[94] On this same basis, compelling arguments have recently been made to privilege the perspective of mandate providers (especially states) in the evaluation of the effectiveness of international courts. See Yuval Shany, *Assessing the Effectiveness of International Courts* (Oxford: Oxford University Press, 2014).

[95] See Chapter 1, this volume.

European court, with CJEU cases shown on the left and ECtHR ones on the right. More concretely, the table displays the five instances in which governments submitted the most third-party interventions (TPIs).[96] Peer mobilization appears to be more common before the CJEU than the ECtHR. One state agent to the latter explained this fact by referring to the more limited resources that are available for regular interventions in Strasbourg.[97] Still, the *Tarakhel* ruling (delivered in November 2014) possibly indicates a change in practice in very salient Strasbourg cases, as it sets a new record regarding the number of government TPIs. In contrast, Member States routinely file TPIs before the CJEU. Like *Tarakhel*, the case with the most TPIs by governments in Luxembourg (*N.S. and M.E.*) concerned the application of the Dublin regulation. As previously mentioned, in two of the 'popular' CJEU cases – *N.S. and M.E.* and *Zambrano* – intervening governments drew particularly gloomy scenarios regarding the consequences of rights-confirming judgments. Regarding *Zambrano*, the 2011 annual report of the Dutch Ministry of Foreign Affairs on the jurisprudence of the CJEU actually underlines that the Court 'diverged from the point of view of the Commission and all intervening EU States, including the Netherlands'.[98]

The idea of peer mobilization implies that states will encourage and coordinate their TPIs. Several interviewees suggested that this is indeed the case, although degrees of coordination and formality vary. With governments intervening more rarely in Strasbourg, connections between states remain mostly informal. Peer mobilization is consequently ad hoc, with agents asking their colleagues for support only when cases are particularly salient.[99] One interesting (although somewhat atypical) example in this context is the case of *Ramzy v. the Netherlands*, where the UK used its Presidency of the Council of the EU to inform other EU Member States about 'the possibility for the European Court of Human Rights of revisiting an earlier Court decision in the 1996 Chahal case'.[100] Lithuania, Portugal and Slovakia joined the UK as interveners, arguing that the ECtHR should reconsider the extent to which Article 3 of the ECHR was to be

[96] The number of interventions is indicated on the official judgments and thus publicly available on the InfoCuria and the HUDOC database.

[97] Interview with government representative, February 2015.

[98] Ministerie van Buitenlandse Zaken, *Jaarbericht 2011: Procesvertegenwoordiging Hof van Justitie van de EU* (Den Haag: Het ministerie van Buitenlandse Zaken, 2012), 21 (own translation).

[99] Interview with government representative, February 2015.

[100] Council of the European Union, Press Release 2683rd Council Meeting Justice and Home Affairs, Luxembourg, 12 October 2005, 12645/05 (Presse 247), 12.

applied in expulsion cases, especially where an applicant was suspected of terrorist activities, thus posing a risk to national security.[101] Peer mobilization was therefore combined with an argument regarding policy consequences, as discussed above.

Arrangements seem to be more standardized in some of the CJEU cases. For instance, some governments promised to submit TPIs whenever a certain issue was at stake.[102] In both courts, TPIs were especially made in the 'Dublin cases', probably because many governments faced similar situations with sometimes hundreds of appeals pending. Yet, peer mobilization is more subtle and uncoordinated in other cases. As one government official notes, submissions of more powerful states might embolden the smaller ones to follow suit or, where they are the respondents, to pick a fight when they usually would not.[103] However, states do not always adopt the same points of view. The judgment in *N.S. and M.E.* shows that the thirteen intervening governments proposed quite different arguments. But even in this instance, there were groups of states which shared and defended the same position.

As with other factors, the confidentiality of judicial deliberations in European courts makes it difficult to estimate the impact of peer mobilization on specific judgments. Cases like *Zambrano* prove, on the one hand, that even the intervention of a large number of governments with similar points of view does not necessarily bring about the outcome they desire. On the other hand, interviewees argued that European courts do not ignore such efforts. As one CJEU judge stated, 'the general tendency is to take very serious[ly] what the Member States are saying, particularly in [a] situation where . . . a large number are intervening'.[104] One government official argued with regard to the ECtHR that by increasing the pressure, they can at least postpone undesired rulings in some cases.[105] NGO members, therefore, stress the need to rally multiple civil society organizations

101 See *Ramzy v. the Netherlands*, European Court of Human Rights, Application no. 25424/05, 27 May 2008 (admissibility), paras 125–30. The case was eventually struck off the list before being considered on the merits as the Court concluded that the applicant had lost interest in his application, not having been in contact with his lawyers for over two years.

102 As one interviewee suggested, at some point three major EU Member States agreed to submit supporting TPIs in all cases concerning the Turkish Association agreements to stress the political relevance of the issue to the CJEU. Interview with former government representative, August 2014.

103 Interview with government representative, December 2014.

104 Interview with CJEU judge, June 2014.

105 Interview with government representative, December 2014.

as a counterweight to governments.[106] Given the growing number of government TPIs in migration cases before the ECtHR, it is not far-fetched to hypothesize a sort of 'judicial arms race'. As the political deadlock forces a growing number of lawyers and support groups to take their struggle to the European courts, peer mobilization might become an essential tool for governments to defend their primacy in this policy domain.

While peer mobilization is both strategically sensible and corroborated by some evidence from qualitative interviews, further research is certainly needed to clarify the spread of this practice and the circumstances of its usage. Particularly interesting is the question of whether efforts have become more coordinated in recent years.

5.6 Post-Judgment Positioning

Finally, a strategic approach of governments can sometimes also be identified in the follow-up to judgments. More concretely, where other in-court or litigation strategies have not been employed or where these have failed to prevent an adverse decision, governments might try to attach a narrative to a certain judgment. While simply refraining from offering any reaction in some cases, they adopt deliberate and even surprising positions in others. The goal is generally to contain the impact of adverse European court rulings, although precise objectives vary depending on the case and the political affiliation of a government. Such post-judgment positioning in the migration context highlights that practices of interpretative framing often do not end at the moment when a judgment has been handed down. Rather, they also appear afterwards, in the 'tribunal of public opinion', where they frequently take on an overtly political character. At times, post-judgment positioning even challenges the authority of a European court as an institution rather than merely dealing with the concrete policy questions at stake in a certain case.

Confronted with adverse decisions in migration cases, the most common position is to seek an alignment with the European court while downplaying the gravity of the violation and the political significance of a case. For example, the Swiss authorities took 'interested notice' of the *Tarakhel* judgment, pledging analysis and verification of measures required for compliance.[107] At the same time, they seemed to convey the impression

[106] Interview with civil society representative, February 2015.

[107] Bundesamt für Justiz, 'EGMR verlangt Garantien vor der Überstellung einer afghanischen Familie nach Italien', Schweizerische Bundeskanzlei, 2014, www.news.admin.ch/message/index.html?lang=de&msg-id=55075 (accessed 28 May 2015) (own translation).

that this 'individual case' did not cast doubt on the Dublin system.[108] In *Hirsi*, most Italian government officials expressed their respect for the ECtHR as a supreme judicial organ, promising to examine the situation and to establish a 'clear, transparent and fair immigration policy'.[109] But seemingly in contradiction to this attitude, the Ministry of Foreign Affairs also stated that 'the treatment of rescued migrants and refugees has always been in line with international obligations'.[110] Such deflections can be particularly effective where anticipatory measures have created a temporarily acceptable human rights situation. Migrant supporters are then unable to direct attention to specific questionable practices. However, short-term compliance after or at the time of a ruling might not at all be indicative of the longer-term approach. While not performing overt 'pushbacks' after the *Hirsi* judgment, Italy continued to engage in policies that are dubious from a human rights standpoint even after the judgment. Only the death of around 300 migrants in a shipwreck close to the Italian island of Lampedusa in 2013 led to a more humanitarian approach in the form of search-and-rescue operations such as *Mare Nostrum*. However, according to a 2014 report by Amnesty International, the authorities still closely cooperated with Libya in questions of migration control while falling short of offering effective asylum procedures in the context of its operations in the Mediterranean.[111] In spring 2015, the government introduced a new proposal at the EU level, focusing especially on the creation of detention centres and the stepping up of coastal guard capabilities in countries like Tunisia and Egypt.[112]

The second and more confrontational approach consists of highlighting one's dissatisfaction with judicial outcomes and shifting the blame to other

[108] Carlos Hanimann, 'Ein Urteil gegen die Gleichgültigkeit', Die Wochenzeitung, no. 45/2014, 6 November 2014, www.woz.ch/-5665 (accessed 29 May 2015) (own translation).

[109] Polchi, Vladimiro, 'Strasburgo, l'Italia condannata per i respingimenti verso la Libia', La Repubblica, 23 February 2012, www.repubblica.it/solidarieta/immigrazione/2012/02/23/news/l_italia_condannata_per_i_respingimenti-30366965/ (accessed 29 May 2015) (own translation).

[110] Ibid.

[111] Amnesty International, 'Submission to the Council of Europe Committee of Ministers: Hirsi Jamaa and Others v. Italy (Application no. 27765/09)', Amnesty International, 2014, www.amnesty.eu/content/assets/Doc2014/B1525_-_second_submission_Hirsi_-_11_Feb_2014.pdf (accessed 30 May 2015).

[112] Manasi Gopalakrishnan, 'The EU's Plan to Restrain Migrants in North Africa Worries Rights Groups', Deutsche Welle, 26 March 2015, www.dw.com/en/the-eus-plan-to-restrain-migrants-in-north-africa-worries-rights-groups/a-18342598?maca=en-rss-en-eu-2092-rdf (accessed 10 July 2015).

actors. For instance, in the aftermath of *M.S.S.*, the Belgian State Secretary of Asylum and Migration overtly criticized Greece, stating that he 'cannot accept that a country like Belgium is being condemned by the European Court of Human Rights because another country does not respect Community law'.[113] More often, however, governments will oppose the position taken by the court in question. This is particularly true for the Strasbourg Court, which is increasingly confronted with strong criticism directly challenging its institutional legitimacy.[114] The strategy is then used to rally the conservative and nationalist parts of the electorate, which are usually opposed to both immigration and interferences of the European courts in domestic politics. As Myjer points out, '[t]he political message is a simple one: blame the Court, emphasize that the State should take care of its 'own' people first, and the last word on immigration matters should not be given to international judges'.[115] In *Hirsi*, for example, some (former) Italian officials displayed such defiant behaviour, going as far as challenging the legality of the judgment. Indeed, the Italian defence attorney declared that the Court had formulated 'an ideological manifesto against Italy and its policies' and that this was 'not the place to debate this matter'.[116] Roberto Maroni, though 'only' the former Minister for the Interior at that time, lamented 'an incomprehensible blow by hypocritical do-gooders'.[117] The *Hirsi* case illustrates that post-judgment positions might differ according to the political affiliation of governments or even individual officials, possibly resulting in a multitude of government positions. Still, where this diversity of views successfully caters to various political interest groups at once (as for example Europhiles and Eurosceptics), it

113 Pascal Martin, 'Asile: Dresser des murs ne résoudra rien', Le Soir, 29 March 2011, www.lesoir.be/archives?url=/actualite/belgique/2011–03–29/asile-dresser-des-murs-ne-resoudra-rien-831147.php (accessed 30 May 2015) (own translation).

114 See Barbara M. Oomen, 'A Serious Case of Strasbourg-Bashing? An Evaluation of the Debates on the Legitimacy of the European Court of Human Rights in the Netherlands' (2016) 20 *The International Journal of Human Rights* 407–25 and Spyridōn L. Phlogaitēs, Tom Zwart and Julie Fraser (eds), *The European Court of Human Rights and Its Discontents: Turning Criticism into Strength* (Cheltenham, UK: Edward Elgar, 2013).

115 Egbert Myjer, 'Why Much of the Criticism of the European Court of Human Rights is Unfounded', in Phlogaitēs, Zwart and Fraser (eds), *The European Court of Human Rights and Its Discontents*, 41.

116 Arnd Riekmann, 'Italy Told Not to Send Back Intercepted Refugees', Deutsche Welle, 24 February 2012, www.dw.de/italy-told-not-to-send-back-intercepted-refugees/a-15765553 (accessed 30 May 2015).

117 Polchi, 'Strasburgo, l'Italia condannata per i respingimenti verso la Libia' (own translation).

might end up benefiting the popularity of a government despite apparent inconsistencies.

Finally, some interviewees made the interesting point that governments may, at times, seek a confrontation with the European courts. One government official explained, for instance, that at one point the election of a right-wing government brought about a strategy of pushing the boundaries of European law with particularly narrow interpretations to, 'in the end, have the Court . . . tell you that it is not possible what you are doing'.[118] The result would either be the approval of the policy or a new opportunity to contest the authority of the European court in question. According to an NGO representative from the same country, governments can thus shift political blame in a way that is usually not possible with domestic courts.[119] Put more simply, when unassertive domestic judiciaries force the European courts to be active in the enforcement of migrant rights, governments might successfully combine highly restrictive migration policies with a confrontational post-judgment positioning. To borrow a concept that has been developed with regard to judicial strategies,[120] governments are able 'to walk on the brink of noncompliance' with human rights obligations while risking very little given the critical attitude of their electorates. While future research needs to inquire into the spread of such tactics among right-wing governments, this plausible scenario shows the potential import of post-judgment positioning into EC litigation on migrant rights.

5.7 Conclusion

Focusing on cases dealing with the human rights of migrants and asylum seekers, this chapter has sought to identify and explain a number of government strategies aimed at managing the influence of the European courts and maximizing their 'sovereign manoeuvrability' in the European legal order(s). While the varying political impact of international courts has recently come under closer scrutiny in scholarship, such practices of political contestation in legal engagement have so far remained under-researched. Based on original research and some general observations, this chapter has tried to elucidate four particular strategies, namely legal

118 Interview with former government representative, August 2014.

119 Interview with civil society representative, February 2015.

120 See Shai Dothan, *Reputation and Judicial Tactics: A Theory of National and International Courts* (Cambridge: Cambridge University Press, 2014), 117–22.

argumentation in court, anticipatory measures, peer mobilization and post-judgment positioning. The first aspect refers to the practice of trying to persuade the European courts during the proceedings of the application or the interpretation of legal provisions, especially where they relate to the scope of legal instruments, policy implications and the 'correct' application of procedural requirements. The adoption of anticipatory measures such as the granting of temporary residence permits or partial legislative changes are meant to remove cases from the courts or to temper public reactions to imminent adverse judgments. Moreover, states are found to mobilize their peers to intervene alongside them in particularly politically salient cases, thus increasing the pressure on the European courts to respect the preferences of contracting states. Finally, governments may adopt different positions in the aftermath of negative rulings in migration-related cases, trying either to show respect and alignment with the European court or to directly confront judicial authority.

To be sure, governments do not always act in strategically optimal ways. For instance, the UK arguably 'lost' the case of *Sufi and Elmi* by submitting a report of poor quality about the human rights situation in Somalia at that time.[121] The ECtHR consequently concluded that a return of asylum seekers is not permissible under the Convention. However, the increasing reliance on the European courts by organizations and lawyers supporting migrants is likely to inspire more calculated, resourceful and coordinated government strategies in the future. This trend is already visible in the growing number of TPIs by governments, especially in cases relating to the Dublin regulation. As the most significant judicial interventions in the migration area are quite recent, it is not unlikely that actors will engage in a sort of 'judicial arms race' before the European courts for at least as long as the political platforms remain deadlocked.

The examples discussed in this chapter illustrate how governments employ various strategies before, during and after European courts litigation. This finding confirms the general observation in this volume that the practices in international law are changing as governments act increasingly strategically to maximize their political room for manoeuver. However, having focused only on the European courts and the migration area, it needs to be seen how this trend plays out across international courts and other policy areas. The strategies identified here are generic in the sense of being transferable to other domains even if the adoption of anticipatory measures, for example, seems particularly 'promising' in the context

[121] Interview with civil society representative, January 2015.

of migration. But the motivations for the application of various measures might differ, with governments either trying to retain control over certain particularly salient policy areas or simply being afraid of general reputational costs. Furthermore, the chapter illustrates that it is difficult to assess the actual effectiveness of these strategies. The fact that governments had to accept negative outcomes in many of the examples cited here does not disprove their value. The question is rather: what would the courts have decided in their absence? The analysis thus finally highlights the ambiguity of judicial outcomes. Even the reinforcement of a legal regime by a strong and assertive international court does not necessarily lead to its promotion. More clarity about the prevalence and effectiveness of government strategies will be necessary for a differentiated evaluation of the influence of the growing number of international courts on the changing practices of international law.

6

The Disaggregated Law of Global Mass Surveillance

ITAMAR MANN*

6.1 Introduction

As the editors of this volume remind us, tensions between various bodies of law coexisting in the transnational legal environment are not only matters of competing legal vocabularies.[1] They are matters of politics. When a lawyer pens an international agreement that adroitly bypasses a domestic constitutional provision, her work is a play of power.[2] One set of rules is often deployed precisely to avoid, thwart or mitigate the consequences of another. In the editors' terms, law is used against law.[3] At times, entire legal arsenals are designed specifically to outdo other legal rules. If design is successful, this work will have thoroughgoing effects. Sometimes these are effects on how opportunities to participate in the actions of government are distributed. As the Edward Snowden revelations have shown, mass surveillance is a fruitful field for examining such design. Mass surveillance is not only a challenge to law. It's also the result of nimble legal craftwork. It provides a quintessential case in point within a more general account of 'legalization', which Gammeltoft-Hansen and Aalberts identify.

This chapter aims to outline the way in which legal manoeuvring has occurred in the context of the cooperative intergovernmental collection of signals intelligence ('sigint'). It focuses on a number of Memoranda of

* I would like to thank Ashley Deeks and the participants of the Summer 2015 Georgetown faculty workshop for invaluable comments, during time I spent at Georgetown as the National Security Fellow. The editors of this volume have also provided tremendously insightful suggestions. Usual caveats apply.

[1] See International Law Commission, *Fragmentation of International Law: Difficulties Arising from Diversification and Expansion of International Law* (2006).

[2] See also David Kennedy, *Of War and Law* (Princeton, NJ: Princeton University Press, 2006); David Kennedy, 'The Mystery of Global Governance' (2008) 34 *Ohio Northern University Law Review* 827–60.

[3] Chapter 1.

Understanding (MOUs) and other legal documents to show how surveillance and its products have been shared. But the objective is not to provide a comprehensive account of this legal world. Part of the challenge is that such an account isn't possible. Writing about the law facilitating cooperative sigint collection depends on sporadic leaks, and therefore generates a necessarily partial picture. Yet the available material does suffice for some limited analysis characterizing a problem with 'the law of global mass surveillance'. I will argue that the legal instruments facilitating such activities have not only led to violations of privacy (a proposition now well understood). They have also influenced how states interpret their own laws, including their constitutions. The results of this influence are reduced opportunities for political participation among citizens in multiple states and an erosion of the rule of law.

Public international law scholars are accustomed to focusing on highly visible legal materials: treaties are the centrepiece of the discipline; customary international law is based on states' behaviour and authoritative pronouncements of their obligations (opinio juris). More recently, scholars and practitioners have also studied executive agreements, MoUs, and other 'soft law' instruments. Though not formally recognized as sources of international law, these instruments are incredibly consequential in a vast array of fields, including trade, investment, tax and environmental law.[4] But they are also often buried deep in intergovernmental bureaucracies, coded in technical terms or simply classified.[5] As became abundantly clear, e.g. in debates on trade, secret agreements between executive branches have often sought to prevent domestic political debate in legislative branches and thus among citizens.[6]

When examining leaked documents on mass surveillance, international lawyers encounter a tip of yet another legal iceberg, that of intergovernmental cooperation in the national security sphere.[7] Reading them, legal

[4] See e.g. Oona Hathaway, 'Treaties End: The Past, Present, and Future of International Law Making in the United States' (2008) 117(7) *The Yale Law Journal*, at 1236.

[5] On this problematic, see Kennedy, 'The Mystery of Global Governance'.

[6] See e.g. David Singh Grewal, 'Another Leaked Trade Agreement, Another Reason to Oppose Fast Track', *The Huffington Post*, 6 April 2015, www.huffingtonpost.com/david-singh-grewal/tisa-leak_b_7514314.html; Amy Kapczynski, 'The Trans-Pacific Partnership – Is It Bad For Your Health?' (2015) 373 *The New England Journal of Medicine* 373 at 201–3, www.nejm.org/doi/full/10.1056/NEJMp1506158?af=R&rss=currentIssue&.

[7] There is a body of work on the legal 'black hole' in the context of American national security policy, especially centred on detention at the facility in Guantanamo Bay. See Chapter 3, this volume, and e.g. *Abassi v. Secretary of State for Foreign and Commonwealth Affairs* [2002] EWCA Civ 1598, CA; Johan Steyn, 'Guantanamo Bay: The Legal

scholars can analyze the underwater texture of this iceberg. The law facilitating mass surveillance is part of a larger cooperative national security legal apparatus still left relatively unexamined by international law scholars;[8] It sheds a different light both on the traditional discussion of 'sources', and on the by now established literature on soft law. And it demonstrates how international and domestic law are amalgamated with internal rules within security agencies, to create new legal assemblages which govern our lives with no real accountability.

Contrary to what the phrase 'law against law' might suggest, the editors of this volume are not so much interested in one register of law violating another. Rather, they invoke law that is generated to comply with other law – while at the same time thwarting law's stated normative commitments.[9] This is precisely what the legal instruments that have facilitated global mass surveillance have done. The main 'strategy' governments use to undo legal limitations on their actions is cooperation. This chapter attempts to map out the cooperative legal and soft law instruments that create such legal loopholes. Whereas public international law is based on common norms agreed upon ex-ante, the law of global mass surveillance presents a much more flexible set of possibilities, more reminiscent of private contract and corporate law.

The roadmap of the law of mass surveillance remarkably reproduces the world legal theorist Anne-Marie Slaughter painted in her now-classical work on 'disaggregated sovereignty'. Disaggregated sovereignty is a mode of governance premised on low-level coordination between executive agencies rather than formal international law, agreed upon by states. As Slaughter explained starting from the 1990s, in a context of disaggregated sovereignty, executive agents become diplomats.[10] Regulatory and enforcement agencies generate a new kind of international law, based upon networks of executive agencies. Such networks made global mass surveillance possible.

Black Hole' (2004) 53(1) *International and Comparative Law Quarterly* at 1–15; Fleur Johns, *Non-Legality in International Law: Unruly Law* (Cambridge: Cambridge University Press, 2015) (especially the chapter 'Black Holes and the Outside Within: Extra-Legality at Guantanamo').

8 Ashley Deeks's work is an important exception to this. See Ashley Deeks, 'Intelligence Communities, Peer Constraints, and the Law' (2015) 7 *Harvard National Security Journal* at 1–54; Ashley Deeks, 'Checks and Balances from Abroad' (2015) 83(4) *The University of Chicago Law Review* at 65–88.

9 Chapter 1, this volume.

10 Anne-Marie Slaughter, *A New World Order* (Princeton, NJ: Princeton University Press, 2004), 36.

Slaughter's was an optimistic account, according to which disaggregated sovereignty would promote liberal values. And it was an enormously influential one, shaping the Weltanschauungs of foreign policy professionals in the US (most remarkably Hilary Clinton's).[11] Diverting attention from privacy concerns to legal infrastructure allows us to see mass surveillance's more rarely acknowledged harms. Precisely because of its disaggregated structure, the law of global mass surveillance eroded democratic values, which Slaughter purportedly held dear. Indeed, disaggregated sovereignty created a new democratic deficit in national security policy. The chapter builds on work by others as well as my own, to expand a picture of the 'dark sides' of disaggregated sovereignty.[12] It illustrates the perception, discussed in the introduction to this volume, that 'legalization' can undermine democratic decision making and popular sovereignty.

This chapter takes no position on the magnitude of the security risks that transnational terrorism reflects for any particular polity. At the wake of continued attacks on cities around the world, the needs of security are as great as ever. Some modes of sigint collection – and indeed sigint sharing – likely help in preventing such awful attacks. However, when striking the balance between national security and civil liberties one must remain cognizant of the democratic basis for both. How to provide security for any particular political community should be the decision of that community; And the legal locus for political community is, as far as international law is concerned, still that of sovereign states.[13] The way political communities have been sidestepped by national security

[11] See Hillary Clinton, *Hard Choices* (New York: Simon and Schuster), 458–59 ('Her [Slaughter's] concept of networks keyed off the architecture of the internet, but it was bigger than that. It had to do with all the ways people were organizing themselves in the 21st century, collaborating, communicating, trading, even fighting').

[12] See generally David Kennedy, *The Dark Side of Virtue* (Princeton, NJ: Princeton University Press, 2005); Thomas Gammeltoft-Hansen and Jens Vedsted-Hansen, *Human Rights and the Dark Side of Globalization* (New York: Routledge, 2017); Itamar Mann, 'Dialectic of Transnationalism: Unauthorized Migration and Human Rights, 1993–2013' (2013) 54(2) *Harvard International Law Journal*, at 315.

[13] Alongside the discipline's clear preference for stability and security, social contact theory provides the normative bulwark for positive international law. See Patrick Capps and Julian Rivers, 'Kant's Concept of International Law' (2010) 16 *Legal Theory* at 229–57. (Explaining how Kant's theory of law, based on the social contract, grants legitimacy to international law understood as an interstate system); Guglielmo Verdirame, 'A Normative Theory of Sovereignty Transfers' (2013) 49 *Stanford Journal of International Law* at 371–426 (arguing that international law has developed and should develop a theory of sovereignty based on liberal self-government, derivative from enlightenment social contract theory).

networks is probably one among several reasons for the recent 'populist' blowback.[14]

Privacy violations have become the pervasive framing of the problem with global mass surveillance. But the law of global mass surveillance raises more fundamental questions. Rather than individual human rights violations, the law of global mass surveillance reveals the ways in which disaggregated sovereignty curtails collective political participation. At stake are the possibility of democratic government and the rule of law in the twenty-first century.

Section 6.2 concisely explains what is 'mass surveillance', and introduces basic aspects of how it has been conceptualized as a violation of international law. Section 6.3 aims to demonstrate the ways in which a particular genre of international law, so far seldom recognized as such, has in fact facilitated rather than limited mass surveillance. Section 6.4 is dedicated to a close reading of legal documents facilitating mass surveillance in several bilateral relationships the US National Security Agency (NSA) with partners abroad: Germany, Sweden, Saudi Arabia and Israel. Section 6.5 shows how the law of mass surveillance continues and develops Slaughter's idea of the disaggregation of sovereignty. Section 6.6 advances a critique of the counter-democratic pull embedded in the law of mass surveillance. Section 6.7 briefly concludes, adding an inchoate normative proposal.

6.2 What Is Mass Surveillance?

'Mass surveillance' refers to the simultaneous harvesting of data regarding a population, conducted by government agents, often relying on private companies. Such policies took centre stage in political debate around the world starting from June 2013.[15] Then, former contractor Edward Snowden began leaking classified documents obtained from the NSA.

Mass surveillance is most often aimed to defend national security objectives, and protect civilian and military targets from militant attack. In January 2015, NSA internal procedures indicated that information collected 'in bulk' will only be used for national security purposes.[16] Yet, as revealed

14 See e.g. Pankaj Mishra, *Age of Anger: A History of the Present* (New York: Farrar, Straus and Giroux, 2017).

15 See account of first leaks in Glenn Greenwald, *No Place to Hide: Edward Snowden, The NSA, and the U.S. Surveillance State* (New York: Metropolitan Books, 2014), 33–89.

16 USSID SP0018: Supplemental Procedures for the Collection, Processing, Retention, and Dissemination of Signals Intelligence Information and Data Containing Personal Information of Non-United States Persons, Section 5 (U) 5.2, www.statewatch.org/news/2015/feb/nsa-USSID-non-us-people.pdf.

in the Snowden documents, mass surveillance was for a long time not in fact limited to such objectives, and had served, e.g. border security and commercial needs.[17]

Mass surveillance does not necessarily refer to the *content* of communications between individuals, whether sent via email, social networks or by phone. The debate has partly revolved around the collection of 'metadata': data about when and where a communication was placed or was received, and its duration. This information can be important and indeed crucial. As former head of NSA and CIA Michael Hayden confirmed referring to lethal drone attacks, 'We kill people based on metadata'.[18]

Mass surveillance has, in recent years, generated an intense debate over its potential violation of both domestic and international law. A considerable part of the discussion has focused on the domestic law of the US. In the US context, critics have charged that the NSA's surveillance programme violates the rights of American citizens under the US Constitution, and under statute.[19] The provisions that had originally established the domestic legal infrastructure of mass surveillance – Section 215 of the Patriot Act, Section 702 of the Foreign Intelligence Surveillance Act, and Executive Order 12333, have all come under considerable attack. As the debate on these provisions emerged, many have found them overly broad, or believed security agencies violated or bent them – ultimately rendering them hollow.

Siding with the critics, the Second Circuit ruled that Section 215 did not in fact authorize the bulk collection of metadata.[20] In June 2015, this

[17] The US has been collecting all telephony metadata and call contents in the Bahamas. The reported reason is fighting narcotics trafficking. See Ryan Dvereux, Glenn Greenwald and Laura Poitras, 'Data Pirates of the Caribbean: The NSA is Recording Every Cell Phone Call in Bahamas', *The Intercept*, 19 May 2014. On mass surveillance and economic and commercial interests, see Greenwald, *No Place to Hide*, 134.

[18] See David Cole, 'We Kill People Based on Metadata', NYBRblog, 10May 2014, www.nybooks.com/blogs/nyrblog/2014/may/10/we-kill-people-based-metadata/. Whether there is any evidence supporting the claim that bulk collection of metadata actually advances concrete national security objectives remains a contested question. See e.g. Alvaro M. Bedoya, 'Big Data and the Underground Railroad', *Slate*, 7 November 2014, www.slate.com/articles/technology/future_tense/2014/11/big_data_underground_railroad_history_says_unfettered_collection_of_data.html.

[19] See Laura Donohue, 'Bulk Metadata Collection: Statutory and Constitutional Considerations' (2014) 37 *Harvard Journal of Law and Policy* at 757–900.

[20] For the Second Circuit Opinion holding that the NSA's bulk telephone metadata programme is not authorized by section 215 of the USA Patriot Act, *see American Civil Liberties Union v. James R. Clapper*, Case 14–42 (2015), http://justsecurity.org/wp-content/uploads/2015/05/14–42.majority.pdf.

section of the USA PATRIOT Act expired, and Congress introduced the USA Freedom Act, seeking to prevent government agencies from warrantless access to bulk data about American citizens. Whether this reform will ultimately prove successful or not, the thrust of the critique is that mass surveillance subverts the American people's privacy. Privacy is not conceived only as a negative right against state intervention, but also as a positive right enabling meaningful civic participation.[21] Philosophically, this critique is firmly rooted in ideas of social contract theory and popular sovereignty.[22]

In the US, both case law and statutory reform have left mass surveillance of non-American citizens outside of US territory wholly unimpeded. Yet both the courts and the legislative branches of other countries – especially European allies of the US – have pushed back.[23] Unlike in the US, in Europe human rights law generally has extra-territorial application. The International Covenant on Civil and Political Rights, the European Convention on Human Rights, and the Charter of Fundamental Rights, protect *all* humans, inasmuch as they are within the de facto or de jure jurisdiction of an actor that is bound by them. This, however, has not changed a basic feature of the debate on mass surveillance: like in the US, the pushback has aimed to protect *European* citizens. In its national and regional enforcement mechanisms, human rights law has thus figured as a quasi-constitutional law oriented primarily towards legal protections at home. Nowhere have the protections of privacy been granted *universal* enforcement.

Within the work of public international law institutions and some NGOS, the invocation of the right to privacy does, of course, have universal aspirations.[24] On 30 June 2014, UN High Commissioner for Human Rights Navi Pillay published *The Right to Privacy in the Digital*

[21] See e.g. David Cole, 'Is Privacy Obsolete?', *The Nation*, 6 April 2015, www.thenation.com/article/198505/privacy-20-surveillance-digital-age# (arguing that 'unless we insist on new rules to govern and regulate the use of these new technologies, it's not only our privacy that will be lost, but all that depends on privacy as well – including democracy itself')

[22] See Marko Milanovic, 'Human Rights Treaties and Foreign Surveillance: Privacy in the Digital Age' (2015) 56(1) *Harvard International Law Journal*, at 81–146.

[23] Perhaps most importantly, see the Court of Justice of the European Union's judgment on the 'safe harbour' scheme: Judgment of the Court (Grand Chamber), 6 October 2015 in Case C-362/14, http://curia.europa.eu/juris/document/document.jsf?text=&docid=169195&pageIndex=0&doclang=en&mode=req&dir=&occ=first&part=1&cid=430261.

[24] Exceptions to this are few references to customary norms such as territorial integrity and the Vienna Convention on the Law of Treaties.

Age.[25] The High Commissioner made resounding findings: 'many states ... contributed to a lack of accountability for arbitrary or unlawful interference in the right to privacy'.[26] Another report, by Special Rapporteur Ben Emmerson, followed in September.[27] Emmerson concluded that mass surveillance 'undoubtedly impinges on the very essence' of the right to privacy, under Article 17 of the International Covenant on Civil and Political Rights (ICCPR).[28] He deemed this interference 'systematic',[29] and warned: 'the use of mass surveillance effectively does away with the right to privacy of communications on the internet altogether'.[30] These reports set the stage for the new mandate the UN Human Rights Council has created for a Special Rapporteur on the Right to Privacy.[31]

Both the Pillay and the Emmerson reports signalled a clash between UN interpretations of international law and the practices of global mass surveillance.[32] As far as these reports were concerned, international law squarely prohibits contemporary mass surveillance policies led by the US. But is the international legal case against mass surveillance so clear-cut? A particular genre of international law has been involved in facilitating (rather than limiting) global mass surveillance. Understanding this law reflects how the attempt to apply a universal standard of privacy probably misses many of its most important consequences. With no international citizenship and no international public sphere to speak of, privacy is still largely an individual right of negative character.[33]

6.3 A Surveillance Charter

Mass surveillance relies upon international law. International law is an important precondition – I dare say as important as technology – for the

25 See Human Rights Council, 'The Right to Privacy in the Digital Age', 30 June 2014, A/HRC/27/37.

26 Ibid., 15–16.

27 See Report of the Special Rapporteur on the promotion and protection of human rights and fundamental freedoms while countering terrorism (23 September 2014), A/69/397.

28 Ibid., 8. 29 Ibid., 5. 30 Ibid., 6.

31 See Human Rights Council, 'The Right to Privacy in the Digital Age', 24 March 2015, A/HRC/28/L.27.

32 One commentator has gone so far as calling this 'universal state practice'. See Peter Marguiles, 'Sweeping Claims and Casual Legal Analysis in the Latest U.N. Mass Surveillance Report', *Lawfare Blog*, 20 October 2014, www.lawfareblog.com/2014/10/sweeping-claims-and-casual-legal-analysis-in-the-latest-u-n-mass-surveillance-report/.

33 On the traditionally negative nature of the right to privacy in international law, see summary in the Max Planck Encyclopedia of International Law: Ineta Ziemele, Privacy, Right to, International Protection, http://opil.ouplaw.com/view/10.1093/law:epil/9780199231690/law-9780199231690-e863?rskey=ZwM8D2&result=1&prd=EPIL.

global proliferation of mass surveillance. To understand this, one must first understand that no single government generated mass surveillance on its own. As Pillay recounts, 'together, the National Security Agency in the United States of America and General Communications Headquarters in the United Kingdom of Great Britain [GCHQ] and Northern Ireland have developed technologies allowing access to much global internet traffic'.[34] For better or worse, mass surveillance has been a cooperative, shared endeavour.

The signals intelligence (sigint) cooperation treaty known as the UKUSA Agreement – the foundational international law instrument mass surveillance rests upon – was concluded only a few months after the adoption of UN Charter in 1945. This UKUSA agreement, for many years unacknowledged by its members, has evolved into the contemporary 'Five Eyes' framework. The legal basis of the five eyes framework is not public. We don't know if it is a multilateral agreement, a number of bilateral agreements, or (likely) a combination thereof. One way or another, it gradually joined together national security agencies of the US, the UK, Canada (1949) and Australia and New Zealand (1952). Its emergence is coeval with the (much more widely known) treaty-based security organization, the North Atlantic Treaty Organization (NATO), established 1949. Like the UN Charter rests at the basis of modern public international law, the UKUSA Agreement is a Charter for the law of mass surveillance.

Whatever the Five Eyes framework's particular legal structure, it has not gone through the formal ratification processes characteristic of treaties in the domestic legal orders of its member states. It does not fall under the definition of a 'treaty' in the Vienna Convention on the Law of Treaties. It is thus not comfortably reducible to any one of the sources of international law in the International Court of Justice Statute. Indeed, the UN Charter goes so far as prohibiting secret treaties (Article 102).[35] For these reasons, some may believe the Five Eyes framework is not part of international law at all. But many legal instruments – executive agreements and other 'soft law' instruments – fall into this category. Taking one's cue from the extensive literature on 'soft law', it is both coherent and fruitful to think about the instruments facilitating intelligence cooperation in a specifically legal context.[36]

[34] Pillay, 'The Right to Privacy', 3.

[35] The legacy of Art. 102 goes back to the Covenant of the League of Nations. At the time the secrecy of the Molotov-Ribbentrop Pact was perceived as a cause for the war's carnage.

[36] Compare with Eric Posner, 'Treaty-ish', *Slate*, 28 August 2014, www.slate.com/articles/news_and_politics/view_from_chicago/2014/08/obama_s_proposed_climate_change_agreement_good_for_the_planet_and_perfectly.html.

The historical roots of the Five Eyes framework lie in joint British-American naval operations in the inter-war period.[37] During WWII, the two parties agreed to share 'all special intelligence derived by cryptanalysis of the communications of the military and air forces of the axis powers, including their secret services'.[38] Washington's War Department and the British Government Code and Cipher School expressly stated that civilian communications were excluded.[39] After the war, the parties' mutual interests in peacetime intelligence opened the way for broader activities. They sought to establish a steadier and more formalized relationship.

The 1946 arrangement was to be at one and the same time flexible and bounded – inviting further development and construction. 'These regulations', write the drafters, 'shall be the basis of all regulations for the security and dissemination of Communication Intelligence information'.[40] The agreement resembles not only the establishment of an intergovernmental organization, but also a charter incorporating a new business enterprise. The very fact that this agreement was put into writing is remarkable evidence of a 'legalization' of intelligence cooperation.[41]

The Agreement's drafting history unmistakably exposes a legal consciousness at play.[42] Until they reached the sought-after meeting of the minds, the US and the UK agents exchanged amended versions in a kind of 'battle of forms'. 'To insure uniform interpretation', they specify, each party would have to refer any change in the regulatory framework to the

[37] Sir Stephen Lander, 'International Intelligence Cooperation: an Inside Perspective' (2013) 17(3) *Cambridge Review of International Affairs* at 481, 485.

[38] War Department, Memorandum for the Chief of Staff, 10 June 1943, www.nsa.gov/public_info/_files/ukusa/spec_int_10jun43.pdf.

[39] Ibid.

[40] Appendix to British–U.S. C.I. Agreement British – U.S. Communication Intelligence Security and Dissemination Regulation, 30 January 1946, www.nsa.gov/public_info/_files/ukusa/security_diss_regs_30jan46.pdf (hereiafter: 'Appendix').

[41] On 'legalization', see Chapters 1 and 7, this volume.

[42] On legal consciousness, see e.g. Duncan Kennedy, 'Toward an Historical Understanding of Legal Consciousness: The Case of Classical Legal Thought in America, 1850–1940' (1980) 3 *Research in Law and Sociology* at 3, 6 (Kennedy explains: 'The notion behind the concept of legal consciousness is that people can have in common something more influential than a checklist off acts, techniques and opinions. They can share premises about the salient aspects of the legal order that are so basic that actors rarely if ever bring them consciously to mind. Yet everyone, including actors who think they disagree profoundly about the substantive issues that matter, would dismiss without a second thought [. . .] an approach appearing to deny them. [. . .] Among these premises, there are often links creating subsystems with their own internal organization and rules of operation. These change. For example, they expand and contract to cover – or not cover – a greater or lesser number of the aspects of legal reality that are within legal consciousness at a given time').

other's prior approval.[43] Enforceability too was contemplated. The Britons attested to their commitment to carry out the terms as agreed upon, warning their American partners not to question their 'good faith'.[44]

Indeed, the UKUSA agreement did not only *open* cooperative possibilities. It also limited the parties in certain ways, e.g. in prohibiting commercial use of shared information.[45] The drafters presumably sought to cabin their mutual interests in security from potential economic competition. The American negotiators questioned British commitment to this provision in particular. The British responded to this concern, explaining that Foreign Minister Bevin 'had lived up completely and wholeheartedly to his agreements – he had debated vigorously and sometimes harshly before entering into them, but having once committed himself he would carry out his *contracts* to the full' (emphasis added).[46] The underlying moral imperative is familiar to any lawyer: *pacta sunt servanda*.

While the US and the UK entered this Agreement with comparable power, other Anglophone partners had far less political clout. Gradually a US-UK power asymmetry developed as well.[47] Yet mutual interests during the Cold War provided a bulwark for continued sharing of surveillance products. Sir Stephen Lander, former Director General of the UK Security Service, explained that the members of the core group conveniently included multiple 'islands with aerials'. As a former colonizer, the UK Enjoyed not only physical access to remote locations. It could also offer deep connections in regions of interest, alongside linguistic expertise.[48] Starting from the 1960s when 'the troubles' began, the British brought to the table 'unrivalled experience of dealing ... with a major and long-running terrorist threat'.[49]

When the 9/11 attacks occurred, The Five Eyes were already firmly positioned at the epicentre of a global surveillance regime based on a multilateral framework. As President George W. Bush began the so-called War on Terror, these countries were included in 'Tier A': the first circle of partners

[43] Appendix, note 41 above.

[44] Intelligence communication from February 8, 1946, www.nsa.gov/public_info/_files/ukusa/comms_int_8feb46.pdf.

[45] Appendix, note 41 above, Art. 16 ('Communication Intelligence shall never under any circumstances and in any from be disseminated to any ministry, department, agency, office or individual from which or from whom it might reasonably be expected to finds its way, officially or extra-officially, into the possession of any person or group who would use it for commercial competition or commercial gain or advantage').

[46] Ibid. [47] Lander, 'International Intelligence Cooperation'. [48] Ibid.

[49] Ibid. The retired British spy compares and contrasts the Northern Irish threat to that of Al-Qaeda.

in its surveillance programmes. This framework simultaneously gave rise to multiple other partially overlapping multilateral frameworks. Consider *Lustre*, the secret surveillance treaty between the Five Eyes and France.[50] This agreement, formalized in 2011, facilitated the transfer of metadata from the French Director General of External Security to the NSA. Other interconnected networks were the Sigint Seniors Europe (SSEUR),[51] the Sigint Seniors Pacific and the Afghanistan Sigint Coalition.[52] If we are to believe Vanee' Vines, NSA spokeswoman, these relationships are not only beneficial, but also rule governed in some significant sense.[53] Even if they provide a more flexible basis for governing interstate relations than treaty law or domestic legal obligations, these agreements and MoUs may still be 'legal' in nature in that they are produced by lawyers and directly influence governmental enforcement tasks. To use a felicitous title carried by a book about the Five Eyes Framework, these are *The Ties that Bind*.[54]

6.4 Mass Surveillance Bilateralism

Multilateral frameworks like the 'Five Eyes' network are supplemented with bilateral and ad hoc arrangements. After the Cold War, this second kind of instrument became an avenue for considerable US power to redesign and manipulate the law of global surveillance. The US now enjoyed hegemonic status in a uni-polar period. A kind of euphoria expressed, e.g. in Francis Fukuyama's *End of History* (1992), became prevalent in American academe. And a particular kind of liberally minded international legalism emerged, focused on the global role of the US.[55] At

[50] Jacques Follorou, 'Espionnage: comment Orange et les services secrets *coopèrent*', Le Monde, 20 March 2014, www.lemonde.fr/international/article/2014/03/20/dgse-orange-des-liaisons-incestueuses_4386264_3210.html#wymDtqXvfQjtdMMw.99.

[51] SSEUR members are the Five Eyes nations, Belgium, Denmark, France, Germany, Italy, the Netherlands, Norway, Spain and Sweden. See www.eff.org/files/2014/06/23/report_on_an_nsa_sigdev_training_course_for_allied_countries_.pdf.

[52] Please visit http://electrospaces.blogspot.com/2014/09/nsas-foreign-partnerships.html.

[53] 'The fact that the U.S. government works with other nations, under specific and regulated conditions, mutually strengthens the security of all', she said (emphasis added). https://firstlook.org/theintercept/2014/06/18/nsa-surveillance-secret-cable-partners-revealed-rampart-a/.

[54] Jeffrey T. Richardson, *The Ties That Bind: Intelligence Cooperation between the UK/USA Countries* (New York: HarperCollins, 1986).

[55] At that time Harold Koh, for example, argued that the enforcement of human rights law is, in fact, the enforcement of American values. See e.g. Harold Hongju Koh, 'The "Haiti Paradigm" in United States Human Rights Policy' (1993–94) 103 *The Yale Law Journal* 103 at 2434–35.

least some American lawyers openly perceived international law as properly subject to American 'sovereign maneuverability'.[56]

Michael Herman, the UK's former Secretary of the joint Intelligence Committee, described the dynamic in the intelligence sphere:

> The arrangements in the anti-terrorist campaign still appear to be mainly bilateral and *ad hoc*. Intelligence is exchanged, but there is yet no machinery for collective agreement on what that means. Britain has been an intelligence partner, but its position remains exceptional. In intelligence, as in other things, the main pattern is of the U.S. as the hub and others as the spokes.[57]

Herman's quote conveys spying as ungoverned by international law, and as facilitated by 'gentlemen's agreements'. Yet many of these agreements turn out to be professionally intelligible from a lawyer's perspective. Indeed, lawyers have been deeply involved in the relevant drafting process. Bilateral agreements drafted by lawyers were a principal instrument that allowed the NSA to spin a network of connections with the so-called Tier B countries.[58] The heterogonous group includes relatively wealthy and powerful countries, such as Japan, Germany, Saudi Arabia and Israel. But it also includes relatively weak and less affluent ones, such as Macedonia or Jordan.[59] Tier B actors naturally enjoy varying degrees of connections to the network's epicentre. Bilateral instruments help structure these connections.

The Snowden revelations exposed several Memoranda of Understanding (MOUs) pertaining to 'Tier B' countries. Like the multilateral frameworks, the bilateral agreements the MOUs refer to may not be understood as legally binding under a *formal* test. Yet the MOUs come with the unmistakable fingerprints of lawyers. Excluding them from the realm of legal phenomena risks promoting a misunderstanding about the way law works beyond borders. What is and what isn't 'law' is itself a legal question. Precisely *because* these bilateral agreements are *not* a familiar tool in the

[56] This is the term the editors use in Chapter 1.

[57] Michael Herman, '11 September: Legitimizing Intelligence?' (2002) 16(2) *International Relations* at 234.

[58] These are sometimes also referred to as 'third party nations'.

[59] 'Tier B' countries likely include Algeria, Austria, Belgium, Croatia, Czech Republic, Denmark, Ethiopia, Finland, France, Germany, Greece, Hungary, India, Israel, Italy, Japan, Jordan, Korea, Macedonia, Netherlands, Norway, Pakistan, Poland, Romania, Saudi Arabia, Singapore, Spain, Sweden, Taiwan, Thailand, Tunisia, Turkey and UAE. See Greenwald, *No Place to Hide*, 123.

traditional toolbox of an international lawyer, they are an important aspect of understanding *changing* practices of international law.

Like multilateral frameworks, bilateral arrangements take on a contractual form. They divert significantly from traditional treaties, and look more like contracts in the private law sense. Sometimes they resemble relational contracts, i.e. long-term contracts amended by party behaviour.[60] At times they include provisions typical to many standard contracts, such as consideration, interpretation guidelines and provisions foreseeing remedies for breach. To name one example, the NSA reportedly paid the GCHQ more than $150 Million for what The Guardian defined as 'access to and influence over Britain's intelligence gathering programmes'. Parts of this sum were earmarked for particular tasks, such as site development. In negotiating these terms, the CHGQ pursued a marketing strategy, and 'exploited to the full our unique selling points of geography, partnerships [and] the UK's legal regime'.[61] But what does it mean for an intelligence agency to exploit its own country's 'legal regime'?

In their bilateral relations with the NSA, partner countries are not represented in their capacities as sovereign states. The agreements are concluded on the sub-national level, between security agencies within states. Inevitably, the picture we have of them is far from complete. Yet it is possible to give the flavour of a several examples. As will become clear, 'legalization' is at play on the bilateral inter-agency level as well.

The German Bundesnachrichtendienst (BND) has been a particularly important NSA partner. The NSA-BND relationship dates back to 1962. According to a 'top secret' memo from January 2013, it has 'in the past year' been significantly boosted. The document indicates that Germany had displayed enthusiasm to expand cooperation.[62] The German agency 'is eager to present its SIGINT capabilities . . . with the goal of expanding the partnership'.[63] The memo unfolds several seemingly significant

[60] See e.g. Ian Macneil, 'Contracts: Adjustment of Long-Term Economic Relations Under Classical, Neoclassical, and Relational Contract Law' (1977–78) 72 *Northwestern University Law Review*.

[61] Nick Hopkins and Julian Borger, 'Exlusive: NSA Pays £100m in Secret Funding for GCHQ', *The Guardian*, 1 August 2013.

[62] National Security Agency Information Paper, 17 January 2013, www.eff.org/files/2014/06/23/history_and_current_state_of_cooperation_between_the_nsa_and_bnd.pdf.

[63] The document says that officials welcome 'the BND's eagerness to strengthen and expand cooperation with NSA'. See 'Spying Together: Germany's Deep Cooperation with the NSA', Der Spiegel, 18 June 2014, www.spiegel.de/international/germany/the-german-bnd-and-american-nsa-cooperate-more-closely-than-thought-a-975445.html.

'success stories', and accounts for some of the give-and-take between the countries. This quid-pro-quo creates a transactional context.

On the one hand, the NSA has provided '"a significant amount of hardware and software" as well as "analytic expertise". The NSA also exchanged intelligence reporting with the BND on both military and non-military targets'.[64] On the other hand, the BND granted access to communications supporting counter-terrorism (CT), counter-narcotics (CN) and weapons of mass destruction missions. It provided help with translating communications in the Nigerian Igbo language, and what appears to be access to one particular 'high-value, time sensitive' target.[65] Other benefits from the BND included data collection related to force-protection in Afghanistan, as well as to drug trafficking. The agencies pursued a mutually beneficial exchange of services.

One pertinent 'success story' the NSA describes, is that 'The German government modified its interpretation of the G-10 Privacy Law, protecting the communications of German citizens, to afford the BND more flexibility in sharing protected information with foreign partners'.[66] What is not written in the memo – but is of some relevance – is that the G-10 Privacy Law is Article 10 of Germany's constitution, the *Grundgesetz*. In a dramatic 2009 judgment, the German Constitutional Court held that the only 'original' source of law is the *Grundgesetz*. The *Grundgesetz*, according to this view, protects an irrevocable element of sovereignty belonging to 'the German people'.[67] But it is hard to square a reality in which a secret bilateral agreement transforms constitutional doctrine with such an element of sovereignty. Sharing sigint products becomes an incentive for more 'flexible' constitutional protections.

The same constitutional provision, however, is referred to later in the memo under the heading 'Problems/Challenges with the partner'. Here, the story about the relationship between Germans' privacy and the relationship with the NSA is cast in different terms: 'The BND's inability to successfully address German privacy Law (G-10) issues has limited some operations, but NSA welcomed German willingness to take risks and to pursue new opportunities for cooperation with the U.S. particularly in the CT realm'.[68] The question what are the 'risks' involved – whether they

[64] National Security Agency Information Paper, note 66 above.
[65] The identity of the target is redacted.
[66] National Security Agency Information, note 66 above.
[67] BVerfG, Judgment of the Second Senate of 30 June 2009 ('Lisbon Judgment') 2 BvE 2/08 para. 231ff, www.bverfg.de/e/es20090630_2bve000208en.html.
[68] National Security Agency Information Paper, note 66 above.

are security or legal risks – remains open. It does however seem safe to assume that these are *legal* risks: the NSA is unsatisfied that the BND is not sufficiently willing to stretch Germany's constitution. Studying the law of global mass surveillance means considering this sought-after stretch not only as a doctrinal matter, i.e. whether German and international law, as they stand, permit such a stretch. The more important task is assessing its consequences, in particular who stands to win and who stands to lose from it.

In Chapter 1, the editors observe that cooperation presupposes a commitment of participating states to adjust domestic affairs and shift lawmaking powers towards international organizations and other non-state actors. Germany–US cooperation reflects a related dynamic. A commitment to adjust domestic affairs is observable. What's more, the shift of lawmaking powers is towards a security agency within another state (not an international organization or a non-state actor).[69]

Responding to these revelations, Angela Merkel's spokesperson explained that:

> The Federal Intelligence Agency (BND) cooperates within its legal framework with partner agencies, including for decades the NSA [...] This cooperation takes place within strict legal and judicial guidelines and is controlled by the competent parliamentary committee.[70]

The NSA's assessment of Germany's changing privacy norms and the German government's response to these reflect related points. First, the relationship between the two countries has a rule-governed aspect. It protects mutual national security interests while reflecting expectation interests and respective bargaining power. Mass surveillance, in other words, is facilitated by legal design – the law of global mass surveillance.

The ways in which these interests are formalized 'spills' into their larger legal and regulatory environments, including the rights of German citizens. It is completely possible that 'cooperation takes place within strict legal and judicial guidelines' – as Merkel's spokesperson said. The question, from citizens' perspective, is what those guidelines say; and who had and who hadn't an opportunity to shape them. From this perspective, one might question not only if they sufficiently protect the privacy rights of

[69] Cf. Mann, 'Dialectic of Transnationalism', 346–52 (discussing 'disaggregated violence').

[70] Stephen Brown, 'Germany Defends "Strictly Legal" Cooperation with NSA', Reuters, 8 July 2013, www.reuters.com/article/2013/07/08/us-usa-security-germany-idUSBRE9670PM20130708.

the German people. A separate and equally important question is if they truly protect their national security, as *German citizens* would define it.

Sweden is another interesting case. Not as prominent a partner as Germany, the country has a long-standing surveillance-sharing relationship with the Five Eyes, established 1954. As a non-member of NATO, Sweden was considered a neutral country – an appearance that intelligence cooperation sought to preserve. In 2004, FRA (Sweden's sigint intelligence agency) acceded to bilateral relations with the US and the UK. FRA granted the NSA access to its cable collection in 2011, 'providing unique collection on high-priority Russian targets such as leadership, internal politics, and energy'.[71] The NSA characterized the FRA as an 'extremely competent, technically innovative, and trusted Third Party'.[72]

Like relations with Germany, the relations this agreement put in place have had considerable implications on domestic law – particularly constitutional law. Following the establishment of the trilateral partnership with the US and the UK, Sweden introduced the 'FRA law', allowing for warrantless wiretapping and other surveillance techniques.[73]

The Bill almost immediately became extremely controversial, a fact the Swedish Ministry of Justice was apparently very cognizant of. As reflected in one cable, the US Embassy in Stockholm too believed the bill would be a 'very hard sell'.[74] This led the negotiations around the Bill in two directions. First, Swedish executive agents sought to *limit* the US data exchange requests, making sure these were not overly broad. Second, they sought to *shelter* the Bill from public scrutiny provided for by the Swedish Constitution. The two directions are of course not mutually consonant, but they are related. Both express the Swedish agency's attempt to protect its own reputation, while preserving a measure of autonomy and ability to work cooperatively with an important partner.

From the Swedish public's perspective, however, the two dynamics may not be equally welcome. From a democratic perspective, it is generally preferable that the Swedish executive agency represents the interests of the Swedish public in negotiations with a foreign agency. But it is probably not advisable that it shelters negotiations with a foreign agency from domestic deliberative processes. Granted, even in democracies, many national security affairs are traditionally kept behind a dark veil. But there is an

[71] Memorandum of 18 April 2013, www.kvinnonet.org/misc/NSASweden/index.html.
[72] Ibid. [73] Please visit https://wikileaks.org/cable/2008/10/08STOCKHOLM704.html.
[74] Cable from 21 October 2008, https://wikileaks.org/cable/2008/10/08STOCKHOLM704.html.

important difference where this secrecy is not motivated by security reasons, but is kept to prevent deliberative processes. Becoming part of a global network may have costs for domestic checks and balances on the executive branch. As the US Embassy in Stockholm explained:

> the agreement may have to be presented to Parliament under a vague constitutional requirement for 'matters of great importance'. If so, the process will take considerably longer and be subject to public scrutiny, something the GOS [Government of Sweden – I.M.] will want to avoid. As the MOJ [Swedish Ministry of Justice – I.M.] continues to analyze the proposed text, *it is also considering how to craft an arrangement that will avoid the need for parliamentary review.* (emphasis added)[75]

The task of government lawyers within executive branches of two states, engaging in cooperation, is one of avoiding domestic law. Language reveals some of the underlying sensibility, for the word 'craft' denotes not only skilful work, but also cunning. As mentioned above, the question is not so much about *violating* domestic law as it is about avoiding it.

The cable also reveals that the NSA and the GCHQ have both been involved in Swedish legislative processes. Within this triangle, the NSA believed Swedish domestic law more permissive than British law. An April 2013 memo shows that one collection programme ('Quantum') was initially advanced trilaterally, but was considered under threat by UK domestic law. The NSA preferred to remove the programme from the UK, operating it bilaterally with Sweden instead. The law of inter-agency bilateral relations is once again generated to avoid domestic checks and balances. According to this pattern, different intelligence collection agencies may have different and potentially *competing* characteristics. They may not be full substitutes for each other. Yet, the NSA – the strongest partner in the network – is shopping for legal systems.[76] The benefits of professionalism and technical capability are weighed against the 'costs' of exposure to domestic constituencies.[77]

A third bilateral surveillance partnership the Snowden leaks shed some light upon is one with Saudi Arabia – once again through an April 2013 memo. In comparison with the language used with regard to Germany and Sweden, here the American intelligence agency seems much more cautious. The memo again tallies the mutual benefits, as well as challenges to

75 Please visit https://wikileaks.org/cable/2008/10/08STOCKHOLM704.html.

76 Navi Pillay writes as much in her *Right to Privacy in the Digital Age* (note 27 above).

77 See discussion of forum shopping in Chapter 1, this volume.

the bilateral relationships. The quid-pro-quo of inter-agency cooperation is once again made explicit.

The sigint cooperation with the Saudis is traced back to the first Gulf War in 1991. In December 2012, the Director of National Intelligence James Clapper approved an expansion of intelligence sharing with Saudi Arabia. The NSA provides the Saudis with technical advice on sigint topics and technical capabilities, as well as decryption service to the Saudi Ministry of Intelligence on 'terrorist targets of mutual interest'. The Saudis provide the NSA with access to 'remote geography in the Arab peninsula', as well as to 'unique collection containing AQAP terrorist targets of mutual interest'.[78]

As of April 2013, part of the motivation of sharing sigint with Saudi Arabia is protecting an important *humint* asset (a human source). In other words, signal sharing may create mutual trust, and further develop the cover of an informant in Saudi. Consider how the memo reflects that the NSA is conscious of the way its relations with one Saudi security agency will influence its relationship with another one.

It seems that the added value of the Saudi case may be particularly dramatic. In his May 2017 speech in Riyadh, Donald Trump declared the establishment of what seems to be a new international organization – The Terrorist Financing Targeting Center – 'co-chaired by the United States and Saudi Arabia, and joined by every member of the Gulf Cooperation Council'. The news was coupled with the announcement of a $110 billion Saudi-funded arms purchase from the US. It is impossible to know what will become of this initiative. If it will indeed go forward, it is more than likely that the organization will have some surveillance capacities, especially in the context of banking. For the present purpose, and regardless of its unknown results, the announcement illustrates how bilateral arrangements can develop into multilateral ones, continuously facilitating global mass surveillance.

In an analysis of the law of mass surveillance, one must keep in mind that a government is not one unitary actor in the transnational environment. Within the 'black box' of sovereignty, different organs of the same government have *independent* commitments towards foreign agencies, which may be in tension or even contradictory. In the Saudi non-democratic context, an analysis of domestic checks and balances

[78] Information Paper: NSA Intelligence Relationship with Saudi Arabia, 8 April 2013, www.eff.org/files/2014/07/29/saudi-arabia-information-paper.pdf (hereinafter Saudi Arabia Information Paper).

seems far less pertinent than in the German or Swedish cases above. Yet internal relations between branches may still illuminate the level of accountability a non-democratic government may have, when it exercises authority.

Israel too enjoys heightened bilateral relations with the NSA – probably even in comparison with Five Eyes members.[79] While mass surveillance is the focus of this chapter, 'This SIGINT relationship has increasingly been the catalyst for a broader intelligence relationship between the United States and Israel'.[80] Israeli and American intelligence organizations engaged in other national security activities – such as the Israeli Mossad, the CIA and the Special Operations divisions – are all agencies with relations in Israel.

According to an NSA assessment, Israel's Sigint National Unit (ISNU, better known as 'Unit 8200') and the NSA both bring to the table comparable 'world class' capabilities. Both agencies have cutting-edge technologies and analytic expertise. The Israelis have a geographic advantage with respect to common intelligence targets in the Middle East and Iran. The NSA, on the other hand, allows the ISNU to purchase equipment in preferable terms. Cooperation is premised on the idea that many of the targets are common to both countries. In July 2012, the bilateral relationship turned into a trilateral one, with the sharing of information expanded to the Egyptian government. This allowed the NSA to 'task for ISNU' when targeting terrorist elements in Sinai. The term 'tasking' suggests a chain of command that crosses national borders, reaching from the NSA to the ISNU. As one Israeli journalist commented, this term would be 'usual among agencies belonging to the same intelligence community'.[81] It brings the category of cooperation to an extreme, suggesting that at times cooperation can transform into inter-agency amalgamation.

An undated NSA MOU provides granular insight into the nature of this form of intelligence bilateralism.[82] Data collected by the NSA is shared

[79] As a leaked memo from April 2013 put it, 'NSA maintains a far-reaching technical and analytic relationship with the Israeli SIGINT National Unit, sharing information on access, intercept, targeting, language, analysis and reporting'.

[80] Amir Oren, 'Leaked Classified Memo Reveals U.S.-Israeli Intel Cooperation on Egypt, Iran', Haaretz, 5 August 2014, www.haaretz.com/news/diplomacy-defense/.premium-1.608802.

[81] Ibid.

[82] The document refers to an earlier agreement 'in principle' reached in 2009. Memorandum of Understanding between the National Security Agency/Central Security Service (NSA/CSS) and the Israeli Sigint National Unit (ISNU) Pertaining to the Protection of U.S. Persons, www.eff.org/files/2014/04/09/20130911-guard-israel_sharing_0.pdf (hereinafter NSA-ISNU MOU).

with ISNU, 'Before filtering out Americans' information'.[83] In doing so, the NSA apparently contradicted previous statements by the Administration: since the Snowden leaks, the government said that before Americans' data are shared, 'the data are protected by strict 'minimization procedures' that prevent the information from being misused'. This has not been the case with Israel's ISNU.[84]

Perhaps more interestingly, the agreement is far from *ignoring* limitations on the use of data under US domestic law. Whether it does so successfully or not, its entire objective is to implement such limitations within an executive-to-executive institutional structure.[85] The idea is to *outsource the application of such legal limitations to the Israeli agency*. The NSA expects Israelis to apply the President's Executive Order and the US Constitution's Fourth Amendment (which secures the right of 'the people' against 'unreasonable' and warrantless 'searches and seizures').

But how is this done? A managerial approach is adopted. The NSA prescribes specified 'procedures and responsibilities'.[86] It trains ISNU agents on how to implement these procedures.[87] And it puts in place a reporting mechanism that requires the ISNU to demonstrate its compliance periodically.[88]

The drafters of the agreement were evidently concerned by how the agreement fits into the tapestry of the Five Eyes framework. The agreement thus specifies that protections 'similar' to those granted to Americans must be given to citizens of all Anglophone countries.[89] The outcome is a rather unusual institutional setting. Within its bilateral relations with the NSA, the *Israeli* intelligence unit is expected to grant protections equivalent to those of the US Constitution to, e.g., New Zealanders. National security rights and duties are redistributed among state actors

83 See Andrea Peterson, 'The NSA Is Sharing Data with Israel. Before Filtering Out Americans' Information', *Washington Post*, 11 September 2013, www.washingtonpost.com/blogs/the-switch/wp/2013/09/11/the-nsa-is-sharing-data-with-israel-before-filtering-out-americans-information/.

84 Ibid.

85 See NSA-ISNU MOU, note 86 above, Art. I.(a): 'This agreement between NSA and the Israeli SIGINT National Unit (ISNU) prescribes procedures and responsibilities for ensuring that ISNU handling of materials provided by NSA – including, but not limited to, Signals Intelligence (SIGINT) technology and equipment and raw SIGINT data (i.e. signals intelligence information that has not been reviewed for foreign intelligence purposes or minimized) – is consistent with the requirements placed upon NSA by U.S. law and Executive Order to establish safeguards protecting the rights of U.S. persons under the Fourth Amendment to the United States Constitution'.

86 NSA-ISNU MOU, note 86 above, Art. I.a.

87 Ibid., Art. IV.a.1. 88 Ibid., Art. VI. 89 Ibid., Art. I.c.

and individuals, copied and pasted across borders and legal traditions, in a rather creative *assemblage*.[90]

As is expressly stated, 'This agreement is not intended to create any legally enforceable rights and shall not be construed to be either an international agreement or a legally binding instrument according to international law'.[91] From the present perspective, however, such a provision – rather than reflecting the extra-legal nature of the agreement – reflects how steeped it is in legal practice.[92] Moreover, the agreement implicates rights enshrined both in the domestic legal systems of the countries involved and in international law, such as the right to privacy. It shifts the locus of duties ordinarily corresponding to those rights. The risks that citizens bearing those rights will be exposed to change as well.

While the agreement does avowedly lean on *norms* external to it (such as the Fourth Amendment), it is not possible to enforce in an external *institution*. Article 7, entitled 'Review and Amendments'[93] allows for immediate and unilateral termination in writing (7(a)); it provides for biannual review procedures, alongside review upon the request of either party (7(b)); it specifies writing and mutual-agreement requirements for any future amendments (7(c)); and bars both parties from any 'attempt to enforce the terms of the MOU in any domestic, third party, or international court or tribunal'. Disputes, rather, 'will be resolved through discussion by all parties'.[94] While the process of judicialization, described in the introduction, may occur in other areas of law, here legalization is internal to executive branches. Legalization thus seems to be as much about *insularity* from judicial bodies, national or supranational.

Israeli intelligence agents are expected to comply simply of interest in the preservation of the cooperative framework. But this interest may not be negligible after all. Freed from the formalities of a 'binding instrument', the agreement may in fact have *increased* enforceability – precisely *because* it avoids the limitations of public international law.

6.5 The Disaggregated Law of Global Mass Surveillance

The networked environment described above reproduces the basic tenets of Anne-Marie Slaughter's understanding of 'disaggregated sovereignty'.[95] Slaughter published the major articulations of her theory starting from the

[90] On the notion of 'assemblage', see Saskia Sassen, *Territory, Authority, Rights: From Medieval to Global Assemblages* (Princeton, NJ: Princeton University Press, 2006).

[91] NSA-ISNU MOU, note 86 above, Art. I.d.

[92] Fleur Johns.

[93] Ibid., Art. VII.

[94] Ibid.

[95] Slaughter, 'A New World Order'.

early 1990s. These culminated in 'A New World Order', a classic of liberal international thought that came out in 2004.[96] The same period was also crucial in the development of the law of global mass surveillance. Since then, the basic insights Slaughter advanced have been taken up by a large literature referred to loosely under the umbrella of 'transnational law'. The terrain of global mass surveillance reveals close links with Slaughter's original iteration.

For Slaughter, binding treaties were no longer at the centrepiece of international law. Instead, Slaughter emphasized the potential of cross-border networks of bureaucrats and professionals to generate policy solutions through informal coordination. Slaughter was especially interested in how the separate branches of government – most importantly executive agencies – can form direct ties with other executive agencies abroad. In the post–Cold War world, she argued, the billiard-ball vision of unitary sovereigns interacting with each other was no longer descriptively accurate. She thus conceptualized states as multiple different organs acting on the international sphere, each able to advance its own foreign policy and to its own goals.

At the centre of this turn was a new (and now very familiar) globalized rhetoric about threats. Threats ostensibly no longer divided states into separate units. The most important policy questions – environment, financial or law enforcement related – came to be understood as implicating multiple stakeholders beyond borders. Counter-terrorism, though not enormously developed in Slaughter's account, fit neatly into this more general picture.[97] It too seemed to demand policies addressing mutual threats and cutting across multiple jurisdictions. In this regard, 9/11 was the truly momentous milestone. As George W. Bush's National Security Advisor Stephen Hadley explained in a 2007 meeting with German partners: 'Threats are global and we need to eliminate barriers to cooperation'.[98]

It may already be evident how the law of global mass surveillance, starting from the 1946 UKUSA agreement, relates to the notion of 'disaggregated sovereignty'. In this strain of post-war law, executive agencies

[96] Ibid.

[97] See in this regard more recently Cian C. Murphy, 'The Dynamics of Transnational Counter-Terrorism Law: Towards a Methodology, Map, and Critique', forthcoming in Jackson and Fabbrini (eds), *Constitutionalism across Borders in the Struggle against Terrorism* (Cheltenham, UK: Edward Elgar, 2015).

[98] See NSA Hadley's Meeting with German Interior Minister Schauble, 6 March 2007, https://wikileaks.org/plusd/cables/07BERLIN457_a.html.

acting quasi-independently are the protagonists. They generate arrangements with their peer executive agencies across borders. They are relatively independent from other branches of government, and possibly even from chief executives at home. Indeed, an alternative genealogy of modern international law, starting with the UKUSA agreement instead of with the UN Charter, exposes the Cold War roots of post–Cold War disaggregated sovereignty. The actual practice of disaggregated sovereignty significantly preceded its labelling and conceptualization in Slaughter's work.

Slaughter emphasized that global interests are advanced not only through discourse, but also through action. An important aspect of this was training and the exchange of technical expertise and technology. All of these came into play in the emergence of mass surveillance as global reality. In all the different contexts Slaughter describes – just like in the surveillance area – 'non-binding' notes and MOUs are favorited instruments. Consider the careful institutional design reflected in the MOU with Israel (described in Section 6.4). The MOU emphasizes internal networked oversight, capacity building, technical assistance and training. Taken together, these aspects of governance realize the various components of Slaughter's vision of 'enforcement networks'. Indeed, Slaughter referred in passing to 'intelligence sharing' as one case in point. She could not anticipate the way intelligence sharing transformed into a law of mass surveillance, but this transformation is intimately related to the legal and political structures she described.

Disaggregated sovereignty is not only about networks, but also about what Slaughter called 'networks of networks'. In the surveillance context, a multi-tiered structure of networks in revealed. Political power is wielded through numerous networks, with various networks having ranging levels of binding force, budgets, as well as different strategic benefits. The multilateral 'Charter' of global mass surveillance – the Five Eyes framework – is one particularly close-knit network. But the Five Eyes framework has multiple connections with other networks. Some of them are additional multilateral networks. Others are bilateral agreements. Disaggregated enforcement occurs not only through new contracts, as emphasized above. Inter-agency contracts are concluded against the backdrop of similar existing ones, furnishing an entire environment. Agencies compete with one another to provide efficient services. Contracting with an agency beyond an existing network may modify relationships with previously active ones.

Slaughter was interestingly cognizant of the potential accountability gap I argued disaggregated sovereignty generates. She therefore developed a theory according to which executive agents have a dual role. They are both accountable to their domestic constituency, and to their international partners: 'officials would have to be able to think at once in terms of the national and the global interest and to sort out the relative priorities of the two on a case-by-case basis'.[99]

Perhaps the latest iteration of the tradition Slaughter established is reflected in Ashley Deeks's important work on 'peer constraints' in the collection of intelligence.[100] Deeks describes transnational checks and balances, in which intelligence agencies mutually impose on each other democratic constraints. My own account is intended as the complementary story, told from a more pessimistic perspective.

6.6 'Law against Law'

One important aspect of Slaughter's disaggregated sovereignty is that it was not only a descriptive model. It also claimed to have normative appeal. Slaughter argued that networked government promotes liberal values and a 'just world order'. At the centre of this normative vision is an understanding of horizontal networks. When state agencies were connected to their partners abroad, working with them to find common solutions to common problems, they 'harmonized' international affairs. Inter-agency cooperation is thus understood as an unqualified good, and defended against potential counter-arguments.

Disaggregated sovereignty, Slaughter believed, would promote opportunities for deliberation for all actors involved in cross-border policy issues; foster active dialogue among governments and government agencies; allow for a space for legitimate *differences* among polities; generate a transnational set of checks and balances checking the power of any particular agency or actor; and require that government functions are not removed from the domestic level – unless specific functions cannot be adequately provided by national institutions.

But I believe disaggregated sovereignty failed to deliver on its promise. The law of global mass surveillance exposes the 'dark side' of disaggregated sovereignty.[101] Slaughter perhaps could not expect the way in which in the sigint-sharing realm, disaggregated networks would produce a kind

99 Slaughter, 'A New World Order', 234.

100 Ashley Deeks, 'Intelligence Communities, Peer Constraints, and the Law'; Ashley Deeks, 'Checks and Balances from Abroad'.

101 Cf. Mann, 'Dialectic of Transnationalism'.

of democratic deficit. National security agencies may act diligently to protect citizens of particular states from terrorism threats. Yet in the disaggregated legal environment, civic participation in crucial decisions about both national security and privacy is systematically eroded.

To be sure, disaggregated sovereignty was an extremely prescient *descriptive* account of the world we live in today. But what becomes clear from the example of the law of global mass surveillance, is that disaggregation is a strategy that was deployed precisely to eschew other legal obligations: those obligations that protect the civic participation of domestic populations and the rule of law. According to Edward Snowden, the NSA has established secret intelligence partnerships with many Western governments. The Foreign Affairs Directorate of the NSA is responsible for these partnerships, which, says the whistle-blower, are organized such that foreign governments can 'insulate their political leaders' from public outrage in the event that these global surveillance partnerships are leaked. The analysis of the MoUs and leaks provided above concretizes the critique, which is most visible in the context of democratic states, such as Germany and Sweden.

Pillay's comments in her report, quoted at the beginning of this chapter, present a powerful starting point for a critique of the disaggregated law of global mass surveillance. The former High Commissioner of Human Rights identified some of the perils of this cooperative, informal model for international law. As Pillay points out, the political and legal infrastructure of mass surveillance is not simply about coordination between security services. It is a strategic mode of coordination designed to overcome legal restrictions, or 'loopholes', as she calls them.

Reminiscent of corporations seeking tax breaks or US extra-territorial prisons, powerful governmental agencies like the NSA and the GCHQ divide their work between different localities. As Pillay writes, states 'outsource surveillance tasks to others'.[102] Such practices have been subject to significant criticism from both human rights and more generally progressive perspectives.

In a disaggregated context, the agendas of national security agencies are largely generated from abroad, not by elected officials. And it cannot be emphasized enough: priorities about security are just as important as priorities about privacy. And it is just as important to think of questions related to the very structure of government, as it is to think of privacy. Consider, e.g., about the separation of powers and the scope of judicial

[102] Pillay, 'The Right to Privacy', 10.

review. It is these doctrines that 'the use of law against law' transforms. This has already been articulated in many states as a matter of domestic constitutional law and of administrative law. To name one example, a lively discussion of the need for transparency and committee oversight has emerged. In international law, the work related to structural changes in government is still limited.[103]

We have seen this dual loyalty to both domestic and transnational constituencies, described in Slaughter's work, demonstrated in the Swedish case above. The executive branch seemed to straddle between its domestic accountability, and the demands of the NSA. But this dual role generates an agency worried above all about its own agency-specific interests, rather than its underlying mandate. Powerful international partners are sometimes given preference in shaping collective political participation outside of their own constituencies.

Indeed, transnational and domestic 'accountability' are *qualitatively* different. Domestic accountability rests on democratic legitimacy. The demands of the NSA, on the other hand, emanate from a global power structure, in which the US has more clout than other counterparts. The latter is not properly a question of legitimacy, accountability or the rule of law. it is a question of relative might, as couched in a contractual language.[104] Slaughter's model of a dual accountability towards a domestic constituency and towards global networks invites a conflation of these two very different registers. The law of mass surveillance heralds a breakdown of domestic checks and balances. The critique of mass surveillance rooted in democratic social contract theory and popular sovereignty is familiar from the US domestic context. We need a similar critique conceptualizing harms to social contracts and popular sovereignty the world over.

In Slaughter's view, a transnational set of checks and balances will help complement domestic checks and balances. This is the aspect of her theory most fully adopted in Deeks's work.[105] Twenty years after Slaughter articulated the 'disaggregated sovereignty' model, and with the paradigm still influential in legal Academic circles, it is high time to reconsider these words. To be fair, the jury is still out if such accountability can be attained

[103] For one example taking on this task to some extent, see Ashley Deeks, 'An International Legal Framework for Surveillance' (2015) 55 *Virginia Journal of International Law* 55.

[104] Think in this context of H. L. A. Hart's classic critique of Austinian positivism: 'law' requires not only a command backed by a sovereign but also obligation. Hart, *The Concept of Law* (Oxford: Oxford University Press, 2012).

[105] Ashley Deeks, 'Intelligence Communities, Peer Constraints, and the Law'; Ashley Deeks, 'Checks and Balances from Abroad'.

in the future. But privacy is only one of many potential aspects of government in which disaggregated sovereignty can have a structural undemocratic effect. Two things are nevertheless clear. One is that the cooperative and horizontal inter-agency processes described in her work were enormously prescient. The other is the corrosive effect they already have on domestic political participation and on the rule of law.

6.7 Conclusion

This chapter sought to provide a descriptive and analytic account of 'the law of global mass surveillance'. By doing so, it offered a critique of a democratic deficit that disaggregated sovereignty generates, and show how it eroded the rule of law.

The account unfolded above diverges from the standard and by now familiar critique of global mass surveillance in international law circles. The latter focuses on violations of privacy, particularly on Article 17 ICCPR. The violation envisioned by this traditional critique is the collection of personal information about a person by a government. The account provided above, however, addressed a wider dynamic that global mass surveillance has generated. At stake is not only the right to exclude others from personal communications. It is the right to partake in the self-government of a *demos*. Global mass surveillance is not only about my control over my email. I may not want others to read my email. But that shouldn't distract me from noticing that to read my email, my government may also have to politically dis-empower its citizens.

National security has traditionally been at the heart of the 'sovereign prerogative'. Democratically inclined commentators have long criticized this prerogative, claiming that it empowers the executive branch and dis-empowers the legislature (or the people). Yet from an international law perspective, this very prerogative – *if it is kept domestic* – is also a protection for political participation. After all, the domestic executive branch is still more accountable towards the domestic population than an executive branch *abroad*.

While this chapter did not seek to advance policy prescriptions responding to this observation, its basic insight might (hopefully) be useful in that task as well. Having some acquaintance with the law of global mass surveillance, policymakers and advocates might not be satisfied with a policy discussion about personal privacy. They may proceed to what I believe is the natural next step: what are the instruments, both in domestic and international law, which can ensure a measure of democratic accountability in national security policies? One long-standing pillar of international law that I believe should be revived and reinterpreted in this context is the principle of self-determination. Traditionally, self-determination is divided to two: external self-determination protects a people from subjugation by another state, and is related to the principle of non-intervention; internal self-determination protects a people within a state from domination by the central government, and is related to the legitimacy of succession. In the digital communications era, we see an intermediate category arising. We must consider when are the people of one state exposed to subjugation by transnational networks. This type of subjugation and the networked self-determination that protects against it is of course not limited to sigint collection, or to the national security sphere. It may pertain to the much broader worlds of transnational governance and soft law. In the emerging multi-polar world, it may be more feasible than ever to respond to it.

7

Legalization in International Environmental Law

JAYE ELLIS*

7.1 Introduction

International environmental law, despite its relative youth, is a vast and complex body of rules and principles, boasting many elaborate and often highly innovative regimes. It gives the appearance of being a highly legalized field. At the same time, there is much evidence of state reluctance to accept constraints in the form of legal obligations to protect the environment. As the ongoing wrangling over the adequacy of commitments to address climate change made by parties to the Paris Agreement indicates, states are hesitant to strengthen their environmental commitments, often citing economic concerns and fears of competition from other, less environmentally friendly states. There may be a large *quantity* of legal rules and institutions in this issue area, but further questions regarding the *quality* of that law are more difficult to answer. Can it be said that states are deploying law to achieve environmental protection obligations, or that they are merely appearing to do so? Or could one go even further and suggest that international environmental law is structured in such a way as to weigh very lightly on states? I argue that states can be seen to avoid legal obligation even as legalization appears to take hold in the field of environmental protection. They do so primarily through reliance on three strategies: extra-legal deferral; forum shopping; and approaches to regime design that produce inefficiency.

States have been very careful in their approach to the development of international environmental law, leaving themselves room to manoeuvre by crafting a plethora of self-contained, highly specialized regimes in which generally applicable rules of law have little purchase. Central to this

* I would like to thank Tanja Aalberts, Thomas Gammeltoft-Hansen, Claire Stockwell and the anonymous reviewers for their extremely useful feedback and comments on earlier drafts. I am grateful to Boris Kozulin and Erica Sanders for their research assistance. This project benefitted from the support of the Social Sciences and Humanities Council and l'Agence nationale pour la recherche française (ANR-12-GLOB-0001-03 CIRCULEX).

approach has been the creation of decision-making processes within and alongside regimes in which legal reasoning plays a relatively minor role. Tanja Aalberts and Thomas Gammeltoft-Hansen describe this as extra-legal deferral, in which conflicts are deemed to fall partly or entirely outside the boundaries of law, requiring forms of expertise other than legal for their resolution.[1] In the field of environment, deferral to knowledge systems beyond the law is not generally made explicit; law and legality continue to be evoked, and appear to play a fundamental role in international environmental regimes. But if we look more closely at the norms within environmental regimes, we see that they take the form either of very general statements of principle or objectives, on the one hand, and highly specific, technical standards on the other. The former give broad latitude to decision makers to craft solutions to problems that are context-specific and informed by a range of expertise; the latter are not suitable to the application of legal reasoning, and represent a high degree of deference to scientific authority. Seen in this light, the dependence of environmental regimes on expertise other than legal can be seen as a means of demonstrating commitment to environmental objectives while avoiding enmeshment in legal norms whose development states control and influence only partially.

Within international environmental law, the apparent increase of legalization can in fact be understood as a rise of managerialism. As Martti Koskenniemi has argued, managerial regimes place heavy emphasis on problem solving in a highly contextual setting in which non-legal expertise is deferred to and legal rules play little role.[2] This is, I argue, central to the strategy of states as they construct environmental regimes while at the same time resisting the constraint of legal obligation. As Koskenniemi notes, managerialism is also characterized by a focus on material objectives: environmental or human rights protection, promotion of free trade, protection of intellectual property.[3] When, as inevitably occurs, these various objectives are in tension with one another, the rules within each regime cannot readily be called upon to address these tensions. This

1 Chapter 1, this volume.

2 Martti Koskenniemi, 'Constitutionalism as Mindset: Reflections on Kantian Themes about International Law and Globalization' (2007) 8(1) *Theoretical Inquiries in Law* 9–36; Martti Koskenniemi, 'International Legislation Today: Limits and Possibilities' (2005) 23 *Wisconsin International Law Journal* 61–92.

3 Martti Koskenniemi, 'Formalism, Fragmentation, Freedom: Kantian Themes in Today's International Law' (2007) 4 *No Foundations* 7–28; Koskenniemi, 'International Legislation Today'; Koskenniemi, 'Constitutionalism as Mindset'.

promotes engagement with a second strategy, namely forum shopping: if a party seeks to promote the rights of a patent holder, it would be unwise to seek to resolve a dispute within a human rights regime – not because the decision maker would be unable to interpret applicable intellectual property law, but because within a human rights regime, the pursuit of human rights will trump patent protection.[4]

This leads us to consideration of a third strategy: inefficiency. Gammeltoft-Hansen and Aalberts refer to the incomplete and uneven influence of legalization in the international legal system, indicating the existence of 'blind spots, gaps, and inefficiencies'.[5] The sheer quantity of environmental norms and instruments, and number of environmental regimes, speak against environment as a blind spot or gap, but interesting questions stand to be addressed regarding the constraining nature of environmental law. I argue that the inefficiency of international environmental law can be analyzed as a matter of design, that is, a strategy in its own right from which attention is deflected by the heavy investment of states in negotiating and concluding multilateral environmental agreements.

I begin with a framing discussion of legalization as conceived by the scholars who coined the term. I then present a brief account of the trajectory of international environmental law, focusing on early developments in the law of state responsibility and the series of environmental and sustainable development summits that have been held periodically since 1972 before turning my attention to sectoral environmental regimes, including fisheries conservation and management regimes and the United Nations climate change regime. Of particular interest within these regimes are the role of scientific bodies tasked with providing expert advice to the decision-making authority within the regime on one hand, and of compliance mechanisms, which may be seen to be the functional equivalent of adjudication on the other. Interestingly, both of these features are present in the World Trade Organization's Agreement on the Application of Sanitary and Phytosanitary Measures (SPS Agreement) as well, but function differently and play different roles. I then conclude with some reflections

[4] Andreas Fischer-Lescano and Gunther Teubner examine a series of international disputes which they argue can be characterized in different fashions, including as collisions between international regimes. They analyze a dispute between Brazil and the US regarding patents on drugs used to treat patients with AIDS as 'an institutional *conflict between the policies of two international organizations*': the WTO and the WTO. Andreas Fischer-Lescano and Gunther Teubner, 'Regime-Collisions: The Vain Search for Legal Unity in the Fragmentation of Global Law' (2004) 25 *Michigan Journal of International Law* 999–1046, at 1024ff.

[5] Chapter 1, this volume.

on the interactions between science and politics, and a potential role for law in structuring these interactions.

7.2 Legalization: Engagement and Avoidance

The phenomenon of legalization, as analyzed in this volume, is an essentially empirical phenomenon: the 'normative thickening and expansion of law' which generates, or perhaps is accompanied by, a less visible counter-movement that takes the form of a series of strategies to avoid one potential consequence of this expansion, namely increasing constraints on states' margin of manoeuvre. My analysis of legalization in the field of environment has led me to observe that states seem to be operating on the basis of a narrow set of assumptions regarding the nature and role of law, assumptions that are well captured by a different take on legalization, presented by Kenneth Abbott, Robert O. Keohane, Andrew Moravcsik, Anne-Marie Slaughter and Duncan Snidal in 2000.[6] Legal scholars commenting on this work at the time of its publication often noted how different their own understandings of law's structure and function were from the concept of legalization as developed in the analyses conducted by Abbott et al.[7] Yet their understanding of legalization bears a striking resemblance to the recent development of international environmental law. What makes this resemblance so interesting is that, at the same time, key design features of this emerging body of law seem destined to *avoid* or *reduce* constraint, rather than enhance it. Central to this complex undertaking, I argue, is deference to expertise, notably scientific expertise – but only up to a certain point. Environmental issues are treated as highly material, largely technical matters; a largely instrumental approach to law is taken; and environmental disputes are cast as problems that are best addressed in an ad hoc, context-dependent and expert-driven manner rather than in light of general rules and generalizable conclusions about their interpretation and application. In this manner, legal rules and the institutions responsible for their interpretation and application end up having relatively little purchase.

The strategies deployed to avoid the constraint of legal rules in the field of environment are thrown into relief when international

[6] The centrepiece of the edition is Kenneth W. Abbott et al., 'The Concept of Legalization' (2000) 54(03) *International Organization* 401–19.

[7] See e.g. Martha Finnemore and Stephen Toope, 'Alternatives to "Legalization": Richer Views of Law and Politics' (2001) 55(03) *International Organization* 743–58.

environmental law is contrasted with another highly technical, expert-driven sub-field, namely trade law, and more in particular the SPS Agreement. This agreement is relevant to the present discussion for four main reasons. First, as noted, SPS measures and the agreement that governs them are highly dependent on expert, particularly scientific, input. Second, the SPS Agreement is, like international environmental law, an excellent example of legalization. Third, it is no exaggeration to describe the SPS Agreement as an environmental agreement, in that it has significant implications for environmental law and governance. Fourth, the SPS Agreement differs from international environmental law in one important respect: it is highly constraining. Many of the strategies that states employ to embrace legalization while holding the constraint of legal obligation at bay are not apparent in the SPS regime.

Abbott et al.'s exploration of legalization begins, naturally enough, with H. L. A. Hart's *The Concept of Law*. In that work, Hart described his task as being to 'isolate and characterize a central set of elements which form a common part of the answer' to three questions: '[h]ow does law differ from and how is it related to orders backed by threats? How does law differ from, and how is it related to, moral obligation? What are rules and to what extent is law an affair of rules?'[8] Abbott et al. have a different set of objectives: having observed the increased prevalence of a particular phenomenon in international institutions, and furthermore, having noted that this phenomenon has more purchase in some domains than others, they seek explanations. They ask:

> Why and when do states choose legalized institutional forms when their autonomy would be less constrained by avoiding legalization? How do legalized constraints operate to change government behavior, if they do? Are efforts to legalize certain issue-areas in world politics realistic attempts to facilitate cooperation or misguided attempts to construct a stable order on the basis of fragile norms rather than the realities of power politics?[9]

Whereas Hart explores what makes law *law*, Abbot et al. are interested in the extent to which, and the conditions under which, law causes changes in state behaviour. To the extent that it does, states can pursue legalization as a strategy to achieve their ends. Abbott *et al.* seem to assume that legalization – and, by extension, law – have to do with the imposition of more, and more effective, constraints upon actors. Hart's three categories of secondary rules – rules of recognition, rules for change and rules for

[8] H. L. A. Hart, *The Concept of Law*, 2nd edn (Oxford: Oxford University Press, 1997).
[9] J. O. Goldstein et al., 'Introduction: Legalization and World Politics' (2000) 54(03) *International Organization* 385–99.

adjudication – are recast by Abbott et al. as obligation, precision and delegation. The emphasis shifts from law to rules – from the concept of law as a system to law as a series of rules imposing behavioural constraints.

7.2.1 *Forum Shopping: (Non)-Adjudication of Environmental Norms*

Recent developments in international environmental law exhibit all three phenomena – obligation, precision and delegation – while at the same time indicating efforts to avoid constraint. One way in which these two apparently contradictory goals are pursued is through resistance to the development, notably through interpretation and application, of the body of general environmental norms, that is, norms of general application to environmental disputes that are in turn embedded in the overarching system of international law. International environmental law is a highly fragmented body of law, featuring a range of issue- and region-specific regimes with very little connective tissue running between them. Nor have environmental norms had much purchase in other fields of international law, though efforts have been made to bring such norms to bear in fields such as trade law and human rights.[10] Fragmentation provides fertile ground for the apparent embrace but actual avoidance of legal obligation.[11] This is the result of the convergence of two phenomena: the reluctance of states to submit environmental disputes to adjudication, and the tendency for specialized regimes to interpret legal norms through the lens of the material objective – free trade, investment protection, human rights – that they were designed to pursue.[12] As a result, states are likely to feel confident that

[10] One such example is the invocation by the European Communities of the precautionary principle in the *Hormones* case: *EC – Hormones (European Communities – Measures affecting the Approval and Marketing of Biotech Products*, Reports of the Panel, WT/DS291/R; WT/DS292/R; WT/DS293/R, 2006). Some headway has been made to address the human rights aspects of environmental protection in the European Union, but much less progress has been made internationally. Alan E. Boyle, 'Human Rights and the Environment: Where Next?' (2012) 23 *European Journal of International Law* 613.

[11] For an analysis of self-contained regimes and fragmentation, see Wouter Werner, 'The Politics of Expertise: Applying Paradoxes of Scientific Expertise to International Law', in Monika Ambrus and others (eds), *The Role of Experts in International and European Decision-Making Processes* (Cambridge: Cambridge University Press, 2014), particularly at 65ff.; International Law Commission, *Fragmentation of International Law: Difficulties Arising from the Diversification and Expansion of International Law*, Report of the Study Group of the International Law Commission, A/CN.4/L.682 (2006).

[12] This phenomenon has been analyzed from different perspectives by Martti Koskenniemi (Koskenniemi, 'Formalism, Fragmentation, Freedom'; Koskenniemi, 'Constitutionalism as Mindset'; Koskenniemi, 'International Legislation Today') and Andreas Fischer-Lescano and Gunther Teubner, 'Regime Collisions'.

they can submit disputes to adjudication with little risk of environmental norms being deemed relevant and brought to bear.

There are some interesting and instructive counter-examples in which states have presented claims regarding environmental degradation and have argued both regime-specific and general rules and principles of international environmental law; furthermore, the adjudicatory bodies in two recent cases have not sought to bracket the environmental aspects of the dispute nor to conclude that procedural and substantive rules of environmental law are not relevant or applicable.[13] The small number of counter-examples and their recent vintage make the drawing of conclusions difficult, but the possibility that states, international regimes, and international adjudicatory bodies could learn to work with environmental obligations and to perceive the potential benefits of the constraints they impose ought to be taken seriously. At present, however, the dearth of environmental adjudication and the tendency of specialized adjudicatory bodies to treat environmental law as relevant to disputes appearing before them continue as dominant trends. States' confidence in the lack of interest in and engagement with environmental norms by other states and by adjudicatory bodies is likely warranted at the present time, but we may be witnessing some interesting deviations that could prove to be game-changing.

7.2.2 *Extra-Legal Deferral: Expertise as Legitimation and Excuse*

Fragmentation creates an opportunity for the deployment of another strategy, namely extra-legal deferral. As is often the case, this strategy takes

[13] Three of the most interesting cases are *EC – Hormones*, *Pulp Mills* (International Court of Justice, *Pulp Mills on the River Uruguay* (*Argentina v. Uruguay*), 20 April 2010), and *South China Sea* (In the matter of the South China Sea Arbitration before an arbitral tribunal constituted under Annex VII to the 1982 United Nations Convention on the Law of the Sea, PCA Case N° 2013–19 [*Republic of the Philippines v. People's Republic of China*], 12 July 2016). In all three cases, one party to the dispute invested heavily in environmental arguments and explicitly invoked environmental rules and principles. Clearly, these parties saw the risk of the further development of environmental normativity, and, as a potential consequence, its increased constraining capacity, as a risk worth taking. In *Pulp Mills* and *South China Sea*, while one can certainly dispute the interpretations or the conclusions, the adjudicator placed heavy emphasis on environmental norms and reached conclusions regarding their interpretation and application that have great potential to contribute to understandings of the norms' content.

The third case, *Hormones*, is a textbook case of fragmentation. The WTO Appellate Body, invited by the European Communities to consider the precautionary principle as a customary legal rule, concluded that its status as a customary rule of *environmental* law could be contemplated, but that it was clearly not a customary rule of *international* law. Citations to numerous sources do not support this distinction between international *environmental* law and *international* law *tout court*.

a slightly different form in the environmental context, but with similar results as concerns avoidance of the constraint of legal obligation. Extra-legal deferral is closely allied with forum shopping in this context, as both strategies are grounded in the instrumental, objective-driven approach increasingly taken by international regimes. Whereas forum shopping is based on an assumption that disputes can find a safe haven – an adjudicatory body that will not rely heavily on environmental norms – extra-legal deferral involves the exclusion of environmental considerations by reason of their scientific, technical – read non-legal – characteristics. As Martti Koskenniemi's concept of managerialism has so clearly demonstrated, legal regimes can simultaneously embrace and exclude law through a patina of normativity over deference to expertise. That environmental law is heavily engaged with scientific, economic and a range of other expertise should not give cause for concern – quite the contrary. The field depends on a range of inputs. But international environmental norms are often framed, or interpreted, as not merely incorporating but waiting on such input. The independence of legal norms from substantive input can be difficult to discern: the substance often remains to be completed by processes of generation of expert knowledge, and the legitimation of such norms often depends to an unhealthy extent on the authority of substantive expertise, rather than the legitimacy of political and legal authority or the validity of legal rules.

As noted above, environmental regimes are increasingly fragmented and issue-specific, and legal norms are framed in highly instrumental terms: rather than aiming at overarching objectives such as fairness, consistency, reasonableness or stability, they are at the service of the regime's objectives. In this manner, the formation and interpretation of legal rules comes to depend on substantive expertise relevant to the sub-field in which the regime operates and the goals which the regime has been formed to pursue. Koskenniemi describes this as deformalization: the retreat of law to procedures and directives to experts, whose task it is to do the real work of problem solving within the regime.[14] Deference to expertise sharply limits the space for legal analysis, but it also deflects attention away from the political aims that are being pursued through regimes. To present decision making within these regimes as essentially political is dangerous; after all, they are meant to govern the behaviour of sovereign states. What remains is the authority of science: given the nature of environmental degradation and of measures to mitigate it, scientific contributions to environmental law and politics are essential. But

[14] Koskenniemi, 'Constitutionalism as Mindset', 13.

as we will see below, states, through their adherence to environmental regimes, do not submit to the conclusions of scientific experts; they retain decision-making power. This is ultimately a dangerous strategy: states often emphasize uncertainty in scientific knowledge to justify decisions that do not closely reflect such knowledge, which can leave decisions open to the charge of arbitrariness and, ultimately, could erode confidence in science as a basis for environmental decision making.

As Wouter Werner has argued, international environmental law is one of the 'functional sub-fields' within international law in which 'legal norms can often only be applied on the basis of scientific expert knowledge'.[15] Many of the legal rules in this field cannot be made to appear to be doing the work of the decision maker: they are too obviously indeterminate, leaving significant leeway to decision makers to choose the outcome that they prefer. Political decision makers rarely wish to absorb the responsibility for decisions on highly technical matters, so experts are called in to present cases based on scientific data and cost-benefit analysis.[16] It has, however, become quite obvious to even casual observers that choices made on the basis of political preferences and values are not thereby eliminated. Besides, political authorities cannot defer to experts for long without being accused of promoting technocracy. The result, as Jan Klabbers describes it, is oscillation between politics and expertise.[17] It has not always been thus, however. As we shall see below, when environmental protection first earned a place on the international agenda, law was seen as central to its pursuit.

7.3 Trajectory of International Environmental Law

Two important streams in the development of international environmental law will be explored here: first, efforts to adapt the general framework of state responsibility to the phenomenon of environmental degradation, particularly at the International Law Commission; and second, the environmental and sustainable development summits that identified broad objectives for environmental protection and articulated sweeping plans to

15 Werner, 'The Politics of Expertise'.

16 Jan Klabbers, 'The Virtues of Expertise', in Monika Ambrus and others (eds), *The Role of Experts in International and European Decision-Making Processes* (Cambridge: Cambridge University Press, 2014), 85.

17 Jan Klabbers, 'Of Round Pegs and Square Holes: International Law and the Private Sector', in Paulius Jurčys, Poul F. Kjaer and Ren Yatsunami (eds), *Regulatory Hybridization in the Transnational Sphere* (Leiden, Netherlands: Martinus Nijhoff, 2013), Section 5.3.

meet those objectives. Following both these streams, we observe that law was central in the 1970s when environmental protection was inscribed on the international agenda, but has gradually been eclipsed. It remains superficially important in the complex administrative regimes that now dominate the landscape, but, as we will see in the next section, there too it has ceded ground to expert-based policy.

7.3.1 *State Responsibility: Work of the International Law Commission*

To what extent do we observe the phenomenon of legalization in international environmental law? During the early days of international environmental law, private law models and structures were highly influential, and remained predominant as states began building up a huge body of multilateral environmental agreements and international administrative regimes. At the same time, work was ongoing on the articulation of international environmental principles which could serve as a common normative framework for the body of law as a whole. But as environmental regimes became more highly specialized and elaborate, forms of expertise other than legal came to predominate, notably science and economics.[18]

Between roughly 1960 and 1980, jurists worked to adapt private law institutions of contract, tort or delict, nuisance or *bon voisinage* and property to the society of states, seeking to develop legal bases upon which states could be held responsible for pollution and other environmental threats that emerged on their territory,[19] even when – as is almost always the case – the environmental harm could not be directly attributed to the state.[20] Dicta in the *Island of Palmas*[21] and *Corfu Channel*[22] cases in which the state is described as possessing, in virtue of the authority that it wields over its territory and population, obligations to prevent harm to its neighbours from arising on its territory were recast as the foundation for obligations to prevent trans-boundary environmental harm. The new interest in trans-boundary environmental damage led to a growing interest in

18 The importance of economic expertise to international environmental regimes is great; however, the focus of the present discussion will be on scientific expertise.

19 Klabbers, 'Round Pegs'.

20 See e.g. L. F. E. Goldie, 'Liability for Damage and the Progressive Development of International Law' (1965) 14(04) *International & Comparative Law Quarterly* 1189–264; C. Wilfred Jenks, 'Liability for Ultra-Hazardous Activities in International Law' (1966) 117 *RCADI* 99.

21 *Island of Palmas Case (Netherlands/United States)* (1928), 2 RIAA 829.

22 *Corfu Channel Case (United Kingdom/Albania)* [1949] ICJ Rep. 4.

liability, obligations of result, responsibility for causing risk and related notions. Huge efforts were devoted over this period, notably by the International Law Commission (ILC), to the development of a general body of norms to address trans-boundary environmental harm,[23] but a number of obstacles proved insurmountable. These included state will: the notion that a state might be liable for damage due to the sub-standard nature of its environmental protection law and policy was unpalatable even to industrialized states with reasonably robust environmental protection frameworks. Beyond that, however, there were genuine difficulties whose sources lay, in part, in the nature of environmental damage itself.[24] The fact that the most environmental harm is caused by private individuals whose acts are not attributable to the state also gives rise to difficulties. The responsibility of states must thus be grounded on the breach of a separate set of obligations, along the lines sketched out in *Island of Palmas*, *Corfu Channel*, and *Trail Smelter*,[25] relating to the proper exercise of sovereignty to protect the interests of other states, which, by the 1970s, were understood to include their interest in a healthy environment. However, confidence in the capacity of legal institutions structured along private law lines soon waned, and attention turned to the construction of highly complex administrative regimes such as those devoted to systemic threats such as ozone layer depletion and global climate change. These regimes, geared towards the achievement of environmental or ecosystem protection, were preceded by often highly institutionalized international regimes for the management of shared resources, particularly in the areas

23 The centre of activity was the instrument that had initially been intended to articulate liability without fault for trans-boundary environmental harm or certain categories thereof, but which, in its final form, restated the obligation of means to prevent trans-boundary harm and a series of procedural obligations: International Law Commission, Draft articles on Prevention of Transboundary Harm from Hazardous Activities, 2001. A companion text, the Draft principles on the Allocation of Loss in the case of Transboundary Harm arising out of Hazardous Activities, 2006, provides for the channelling of liability to private operators. See A. E. Boyle, 'Globalising Environmental Liability: The Interplay of National and International Law' (2005) 17 *Journal of Environmental Law* 3–26; Julio Barboza, *The Environment, Risk and Liability in International Law* (Leiden, Netherlands: Martinus Nijhoff, 2011).

24 These include the temporal and spatial scales over which environmental impacts are felt; the difficulty of detecting these impacts and understanding their causes; the beneficial aspects of acts and activities that set environmental degradation into motion; and the difficulties of coming to terms with 'nature' as dynamic and even chaotic rather than static. Kerry H. Whiteside, *Precautionary Politics: Principle and Practice in Confronting Environmental Risk* (Cambridge, MA: MIT Press, 2006).

25 *Trail Smelter Arbitration (United States/Canada)* (1931–41), 3 RIAA 1905.

of fisheries and shared watercourses.[26] Following this turn to regime-building, international environmental law is no longer predominantly based on private law;[27] it is now largely administrative law, increasingly characterized by managerialism. Before turning to international environmental regimes, however, consideration will be given to the series of environmental and sustainable developments convened by the United Nations beginning in 1972 that ran parallel to the ILC's efforts to articulate generally applicable environmental rules.

7.3.2 *The Environmental Summits*

The first two environmental summits, Stockholm 1972 and Rio 1992, resulted in declarations which contained provisions setting out a series of principles, along with much longer texts, the Stockholm Action Plan for the Human Environment and Rio's Agenda 21, which lay out a broad and ambitious series of objectives and the steps required to attain them. The declarations are not legally binding, but in form and content they resemble legal norms, and they have been regularly invoked in discussions and negotiations in subsequent decades over the development of international environmental law. The relevance of law is further flagged by numerous references in these documents to the need for the development of legal norms and institutions.[28]

The picture changed dramatically at the 2002 summit in Johannesburg. The means identified at this summit to pursue sustainable development include collaboration, investment, research, capacity building and the pursuit of good governance, while law and legal institutions receive very little attention. At Rio +20 in 2012, the declaratory form was foregone altogether, and the product, *The Future We Want*, is a lengthy and highly

[26] The International Commission of the Northwest Atlantic Fisheries was founded in 1949 and the North-East Atlantic Fisheries Commission in 1959. The Danube Commission was created in 1948; its predecessor, the European Danube Commission, was established in 1856. The International Joint Commission was created in 1909.

[27] Klabbers, 'Round Pegs'.

[28] In Agenda 21, there is a heavy emphasis on policy development, but attention turns to law at a number of points in the document. Chapter 39 is devoted entirely to 'legal instruments and mechanisms'. In addition, chapters on the integration of sustainable development into decision-making and on international institutional arrangements contain sections on legal and regulatory frameworks. Law is central to all the activities that are identified for the pursuit of the objectives outlined in the chapter. Law comes to the fore in the chapters on toxic chemicals and radioactive waste, not surprisingly; it also receives attention in chapters on human rights and on business and industry.

ambitious plan of action which avoids reference to rights, obligations or standards except in oblique ways. Terms such as 'law' or 'legislation' appear infrequently, usually in reference to the need to respect national and international law; the term of choice is 'policy'.

Already in Agenda 21 one can discern some uncertainty regarding the role of law, despite its prominence in that document. In the chapters on particular sectors or environmental media, the emphasis is on policy rather than legal development. Chapters devoted to law and to legal institutions, respectively, indicate a conviction that they are important, while at the same time conveying uncertainty as to how they could be deployed – or perhaps a reluctance to be too specific about their deployment. By 2002, the main mechanism for achieving sustainable development came to be understood to be economic policies. By 2012, environmental protection appeared as one part of a vast agenda, best pursued in an indirect manner through a variety of avenues as indicated in paragraph 4 of the document:

> We recognize that poverty eradication, changing unsustainable and promoting sustainable patterns of consumption and production, and protecting and managing the natural resource base of economic and social development are the overarching objectives of and essential requirements for sustainable development. We also reaffirm the need to achieve sustainable development by: promoting sustained, inclusive and equitable economic growth, creating greater opportunities for all, reducing inequalities, raising basic standards of living; fostering equitable social development and inclusion; and promoting integrated and sustainable management of natural resources and ecosystems that supports inter alia economic, social and human development while facilitating ecosystem conservation, regeneration and restoration and resilience in the face of new and emerging challenges.

With the adoption of such an ambitious set of objectives, the stage is set for a move to managerialism.

7.4 International Environmental Regimes: From Legalization to Managerialism

In this section, legalization and managerialism will serve as frameworks for an analysis of two features of international environmental regimes, namely the reliance on scientific expertise, and the development of compliance mechanisms as functional equivalents to adjudication. These features of regimes are suggested by a legalization analysis: while the (legally binding) provisions of international environmental conventions and protocols often lack precision, the appendices and annexes in which sector-specific environmental standards are set out are often very precise, and highly technical. As for delegation, this occurs in a modest way within environmental regimes through two main avenues: first, through a division of labour between expertise and political authority within regimes, with expert bodies investigating various policy issues and providing recommendations to decision-making bodies within regimes; and second, through compliance mechanisms through which instances of alleged non-compliance with the regime's obligations can be investigated and addressed. As I will argue below, these features of environmental regimes can also be understood to be driven by the managerial mind-set. States can at one and the same time subject themselves to rules designed to constrain their behaviour in the furtherance of environmental protection goals (legalization) and manage the substance and application of those rules (managerialism). States cannot altogether avoid the turn to law in the field of environmental protection, but they do have opportunities to limit the constraining effect of legal obligation.

7.4.1 Scientific Expertise in Environmental Regimes

Environmental regimes tend to share a common structure. The central decision-making organ consists of representatives of the parties. A fairly parsimonious statement of principles or objectives is accompanied by processes through which decisions on more detailed measures are to be taken in pursuit of those principles or objectives. Much of the work within these regimes is accomplished through the adoption of often highly technical measures and standards based, to varying degrees, on scientific input provided by bodies of experts responsible for scientific advice and recommendations. In some of the newer regimes, expert bodies are heavily involved in decision making. For example, under the Stockholm Convention on Persistent Organic Pollutants, a Persistent Organic Pollutants Review Committee is tasked with examining proposals for the listing of substances and proposing measures to manage the risks posed by those substances.[29] The final decision on listing is made by the COP by consensus or, failing that, by a three-quarters majority;[30] however, parties may opt out of the decision.[31]

[29] The Committee is created in virtue of Art. 6 of the Stockholm Convention on Persistent Organic Pollutants (Stockholm 2001), and its mandate outlined in Art. 8. The Committee is responsible for applying a set of screening criteria (Annex D), preparing a draft risk profile (Annex E), making a determination on the risk posed by a substance to human health and environment (Art. 8(7)(a)) and preparing a risk management evaluation (Arts 8(9); 21(1–3) and 22).

[30] Stockholm Convention, Art. 19(6)(c).

[31] Stockholm Convention, Art. 22(3)(b).

In older conventions, such as the Convention on International Trade in Endangered Species (CITES), adopted in 1973, the process by which species came to be listed as threatened with extinction and therefore subject to trade restrictions was initially much looser, being left largely to the discretion of the parties.[32] Once scientific committees were created, in 1987, their role was left rather open-ended, with emphasis on providing scientific information generally rather than preparing proposals for listing of species for protection.[33] In 1994, criteria were adopted for the drafting of listing proposals that required much greater attention to scientific evidence,[34] though decisions on listing remain in the hands of the Conference of the Parties.[35]

Fisheries commissions provide further examples of the extent to which states have retained a free hand in the adoption of measures, in this case total allowable catch, the distribution of quotas among member states, and other conservation and management measures. The language in the conventions respecting the role of scientific advice in decision making is very general, obliging fisheries commissions to take account of, or make decisions on the basis of, such advice.[36] In each case, however,

32 Thomas Gehring and Eva Ruffing, 'When Arguments Prevail over Power: The CITES Procedure for Listing of Endangered Species' (2008) 8 *Global Environmental Politics* 123–48.

33 Report of the Sixth Meeting of the Conference of the Parties to the Convention on International Trade in Endangered Species (Ottawa 1987). The current structure, an Animals Committee and a Plant Committee, was adopted much later: Resolution Conf. 11.1, Meeting of the Conference the Parties to CITES, Gigiri, Kenya, 10–20 April 2000. See P. H. Sand, 'Whither CITES? The Evolution of a Treaty Regime in the Borderland of Trade and Environment' (1997) 8 *European Journal of International Law* 29–58, at 8.

34 Fort Lauderdale Criteria, CITES Conf. 9.4, revised CoP 14, 1994. See Gehring and Ruffing, 'When Arguments Prevail over Power', 130; Shaun A. Goho, 'Note: The CITES Fort Lauderdale Criteria: The Uses and Limits of Science in International Conservation Decisionmaking' (2000–2001) 114 *Harvard Law Review* 1769–92, at 1781ff.

35 Decisions are made by two-thirds majority (CITES, Art. XV(2)(g)), subject to reservations by states (CITES, Art. XV(3)).

Thomas Gehring and Eva Ruffing argue that the regime assigns a major role to the convention's Secretariat, which is responsible for receiving state proposals, gathering further information from other states and from expert bodies, elaborating proposals, and making recommendations to parties: Gehring and Ruffing, at 124. It is true that the Secretariat is heavily implicated in the process and has an enormous amount of influence over the shape the proposal, and scientific evidence in support of it, will take. But states remain free to go their own way when the proposal comes to a vote.

36 The Convention on Future Multilateral Cooperation in North-East Atlantic Fisheries (London 1980), Art. 4 requires the Commission to 'ensure that [its] recommendations are based on the best scientific evidence available'. The Convention on the Conservation and Management of Fisheries Resources in the South East Atlantic Ocean (Windhoek 2001) calls for measures to be 'based on the best scientific evidence available' (Art. 3(a)). The Northwest Atlantic Fisheries Convention (Ottawa 1979) calls upon the Commission to

decision-making authority resides with the commission, made up of representatives of the parties. In many instances, decision making is by majority or qualified majority voting;[37] in others, by consensus,[38] with a procedure for opting out of adopted measures[39] which is resorted to not infrequently.[40]

That states are unwilling to delegate decision making to scientific experts or to otherwise constrain themselves to follow scientific advice in the making of decisions on environmental protection and resource conservation issues might seem unremarkable. States naturally wish to maintain a free hand, and not for altogether cynical reasons: the scientific community is not the only source of knowledge relevant to the making of decisions which have significant social, economic and often cultural impacts. However, there is an interesting counter-example of the division of labour between expertise and political authority under the SPS Agreement to which we will turn following an examination of adjudication in international environmental law.

7.4.2 *Adjudication and Compliance*

For Abbott et al., adjudication is significant, implying as it does a loss or at least diminution of control by states over outcomes of decision-making processes. There is very little litigation of environmental disputes before

'take into account' scientific information and advice (Art. XI(2)). Slightly stronger language is found in the Convention on the Conservation of Antarctic Marine Living Resources (1980): the Commission is to 'take full account of the recommendations and advice of the Scientific Committee': CCAMLR, Art. IX(4).

It is often noted that scientific advice appears to be disregarded or discounted by fisheries commissions: see, for example, Tim Daw and Tim Gray, 'Fisheries Science and Sustainability in International Policy: A Study of Failure in the European Union's Common Fisheries Policy' (2005) 29 *Marine Policy* 189.

[37] Northwest Atlantic Fisheries Convention, Art. XIV(2); North-East Atlantic Fisheries Convention, Art. 5; Agreement for the Establishment of the General Fisheries Commission for the Mediterranean, 1997, Art. V.

[38] Convention on the Conservation and Management of Fisheries Resources in the South East Atlantic Ocean, Art. XII(1).

[39] Convention on the Conservation and Management of Fisheries Resources in the South East Atlantic Ocean, Art. IX(6); Convention on Future Multilateral Cooperation in North-East Atlantic Fisheries, Art. 12; Agreement for the Establishment of the General Fisheries Commission for the Mediterranean, Art. V.

[40] The European Union famously opted out of the measure assigning its quota of 13 per cent of the total allowable catch in 1995, unilaterally assigning itself a quota of 70 per cent. Derrick M. Kedziora, 'Gunboat Diplomacy in the Northwest Atlantic: The 1995 Canada-EU Fishing Dispute and the United Nations Agreement on Straddling and High Migratory Fish Stocks' (1996) 17 *Northwest Journal of International Law and Business* 1132–62.

adjudicative bodies and, if one excludes cases not heard on the merits,[41] the number dwindles even further.[42] It has been argued that environmental disputes are difficult for generalist courts to address, given their often highly technical nature, but the creation of an environmental chamber of the International Court of Justice, which went at least some distance to address this concern, has been wound down after having seen no disputes submitted to it. While it is true that three cases with an environmental component have been adjudicated on their merits before the ICJ since the late 1990s,[43] it is hard to know whether this can be seen as a trend.

One could explain the lack of adjudication by reference to a trend towards the creation of implementation and compliance mechanisms within environmental regimes.[44] Arguments can be made that environmental degradation is not well suited to adversarial adjudicative processes in which general, formal rules are applied by judges or arbitrators possessing little or no scientific expertise, and that the main point

41 These include as preliminary motions: *Southern Bluefin Tuna Cases* (*New Zealand v. Japan; Australia v. Japan*), nos 3 & 4, 27 August 1999; *MOX Plant Case* (*Ireland v. United Kingdom*), no. 10, 3 December 2001; denial of jurisdiction: *Fisheries Jurisdiction Case (Spain/Canada)* [1998] ICJ Rep. 432; and findings that avoid consideration of arguments regarding responsibility for environmental harm: *Nuclear Test Cases (Australia/France; New Zealand/France)* [1974] ICJ Rep. 253.

42 There are important international cases, such as *Island of Palmas* and *Corfu Channel*, which have no environmental component to them but which are heavily relied on to ground state obligations respecting environmental protection, but my argument centres on the unwillingness of states to submit environmental disputes to adjudication.

43 International Court of Justice, *Case Concerning the Gabčíkovo-Nagymaros Project* (*Hungary/Slovakia*), Judgment of 25 September 1997; *Pulp Mills*, and International Court of Justice, *Whaling in the Antarctic* (*Australia v. Japan*: New Zealand intervening), 31 March 2014. In *Gabčíkovo*, while environmental damage was not central to the dispute, it did play a role, and gave the Court the opportunity to discuss environmental principles. As for *Whaling*, while it did not turn on the ecosystemic implications of Japan's whaling programme, it was nevertheless an important decision for environmental law in that it speaks to the relationship between scientific and legal justifications for action. One could also mention two requests for provisional measures before the International Tribunal for the Law of the Sea: *Bluefin Tuna Cases* (no. 38); *MOX Plant Case*.

The environmental aspects of the *South China Sea Arbitration* were also considered on their merits by an arbitral tribunal composed of renowned experts on the law of the sea and international environmental law, suggesting that barriers to international environmental litigation may be descending if not coming down altogether.

44 The best-known examples of such mechanisms are the pioneering Non-Compliance Procedure adopted by the parties to the Montréal Protocol on Substances that deplete the Ozone Layer (Montréal 1987) at their eighth meeting in 1998 (Decision X/10, adopted in virtue of art. 8 of the Protocol), and the Compliance Committee, established in 2005 by the parties to the Kyoto Protocol to the United Nations Framework Convention on Climate Change (Kyoto 1998), in virtue of art. 18 of the Protocol (Decision 27/CMP 1).

of compliance with environmental obligations is not punishment of violations but rather promoting the achievement of environmental protection objectives.[45] What is required, arguably, is problem solving rather than enforcement of rules for the rules' sake.[46] It is true that the compliance mechanisms of the Montréal and Kyoto Protocols have been quite active, the former in particular.[47] It may well be, then, that delegation simply takes a different form in these regimes.

Arguments in favour of adjudication can also be made, however. At its best, adjudication allows, at one and the same time, for the resolution of individual disputes and for the ongoing development of the legal system. The interpretation and application of rules is not a mechanical process; the rules themselves, as well as relationships between different rules, can come to be understood differently as they are brought to bear on problems that are different from those considered in the past. Astute judges attend not only to the dispute at hand but also to the implications of various possible interpretations of legal rules for the coherence of the legal system.[48] Compliance, as noted above, focuses instead on problem solving: the point is not (necessarily) to punish parties who are in violation of their obligations but to seek to understand the reasons for violations,

45 Annex V of Decision X/10 ibid. contains an 'indicative list' of measures that could be taken in response to non-compliance, which includes the provision of assistance and the issuing of cautions, but which also includes suspension of rights and privileges under the regime. Similarly, the Facilitative Branch of the Kyoto Protocol's Compliance Committee may give advice, facilitate assistance, and make recommendations to the party not in compliance: Decision 27/CMP.1: Procedures and mechanisms relating to compliance under the Kyoto Protocol (hereinafter Procedures and Mechanisms), FCCC/KP/CMP/2005/8/Add.3, 30 March 2006, Section XIV: Consequences applied by the Facilitative Branch.

46 MA Fitzmaurice and C Redgwell, 'Environmental Non-Compliance Procedures and International Law' (2000) 31 *Netherlands Yearbook of International Law* 35–65; Gunther Handl, 'Compliance Control Mechanisms and International Environmental Obligations' (1997) 5 *Tulane Journal of International and Comparative Law* 29–49.

47 There were a few years near the beginning of its life, in 1998, when the Implementation Committee established under the Montréal Protocol did not consider the compliance of any state, but since then the Committee has worked on a steady stream of compliance issues respecting a range of states. The Kyoto Protocol's compliance committee, established in 2005, has considered a much smaller number of cases concerning eight states, of which all but two (Greece and Canada) are so-called countries with economies in transition, which benefit from some special consideration under the Protocol. In all but one case (Canada), a finding of non-compliance was made and benefits under the Protocol suspended. None of these cases involved compliance with emissions reductions obligations directly, but, as will be discussed below, the question of Canada's compliance with those obligations was raised by the Facilitative Branch of the Compliance Committee. For an overview of each of these cases, see http://unfccc.int/kyoto_protocol/compliance/items/2875.php.

48 See Koskenniemi, 'Constitutionalism as Mindset'.

address underlying problems, and bring parties into compliance through a combination of incentives and disincentives that are calibrated to the particular circumstances.[49] Because of the technical nature of many of the rules whose violation is at issue, the finding of a violation requires no legal expertise. Decisions produced by these bodies are framed as progress reports not judgments. Central to the processes is the drafting and submission of a plan by the party in breach setting out steps to be taken to return to compliance; this plan is then evaluated to determine whether it will likely bring about a return to compliance, and progress towards the implementation of the plan is subsequently considered.

I noted above that compliance could be understood to be better suited to international environmental regimes than adjudication. However, there is another potential explanation for the prevalence of compliance and the dearth of adjudication. To the extent that adjudication can contribute to the development of the legal system, as well as to stronger ties among individual regimes and with the general body of international law, it could lead to the weaving of an ever denser, more determinate web of legal obligations. This is much less likely to happen under the conditions of fragmentation that we observe in international environmental law. Compliance bodies within self-contained regimes do not have a mandate to consider rules from beyond the regime, and their decisions, while relevant to the parties before them in the context of the alleged violation in question, contribute little to the development of law within the regime and even less to the general body of international environmental law. As a result, states are better able to manage their obligations: there is virtually no opportunity for the gradual accumulation of judgments regarding the meaning of rules and their application in particular situations, and therefore little danger that the rules of the regime will begin to take on a life of their own through the development of an environmental jurisprudence. It should be noted, however, that some states are better positioned than others to do so.

In many cases, compliance bodies focus little attention on wealthy states. For example, much of the activity of the Montréal Protocol's Implementation Committee relates either to developing states or to the so-called states with economies in transition, that is, the states of the former

[49] Handl, 'Compliance Control Mechanisms and International Environmental Obligations', 34; Martti Koskenniemi, 'Breach of Treaty or Non-Compliance? Reflections on the Enforcement of the Montreal Protocol' (1992) 3 *Yearbook of International Environmental Law* 123–62.

Eastern Bloc and Soviet Union.[50] The situation is different in the climate change regime, whose Compliance Committee was primarily interested in the performance of developed states, as these were the only states to have accepted binding emissions reduction obligations under the Kyoto Protocol. Furthermore, while the Facilitative Branch was concerned with removing obstacles to compliance,[51] the Enforcement Branch had the competence to make a finding of breach and to impose sanctions.[52]

Because respecting emissions reduction obligations requires a significant investment on the part of states, it was reasonable for states party to the Kyoto Protocol to seek assurances that some states are not free-riding on the investments of others.[53] However, the threat of sanctions in the climate change regime should not be overstated. One of the most important sanctions that the Enforcement Branch could impose was a penalty in the form of additional emissions reductions in the commitment period subsequent to that defined by Kyoto, which ended in 2012. As that subsequent commitment period did not materialize until some years later, in the form of the Paris Agreement, this was an empty threat.[54] While both

[50] In 1995, Russia became the first state to be subjected to the compliance procedure. Interestingly, the decision to bring Russia before the Implementation Committee was made by Russia itself, in virtue of para. 4 of the Non-Compliance Procedure: Report of the Tenth Meeting of the Implementation Committee under the Non-Compliance Procedure for the Montreal Protocol, Geneva, 25 August 1995, UNEP/OzL.Pro/ImpCom/10/4, 30 August 1995. See Jacob Werksman, 'Compliance and Transition: Russia's Non-Compliance Tests the Ozone Regime' (1996) 56 *Zeitschrift für ausländisches öffentliches Recht und Völkerrecht* 750–73.

For some time, states of the former Soviet Union and Eastern Block occasionally appeared before the Committee; in 2001, developing states began to appear at a rapid rate. Developed states such as Canada, New Zealand, Switzerland and Israel have also drawn the Committee's attention for failure to respect reporting obligations, and Greece was found to be in non-compliance in 2007.

[51] Kenneth W. Abbott and Duncan Snidal, 'Hard and Soft Law in International Governance', in Judith L. Goldstein et al. (eds), *Legalization and World Politics*, (Cambridge, MA: MIT Press, 2001), 37–72; Decision 27/CMP.1: Procedures and mechanisms relating to compliance under the Kyoto Protocol (hereinafter Procedures and Mechanisms), FCCC/KP/CMP/2005/8/Add.3, 30 March 2006, Section XIV: Consequences applied by the Facilitative Branch.

[52] Procedures and Mechanisms, Section XV: Consequences applied by the Enforcement Branch.

[53] Abbott and Snidal, 'Hard and Soft Law in International Governance', 42.

[54] Post-Kyoto reduction obligations have been conditionally undertaken by forty-two developed states. Most of the conditions relate to the adoption of a comprehensive agreement on emissions reductions: UNFCCC, Nationally Appropriate Mitigation Commitments or Actions by Developed Country Parties, http://unfccc.int/focus/mitigation/items/7223.php.

the Facilitative and Enforcement Branches of the Compliance Committee had dealings with developed states, including Canada,[55] the results fell far short of findings of breach or imposition of penalties. In any event, Canada placed itself beyond the reach of the Compliance Committee by taking the extremely unusual step in December 2011 of withdrawing from the Kyoto Protocol, thus avoiding penalties that it could have faced given its failure to meet its emission reduction obligations.[56] However, the conclusion that Canada got cold feet when it realized that Kyoto's commitment device could impose real costs is too hasty: a very large number of states failed to meet their 2012 targets, and no other state withdrew from the convention. Canada's withdrawal can be explained much more readily by a change in government and resulting change in orientation on climate change.

In the above discussion on scientific expertise and compliance within international environmental regimes, I have sought to show that the three features of legalization – obligation, precision and delegation – are present, but only at a superficial level. The approach taken much more closely resembles managerialism, which is itself the product of strategies to create the appearance of legal constraint while in fact retaining a reasonably high degree of flexibility. Legal obligations whose content is informed by science, and bolstered by science's authority, are much less constraining than they appear. As noted above, political authorities do not adopt wholesale the recommendations of scientific bodies, and decisions are context-specific with little or no precedential value. However, there are cases in which states do submit to constraints. In the following section, I will

55 See UNFCCC, Questions of Implementation – Canada: http://unfccc.int/kyoto_protocol/compliance/enforcement_branch/items/5298.php. Canada was required by the Enforcement Branch to submit information on its national registry, which permits the tracking of greenhouse gas emissions credits. The Enforcement Branch considered the matter but in the end did not proceed: Informal Information Note by the Secretariat: The Compliance Procedure with respect to Canada, http://unfccc.int/files/kyoto_protocol/compliance/application/pdf/informal_information_note_by_the_secretariat_on_the_comp_proc_wrt_canada.pdf. The full set of documents relating to these proceedings is available at http://unfccc.int/kyoto_protocol/compliance/enforcement_branch/items/5298.php. See Sebastian Oberthür and René Lefeber, 'Holding Countries to Account: The Kyoto Protocol's Compliance System Revisited after Four Years of Experience' (2010) 1 *Climate Law* 133–58.

56 Adam Vaughan, 'What Does Canada's Withdrawal from Kyoto Protocol Mean?', The Guardian, 13 December 2011, www.theguardian.com/environment/2011/dec/13/canada-withdrawal-kyoto-protocol. The question of Canada's non-compliance was raised by the Facilitative Branch in February 2012, after Canada had announced its withdrawal but before it became effective: Report on the 11th Meeting of the Facilitative Branch, 6–8 February 2012, CC/FB/11/2012/2, 27 February 2012, para. 13.

consider an environmental regime in a different sense of that term, namely the SPS Agreement. The objective of this agreement is not environmental protection, but rather promotion of free trade, yet it has important implications for domestic and international environmental measures. Unlike the environmental regimes considered above, the SPS regime displays a high degree of deference to expertise, and provides for binding third-party dispute resolution. The constraints which this agreement imposes on state behaviour are much more difficult for most states to manage than is the case with the environmental regimes considered above. Yet law is implicated in these constraints in a superficial manner; the regime remains highly managerial despite its differences from regimes oriented towards environmental protection.

7.5 Legalization and the SPS Agreement

I have argued that the regime for the governance of sanitary and phytosanitary measures, to which the SPS Agreement is central, bears many important similarities to international environmental regimes, but differs in one important respect: the degree of constraint which it imposes on states. It is therefore of great interest to observe the strategies at work within and around this regime and to contrast them to strategies at work in the area of environment. The SPS Agreement submits domestic health and environmental measures to scrutiny to determine whether they are 'necessary for the protection of human, animal or plant life or health',[57] as established by science,[58] whether they are discriminatory, or whether they constitute a disguised restriction on international trade.[59] If a measure is in conformity with an international standard, it will be deemed necessary,[60] but stricter measures, or measures pertaining to an issue for which international standards have not been developed, must be scientifically justified.[61] Furthermore, in designing their measures, states must take into account the economic impact of the measure, of the harm that it is intended to avert, and of alternative measures – in other words, they must conduct a cost-benefit analysis of the measure and available alternatives.[62]

Viewed from one angle, the Agreement represents a high degree of legalization, at least as understood by Abbott et al.: the rules are binding

[57] WTO Agreement on the Application of Sanitary and Phytosanitary Measures (SPS Agreement) Marrakesh 1994), Art. 2(1).

[58] Ibid., Art. 2(2). [59] Ibid., Art. 2(3). [60] Ibid., Art. 3(2).

[61] Ibid., Art. 3(3) and Art. 5(1) and (2). [62] Ibid., Art. 5(3) to 5(6).

(obligation); while the rules in the Agreement itself are often imprecise, the standards to which the rules refer are not (precision); and the Dispute Settlement Body (DSB) rules on disputes submitted to it and has the capacity to permit the imposition of penalties on parties found to be in violation of WTO law (delegation). It is striking to see how far along the legalization spectrum states have gone in this regard, in contrast to legalization in environment. But it is equally striking to observe that, despite the fairly high degree of conformity of the SPS Agreement to Abbott et al.'s concept of legalization, the Agreement nevertheless marginalizes law in favour of non-legal, notably scientific, expertise. This suggests that Abbott et al.'s conception of legalization is more akin to managerialism than to governance by law.

It is possible to read the SPS Agreement as imposing a series of procedural obligations on states wishing to enact health and environmental measures, the essentials of which are set out in art. 5: conduct a risk assessment; consider costs and benefits of the measure and of alternatives, consider negative trade effects, avoid arbitrary or unjustifiable distinctions resulting in discrimination or disguised restrictions on trade. This is not, however, how it has come to be interpreted. The measures themselves and the decision-making process that led to them are subject to fairly or very close scrutiny, which, because of the highly technical nature of the issues in play, must be mediated by scientific and economic expertise.

An excellent example is provided by conclusions reached by the DSB concerning what constitutes a risk assessment for the purposes of art. 5.1. That text reads as follows:

> Members shall ensure that their sanitary or phytosanitary measures are based on an assessment, as appropriate to the circumstances, of the risks to human, animal or plant life or health, taking into account risk assessment techniques developed by the relevant international organizations.

In *EC – Biotech*, Austria submitted a document setting out reasons for its measures with respect to certain GM products.[63] The Panel was critical of the methodology used in the study,[64] and of the fact that the potential for health and environmental impacts had been noted in the studies, but that

[63] Austria, along with a number of other Member States, availed itself of the possibility provided for under the EC's regulatory scheme on genetically modified products to take 'safeguard measures' with respect to products that had been approved under that scheme.

[64] *EC – Hormones* (n 8), paras 7.3094–98. See Robert L. Howse and Henrik Horn, 'European Communities – Measures Affecting the Approval and Marketing of Biotech Products' (2009) 8 *World Trade Review* 49–83, at 73–74.

neither had sought to estimate the likelihood of these impacts occurring nor to evaluate them. As a result, the Panel concluded, the document did not constitute a risk assessment and the measure could therefore not pass muster under para. 5.1.[65]

As observed by Robert L. Howse and Henrik Horn, there is no basis in the SPS Agreement for such a strictly defined approach to risk assessment, particularly in light of the Appellate Body's conclusion in *EC – Hormones* that states were entitled to take into account minority views that did not accord with the mainstream scientific studies relied on in the risk assessment, if those minority views gives rise to doubts regarding the adequacy of the risk assessment.[66] Yet here, the Panel did not limit itself to an assessment of the reasonableness of the decision-making procedure followed by Austria and the extent to which it conformed to requirements set out in the Agreement. It entered the scientific and policy debate, evaluating the evidence and examining the methodology.[67]

Panels do not limit themselves to reviewing the reports on which parties' policy decisions are based; they also consult experts directly,[68] using a process that was developed on an ad hoc basis by a series of panels.[69] In addition to hearing from the experts as witnesses, panels also submit questions to the experts to which they respond in writing if they feel they have the requisite competence.[70] Lucasz Gruszczynski refers to an interesting feature of exchanges between panel members and experts: the words in the relevant text are meant to have a specific meaning or range of meanings which, given that they are legal texts, lawyers are understood to be expert in interpreting. Naturally, the legal meaning ascribed to a word by a jurist

65 *EC – Hormones* ibid. paras 7.3094–7.3098; Howse and Horn, 'European Communities'.

66 Howse and Horn, 'European Communities', 76.

67 See e.g. the questions and summaries of responses in *Japan – Measures Affecting Agricultural Products*, Report of the Panel, WT/DS76/R, 1998; *European Communities – Measures Affecting the Approval and Marketing of Biotech Products (EC – Biotech), Report of the Panel, WT/DS291/R WT/DS292/R WT/DS293/R*, 29 September 2006, Annex H: Replies by the Scientific Experts advising the Panel to Questions Posed by the Panel, which is 256 pages long.

68 Art. 11.2 DSU.

69 As Gruszczynski notes, well-articulated guidelines on the consultation of experts were developed in a series of reports: Japan – Agricultural Products in 1998; US/Canada Continued Suspension in 2008; and Australia – Apples in 2010: Lucas Gruszczynski, 'The Role of Experts in Environmental and Health-Related Trade Disputes in the WTO: Deconstructing Decision-Making Processes', in Monika Ambrus and others (eds), *The Role of Experts in International and European Decision-Making Processes* (Cambridge: Cambridge University Press, 2014), 221.

70 Gruszczynski, 'The Role of Experts'.

may not be evident to a scientist. Gruszczynski points to an example of a lawyerly distinction drawn between the words possibility and potential, on one hand, and probability, on the other. When a question about the potential for adverse effects was put to an expert, he responded in the language of probability, noting that (for a scientist) a risk scenario, no matter how improbable or unlikely, could always be said to be *possible*.[71] That the same words and concepts are likely to mean different things in different disciplines is a point that seems too obvious to require emphasis, yet it does not appear to have been recognized by the DSB. This may well be because the lawyerly meaning of the text has, in this context, become less important, while the meaning attributed to it by scientific and economic experts is now taken to be the most relevant, authoritative one.

Central to this loss of authority on the part of legal interpretation is its incapacity to produce a precise result: legal texts such as the SPS Agreement are subject to multiple interpretations, giving rise to perceptions that legal interpretation is imprecise, ambiguous and highly vulnerable to politicization. For jurists, the open texture of legal texts is not necessarily seen as a problem, as we understand that it is the arguments in favour of one interpretation over another that make a non-arbitrary choice among interpretations possible. However, as Werner has noted, selecting among interpretations depends on reference to shared understandings regarding the interpretive process. Werner argues that jurists 'can only make their claims *qua legal* expert if they base their arguments on criteria for validity that are accepted in a broader community of international lawyers'.[72] This means that '[l]egal argumentation … is only possible when participants assume that there are some criteria and a body of knowledge that can be used to validate or invalidate specific claims if they *also* act as members of Schachter's 'invisible college' and not just as advocates'.[73] But the conditions for deference to such an invisible college are not met within the WTO: the most obvious reason has to do with what is at stake. Panels are charged with nothing short of determining the appropriateness, effectiveness, and, of course, trade friendliness of states' health and environmental measures, as compared with other available alternatives. This is not a task for legal expertise; it is a political matter. The hearings at which advocates for the various positions face off against one another, followed by the deliberation and reasoned decisions of the panels, all on the basis of legal rules, cannot bear the legitimation burden imposed by this task. Scientists in

[71] Ibid. [72] Werner, 'The Politics of Expertise', 59. [73] Ibid., 61.

particular are called upon to communicate scientifically proven facts, and the outcome of the dispute is made to depend heavily on these scientific facts – or to appear to, in any event. I take the point made by Howse and Horn that, in fact, neither the SPS Agreement itself nor previous WTO rulings required the panel in *Biotech* to take such a strict interpretation of risk assessment. Furthermore, it makes policy sense to give states some leeway to be cautious in the face of scientific evidence that aspects of a completed risk assessment may have been flawed. Nevertheless, the SPS Agreement and the WTO's Dispute Settlement Understanding together impose real constraints on the adoption by states of health and environmental measures that do not conform to internationally recognized standards. The robustness of WTO dispute settlement and the approach taken to scientific justification of measures may have taken some states by surprise, but it also serves the ends of states that face pressure from constituents to adopt stringent environmental law and policy that would not find favour with powerful economic actors.

I have noted that the capacity of states to manage the constraining effect of the SPS Agreement varies. In the section that follows, I address certain means by which some states manage constraints. States may be subject to binding third-party dispute settlement within the SPS regime, and may have delegated significant authority to bodies such as the *Codex Alimentarius* Commission, but wealthy states have the capacity to exercise significant influence in the standard-setting process. The advantage to states that have this capacity is that their influence over standard-setting is much more difficult to detect than in environmental regimes, where the distance between scientific recommendations and decisions by political authorities can readily be observed and measured.

7.5.1 Opening the Black Box: Inside Standard-Setting Bodies

Bodies such as the *Codex Alimentarius* Commission attracted little attention prior to the conclusion of the SPS Agreement: the standards established by such bodies were voluntary, and their highly technical nature made them inaccessible to general audiences. Members were named to such bodies based on their expertise, and their work was seen to be technical not political in nature. This changed with the advent of the SPS Agreement: states with the capacity to do so began selecting delegates based not only on their expertise but on their interest in pursuing a particular outcome. This soon prompted closer scrutiny of practices within such bodies. Arguments came to be made that the work of such bodies ought not to be seen as 'merely' technical and therefore apolitical and objective, building on insights from various bodies of literature which examine the ways in which scientific knowledge is produced, and the range of processes through which scientific judgments and conclusions come to be understood as reliable, valid or accurate.[74] These insights could not be ignored by political and legal authorities for long, as the highly visible and bitter debates around 'Climategate' have made painfully clear.[75] On many occasions, concerns on the part of members of the public about the soundness and reliability of the science being relied on by political authorities are understandable: faith in science and in political decision-making processes that draw heavily on scientific input has been severely shaken by food safety crises in Europe, for example. This poses a dilemma to states: they need their decisions to be seen to rest on science in order to lend them the appearance of objectivity, but this reliance can make them vulnerable to charges from various quarters that they are not taking their responsibilities as public authorities seriously. Even worse, state authorities can find themselves being caught up in controversies over perceptions that science has become politicized, particularly in the realm of so-called post-normal science, involving issues in which both uncertainty and stakes are high.[76]

Until relatively recently, it was normal for members of expert bodies within environmental regimes to be, in essence, political appointees. This is changing: increasingly, experts are selected on the basis of their expertise, though their nationality remains relevant, as expert bodies formed more recently still require regional representation. One of the best-known expert bodies, the Intergovernmental Panel on Climate Change, devotes

[74] Clark A. Miller, 'Challenges in the Application of Science to Global Affairs: Contingency, Trust, and Moral Order', in Clark A. Miller and Paul N. Edwards (eds), *Changing the Atmosphere: Expert Knowledge and Environmental Governance* (Cambridge, MA: MIT Press, 2001); Clark A. Miller, 'Democratization, International Knowledge Institutions, and Global Governance' (2007) 20 *Governance* 325–57; William Rehg, *Cogent Science in Context: The Science Wars, Argumentation Theory, and Habermas* (Cambridge, MA: MIT Press, 2009).

[75] See e.g. Myanna Lahsen, 'Climategate: The Role of the Social Sciences' (2013) 119 *Climatic Change* 547–58; Naomi Oreskes and Erik M. Conway, *Merchants of Doubt: How a Handful of Scientists Obscured the Truth on Issues from Tobacco Smoke to Global Warming* (New York: Bloomsbury Press, 2010).

[76] S. O. Funtowicz and J. R. Ravetz, 'The Emergence of Post-Normal Science', in René von Schomberg (ed.), *Science, Politics and Morality. Scientific Uncertainty and Decision Making* (Berlin: Kluwer, 1993).

an enormous amount of attention and resources to ensuring not only that its work is sound and accurate but that it is credible and trustworthy, and perceived as such.[77] Similarly, the *Codex Alimentarius* Commission has begun to focus its attention on questions relating to trustworthiness and credibility.[78] Questions have been asked, for example, about the impact on standards of the unequal ability of states to participate in the work of the Commission, and the frequency with which standards are aligned with the interests of economically powerful states has been noted.[79] Political authorities may seem to be constrained by the decisions of nameless, faceless experts, but when one digs deeper, one finds these authorities – at least in wealthy states[80] – sending industry representatives to participate in their state's delegation to Commission sessions.[81] What we see is political authority seeking to cloak itself in the authority of science while maintaining as free a hand as possible – extra-legal deferral with an added dimension, namely the latitude that can be won by framing a question as economic or scientific rather than legal,[82] but this may be changing as a result of increased focus on the interactions between science and politics.

Law and politics must rely heavily on science in the field of environmental protection, but the nature of this reliance requires careful consideration. The complexity and uncertainty inherent in areas such as climate

[77] Clark Miller, 'Hybrid Management: Boundary Organizations, Science Policy, and Environmental Governance in the Climate Regime' (2001) 26 *Science, Technology & Human Values* 478–500; Miller, 'Challenges in the Application of Science to Global Affairs'; Sandrine Maljean-Dubois and Mattieu Wemaëre, *La diplomatie climatique: Les enjeux d'un régime international du climat* (Paris: Pedone, 2010), 30ff.

[78] Ève Truilé-Marengo, 'Consensus comme modalité d'adoption des normes au sein du Codex Alimentarius', in Estelle Brosset and Ève Truilhé-Marengo (eds), *Les enjeux de la normalisation technique internationale: Entre environnement, santé et commerce international* (Centre d'études et de recherches internationales et communautaires, Université d'Aix-Marseille III, 2006), 105–19; Bhupinder S. Chimni, 'Co-Option and Resistance: Two Faces of Global Administrative Law' (2004) 37 *NYU Journal of International Law and Politics* 799–827; Michael A. Livermore, 'Authority and Legitimacy in Global Governance: Deliberation, Institutional Differentiation, and the Codex Alimentarius' (2006) 81 *NYU Law Review* 766–801.

[79] Nathalie Thomé, 'Participation et représentation des États dans l'élaboration des normes du Sein du Codex Alimentarius', in Estelle Brosset and Ève Truilhé-Marengo (eds), *Les enjeux de la normalisation technique internationale: Entre environnement, santé et commerce international* (Centre d'études et de recherches internationales et communautaires, Université d'Aix-Marseille III, 2006), 102.

[80] Thomé, 'Participation et resprésentation des États', notes that not all states have the capacity to send large and well-briefed delegations to these meetings, at 99ff.

[81] Ibid., 102. [82] Koskenniemi, 'International Legislation Today', 79–80.

change, toxic substances, or endangered species make it impossible for scientists to provide clear predictions about the consequences of various courses of action. Furthermore, as Werner has noted, the fragmentation of scientific knowledge has a significant impact on the capacity of scientific experts to influence decision making:

> Knowledge societies may even involve more politics than before *because* of the pivotal role of scientific experts. While experts are called in to reduce complexity and provide legitimacy by enabling well-informed decision making, in practice their answers are often partial, conditional and contested. Using experts in decision making may then yield opposite results: an increase in complexity, openly contested decisions and a struggle over alternative definitions of problem situations.[83]

Extra-legal deferral may be running out of steam. States may then be obliged to acknowledge the essentially political nature of their decisions – or they may need to find innovative ways to resort to law, and more in particular to a legal system that functions in a very different manner than that depicted through the concepts of legalization and managerialism.

7.6 Conclusion

It is tempting to see in the short history of international environmental law a series of attempts on the part of states to create regimes whose constraints and disciplines can be carefully managed and avoided. The breathtaking scope of the task that the participants in the Rio +20 Summit set for themselves suggests an attempt to define the problem in such a way that progress towards addressing it cannot be measured, and that states cannot be blamed for a failure to reach their stated objectives. The delayed adoption of a new round of commitments to slow climate change, and the inadequate nature of the commitments that have been adopted under the auspices of the Paris Agreement, could be due to conclusions on the part of states that the Kyoto Protocol was too constraining. Trade and investment regimes create some downward pressure on environmental standards – or perhaps simply an excuse for states to underperform. There seems to be no equivalent site in international law for the operation of countervailing upward pressure. In short, states' approaches to international environmental law could be understood in terms of obfuscation and avoidance in the form of the inefficient design of environmental regimes.

[83] Werner, 'The Politics of Expertise'.

Yet we must also note that environmental law seems to have lost its way for reasons that may have as much to do with a lack of imagination and a narrow conception of the form of law as with a lack of state will. States have proven much less willing to adopt stringent environmental obligations and to create institutional structures for their implementation and enforcement than is the case with trade and investment law, for example, but this may be due in part to uncertainty as to how to go about this. At this stage in the development of international environmental law, particularly in light of the conditions of uncertainty and complexity under which political authorities have to operate, and given the immense contributions expected of science, it is time to devote more attention to the form of law, and to the roles and functions appropriate to law.

If law were indeed an important form of expertise in environmental regimes, one would expect to see the interpretation and application of legal norms overshooting their context, holding relevance for future disputes in which the same sets of norms, or the same types of problems, or both, stand to be addressed. Each instance of problem solving in the light of environmental norms would generate expectations that not only the material problem at hand but also the integrity of applicable norms and the system to which they belong would be attended to. In this manner, one might detect a tendency for legal norms to take on a life of their own. Resolutions of disputes would be evaluated not only from the point of view of the objectives of a given regime but on other bases as well, including procedural and substantive fairness and coherence with previous applications of rules, both within and between regimes. However, there is a strong tendency in international environmental law for legal reasoning to be subordinated to other forms of reason or logic, and for the objectives of individual regimes to hold priority over the coherence of legal discourse across regimes and issue areas.

8

Search and Rescue as a Geopolitics of International Law

THOMAS GAMMELTOFT-HANSEN AND TANJA AALBERTS*

8.1 Introduction

The notion of Europe being 'flooded' or 'invaded' by boat migrants is one of the most often invoked examples by those arguing that globalization is fundamentally eroding state sovereignty. In the wake of the current global refugee crisis, hundreds of thousands of refugees and migrants risk their lives each year in the attempt to irregularly reach Europe. Many others never make it that far. In 2016, more than 5000 migrant deaths were recorded in the Mediterranean – accounting for nearly two-thirds of all migrant fatalities worldwide.[1] Given the clandestine nature of these crossings, the real number may well be substantially higher.

From the perspective of European states, the irregular migrant has become the embodiment of the inability to protect and control access to that most sacred property of statehood, the sovereign territory. Hence, maritime border controls have been expanded and transformed with navy vessels, surveillance planes and radar stations creating a 'virtual border' across the Mediterranean. In addition, transit and origin countries are increasingly conscripted to grant access to their territorial waters or through their own authorities effect migration control on behalf of

* This chapter draws partly on two earlier publications: Tanja E. Aalberts and Thomas Gammeltoft-Hansen, 'Sovereignty at Sea: The Law and Politics of Saving Lives in Mare Liberum' (2014) 17 *Journal of International Relations and Development* 439–468; Thomas Gammeltoft-Hansen, 'The Perfect Storm: Sovereignty Games and the Law and Politics of Boat Migration', in Violeta Moreno-Lax and Efthymios Papastavridis (eds), *'Boat Refugees' and Migrants at Sea: A Comprehensive Approach: Integrating Maritime Security with Human Rights* (The Hague: Brill, 2016), pp. 60–79.

[1] https://missingmigrants.iom.int/latest-global-figures.

the European Union (EU) and its Member States.[2] While these policies involving maritime interception and international cooperation to prevent migrants from departing are often framed in humanitarian terms – as 'search and rescue' operations intended to prevent the loss of lives at sea – the fact is that these measures only tend to drive up prices and to force migrants to take longer, more risky and dangerous journeys.[3]

The present chapter examines the different approaches pursued by Mediterranean states in order to manage boat migrants and eschew responsibility for people in distress at sea in the context of the maritime 'search and rescue' rules established as a matter of international law. As will be shown, not only does the current politicization of migration issues in Europe provide for evermore draconian policies, the particular legal geography in which this issue is embedded also provide a particular apt case for illustrating several of the different state strategies outlined in Chapter 1.

As a result, the boat migrant finds herself embedded in a complex international legal field, involving multiple bases for jurisdiction and interlocking legal regimes in the context of rescue at sea and international human rights law. Developments in both regimes have further taken place, leading to processes of both de- and re-territorialization. This opens up a particular playing field between international law and politics, where states are able to simultaneously capitalize on policy innovations and legal developments in order to address the political imperative of managing irregular migration. Over the last decades, the governments of the Mediterranean have thus repeatedly locked horns over respective obligations vis-à-vis migrants lost at sea, several claims have been made that neighbouring countries were deliberately dumping rescuees in foreign territorial waters or search and rescue regions, and regular testimonies by survivors report about both commercial vessels and navy ships ignoring pleas to assist migrant boats in distress.[4]

[2] Thomas Gammeltoft-Hansen, *Access to Asylum: International Refugee Law and the Globalisation of Migration Control* (Cambridge: Cambridge University Press, 2011).

[3] Thomas Gammeltoft-Hansen and Ninna Nyberg Sørensen (eds), *The Migration Industry and the Commercialization of International Migration* (London: Routledge, 2013). See also www.borderdeaths.org/.

[4] See e.g. Comisión Espanola de Ayuda al Regiado, 'Report on Certain Border Externalisation Practices Pursues by the Spanish Government That Violate the Rights Both Now and in the Future of Immigrants Who May Seek to Reach Spain Via the Southern Border', 30 May 2007. Consiglio Italiano per i Rifugiati, 'Report Regarding Recent Search and Rescue Operations in the Mediterranean', 1 June 2007.

8.2 The Law and Politics of Saving Lives in the *Mare Liberum*

Traditionally, the high seas are defined exactly as a space of non-sovereignty.[5] Since Grotius it has been accepted that the high seas can be subject to no national jurisdictions and are governed by a residual principle of freedom allowing vessels of all nations the right of passage, trade and exploitation.[6] On the high seas different and fewer rules supposedly apply; what happens here is not necessarily subordinated to the sovereign sphere and national laws of a single state. This is the truly *inter*-national sphere, containing both an inherent freedom to exercise sovereign power, but as a result also innate potential for conflict in the absence of neat delineations between competing claims.

To some extent, Grotius's principle of the *Mare Liberum* survives to this day. The 1958 Convention on the High Seas states that '[t]he high seas being open to all States, no State may validly purport to subject any part of them to its sovereignty' (Art. 2) and it affords all states the same basic freedoms of navigation, fishing, infrastructure and overflying.[7] Yet, despite its name, the *Mare Liberum* is hardly a space devoid of regulation. The law of the sea imposes a complex set of norms on the maritime environment, charting out a web of intersecting rights and obligations for both states and private actors. Equally important, modern international law provides for a host of competing and often overlapping claims in the maritime environment, in which territorial waters, the contiguous zone, nationality, flag state jurisdiction, nearest port of safety, next port of call, and regional search and rescue zones may all be invoked for the purpose of establishing authority or responsibilities.

5 As a matter of modern international law, a state's territorial waters may extend twelve nautical miles (twenty-two kilometres) from the baseline, which the low water mark or internal waters (Art. 3 of the Convention on the Law of the Sea, Montego Bay, 10 December 1982, in force 1 November 1994, 1833 UNTS 397). This belt is regarded part of the state's sovereign territory for all purposes, save that international maritime law demands that states allow foreign ships innocent passage. Certain sovereign functions may additionally be exercised within an additional contiguous zone extending up to 24 miles from the low water mark. While the contiguous zone is technically considered the high seas, states are allowed to exercise control and checks to 'prevent infringement of its customs, fiscal, immigration or sanitary laws and regulations' (Art. 24(1) of the Convention on the Territorial Sea and Contiguous Zone, Geneva, 29 April 1958, in force 10 September 1964, 516 UNTS 205). Finally, states may extend exclusive claims to e.g. fishing within the exclusive economic zone, extending 200 miles from the baseline (Art. 56 of the Convention on the Law of the Sea).

6 Hugo Grotius, *The Freedom of the Seas* (Oxford: Oxford University Press, 1916).

7 Convention on the High Seas, Geneva, 29 April 1958, in force 30 September 1962, 450 UNTS 11.

In contrast, international human rights law normally presumes a binary relationship between a single state and individuals within its jurisdiction. The major achievement of the human rights movement was exactly to introduce to international law a set of norms that did not simply concern the *horizontal* relationship between states, but a *vertical* obligation between each state and its subjects and aliens within its territory.[8] This is also reflected in the international refugee protection regime and the 1951 Refugee Convention. International refugee law deliberately shies away from placing any obligations on the countries of origin,[9] and despite a call for international cooperation in the Convention's preamble, the basic legal mechanism for dividing responsibility among states remains individualized and based on territorial proximity.[10]

Both the law of the sea and international human rights law impose obligations upon states even outside their territorial waters. Grotius himself underscored that the correlate of the sovereign freedom afforded on the high seas is a common obligation to obey by 'the law of hospitality which is of the highest sanctity'.[11] Both the duty to render assistance to migrants and others lost at sea and to allow disembarkation of those rescued at a place of safety are both old and universal norms of international law.[12] In their modern iteration, every state must require the captain of a ship flying its flag to 'render assistance to any person found at sea in danger of being lost' and 'to proceed with all possible speed to the rescue of persons in distress, if informed of their need of assistance'.[13] Beyond imposing an

[8] Henry Steiner, 'International Protection of Human Rights', in Malcolm D. Evans (ed.), *International Law*, 2nd edn (Oxford: Oxford University Press, 2006), 753–82, at 769; Sigrun Skogly and Mark Gibney, 'Transnational Human Rights Obligations' (2002) 24 *Human Rights Quarterly* 781–98, at 782

[9] Indeed, certain refugee instruments have been explicit in stating that the granting of asylum is not to be considered as an 'unfriendly act' towards countries of origin. See e.g. the preamble of the UN Declaration on Territorial Asylum. UNGA resolution 2312 (XXII), 14 December 1967.

[10] Arguably, certain later policy developments would seem to complicate this picture by invoking competing jurisdictions through e.g. safe third-country and safe country of origin policies.

[11] Grotius, *The Freedom of the Seas*, 1.

[12] Both principles are considered international customary law as well as codified within the global maritime search and rescue regime. See in particular Art. 98 in the Convention on the Law of the Sea; the International Convention for the Safety of Life at Sea, London, 1 November 1974, in force 25 May 1980, 1184 UNTS 3; and the International Convention on Maritime Search and Rescue, Hamburg, 27 April 1979, in force 22 June 1985, 1403 UNTS.

[13] Art. 98(1) of the Convention on the Law of the Sea; Chapter V, Regulations 10(a) and 33 of the International Convention for the Safety of Life at Sea. This entails a positive

obligation for both official and private vessels to rescue anyone encountered in distress, coastal states further have a positive duty to maintain 'an adequate and effective search and rescue service' and to ensure co-ordination of search and rescue operations.[14] To that end the international search and rescue regime has led to the division of the world's oceans into national search and rescue regions, within which each coastal state has the primary responsibility for ensuring that distress calls are received and responded to.[15]

In parallel, the corner-stone of international refugee law, the principle of *non-refoulement*, requires states not to return in any manner a person with a well-founded fear of persecution.[16] While the *non-refoulement* principle has previously been interpreted as applying only to refugees who have already arrived at a state's territory, both international human rights law and international refugee law has come to understand this principle to apply wherever states exercise jurisdiction.[17]

For a long period, the issue of disembarkation and subsequent return to the country of origin of persons rescued at sea was a nominally minor issue mainly related to sailors. As such, the obligations imposed by international law in regard to boat migrants were seen as reciprocal and reconcilable to the perceived self-interest of relevant states. Similarly, the modern refugee protection regime came about as an attempt, albeit imperfect, to resolve the problem of those occupying the undesirable and in systemic terms impossible position in between mutually exclusive sovereign states. During the first decades of the Cold War, receiving refugees was entailed scoring ideological value for states, allowing people 'to vote with their feet' by admitting the enemies of one's enemy.

A combination of several factors has fundamentally changed this picture, however. New refugee flows emerged from proxy wars fought in the Global South in the 1980s.[18] A decade before, the oil crisis meant that

obligation of flag states to adopt domestic legislation that imposes penalties on shipmasters who ignore or fail to provide assistance, see Michael Pugh, 'Drowning Not Waving: Boat People and Humanitarianism at Sea' (2004) 17 *Journal of Refugee Studies* 50–68. In practice, however, many states have failed to do so and enforcement often remains difficult, see Sophie Cacciaguidi-Fahy, 'The Law of the Sea and Human Rights' (2007) 19 *Sri Lanka Journal of International Law* 85–107.

14 Art. 98(2) of the Convention on the Law of the Sea.

15 International Convention for the Safety of Life at Sea, as amended.

16 Art. 33(1) of the Convention Relating to the Status of Refugees. 28 July 1951. 189 UNTS 2545.

17 Gammeltoft-Hansen, *Access to Asylum*, 94–99.

18 Laura Barnett, *Global Governance and the Evolution of the International Refugee Regime*, New Issues in Refugee Research no. 54, United Nations High Commissioner for Refugees,

most European countries abandoned their welcoming labour immigration schemes, placing additional stress on the asylum institution. And at the same time, globalization allowed new patterns of migration and refugee flight by air and by sea, leading to mixed flows of irregular migrants, often facilitated by human smugglers specialized in avoiding traditional forms of border control.[19] Last, but not least, the advent of large-scale boat migration from refugee producing countries made receiving states concerned that asylum processing and protection responsibilities would follow from search and rescue operations. As a result, the hitherto relatively trivial issue of disembarkation of those rescued became politicized and subject to a variety of interpretations and resulting political stalemates between states each arguing against taking responsibility.[20]

In this context, both the *non-refoulement* principle and the duty to perform search and rescue have come to constitute significant fetters upon states' prerogative to perform border controls. As the drafting committee of the 1951 Refugee Convention made clear, the *non-refoulement* clause constitutes 'an exceptional limitation of the sovereign right of states to turn back aliens to the frontiers of their country of origin'.[21] As such, refugee and human rights law require border officials to immediately address those claiming to be in need of international protection before applying any generalized measures to block or return irregular boat migrants. Similarly, search and rescue rules are often triggered in the conduct of maritime border control where migrant vessels are either deemed unseaworthy or capsize during the encounter, either deliberately as migrants seek to provoke a rescue operation, or involuntarily if the weight of those on board the often-overcrowded ships shifts too much to one side.[22]

Both legal regimes have sought to respond to this new reality. Within international human rights law e.g. by expanding the application of the *non-refoulement* principle and other human rights norms in situations

Geneva (2002); Aristide Zolberg, 'Beyond the Crisis', in Peter M. Benda and Aristide Zolberg (eds), *Global Migrants, Global Refugees* (New York: Berghahn Books, 2001), 1–19.

19 Matthew J. Gibney and Randall Hansen, *Asylum Policy in the West: Past Trends, Future Possibilities*, WIDER Discussion Paper, UNU/WIDER, Helsinki, Finland (2003); Stephen Castles and Mark J. Miller, *The Age of Migration: International Population Movements in the Modern World*, 3rd edn (New York: Palgrave-Macmillan, 2003).

20 Violeta Moreno-Lax and Efthymios Papastavridis (eds), *'Boat Refugees' and Migrants at Sea: A Comprehensive Approach: Integrating Maritime Security with Human Rights* (The Hague: Brill, 2016).

21 Remark made by the Israeli delegate, Nehemiah Robinson. Ad Hoc Committee on Statelessness and Related Problems. First Session, 20th meeting. E/AC.32/SR.20, para. 49.

22 Interview with Spanish naval captain, Las Palmas, 23 April 2007.

where states perform migration control extra-territorially, and within search and rescue by seeking to resolve issues relating to the division of responsibilities and disembarkation for rescued migrants. Nonetheless, legal developments have not necessarily resulted in better protection of irregular boat migrants on the high seas, as evidenced by the growing death toll[23] and repeated political clashes in relation to this issue.

As will be argued in the following, rather than reducing the room for politics, paradoxically the development and expansion of international law on the high seas has enhanced the possibility of political manoeuvring. Context matters here. In comparison with *terra firma*, on the high seas the precise division and content of the sovereign rights and obligations are more open to interpretation and subject to varying interpretations. In this space, a particular geopolitics emerges, in which the zonal divisions of each state's search and rescue obligations and territorial logics in regard to asylum obligations clash with the more functional divisions of authority and assertions of power pertaining to migration control at sea. As a result, boat migrants find themselves subjected to an increasingly complex field of governance, in which participating states may successfully barter off and eschew their international obligations by reference to traditional norms of sovereignty and international law. Thus, rather than simply a space of non-sovereignty per se, the high seas become the venue for a range of competing claims and disclaims to sovereignty and responsibility.

In the following, we identify a number of politico-legal strategies pursued by states in this area, notably interpretive framing, regime shopping, jurisdiction shopping and international cooperation. While developments in both the law on search and rescue and international human rights law intended to improve the protection of irregular migrants have changed the modalities of these practices, the sovereignty game around search and rescue remains in place.

8.3 The Politics of Interpretation

The political struggles over search and rescue are facilitated by the continued unclarity in terms of the international legal framework. While few states have challenged the existence of search and rescue obligations at the general level, several issues of how to interpret the more specific obligations remain hotly contested. Neither the 1979 Search and Rescue nor the 1974 Safety of Life at Sea conventions provide a solid definition of what

[23] www.borderdeaths.org/.

constitutes 'distress'.[24] Instead, the captain of the intercepting ship is given authority to judge when a vessel is in need of rescue. Malta, for example, appears to apply a particularly narrow definition, effectively distinguishing between 'being in need of rescue' and general 'unseaworthiness' by modern standards. According to a senior officer of the Armed Forces of Malta, distress is defined as 'the imminent danger of loss of lives, so if they are sinking it is distress. If they are not sinking it is not distress' and hence no rescue operation is required.[25]

The problematic nature of this kind of discretion is compounded by the unavailability of the regular accountability mechanisms that usually accompanies such measures within the territory of liberal states. Compared to the migrant or asylum seeker arriving at the territory of his or her destination state, migrants who find themselves in distress or encounter migration control on the high seas will have obvious difficulties in accessing NGOs, medias, lawyers, or relevant authorities to plea their case and protection claims thus easily risk being 'overheard'.[26] Maltese authorities have thus been accused of encouraging and even supplying migrant boats with water and fuel to sail on to Italian waters and thereby 'pass the buck'.[27]

Secondly, disputes relate to the division of responsibilities. The search and rescue regime entails the division of the high seas into geographical

[24] Pugh, 'Drowning Not Waving', 58. The Search and Rescue Convention defines distress as 'situation wherein there is a reasonable certainty that a vessel or a person is threatened by grave and imminent danger and requires immediate assistance'. In 2012 the Parliamentary Committee of the Council of Europe emphasized that a situation of distress should be evaluated based on several factors, including the number of persons on board the vessel relative to its size, the number of persons showing signs of distress and the distance of the vessel from shore. Parliamentary Assembly of the Council of Europe, 'Lives Lost in the Mediterranean Sea: Who Is Responsible?', Doc. 12895 (2012).

[25] Silja Klepp, 'Illegal Migration and Migrant Fatalities in Malta', paper presented at the Human Cost of Border Control in the Context of EU Maritime Migration Systems, Vrije Universiteit, Amsterdam, 25–27 October 2009.

[26] Gammeltoft-Hansen, *Access to Asylum*, 209–30.

[27] In August 2009, Italian authorities rescued a boat with five Eritreans close to Lampedusa. The seventy-five other passengers originally on board had died of dehydration and starvation during the three weeks the boat had been at sea. The survivors claimed that at least ten ships had passed them by without rescuing them. In addition, the Italian Ministry of the Interior accused Malta's Maritime Squadron of spotting the boat two days prior to the Italian interception. According to the survivors, the Maltese authorities had supplied them with water and food supplies but not taken any steps to rescue them. A spokesperson from Malta's Armed Forces acknowledged that they had encountered the boat, but claimed the vessel and passengers appeared to be 'in very good shape' and that the migrants had refused assistance.; see further Repubblica, 22 August 2009.

search and rescue regions, in which each coastal state maintains overall responsibility for coordinating search and rescue operations. The importance of these zones was emphasized in the 2004 amendments to the Search and Rescue and Safety of Life at Sea conventions.[28] The amendments specify that persons rescued at sea are to be taken to a place of safety and the accompanying guidelines stress the importance of the *non-refoulement* principle in that disembarkation should be avoided in 'territories where the lives and freedoms of those alleging a well-founded fear of persecution would be threatened'.

At the same time, however, no direct obligation is placed upon states to allow rescued persons' access to their territory. Instead, contracting states shall 'co-ordinate and co-operate' to ensure that a place of disembarkation is found with a minimum further deviation from the ships' intended voyage whilst still respecting safety of life at sea. Where this does not happen on its own, a fall-back mechanism is inserted by noting that the state 'responsible for the search and rescue region in which such assistance is rendered shall exercise primary responsibility for ensuring such coordination and co-operation occurs'.[29] This residual obligation places additional emphasis on organizing disembarkation according to the existing division of the high seas into national search and rescue regions, which has been confirmed by the IMO Facilitation Committee.

If previously the law of the sea provided little guidance as to the resolution of conflicts over where rescued persons should be put ashore, the 2004 amendments implies a significant narrowing of the interpretative scope towards placing responsibility to ensure disembarkation with the state in charge of the SAR region. Under such an interpretation, carrying out migration control and search and rescue operations within North African states' territorial waters and SAR regions naturally becomes an attractive strategy for EU member states. Indeed, the intensified patrols by EU's border agency, Frontex, means that European patrol vessels are increasingly operating inside foreign search and rescue regions in the Mediterranean. Yet, if the above interpretation of disembarkation responsibilities is accepted, the amended SAR regime establish a normative structure for jurisdiction shopping. Barring any EU states offering disembarkation, the

28 Amendments to Chapter V of the International Convention for the Safety of Life at Sea and 2–4 of the Annex to the International Convention on Maritime Search and Rescue, entry into force 1 July 2006.

29 International Maritime Organization, Guidelines on the Treatment of Persons Rescued at Sea, MSC.167(78), 20 May 2004, Principle 6.17.

assumption would be that the respective third state would be responsible for allowing disembarkation of persons rescued during operations taking place within their search and rescue zone, and from then on presumably take on any asylum claims or enforce returns to the country of origin.

International agreement on this issue is still not uniform, however, and the language is clearly a compromise as indicated by the continued use of softer language such as 'coordinate' and 'should' in the aforementioned article in the IMO guidelines.[30] Several states continue to dispute the SAR region divisions or apply different interpretations in regard to disembarkation. Malta, which maintains an excessively large SAR region (a remnant of when Malta was under British colonial rule), has so far refused to ratify the 2004 amendments for fears that it would impose unrealistic obligations to disembark migrants rescued by other states and private vessels. Malta instead maintains that the coordinating country's obligation is to disembark rescued persons at the 'nearest safe port of call'.[31] This has led to further tensions between Malta and Italy following a series of incidents where migrants were rescued in Malta's SAR region yet were geographically closer to the Italian islands Lampedusa and Pantellaria than Malta's mainland. As neither country has been willing to allow disembarkation, the result has been lengthy stand-offs, in some cases leading to migrant deaths, and a number of confrontations between Italian and Maltese naval vessels literally trying to block each other from entering its territorial waters and disembark rescued migrants.[32]

8.4 Regime Shopping

The high seas furthermore provide a rather different legal environment than that normally encountered by migrants and refugees arriving at the territory of a host state. As noted above, the refugee regime in particular pays homage to the principle of territoriality. While the *non-refoulement* principle is generally accepted to apply wherever states exercise jurisdiction,[33] it remains a reactive obligation in the sense that it presupposes some kind of qualified contact between the state and the

[30] See further Seline Trevisanut, 'Search and Rescue Operations in the Mediterranean: Factor of Cooperation or Conflict?' (2010) 25 *International Journal of Marine and Coastal Law* 523–42.

[31] Raphael Vassallo, 'Between a Rock and a Hard Place', *Malta Today*, 13 September 2009.

[32] Derek Lutterbeck, 'Migrants, Weapons and Oil: Europe and Libya after the Sanctions' (2009) 14 *The Journal of North African Studies* 169–84.

[33] Gammeltoft-Hansen, *Access to Asylum*, 94–99.

asylum seeker. The importance of territorial delineations becomes even more evident when moving past this fundamental obligation and looking at the wider set of protections guaranteed by the international refugee protection regime. The rights stemming from the 1951 Refugee Convention are not granted *en bloc*, but rather progressively according to the 'level of attachment' a refugee obtains to a given country. Thus, the more sophisticated rights, such as access to welfare, employment and legal aid, are only granted when the refugee is 'lawfully staying' or 'durably resident' in the territory of the host state. Conversely, refugees or asylum seekers who are not present in a state's territory but nonetheless under its jurisdiction, such as on the high seas or in the territory of a third state, are only entitled to a basic set of rights centred around the *non-refoulement* obligation.[34]

The incremental approach reflects a sensible concern of the drafters not to immediately extend the full scope of rights in situations where refugees may arrive spontaneously in large numbers.[35] Yet, at a time when several states are moving both migration control and asylum processing offshore, this notion of progressive realization of rights risks being cut short, as refugees and asylum seekers may never reach the territory of the acting state.

In contrast with the territorial focus of refugee law, the law of the sea is generally informed by a 'functional' logic.[36] The law of the sea accepts that certain prerogatives short of full sovereignty may be projected beyond the state's territorial jurisdiction. This includes the right to exercise migration control within the 24-mile contiguous zone,[37] and the extension of exclusive claims to e.g. fishing within the exclusive economic zone, extending 200 miles from the baseline.[38]

In the context of boat migrants, this shift creates a pretext for political attempts to sever the bond between authority and responsibility, leaving states free to assert sovereign prerogatives in regard to migration

[34] The most pertinent rights under the Refugee Convention that are specifically granted without reference to being present or staying at the territory include Art. 33 (*non-refoulement*), Art. 16 (access to courts) and Art. 3 (non-discrimination). Somewhat more specific and limited in their extraterritorial remit Arts. 13 (property), Act. 22 (education) and Act. 20 (rationing) also apply extraterritorially. James Hathaway, *The Rights of Refugees under International Law* (Cambridge: Cambridge University Press, 2005), 160ff.

[35] Hathaway, *The Rights of Refugees under International Law*, 157ff.

[36] Maria Gavouneli, *Functional Jurisdiction in the Law of the Sea* (The Hague: Martinus Nijhoff, 2007); Brian D. Smith, *State Responsibility and the Marine Environment: The Rules of Decision* (Oxford: Clarendon Press, 1988).

[37] Art. 24(1) of the Convention on the Territorial Sea and Contiguous Zone.

[38] Art. 56 of the Convention on the Law of the Sea.

control without taking on the correlate duties that would normally flow from international refugee and human rights law. This argument was made most clearly by the Italian government in the *Hirsi* case.[39] The case concerned Italy's much-criticized interception programme in cooperation with Libya from 2009 to 2011. The Italian government claimed that even though the applicants had been brought on board Italian navy vessels – something that will normally trigger the state's jurisdiction[40] – the Italian authorities had not exercised 'absolute and exclusive control'[41] over the applicants, but merely carried out a search and rescue operation on the high seas in accordance with its obligations under the law of the sea. According to the government:

> The Italian ships had confined themselves to intervening to assist the three vessels in distress and ensuring the safety of the persons on board. They had then accompanied the intercepted migrants to Libya in accordance with the bilateral agreements of 2007 and 2009. The Government argued that the obligation to save human lives on the high seas, as required under the Montego Bay Convention, did not in itself create a link between the State and the persons concerned establishing the State's jurisdiction.[42]

Such attempts towards 'regime shopping' in order to escape human rights obligations are far from limited to maritime interception.[43] Yet, the European Court of Human Rights has so far rejected that parallel obligations under international law – whether part of bilateral and regional arrangements or under multilateral treaties – can displace a state's human rights obligations.[44] In the *Hirsi* case, it did so by making exactly the opposite argument, namely that general international law supported a finding of

[39] *Hirsi Jamaa and Others v. Italy*. European Court of Human Rights. Appl. no. 27765/09. 23 February 2012.

[40] *Medvedyev and Others v. France*. European Court of Human Rights. Appl. no. 3394/03 29 March 2010 GC; *Xhavara and fifteen v. Italy and Albania*. European Court of Human Rights. Appl. no. 39473/98. 11 January 2001 (admissibility).

[41] *Hirsi*, ibid., para. 64. See further Chapter 3, this volume.

[42] *Hirsi*, ibid., para. 65.

[43] Thomas Gammeltoft-Hansen and Jens Vedsted-Hansen (eds), *Human Rights and the Dark Side of Globalisation: Transnational Law Enforcement and Migration Control* (London: Routledge, 2016).

[44] In *Al-Saadoon and Mufdhi v. United Kingdom* (European Court of Human Rights. Appl. no. 61498/08. 2 March 2010), the UK government thus argued that that it was under a bilateral legal obligation to transfer the applicant to the Iraqi authorities, even though such a transfer might constitute refoulement in relation to Art. 2, as there was a serious risk that they would be subjected to the death penalty. While the European Court of Human Rights acknowledged that 'the Convention should be interpreted as far as possible in harmony with other principles of international law . . . [and] . . . recognises the importance of international cooperation' (para. 126), it rejected this claim, arguing that 'Article 1 makes no

human rights jurisdiction, and that obligations in relation to different bodies of international law applied cumulatively:

> The Court observes that by virtue of the relevant provisions of the law of the sea, a vessel sailing on the high seas is subject to the exclusive jurisdiction of the State of the flag it is flying. This principle of international law has led the Court to recognise, in cases concerning acts carried out on board vessels flying a State's flag, in the same way as registered aircraft, cases of extra-territorial exercise of the jurisdiction of that State [. . .] Where there is control over another, this is *de jure* control exercised by the State in question over the individuals concerned.
>
> . . .
>
> Moreover, Italy cannot circumvent its 'jurisdiction' under the Convention by describing the events at issue as rescue operations on the high seas. In particular, the Court cannot subscribe to the Government's argument that Italy was not responsible for the fate of the applicants on account of the allegedly minimal control exercised by the authorities over the parties concerned at the material time.[45]

However important the *Hirsi* judgment was from a human rights perspective, it is unlikely to prove the end of political manoeuvring to avoid human rights obligations in the context of maritime search and rescue. Following the overturn of the Tunisian government, Italy was quick to negotiate a new agreement to deploy its naval assets in international waters north of Tunisia's coastline.[46] Yet in contrast to the Libya scheme, Italy's role is in this case limited to notifying its Tunisian counterparts whenever migrant vessels are leaving the coast. As it is Tunisia's authorities undertaking the interception before the boats leave territorial waters, Italy thus claims to avoid triggering any direct human rights responsibility.[47]

distinction as to the type of rule or measure concerned and does not exclude any part of the Contracting Party's "jurisdiction" from scrutiny under the Convention' (para. 128).

45 *Hirsi*, ibid., paras 77 and 79.

46 Ministry of the Interior, 'Siglato l'Accordo tra Italia e Tunisia', press release, 6 April 2011. Available from www.interno.it. See further Matteo Tondini, 'The Legality of Intercepting Boat People under Search and Rescue and Border Control Operations with Reference to Recent Italian Interventions in the Mediterranean Sea and the Ecthr Decision in the Hirsi Case' (2012) 18 *Journal of International Maritime Law* 59074, at 74

47 Customary international law does establish principles whereby a secondary responsibility may fall upon Italy for 'aiding or assisting' another state in the commission of an internationally wrongful act. See in particular the International Law Commission, Articles on State Responsibility, Art. 16. Yet, in practice this sort of indirect obligation has proved difficult to invoke in regard to human rights, and it demands that both states are bound by the same international treaties. See Tom de Boer, 'Closing Legal Black Holes: The Role of Extraterritorial Jurisdiction in Refugee Rights Protection' (2014) 28 *Journal of Refugee Studies* 118–34 and Thomas Gammeltoft-Hansen and James C. Hathaway,

Vice versa, for an institution such as the European Court of Human Rights, precedent is likely to structure the ongoing development of interpretation in this area. Even if a more 'functional' approach to establishing extra-territorial responsibility may be finding its way into the jurisprudence of the European Court of Human Rights,[48] existing case law retains a strong affinity to territoriality principles,[49] resulting in the rather strenuous tests for 'effective control over territory' and 'personal authority' that are likely to exclude certain instances of offshore migration control.[50]

8.5 Marketization and Jurisdiction Shopping

Third and finally, the boat migrant is caught up in a more general shift towards neoliberal governance. As aforementioned, migration control is traditionally considered an inalienable sovereign function of the state. Yet today, migration management is fast becoming a key foreign policy issue or even commodity, where deals are being struck between developed states and the countries of origin and transit.[51] In February 2017 Italy, backed by the EU Council, concluded an agreement with Libya's GNA government, promising to provide both funding and equipment to Libya's struggling coastguard in exchange for the fragile government's support in

'Non-refoulement in a World of Cooperative Deterrence' (2015) 53(2) *Columbia Journal of Transnational Law* 235–85, at 267ff.

48 See e.g. *Pad and Others v. Turkey*. European Court of Human Rights. Appl. no. 60167/00. 28 June 2007 and *Al-Skeini and Others v. United Kingdom*. European Court of Human Rights. Appl. no. 55721/07. 7 July 2011, para. 135. See further Gammeltoft-Hansen and Hathaway, 'Non-Refoulement', 266ff.

49 Notably *Bankovic and Others v. Belgium, Czech Republic, Denmark, France, Germany, Greece, Hungary, Iceland, Italy, Luxemburg, Netherlands, Norway, Poland, Portugal, Spain Turkey and the UK*. European Court of Human Rights. Appl. no. 5207/99. 12 December 2001 (Grand Chamber). For critique see e.g. Erik Roxstrom, Mark Gibney and Terje Einarsen, 'The Nato Bombing Case (Bankovic et al. v. Belgium et al.) and the Limits of Western Human Rights Protection' (2005) 23 *Boston University International Law Journal* 56–136; Rick Lawson, 'Life after Bankovic: On the Extraterritorial Application of the European Convention on Human Rights', in Fons Coomans and Menno T. Kamminga (eds), *Extraterritorial Application of Human Rights Treaties* (Antwerp: Intersentia, 2004), 83–123.

50 Gammeltoft-Hansen, *Access to Asylum*, 100–157.

51 Aderanti Adepoju, Femke Van Noorloos and Annelies Zoomers, 'Europe's Migration Agreements with Migrant-Sending Countries in the Global South: A Critical Review' (2010) 48 *International Migration* 42–75; Philippe Fargues and Christine Fandrich, *Migration after the Arab Spring*, Migration Policy Centre Research Report 2012/09, September 2012.

stopping boat migrants towards Europe.[52] Likewise, the 2015 EU-Turkey agreement involved both cooperation on migration control and a return arrangement for asylum seekers arriving in Greece in exchange for the EU speeding up accession talks, visa liberalization, resettlement spaces and a total of 3 billion Euros to provide refugee assistance in Turkey.[53] The political backdrop for the *Hirsi* case mentioned above was the 2007 agreement between Italy and Libya, promising the latter US$5 billion if the Gaddafi regime would set up radar detection facilities on Libya's shores and work with Italy to prevent the departure of unauthorized migrants.[54] Outside Europe, Australia's 'Pacific Solution' saw that country woo the island state of Nauru with offers of free medical care, educational opportunities and sports ovals in return for the warehousing in Nauru of boat migrants intercepted by Australia.[55] That deal was the genesis for subsequent outreach to other neighbouring states, including Indonesia and Papua New Guinea,[56] intended to prevent boats carrying migrants from travelling towards Australia.

The above examples may be seen as evidence of an increasing 'marketization of migration management', in which global migration governance are increasingly adopting the methods and values of the market

52 Nikolaj Nielsen, 'Italy and Libya Cut Migrant Busting Deal', *EU Observer*, 3 February 2017, https://euobserver.com/migration/136781; Council of the European Union, 'Malta Declaration by the Members of the European Council on the External Aspects of Migration: Addressing the Central Mediterranean Route', 3 February 2017.

53 The Agreement builds on the EU-Turkey Joint Action Plan of 15 October 2015.

54 The Treaty on Friendship, Partnership and Cooperation between Italy and Libya was signed on 30 August 2008 and entered into force on 2 March 2009. Cooperation under the treaty was halted in March 2011 following the NATO bombing campaign. See further Human Rights Watch, *Pushed Back, Pushed Around: Italy's Forced Return of Boat Migrants and Asylum Seekers, Libya's Mistreatment of Migrants and Asylum Seekers*, New York, September 2009, 24; Thomas Gammeltoft-Hansen, 'The Externalisation of European Migration Control and the Reach of International Refugee Law', in Elspeth Guild and Paul Minderhoud (eds), *The First Decade of EU Migration and Asylum Law* (Leiden: Martinus Nijhoff, 2012), 273–98.

55 Tara Magner, 'The Less Than "Pacific" Solution for Asylum Seekers in Australia' (2004) 16 *International Journal of Refugee Law* 53–90.

56 In July 2013 Papua New Guinea (PNG) and Australia signed a bilateral agreement to process and resettle an uncapped number of asylum seekers in PNG, to be funded by Australia but administered by PNG. As well as funding the entire arrangement, Australia announced a suite of additional development assistance programmes to the developing state. Regional Resettlement Arrangement between Australia and Papua New Guinea, signed in Brisbane 19 July 2013; Helen Brown, *Indonesia to change visa requirements for Iranians entering the country following request from PM Kevin Rudd*, Australian Broadcasting Commission, 19 July 2013, www.abc.net.au/news/2013-07-18/indonesia-to-change-visa-requirements-for-iranians/4829434.

to guide policy development and implementation. This marketization is premised on a combination of jurisdiction shopping and commercialization of sovereignty itself. As certain states are keen to outsource the less palatable aspects of governments, such as migration control, others states are making their territory and/or authorities available for the same purpose in exchange for funds, development assistance, trade privileges, labour migration quotas or some other form of compensation. The result is that sovereign prerogatives, territory and functions are strategically traded and commodified among states and between governments.[57]

The introduction of such market-based logics into the migration field have deep-seated and troubling consequences for the migrants affected. In terms of human rights accountability, jurisdiction shopping may be seen to achieve a geographic, political and/or legal distancing of the less palatable aspects of migration governance away from the sponsoring state. In the patchwork of national refugee and human rights jurisdictions, shifting the legal geography and/or government responsible for carrying out migration control may simultaneously reduce the acting state's protection responsibilities and shift legal obligations to third states whose 'human rights obligations are either lower, less extensive or less precise than those of the destination State'.[58] Sponsoring states have not shied away from cooperating with non-parties to the 1951 Refugee Convention, such as Libya and Indonesia. Indeed, Nauru's then non-party status may have been part of the reason for Australia choosing it as a place for offshore asylum processing in 2001.[59] Papua New Guinea is party to the Convention but maintains several reservations, affecting core rights, such as non-penalization and freedom of movement, as well as refugees' standard of treatment in regard to housing, employment and education.[60]

As in the above case, both domestic jurisprudence and developments in international human rights law have made inroads to counter this dynamic. For example, the Australian High Court struck down the

[57] Ronen Palan, 'Tax Havens and the Commercialization of State Sovereignty' (2002) 56 *International Organization* 151–76; Gammeltoft-Hansen and Vedsted-Hansen, *Human Rights and the Dark Side of Globalisation*.

[58] Gregor Noll, 'The Politics of Saving Lives: Interception, Search and Rescue and the Question of Human Rights at Sea', paper presented at the Future of Asylum Policy in the European Union, Turku, 10 October 2006.

[59] Nauru acceded to the 1951 Convention Relating to the Status of Refugees as well as the 1967 Protocol on 28 June 2011.

[60] Diana Glazebrook, 'Papua New Guinea's Refugee Track Record and Its Obligations under the 2013 Regional Resettlement Arrangement with Australia', SSGM Discussion Paper 2014/3, Australian National University.

government's scheme to relocate asylum seekers arriving irregularly by boat to Malaysia.[61] In doing so, the court lent support to the general interpretative principle under the 1951 Refugee Convention that a state may only transfer an asylum seeker to a third state if equivalent 'effective protection' is provided there.[62] More generally, international human rights law jurisprudence has developed to accept shared and differentiated responsibility in a range of situations relevant to international cooperation on migration control and asylum processing.[63]

Even so, the market dynamic may in itself be argued to produce 'negative externalities' for the migrant. As in the case of privatization, the introduction of a third-party profit motive into migration management is likely to lead to cost-cutting,[64] and third states may thus be unwilling or unable to make good on promises to ensure effective human rights protection. While this is often suppressed at the political level, it is a foreseeable consequence. The efficiency of a market economy is premised on a feedback loop from consumers to suppliers: if consumers do not like the product, they will not buy it. Yet, the marketization of migration control represents a third-party provider economy, where the end-users (migrants) are not the same as the customers (sponsoring states) footing the bill. Migrants themselves do not get a voice in this equation and oversight and accountability mechanisms as part of these schemes are equally lacking. The result is a 'rights economy' in which human rights and refugee protection is either sought realized at the lowest possible cost or disbanded altogether.[65]

8.6 Understanding the Politics of Law in Regard to Rescue at Sea

How can we account for the developments of the SAR and SOLAS regimes, and their impact on the encounter between irregular boat migrants and

[61] *Plaintiffs M70/2011 and M106 of 2011 v. Minister for Immigration and Citizenship* ('*the Malaysia-Swap Arrangement case*') [2011] HCA 32.

[62] Susan Kneebone, 'The Bali Process and Global Refugee Policy in the Asia-Pacific Region' (2014) 27 *Journal of Refugee Studies* 596–618; Michelle Foster, 'Protection Elsewhere: The Legal Implications of Requiring Refugees to Seek Protection in Another State' (2007) 28 *Michigan Journal of International Law* 223–86, at 230–31; Stephen H. Legomsky, 'Secondary Refugee Movements and the Return of Asylum Seekers to Third Countries: The Meaning of Effective Protection' (2003) 15 *International Journal of Refugee Law* 567–667, at 570.

[63] Gammeltoft-Hansen and Hathaway, 'Non-Refoulement', 272ff.

[64] Gammeltoft-Hansen and Sørensen, *The Migration Industry*.

[65] Thomas Gammeltoft-Hansen, 'Outsourcing Asylum: The Advent of Protection Lite', in Luiza Bialasiewicz (ed.), *Europe in the World: EU Geopolitics and the Making of European Space* (Farnham, UK: Ashgate, 2011), 129–52.

sovereign authorities on the high seas? At face value it might fit a governance framework, characterized by transnational dynamics, the evaporation of boundaries, a growing interdependence between a plurality of state and non-state actors, and the thickening of international regimes and regulation. Within such a framework the emphasis is on the linkages between formally equal members of the international society (networks of interdependence), whose dealings with each other regarding shared problems take place on an equal footing, without relying on centralized, hierarchical and coercive authority structures to create international order. In this view governance is conceived as rescuing the international community from 'sovereignty's worst instincts'.[66] Sovereignty is, in this case, conceived in terms of autonomy and freedom, and works – like traditional conceptions of power – as a zero-sum game.[67]

Yet, such an understanding misses out on the more intricate relationship between sovereignty, power and international law, between freedom, rule and responsibility, that seem to be at play in the encounter between sovereigns and boat migrants at the high seas. The amendments to the SAR and SOLAS conventions do not just connote a development from the international law of co-existence to the international law of cooperation[68] regarding rescue at sea that limits and/or 'tames' state freedom in the *Mare Liberum*. Rather, the cooperative regime in the international realm involves a transformation of the logic of politics and the functioning of power itself in relation to states as the simultaneous masters and subjects of international law.[69]

Crucially, this functioning of power is not separate from the legal realm but part and parcel of the manifestation of sovereign identity as it is embedded in international legal regime at play. In case of the SAR regime, it is the ongoing normative developments that provide the context within which the sovereignty game at the high seas is carried out. For example, the zonal divisions of the *Mare Liberum* through the search and rescue regime not only replicate the powerful imaginary of territorial jurisdiction, but equally can be conceived as a particular way of governing the high seas by linking freedom with responsibility.

66 Michael Barnett and Raymond Duvall, *Power in Global Governance* (Cambridge: Cambridge University Press, 2005), 1.

67 See further Chapter 2, this volume.

68 Wolfgang Friedmann, *The Changing Structure of International Law* (London: Stevens & Sons, 1964).

69 Iver B. Neumann and Ole Jacob Sending, 'The International as Governmentality' (2007) 35 *Millennium* 677–701.

Together this leads to a different analytics of the politics of law in the context of the high seas. International law does not necessarily work through liberal internalization and socialization processes,[70] nor is it a redundant normative layer to the rationalist sovereignty game where the key players are conceived as atomistic subjects that pursue their self-interested strategies regardless of the international normative context in which they encounter each other.[71] Rather, as we argued in the above, it is precisely because of the normative patchwork established by the search and rescue regime, human rights and refugee law that sovereign states take pains to *dis*claim their sovereignty, rather than jealously guard it. It is precisely the increasing codification of the international realm, including the high seas, that at once creates the necessity of disclaiming practices *and* provides the tools to do so.

In the encounter between European authorities and migrants on the high seas, the sovereign in other words makes use of the discretion to interpret legal rules and/or apply different legal regimes and thus seek redefine and demarcate its sovereign responsibility under these diverse systems of rules and regimes.

8.7 Conclusion

The high seas remain one of the few places on earth not subject to a national sovereign legal order, which could be said to make the legal framework rather thin, both legally and, especially, institutionally. The lack of a domestic legal order makes shifts between different legal regimes easier and subject to less oversight and means for resolution. Enforcing and monitoring the application of maritime regimes thus becomes inherently difficult. The lack of legal clarity and protection of migrant lives have led some scholars to describe the situation in the Mediterranean with regard to search and rescue as the 'Wild West'.[72]

It would be misguided, however, to think of the high seas as a space of legal exception per se. The law of the sea, international human right law and EU law together provide a normative framework for governance, albeit with somewhat different arrangements of the relationship between

[70] See e.g. Martha Finnemore and Kathryn Sikkink, 'International Norm Dynamics and Political Change' (1998) 52 *International Organization* 887–917.

[71] See e.g. Stephen D. Krasner, *Sovereignty: Organized Hypocrisy* (Princeton, NJ: Princeton University Press, 1999).

[72] Derek Lutterbeck, 'Small Frontier Island: Malta and the Challenge of Irregular Migraiton' (2009) 20 *Mediterranean Quarterly* 119–41, at 131.

autonomy and responsibility for states engaged in migration control and search and rescue in the Mediterranean. In this chapter, we have tried to show how a geopolitics of the *Mare Liberum* is thereby created through which states may seek to disclaim responsibilities through different strategies, notably regime shopping, legal interpretation and jurisdiction shopping.

While from the perspective of governments these strategies are all coached and enacted in the language of international law, the result easily appears exactly opposite from the perspective of the boat migrant. Rather than creating a dense net that will provide for a better protection of migrants and refugees, the codification of the *Mare Liberum* has simultaneously created loopholes that enable states to barter off their sovereignty at the expense of their responsibility towards those in distress at sea. Consequently, the boat migrant far too often find herself no longer caught in it and consequently out of legality altogether.[73]

[73] Hannah Arendt, 'The Perplexities of the Rights of Man', in Peter Baehr (ed.), *The Portable Hannah Arendt* (New York: Penguin Books, 2000), 31–45, at 34ff.

9

Conclusion

The Dark Side of Legalization

TANJA AALBERTS AND THOMAS GAMMELTOFT-HANSEN

Its expansion since the mid twentieth century is a remarkable achievement for international law, right after two world wars seemed to have signalled the bankruptcy of modern international law before it fully matured. While Hans Morgenthau and his new colleagues in the juvenile discipline of International Relations propagated an agenda of realistic power politics, the process of legalization of international society only got started, resulting in an impressive collection of 158 000 treaties and 125 international courts and tribunals, and legal regimes for each and every issue area in foreign policy by the end of the millennium. As identified by Wolfgang Friedmann, the normative thickening of international life has not just resulted in a significant expansion of treaty law and international judiciaries but also led to qualitative transformations of international law itself, incorporating different subjects and issue areas, such as human rights, international criminal law and climate change. At the same time, it would be naïve to present this transformation of international law as a purely progressive project beyond politics. As has been pointed out by different scholars, international law is both surrounded by and steeped in power politics.[1] Similarly, post-colonial and historical legal scholars remind us how modern international law is rooted in imperialism and complicit in past and present exploitation.[2]

A key problem of celebratory (hi)stories of international law's expansion as a progressive teleology lies with simplistic conceptualizations of

[1] Detlev F. Vagts, 'Hegemonic International Law' (2001) 95 *American Journal of International Law* 843–48; Martti Koskenniemi, 'International Law and Hegemony: A Reconfiguration' (2004) 17 *Cambridge Review of International Affairs* 197–218.

[2] B. S. Chimni, 'Third World Approaches to International Law: A Manifesto' (2006) 8 *International Community Law Review* 3–28; Antony Anghie, *Imperialism, Sovereignty and the Making of International Law* (Cambridge: Cambridge University Press, 2005).

opposing dichotomies: from power politics to norms, from strategy to rules, from sovereignty to international law with one side of the dichotomy always necessary trumping its opposite. Yet, as this volume has argued, the development of international law presents a far more nuanced, complicated and interesting story of the politics of international law. In this concluding chapter, we want to summarize the main findings and contributions of the volume in conceptual, analytical and methodological terms, and make some suggestions for the further development of the research agenda initiated here.

9.1 Conceptual Reorientation

This volume shows how legal proliferation has indeed changed the playing field for members of the international society, and the sovereignty games they play. For most states, big and small alike, moving outside the confines of international law has become more difficult and costly. As such, international law is indeed disciplining politics, but the crucial point is that it does not do so in a unidirectional way, away from politics. In the face of a rather dense net of legal rules, and international law at every corner of foreign affairs, to paraphrase Kennedy,[3] it is the very confines of international law and the meaning of international rules that are the subject of engaged political contestation. Based on the general and somewhat contradictory developments in international law as an elaborate yet fragmented patchwork of rules, the foregoing chapters have analyzed the paradox of increasing legalization leading to increasing politicization through various case studies. More specifically, they have investigated how normative developments both change the obligations and agency of states under international law, yet at the same time, and through international law's proliferation and transformation, provide the backdrop for governmental strategies to instrumentalize legal discourse.

Crucially, this paradox of simultaneous legalization and politicization is not a sign of international law's shortcomings or failure, but rather the result of an extensive legal system at work. If sovereignty is an international ordering device that works by linking freedom and responsibilities,[4]

[3] See quote on p. 5, this volume.

[4] Tanja E. Aalberts and Wouter G. Werner, 'Sovereignty beyond Borders: Sovereignty, Self-Defense and the Disciplining of States', in Rebecca Adler-Nissen and Thomas Gammeltoft-Hansen (eds), *Sovereignty Games: Instrumentalising State Sovereignty in Europe and Beyond* (Houndmills, UK: Palgrave, 2008), 129–50. See further Chapter 2, this volume.

the upshot of the international legal patchwork is that it provides a larger playing field for states to creatively manage this relationship. This is the dark side not only of disaggregated sovereignty, as Mann argues with regard to executive cooperation on mass surveillance,[5] but also of international law's own success story of expansion. Multiple and overlapping regimes and responsibilities enable states to eschew legal obligations, thus resulting in, as Brummer provocatively formulates it in Chapter 3, law's complicity in creating irresponsibility. The expansion of international law thus challenges the rule of law by facilitating 'organized irresponsibility',[6] precisely because there is so much law to draw on and to legally escape, disperse and disavowal responsibilities and shift them elsewhere.

At the conceptual level, what the chapters to this volume have sought to provide is a counter-balance to the progressive image of international law. These critical reflections on the operation of international law should not, however, be understood as a rejection of international law's regulatory significance and potential. As Fleur Johns has argued, 'experiencing law as manipulable rhetoric is not the same as experiencing law as wrong or worthless'.[7] Rather our point is that in order to have a better understanding of the limits and possibilities of the international rule of law, and law as a check on state power, we need to take a step back and analyze how state practices to strategically navigate this normative terrain are intimately connected to developments of international law itself.

9.2 Empirical Reorientation

In line with this conceptual reorientation, the volume has secondly called for an empirical reorientation. To understand how international politics and the international legal order operate in tandem, we need to empirically investigate the concrete ways in which states navigate the international legal order; how states concomitantly play *by* and *with* the rules. The chapters to this volume identify a range of different cases where states rely on international law's complex and fragmented structure in order to turn legal norms and structures to their own advantage, regain sovereign room for manoeuvre and legitimize otherwise controversial policies.

5 Chapter 6, this volume.

6 Scott Veitch, *Law and Irresponsibility: On the Legitimation of Human Suffering* (Abingdon, UK: Routledge, 2007).

7 Fleur Johns, *Non-Legality in International Law: Unruly Law* (Cambridge: Cambridge University Press, 2013), 20.

As a framework for such an empirical analysis, Chapter 1 set out a general repertoire of different strategies, derived from the literature and our previous work: jurisdiction shopping, international cooperation, regime or treaty shopping, judicial forum shopping, interpretive framing and extra-legal deferral. This preliminary typology is intended as starting point for a new empirical research agenda on the politics of international law, and as such not intended to be exhaustive. Thus, while each chapter identifies one or more of these general strategies as part of the various case studies, they also further nuance this framework, showing additional perspectives and connections, as well as pointing to new and different strategies.

One of these perspectives relates to the temporal dimension. As Baumgärtel shows in Chapter 5, states may pursue different strategies at different stages of the legal process; from developing policies in 'grey areas' of international law, to pursuing legal interpretation and mobilizing peer support during court proceedings, and to post-judgment positioning and adjustment of policies. Another important temporal factor is the relative state of legal development. The limited degree of codification in areas such as environmental law and mass surveillance shapes both the form of international cooperation and the kind of strategies pursued. As Mann highlights, executive agreements, Memoranda of Understanding and other soft law instruments have come to shape arrangements on issues such as mass surveillance, migration control, rendition and trade in a way that at once provides political flexibility and shrouds these arrangements from the public eye, effectively limiting political debate and requiring public interest lawyers to pursue different strategies to access and understand the 'underwater part of the iceberg'.[8]

In areas of political sensitivity, the development of international law may further serve a more performative role, not backed by any real interest among states to ensure that new legal instruments effectively regulate the issues at stake. As Ellis argues in regard to international environmental law, poor regulatory design may in itself be seen as a strategy through which states seek to avoid or reduce constraint. Questions may be framed in economic or scientific rather than legal terms, deflecting political-legal struggles to other forms of expertise.[9]

Moreover, the analysis shows that even in light of complex legal constructions involving various forms of international and transnational

[8] Chapter 6, this volume. [9] Chapter 7, this volume.

forms of cooperation, traditional distinctions concerning state sovereignty, the public-private divide and territory far from disappear. This can be seen in regard to the law of sea, where the otherwise universal obligation to perform search and rescue is increasingly tied to geographical divisions of the high seas.[10] More fundamentally, Brummer shows in Chapter 3 how the formation of extra-territorial zones is connected to particular political-legal vocabularies of international law, allowing the legal character of a specific piece of territory to be defined from a multitude of legal bases.

Together the case studies show how the combined quantitative and qualitative transformations of international law further facilitate strategic engagement with the law, or navigating the room for semi-compliance, as Langford et al. formulate it in Chapter 4. The varied patchwork of legal regimes, institutions and instruments enables the invocation of one register of law, not to disregard or violate the law, but to avoid it by 'comply[ing] with other law – while at the same time thwarting law's stated normative commitments'.[11] In other words, the expansion of international law has not eliminated politics, but transformed its operation as states are pursuing their foreign policy goals through a variety of strategies that mobilize international law in sophisticated ways in order to mitigate its constraining effects on the one hand, while legitimizing international politics, on the other.

9.3 Towards a New Research Agenda

The next step for this research agenda is to elaborate on the typology as a template to systematically reflect on international legal practices. The case studies themselves already provided hints for further elaboration. For instance, in Chapter 5, Baumgärtel discusses a strategy of containment in European litigation on migration and asylum, as well as 'peer mobilization' as a specific form of international cooperation. In her analysis of international environmental law, Ellis identifies managerialism as another important transformation of law which facilitates efficiency as another strategy in Chapter 7. Brummer provides an insightful discussion of how jurisdiction shopping takes on different shades in the context of different understandings of what constitutes jurisdiction across different legal regimes.[12] Focusing on international cooperation between executive agencies, Mann shows the

[10] Chapter 8, this volume. [11] Chapter 6, this volume, p. 131.
[12] Chapter 3, this volume.

importance of transnational security networks.[13] Similarly, Langford, Behn and Fauchald point to the intricate interplay between domestic and international law and judiciaries.[14]

Other possible additional strategies to be explored in further research are strategically created treaty conflicts and 'treaty rambling'[15] which relates to, but provides a more specific dynamic than treaty shopping as a more general category; or 'legal inter-textuality' as a more specific strategy of interpretive framing combined with some form of judicial forum shopping.[16] On a more epistemological level, one could trace different modes of reasoning, or 'dialects' within legal reasoning that go back to different paradigms within the disciplinary history of international law, building on natural law, legal positivism or the recent turn to legitimacy and/or managerialism.[17]

Apart from the fine-tuning and/or expansion of the typology of strategies, a further step would be to broaden the analysis to other issue areas and cases. Cases might include the current process surrounding control over resource utilization and access to the Arctic, the global regime for tax evasions as evidenced by the Panama papers, or new types of warfare (with new types of actors, such as private military companies, as well as new weaponry, such as drones and other automated weapon systems) more generally. Such an expansion into other areas of international law would be a crucial contribution to the making of an inventory of strategies as initiated in this volume.

Moreover, our investigation has focused on the repertoire of political-legal strategies, rather than on who and under what conditions these strategies are deployed. A next stage in developing this research agenda should move beyond elaborating and fine-tuning the typology and zoom out to further investigate its workings across the board: which strategies are the most popular, across which issues areas, which states are most active if not successful in their politico-legal strategies (as well as other actors within the transnational legal field – such as executive agencies,

[13] Chapter 6, this volume. [14] Chapter 4, this volume.

[15] Surabhi Ranganathan, *Strategically Created Treaty Conflicts and the Politics of International Law* (Cambridge: Cambridge University Press, 2015).

[16] Philip Liste, 'The Politics of (Legal) Intertextuality' (2010) 4 *International Political Sociology* 318–21.

[17] David Kennedy, *A World of Struggle. How Power, Law & Expertise Shape Global Political Economy* (Princeton, NJ: Princeton University Press, 2016). Martti Koskenniemi, 'Miserable Comforters: International Relations as New Natural Law' (2009) 15 *European Journal of International Relations* 395–422. See also Chapter 7, this volume.

non-governmental organizations and private regulators). Indeed, another aspect coming out of the several chapters relates to the need to differentiate amongst states. Not all states share the same outlook on international law, and great differences persist in terms of resources to design and implement strategies.

Another crucial entry that follows from this concerns the scope conditions, and in particular the political economy, of this form of legalized politics. Even if hegemony does not necessarily trump law, and law can also be an instrument to resist hegemony, it is indeed costly to engage in this kind of legal navigation. For one thing, you will need an army of the cleverest lawyers. Perhaps unsurprising, it is particularly states in the Global North that have engaged in cumbersome and often costly policy schemes to manage international and domestic legal commitments in regard to issues such as migration, prisoner rendition and surveillance. Vice versa, despite a formal emphasis on reciprocity, economic inequality and outlook inevitably shape states' approach to international investment law. At the same time, the asymmetry between states and private parties invariably provide the former with a range of strategic possibilities to exploit their sovereign status in order to resist foreign investor arbitration.[18] So a further step would be to focus on different types of (state) actors to see if and how inequality gets reproduced within the system of equal sovereigns.[19] Of particular interest would be to investigate the specific repertoire of how great powers engage with international law, insofar as they would seem to be best positioned to ignore international law without repercussions.

9.4 Methodological Reorientation

While it has not been made explicit so far, the research agenda proposed in this volume methodologically shares a number of affinities with the recent 'practice turn' in International Relations and International Law, as well as with its elaboration in terms of 'European new legal realism' in international legal theory.[20] In order to further locate this research agenda, it is

[18] Chapter 4, this volume.

[19] Chapter 7, this volume. See also Nico Krisch, 'International Law in Times of Hegemony: Unequal Power and the Shaping of the International Legal Order' (2005) 16 *European Journal of International Law* 369–408.

[20] Nikolas M. Rajkovic, Tanja E. Aalberts and Thomas Gammeltoft-Hansen, 'Introduction: Legality, Interdisciplinarity and the Study of Practices', in Nikolas M. Rajkovic, Tanja E. Aalberts and Thomas Gammeltoft-Hansen (eds), *The Power of Legality: Practices of International Law and Their Politics* (Cambridge: Cambridge University Press, 2016); Jakob

worthwhile to highlight some of the main pointers of a practice approach, albeit only summarily at this stage.

While both International Law and International Relations have been familiar with the notion of 'practice' as a generic or descriptive term, as an analytical approach the practice turn invites us to examine how international practices constitute and transform domains we usually take for granted as given, separate and even juxtaposed. Crucially, in order to do so, a practice approach calls for a move away from a priori theorizing towards empirically investigating what communities of actors are doing in and on the world. In our case, it means putting politics and law as social practices – as an actual, contingent, evolving and productive set of activities that reconstitute the international order – centre stage.[21]

While related to specific epistemologies on knowledge production and its relation to world-making,[22] the practice approach proposed here (investigating *how* practices constitute law) may accommodate different theoretical orientations and explanatory frameworks as to *why* states would engage in this behaviour.[23] In this regard Langford et al. rely on rationalist explanations, whereas Ellis' chapter aligns more with constructivist reasoning, Mann engages with liberal institutionalist concepts, and Brummer's approach is closer to legal realism.[24] What unites the various contributions, however, is a shift away from deductive theory-testing and towards a more bottom-up or inductive investigation of a repertoire of practice. Such a research agenda, we believe, can help avoid theoretical trench wars and instead provide an agora for pluralist dialogue.[25] As

V. H. Holtermann and Mikael Rask Madsen, 'European New Legal Realism and International Law: How to Make International Law Intelligible' (2015) 28 *Leiden Journal of International Law* 211–30.

21 Such a focus on practices remains different from recent calls for an 'empirical turn' seeking to turn legal studies into a more scientific discipline by placing more emphasis on social scientific methods. See below and note 34.

22 Friedrich Kratochwil, 'Making Sense of "International Practices"', in Emanuel Adler and Vincent Pouliot (eds), *International Practices* (Cambridge: Cambridge University Press, 2011), 36–60.

23 See Chapter 2, this volume.

24 See Chapters 4, 6 and 7, this volume. In a previous version of our chapter on the Search and Rescue regime, we engaged with the Foucaultian concept of governmentality. Tanja E. Aalberts and Thomas Gammeltoft-Hansen, 'Sovereignty at Sea: The Law and Politics of Saving Lives in Mare Liberum' (2014) 17 *Journal of International Relations and Development* 439–68.

25 Our own divergent theoretical orientations illustrate how focusing on practices can overcome theoretical standstills. Crucially, our call is for a pluralist agenda which does not seek to synthesize different theoretical approaches into an eclectic hotchpotch.

Dunoff has recently observed, '[t]here is increasing convergence [among mainstream and counter currents] on the proposition that the best teaching and research is problem driven. Scholarship should neither be led, nor constrained, by the structures of the academy or by academic trends'.[26] Even if its label of a 'turn' might indicate another theoretical trench war in the making, the practice turn invites us to reflect upon (inter)disciplinarity as a practice itself, and engage in question-driven research.[27] With its specific focus on politico-legal strategies within a globalized international order, we hope that the current volume puts the practice turn into sharper focus by extending this 'movement' into new fields, events and issues.

9.5 Towards a New Interdisciplinary Agenda

The turn to practices also opens up interesting avenues for interdisciplinary research collaboration.[28] The underlying argument of this volume is that in order to analyze the interplay between politics and international law, we need to move the interdisciplinary agenda beyond a division of labour based on narrow conceptions of how international law and politics work as separate and autonomous practices. Instead, we propose an integrated approach combining legal insight and doctrinal legal analysis with an understanding of the broader context in which international rules operate. Such an approach, on the one hand, requires legal scholars to move beyond a strict focus on (international) law as a body of rules, to focusing on how these rules come to life. International law, in other words, must be seen as 'an activity, and not a thing. Its 'being' is in the 'doing' of the participants within the practice'.[29] On the other hand, the

26 Jeffrey L. Dunoff, 'Perspectives on the Perils, Promise, Politics – and Practice – of Interdisciplinarity', in Nikolas M. Rajkovic, Tanja E. Aalberts and Thomas Gammeltoft-Hansen (eds), *The Power of Legality: Practices of International Law and Their Politics* (Cambridge: Cambridge University Press, 2016), 345–70, at 370.

27 Friedrich Kratochwil, *The Status of Law in World Society: Meditations on the Role and Rule of Law* (Cambridge: Cambridge University Press, 2014).

28 Tanja E. Aalberts and Ingo Venzke, 'Moving Beyond Interdisciplinary Turfwars: Toward an Understanding of International Law as Practice', in André Nollkaemper et al. (eds), *International Law as Profession* (Cambridge: Cambridge University Press, 2016); Rajkovic et al., 'Introduction: Legality, Interdisciplinarity and the Study of Practices'; Dunoff, 'Perils, Promise, Politics'.

29 Dennis M. Patterson, 'Law's Pragmatism: Law as Practice and Narrative', in Dennis M. Patterson (ed.), *Wittgenstein and Legal Theory* (Boulder, CO: Westview Press, 1992), 85–121, at 87. For an analysis of the different communities of practice construing legality in specific areas and times, see Nikolas M. Rajkovic, Tanja E. Aalberts and Thomas Gammeltoft-Hansen (eds), *The Power of Legality: Practices of International Law and Their Politics* (Cambridge: Cambridge University Press, 2016).

approach forwarded here rejects one-sided methodologies to establish the power or irrelevance of international law based on external causalities and behavioural compliance, erasing the importance of doctrinal practices for understanding international law altogether. This kind of external approach has driven large parts of the interdisciplinary agenda between International Law and International Relations over the past few decades,[30] and also finds expression among scholars promoting an 'empirical turn' based on social scientific methods within international law.[31] However, such external perspectives easily risk reducing the politics of international law to measuring and managing rule compliance.[32] In contrast, we argue that an understanding of the specific characteristics of international law as a set of argumentative practices as well as the engagement with the technicalities and craft of developing legal argument are essential for analyzing what, in any particular instance, compliance means in the first place.[33] In other words, we embrace the call by European New Legal Realism that in order to understand the workings of international law, we need to accommodate both the internal dimension of international law as a particular legal form and discourse *and* the social context as the external dimension in which legal argumentation gains its power, and is contested.[34]

[30] For an important overview, see Jeffrey L. Dunoff and Mark A. Pollack (eds), *Interdisciplinary Perspectives on International Law and International Relations: The State of the Art* (Cambridge: Cambridge University Press, 2013).

[31] Gregory Shaffer and Tom Ginsburg, 'The Empirical Trend in International Law' (2012) 106 *American Journal of International Law* 1–46. In the quantitative variant propagated by the Society for Empirical Legal Studies, empirical work is identified with a specific form of data collection and quantitative statistical analysis and thus provides a similar external perspective to law as compliance studies in IR. As such, it stands in stronger opposition to doctrinal work than a practice approach as another form of empirical legal studies. Jakob V. H. Holtermann and Mikael Rask Madsen, 'Toleration, Synthesis or Replacement? The "Empirical Turn" and Its Consequences for the Science of International Law' (2016) 29 *Leiden Journal of International Law* 1001–19.

[32] Koskenniemi, 'Miserable Comforters'.

[33] It should be emphasized that we do not suggest all IR approaches are necessarily external perspectives on law. Such generalizing and homogenizing dichotomies are one of the reasons behind the current deadlock in the IL/IR debate, possibly creating another trench war and even outright rejection of interdisciplinarity altogether. Such a view also goes against the premises of a practice oriented approach and neglects for instance the work by Nicholas Onuf and Friedrich Kratochwil, who share a critical constructivist approach that is adamant to recognize the *proprium* of international law as an argumentative practice and thus provide a critical alternative to the mainstreamed IL/IR agenda. Aalberts and Venzke, 'Moving beyond Interdisciplinary Turfwars'.

[34] Holtermann and Madsen, 'European New Legal Realism'; see also Wouter G. Werner, 'The Use of Law in International Political Sociology' (2010) 4 *International Political Sociology* 304–7.

Last, but not least, we believe that a practice approach can address some of the concerns regarding what a move to politics and inter-disciplinarity entails for the autonomy of international law as an (academic) field.[35] Analyzing the politics of international law from a practice approach allows for an understanding of international law as simultaneously autonomous and political.[36] International law is autonomous as a *social* practice. As such, its autonomy is not an inherent feature emanating from its normative corpus, nor an empirically given thing, but rather a contingent outcome of its different practices. At the same time, despite its distinctive mode of reasoning, international legal argumentation remains an undeniable political enterprise. Legal arguments, in other words, never simply produce substantive outcomes, but always also seek to justify them.[37] As aptly put by Andrew Hurrell: '[I]f there remains an unavoidable need to hold on to the specificity of law as a social institution, neither is it possible to evade the complexity and specificity of politics',[38] and, we would emphasize, the *interplay* between these two.[39] A practice approach provides a way to keep in focus the mutually constitutive relationship between international law and politics, which in turn enables a grounded understanding of how international law is politicized without reducing law to an epiphenomenon of power politics, based on various understandings of what power entails.[40] It also means that, rather than focusing on bodies of rules and legal texts alone, we need to trace day-to-day actions and processes through which international law is produced, performed, disseminated *and* resisted.[41]

If what emerges from this volume is a profound ambivalence about international law and its capabilities, we follow the lead by Veitch who suggests that the response to our schizophrenia with regard to

[35] See e.g. Jan Klabbers, 'The Bridge Crack'd: A Critical Look at Interdisciplinary Relations' (2009) 23 *International Relations* 119–25.

[36] Aalberts and Venzke, 'Moving beyond Interdisciplinary Turfwars'.

[37] Martti Koskenniemi, *From Apology to Utopia: The Structure of International Legal Argument* (1989; repr., Cambridge: Cambridge University Press, 2005), 570.

[38] Andrew Hurrell, 'Conclusion: International Law and the Changing Constitution of International Society', in Michael Byers (ed.), *The Role of Law in International Politics* (Oxford: Oxford University Press, 2000), 327–47, at 333.

[39] See also the forum on international law and international political sociology in (2010) 4(3) *International Political Sociology*.

[40] Michael Barnett and Raymond Duvall, 'Power in Global Governance', in Michael Barnett and Raymond Duvall (eds), *Power in Global Governance* (Cambridge: Cambridge University Press, 2005), 1–32.

[41] See also Johns, *Non-Legality*; Rajkovic et al., *Power of Legality*.

(international) law as either an absolute good or a corrupt force should be not to loose sight of either of these sides, but rather 'to explore in nuanced ways precisely where and how the extremes meet. It is here that we must address how what might appear to be an excess can be, and often is, simultaneously rooted in the norm [. . .], enacting and legitimating disavowals and amnesias of responsibilities'.[42] We hope that this volume has put the inherent ambivalence of the politics of international law to productive scrutiny by empirically exploring politico-legal strategies as specific ways of engagement and contestation in practices of (ir)responsibilities. Not to accuse or dismiss international law as toothless or irrelevant, but as a basis to come to terms with the fact that international law and politics are entangled, and, crucially, that the impulse to create more international law in order to seal up its loopholes is not necessarily the best way forward.

[42] Veitch, *Law and Irresponsibility*, 11.

BIBLIOGRAPHY

Aalberts, Tanja, *Constructing Sovereignty between Politics and Law* (London: Routledge, 2012)

'Playing the Game of Sovereign States: Charles Manning's Constructivism *Avant-La-Lettre*' (2010) 16 *European Journal of International Relations* 247–68

'The Sovereignty Game States Play: (Quasi-)States in the International Order' (2004) 17 *International Journal for the Semiotics of Law* 245–57

Aalberts, Tanja and Thomas Gammeltoft-Hansen, 'Sovereignty at Sea: The Law and Politics of Saving Lives in Mare Liberum' (2014) 17 *Journal of International Relations and Development* 439–68

Aalberts, Tanja and Ingo Venzke, 'Moving beyond Interdisciplinary Turfwars: Toward an Understanding of International Law as Practice', in André Nollkaemper, Jean d'Aspremont, Tarcisio Gazzini and Wouter G. Werner (eds), *International Law as Profession* (Cambridge: Cambridge University Press, 2017), pp. 287–310

Aalberts, Tanja and Wouter Werner, 'International Law and International Political Sociology', in Xavier Guillaume and Pınar Bilgin (eds), *The Routledge Handbook of International Political Sociology* (New York, NY: Routledge, 2017), pp. 36–45

'Mastering the Globe: Law, Sovereignty and the Commons of Mankind', in Rens van Munster and Casper Sylvest (eds), *The Politics of Globality since 1945: Assembling the Planet* (New York: Routledge, 2016), pp. 89–105

'Sovereignty beyond Borders: Sovereignty, Self-Defense and the Disciplining of States', in Rebecca Adler-Nissen and Thomas Gammeltoft-Hansen (eds), *Sovereignty Games: Instrumentalising State Sovereignty in Europe and Beyond* (Houndmills, UK: Palgrave, 2008), pp. 129–50

Abbott, Kenneth W. and Duncan Snidal, 'Hard and Soft Law in International Governance', in Judith L. Goldstein et al. (eds), *Legalization and World Politics* (Cambridge, MA: MIT Press, 2001), pp. 37–72

'Law, Legalization, and Politics: An Agenda for the Next Generation of IL/IR Scholars', in Jeffrey L. Dunoff and Mark A. Pollack (eds), *Interdisciplinary Perspectives on International Law and International Relations: The State of the Art* (Cambridge: Cambridge University Press, 2013), pp. 33–56

Abbott, Kenneth W. et al., 'The Concept of Legalization' (2000) 54(3) *International Organization* 401–19

Adepoju, Aderanti, Femke Van Noorloos and Annelies Zoomers, 'Europe's Migration Agreements with Migrant-Sending Countries in the Global South: A Critical Review' (2010) 48 *International Migration* 42–75

Adler-Nissen, Rebecca and Thomas Gammeltoft-Hansen (eds), *Sovereignty Games: Instrumentalising State Sovereignty in Europe and Beyond* (Houndmills, UK: Palgrave, 2008)

Allen, S., *The Chagos Islanders and International Law* (Oxford: Hart, 2014)

Alschner, Wolfgang, 'The Impact of Investment Arbitration on Investment Treaty Design: Myth versus Reality' (2017) 42 *Yale Journal of International Law* 1–66

Alter, Karen J., 'Agents or Trustees? International Courts in Their Political Context' (2008) 14 *European Journal of International Relations* 33–63

The New Terrain of International Law: Courts, Politics, Rights (Cambridge: Cambridge University Press, 2014)

Alter, Karen J. and Sophie Meunier, 'The Politics of International Regime Complexity' (2009) 7(1) *Perspectives on Politics* 13–24

Altwicker, Tilmann and Oliver Diggelmann, 'How Is Progress Constructed in International Legal Scholarship?' (2014) 25 *European Journal of International Law* 425–44

Alvarez, Jose, 'Contemporary International Law: An "Empire of Law" or the "Law of Empire"' (2009) 24(5) *American University International Law Review* 811–42

'The Return of the State' (2011) 20 *Minnesota Journal of International Law* 223–64

Amoore, Louise, *The Politics of Possibility* (Durham, NC: Duke University Press, 2013)

Anghie, Antony, *Imperialism, Sovereignty and the Making of International Law* (Cambridge: Cambridge University Press, 2005)

Arendt, Hannah, 'The Perplexities of the Rights of Man', in Peter Baehr (ed.), *The Portable Hannah Arendt* (New York: Penguin Books, 2000), pp. 31–45

Avtgis, Alexander, 'Rethinking Article 422: A Retrospective on Ecuador's 2008 Constitutional ISDS Recalibration' (2016) 2(2) *Indiana Journal of Constitutional Design*, 1–21

Baird, Douglas G., Robert H. Gertner and Randal C. Picker, *Game Theory and the Law* (Cambridge, MA: Harvard University Press, 1998)

Bandjunis, V. and Diego Garcia, *Creation of the Indian Base* (San Jose, CA: Writer's Showcase, 2001)

Barboza, Julio, *The Environment, Risk and Liability in International Law* (Leiden: Martinus Nijhoff, 2011)

Barnett, Michael and Raymond Duvall, 'Power in Global Governance', in Michael Barnett and Raymond Duvall (eds), *Power in Global Governance* (Cambridge: Cambridge University Press, 2005), pp. 1–32

Basilien-Gainche, Marie-Laure, 'Immigration Detention under the Return Directive: The CJEU Shadowed Lights' (2015) 17 *European Journal of Migration and Law* 104–26

Baumgärtel, Moritz, 'From Deficit to Dilemma: An Evaluation of the Contribution of Europe's Supranational Courts to the Promotion of the Rights of Vulnerable Migrants', unpublished PhD thesis, Université libre de Bruxelles (2016)

Beck, Robert J., 'International Law and International Relations Scholarship', in David Armstrong (ed.), *Routledge Handbook of International Law* (Abingdon, UK: Routledge, 2009), pp. 13–43

Beck, Robert J., Anthony Clark Arend and Robert D. Vander Lugt (eds), *International Rules: Approaches from International Law and International Relations* (Oxford: Oxford University Press, 1996)

Behn, Daniel, 'Legitimacy, Evolution, and Growth in Investment Treaty Arbitration: An Empirical Evaluation of Recent Decisions' (2015) 46(2) *Georgetown Journal of International Law* 363–415

Behn, Daniel, Tarald Berge and Malcolm Langford, 'Poor States or Poor Governance? Testing Claims of Systemic Bias in Investment Treaty Arbitration' (forthcoming) *Northwestern Journal of International Law & Business*

Benvenisti, Eyal and George W. Downs, 'The Empire's New Clothes: Political Economy and the Fragmentation of International Law' (2007) 60 *Stanford Law Review* 595–631

Bianchi, Andrea, Daniel Peat and Matthew Windsor (eds), *Interpretation in International Law* (Oxford: Oxford University Press, 2015)

Bix, Brian, 'H.L.A. Hart and the "Open Texture" of Language' (1991) 10 *Law and Philosophy* 51–72

Block, Laura and Saskia Bonjour, 'Fortress Europe or Europe of Rights? The Europeanisation of Family Migration Policies in France, Germany and the Netherlands' (2013) 15 *European Journal of Migration and Law* 203–24

Boer, Tom de, 'Closing Legal Black Holes: The Role of Extraterritorial Jurisdiction in Refugee Rights Protection' (2014) 28 *Journal of Refugee Studies* 118–34

Borgen, Christopher J., 'Resolving Treaty Conflicts' (2005) 37 *George Washington International Law Review* 57–80

Bourdieu, Pierre, 'The Force of Law: Toward a Sociology of the Juridical Field' (1987) 38 *Hastings Law Journal* 805–53

Boyle, Alan E., 'Globalising Environmental Liability: The Interplay of National and International Law' (2005) 17 *Journal of Environmental Law* 3–26

'Human Rights and the Environment: Where Next?' (2012) 23 *European Journal of International Law* 613

Broberg, Morten and Niels Fenger, *Preliminary References to the European Court of Justice* (Oxford: Oxford University Press, 2014)

Brown, Chester, *Commentaries on Selected Model Investment Treaties* (Oxford: Oxford University Press, 2013)

Brunnée, Jutta and Stephen J. Toope, 'International Law and Constructivism: Elements of an Interactional Theory of International Law' (2000) 39 *Columbia Journal of Transnational Law* 19–74

Bull, Hedley, *The Anarchical Society: A Study of Order in World Politics*, 2nd edn (London: Macmillan, 1977)

Busch, Mark L., 'Overlapping Institutions, Forum Shopping, and Dispute Settlement in International Trade' (2007) 61 *International Organization* 735–61

Byers, Michael (ed.), *The Role of Law in International Politics: Essays in International Relations and International Law* (Oxford: Oxford University Press, 2000)

Cacciaguidi-Fahy, Sophie, 'The Law of the Sea and Human Rights' (2007) 19 *Sri Lanka Journal of International Law* 85–107

Capps, Patrick and Julian Rivers, 'Kant's Concept of International Law' (2010) 16 *Legal Theory* 229–57

Carty, Anthony, 'Language Games of International Law: Koskenniemi as the Discipline's Wittgenstein' (2012) 13 *Melbourne Journal of International Law* 1–20

'Sociological Theories of International Law', in *Max Planck Encyclopedia of Public International Law* (Oxford: Oxford University Press, 2009)

Castles, Stephen and Mark J. Miller, *The Age of Migration: International Population Movements in the Modern World*, 3rd edn (New York: Palgrave Macmillan, 2003)

Charney, Jonathan I., 'Transnational Corporations and Developing Public International Law' (1983) 4 *Duke Law Journal* 748–88

Chayes, Abram and Antonia Handler Chayes, *The New Sovereignty: Compliance with International Regulatory Agreements* (Cambridge, MA: Harvard University Press, 1995)

Chetail, Vincent, 'The Common European Asylum System: Bric-à-Brac or System?', in Vincent Chetail, Philippe De Bruycker and Francesco Maiani (eds), *Reforming the Common European Asylum System: The New European Refugee Law* (Leiden, Netherlands: Martinus Nijhoff, 2016)

Chimni, B. S., 'Legitimating the International Rule of Law', in James Crawford and Martti Koskenniemi (eds), *The Cambridge Companion to Interntional Law* (Cambridge: Cambridge University Press, 2012), pp. 290–308

'Third World Approaches to International Law: A Manifesto' (2006) 8 *International Community Law Review* 3–28

Chinkin, Christine, 'Human Rights and the Politics of Representation: Is There a Role for International Law?', in Michael Byers (ed.), *The Role of Law in International Politics* (Oxford: Oxford University Press, 2000), pp. 131–48

Clapham, Andrew, *Human Rights Obligations of Non-State Actors* (Oxford: Oxford University Press, 2006)

Clinton, Hilary, *Hard Choices* (New York: Simon and Schuster)

Collins, David, 'Loss Aversion Bias or Fear of Missing Out: A Behavioural Economics Analysis of Compensation in Investor–State Dispute Settlement' (2016) 8(3) *Journal of International Dispute Settlement* 460–82

Conant, Lisa J., *Justice Contained: Law and Politics in the European Union* (Ithaca, NY: Cornell University Press, 2002)

Conroy, J., *Unspeakable Acts, Ordinary People: The Dynamics of Torture* (Berkeley: University of California Press, 2000)

Conway, Gerard, *The Limits of Legal Reasoning and the European Court of Justice* (Cambridge: Cambridge University Press, 2012)

Crawford, James and Martti Koskenniemi, 'Introduction', in James Crawford and Martti Koskenniemi (eds), *The Cambridge Companion to International Law* (Cambridge: Cambridge University Press, 2012), pp. 1–21

Creamer, Cosette, 'Between the Letter of the Law and the Demands of Politics: The Judicial Balancing of Trade Authority within the WTO', working paper (2015)

Cutler, Claire A., 'The Legitimacy of Private Transnational Governance: Experts and the Transnational Market for Force' (2010) 8 *Socio-Economic Review* 157–85

Daw, Tim and Tim Gray, 'Fisheries Science and Sustainability in International Policy: A Study of Failure in the European Union's Common Fisheries Policy' (2005) 29 *Marine Policy* 189

Dawson, Mark, Bruno De Witte and Elise Muir (eds), *Judicial Activism at the European Court of Justice* (Cheltenham, UK: Edward Elgar, 2013)

Deeks, Ashley, 'An International Legal Framework for Surveillance' (2015) 55 *Virginia Journal of International Law* 55

'Checks and Balances from Abroad' (2015) 83(4) *University of Chicago Law Review* 65–88

'Intelligence Communities, Peer Constraints, and the Law' (2015) 7 *Harvard National Security Journal* 1–54

Dembour, Marie-Bénédicte, *When Humans Become Migrants: Study of the European Court of Human Rights with an Inter-American Counterpoint* (Oxford: Oxford University Press, 2015)

Den Heijer, Maarten, 'Reflections on Refoulement and Collective Expulsion in the Hirsi Case' (2013) 25 *International Journal of Refugee Law* 265–90

Donohue, Laura, 'Bulk Metadata Collection: Statutory and Constitutional Considerations' (2014) 37 *Harvard Journal of Law and Policy* 757–900

Dothan, Shai, *Reputation and Judicial Tactics: A Theory of National and International Courts* (Cambridge: Cambridge University Press, 2014)

Dumberry, Patrick, 'Are BITs Representing the "New" Customary International Law in International Investment Law?' (2010) 28(4) *Penn State International Law Review* 675–701

Dunlap, Major General Charles J., 'Lawfare amid Warfare', *Washington Times*, 3 August (2007)

Dunoff, Jeffrey L., 'Perspectives on the Perils, Promise, Politics – and Practice – of Interdisciplinarity', in Nikolas M. Rajkovic, Tanja E. Aalberts and Thomas Gammeltoft-Hansen (eds), *The Power of Legality: Practices of International Law and Their Politics* (Cambridge: Cambridge University Press, 2016), pp. 345–70

Dunoff, Jeffrey L. and Mark A. Pollack (eds), *Interdisciplinary Perspectives on International Law and International Relations: The State of the Art* (Cambridge: Cambridge University Press, 2013)

Easterling, K., *Enduring Innocence: Global Architecture and Its Political Masquerades* (Cambridge, MA: MIT Press, 2005)

Echandi, Roberto and Pierre Sauvé (eds), *Prospects in International Investment Law and Policy* (Cambridge: Cambridge University Press, 2013)

Fabri, H. R., 'Regulating Trade, Investments and Money', in J. Crawford and M. Koskenniemi (eds), *The Cambridge Companion to International Law* (Cambridge: Cambridge University Press, 2012), pp. 352–72

Fearon, James and Alexander Wendt, 'Rationalism v. Constructivism: A Skeptical View', in Walter Carlsnaes, Thomas Risse and Beth A. Simmons (eds), *Handbook of International Relations* (London: Sage, 2002), pp. 52–72

Fecák, Tomáš, 'Czech Experience with Bilateral Investment Treaties: Somewhat Bitter Taste of Investment Protection' (2011) 2 *Czech Yearbook of Public & Private International Law* 233–67

Finnemore, Martha and Kathryn Sikkink, 'International Norm Dynamics and Political Change' (1998) 52 *International Organization* 887–917

Finnemore, Martha and Stephen J. Toope, 'Alternatives to "Legalization": Richer Views of Law and Politics' (2001) 55 *International Organization* 743–58

Fischer-Lescano, Andreas and Gunther Teubner, 'Regime-Collisions: The Vain Search for Legal Unity in the Fragmentation of Global Law' (2004) 25 *Michigan Journal of International Law* 999–1046

Fitzmaurice, M. A. and C. Redgwell, 'Environmental Non-Compliance Procedures and International Law' (2000) 31 *Netherlands Yearbook of International Law* 35–65

Foster, Michelle, 'Protection Elsewhere: The Legal Implications of Requiring Refugees to Seek Protection in Another State' (2007) 28 *Michigan Journal of International Law* 223–86

Foster, Michelle and J. Pobjoy, 'A Failed Case of Legal Exceptionalism? Refugee Status Determination in Australia's "Excised" Territory' (2011) 23 *International Journal of Refugee Law* 1–49

Foucault, Michel, 'Truth and Power', in Colin Gordon (ed.), *Power/Knowledge: Selected Interviews and Other Writings 1972–1977* (Brighton, UK: Harvester Press, 1980), pp. 109–33

Friedmann, Wolfgang, *The Changing Structure of International Law* (London: Stevens, 1964)

Galanter, Marc, 'Why the "Haves" Come Out Ahead: Speculations on the Limits of Legal Change' (1974) 9 *Law and Society Review* 95–160

Gammeltoft-Hansen, Thomas, *Access to Asylum: International Refugee Law and the Globalisation of Migration Control* (Cambridge: Cambridge University Press, 2011)

'The Externalisation of European Migration Control and the Reach of International Refugee Law', in Elspeth Guild and Paul Minderhoud (eds), *The First Decade of EU Migration and Asylum Law* (Leiden, Netherlands: Martinus Nijhoff, 2012), pp. 273–98

'Outsourcing Asylum: The Advent of Protection Lite', in Luiza Bialasiewicz (ed.), *Europe in the World: EU Geopolitics and the Making of European Space* (Farnham, UK: Ashgate, 2011), pp. 129–52

'The Perfect Storm: Sovereignty Games and the Law and Politics of Boat Migration', in Violeta Moreno-Lax and Efthymios Papastavridis (eds), *'Boat Refugees' and Migrants at Sea: A Comprehensive Approach: Integrating Maritime Security with Human Rights* (The Hague: Brill, 2016), pp. 60–79

'Private Security and the Migration Control Industry', in Rita Abrahamsen and Anna Leander (eds), *Routledge Handbook on Private Security* (New York: Routledge, 2015), pp. 207–217

'The Role of International Refugee Law in Refugee Policy' (2014) 27 *Journal of Refugee Studies* 574–595

Gammeltoft-Hansen, Thomas and Rebecca Adler-Nissen, 'An Introduction to Sovereignty Games', in Rebecca Adler-Nissen and Thomas Gammeltoft-Hansen (eds), *Sovereignty Games: Instrumentalising State Sovereignty in Europe and Beyond* (Houndmills, UK: Palgrave, 2008), pp. 1–17

Gammeltoft-Hansen, Thomas and James C. Hathaway, 'Non-Refoulement in a World of Cooperative Deterrence' (2015) 53 *Columbia Journal of Transnational Law* 235–85

Gammeltoft-Hansen, Thomas and Ninna Nyberg Sørensen (eds), *The Migration Industry and the Commercialization of International Migration* (London: Routledge, 2013)

Gammeltoft-Hansen, Thomas and Jens Vedsted-Hansen (eds), *Human Rights and the Dark Side of Globalisation: Transnational Law Enforcement and Migration Control* (London: Routledge, 2016)

Ganty, Sarah and Moritz Baumgärtel, 'Effective Remedies as Capabilities: Towards a User Perspective to Human Rights of Migrants in Belgium' (2014) 8 *Human Rights & International Legal Discourse* 215–34

Garrett, Geoffrey and Barry Weingast, 'Ideas, Interests, and Institutions: Constructing the EC's Internal Market', in Judith Goldstein and Robert Keohane (eds), *Ideas and Foreign Policy* (Ithaca, NY: Cornell University Press, 1993), pp. 173–206

Gavouneli, Maria, *Functional Jurisdiction in the Law of the Sea* (The Hague: Martinus Nijhoff, 2007)

Gehring, Thomas and Eva Ruffing, 'When Arguments Prevail over Power: The CITES Procedure for Listing of Endangered Species' (2008) 8 *Global Environmental Politics* 123–48

Glas, Lize R., 'Changes in the Procedural Practice of the European Court of Human Rights: Consequences for the Convention System and Lessons to be Drawn' (2014) 14 *Human Rights Law Review* 671–99

Goho, Shaun A., 'Note: The CITES Fort Lauderdale Criteria: The Uses and Limits of Science in International Conservation Decisionmaking' (2000-1) 114 *Harvard Law Review* 1769–92

Goldie, L. F. E., 'Liability for Damage and the Progressive Development of International Law' (1965) 14(4) *International & Comparative Law Quarterly* 1189–264

Goldsmith, Jack and Eric A. Posner, *The Limits of International Law* (Oxford: Oxford University Press, 2005)

Goldstein, Judith et al., 'Introduction: Legalization and World Politics' (2000) 54 *International Organization* 385–99

Gordon, Kathryn and Joachim Pohl, 'Investment Treaties over Time: Treaty Practice and Interpretation in a Changing World', OECD Working Papers on International Investment (Paris: OECD, 2015)

Greenwald, Glenn, *No Place to Hide: Edward Snowden, the NSA, and the U.S. Surveillance State* (New York: Metropolitan Books, 2014)

Groenendijk, Kees, 'Recent Developments in EU Law on Migration: The Legislative Patchwork and the Court's Approach' (2014) 16 *European Journal of Migration and Law* 313–35

Grotius, Hugo, *The Freedom of the Seas* (Oxford: Oxford University Press, 1916)

Guilfoyle, Douglas, *Shipping Interdiction and the Law of the Sea* (Cambridge: Cambridge University Press, 2009)

Guzman, Andrew T., *How International Law Works: A Rational Choice Theory* (New York: Oxford University Press, 2008)

Hadfield, Gillian K., 'Privatizing Commercial Law: Lessons from ICANN' (2002) 6 *Journal of Small and Emerging Business Law* 257–288

Hadley, Kate, 'Do China's BITS Matter? Assessing the Effect of China's Investment Agreements on Foreign Direct Investment Flows, Investor's Rights, and the Rule of Law' (2013) 45 *Georgetown Journal of International Law* 255–321

Haftel, Yoram and Alexander Thompson, 'Delayed Ratification: The Domestic Fate of Bilateral Investment Treaties' (2013) 67 *International Organization* 355–87

Haftel, Yoram and Alexander Thompson, 'When Do States Renegotiate Investment Agreements? The Impact of Arbitration' (forthcoming) *Review of International Organizations*

Handl, Gunther, 'Compliance Control Mechanisms and International Environmental Obligations' (1997) 5 *Tulane Journal of International and Comparative Law* 29–49

Harrelson, Jill, 'Blackbeard Meets Blackwater: An Analysis of International Conventions That Address Piracy and the Use of Private Security Companies to Protect the Shipping Industry' (2010) 25 *American University International Law Review* 283–312

Hart, Herbert L. A., *The Concept of Law* (1961; repr., Oxford: Oxford University Press, 1997)

Essays in Jurisprudence and Philosophy (Oxford: Oxford University Press, 1993)

Hathaway, James, *The Rights of Refugees under International Law* (Cambridge: Cambridge University Press, 2005), pp. 1236–372

Hathaway, James and T. Gammeltoft-Hansen, 'Non-Refoulement in a World of Cooperative Deterrence', Law & Economics Working Paper 106 (2014)

Hathaway, Oona, 'Between Power and Principle: An Integrated Theory of International Law' (2005) 71 *University of Chicago Law Review* 469–536

'Treaties' End: The Past, Present, and Future of International Law Making in the United States' (2008) 117(7) *The Yale Law Journal* 1236–1567

Helfer, Laurence R., 'Forum Shopping for Human Rights' (1999) 148 *University of Pennsylvania Law Review* 285–400

'Regime Shifting; the Trips Agreement and the New Dynamics of International Intellectual Property Making' (2004) 29 *Yale Journal of Intenational Law* 1–81

Henkin, Louis, *How Nations Behave* (New York: Columbia University Press, 1979)

Henriksen, Anders, 'Fanger, folkeret og "brite-finter"' [Detainees, international law and 'the British Trick'] (2014) 87 *Økonomi & Politik* 6–15

Herman, Michael, '11 September: Legitimizing Intelligence?' (2002) 16(2) *International Relations* 227–241

Higgins, Rosalyn, 'Human Rights in the International Court of Justice' (2007) 20 *Leiden Journal of International Law* 745–51

Hinsley, F. H., *Sovereignty*, 2nd edn (Cambridge: Cambridge University Press, 1986)

Hirschman, Albert, *Exit, Voice, and Loyalty: Responses to Decline in Firms, Organizations, and States* (Cambridge, MA: Harvard University Press, 1970)

Holmes, Oliver Wendell, Jr, 'The Path of the Law' (1897) 10 *Harvard Law Review* 457–61

Holtermann, Jakob V. H. and Mikael Rask Madsen, 'European New Legal Realism and International Law: How to Make International Law Intelligible' (2015) 28 *Leiden Journal of International Law* 211–30

'Toleration, Synthesis or Replacement? The "Empirical Turn" and Its Consequences for the Science of International Law' (2016) 29 *Leiden Journal of International Law* 1001–19

Hoppe, Carsten, 'Passing the Buck: State Responsibility for Private Military Companies' (2008) 19 *European Journal of International Law* 989–1014

Hurrell, Andrew, 'Conclusion: International Law and the Changing Constitution of International Society', in Michael Byers (ed.), *The Role of Law in International Politics* (Oxford: Oxford University Press, 2000), pp. 327–47

Jackson, Robert H., *Quasi-States: Sovereignty, International Relations and the Third World* (Cambridge: Cambridge University Press, 1990)

Jansen, Sabine, 'Introduction: Fleeing Homophobia, Asylum Claims Related to Sexual Orientation and Gender Identity in Europe', in Thomas Spijkerboer (ed.), *Fleeing Homophobia: Sexual Orientation, Gender Identity and Asylum* (London: Routledge, 2013), pp. 1–31

Jenks, C. Wilfred, 'The Conflict of Law-Making Treaties' (1953) 30 *British Yearbook of International Law* 401–453

'Liability for Ultra-Hazardous Activities in International Law' (1966) 117 *RCADI* 99–200

Johns, Fleur, 'Guantánamo Bay and the Annihilition of the Exception' (2005) 16 *European Journal of International Law* 613–35

Non-Legality in International Law: Unruly Law (Cambridge: Cambridge University Press, 2013)

Johnstone, Ian, *The Power of Deliberation: International Law, Politics and Organizations* (Oxford: Oxford University Press, 2011)

Kalicki, Jean and Anna Joubin-Bret (eds), *Reshaping the Investor-State Dispute Settlement System: Journeys for the 21st Century* (The Hague: Brill, 2015)

Kapczynski, Amy, 'The Trans-Pacific Partnership – Is It Bad for Your Health?' (2015) 373 *New England Journal of Medicine* 373

Kedziora, Derrick M., 'Gunboat Diplomacy in the Northwest Atlantic: The 1995 Canada-EU Fishing Dispute and the United Nations Agreement on Straddling and High Migratory Fish Stocks' (1996) 17 *New Journal of International Law & Business* 1132–62

Keller, Helen, Magdalena Forowicz and Lorenz Engi, *Friendly Settlements before the European Court of Human Rights: Theory and Practice* (Oxford: Oxford University Press, 2010)

Kennedy, David, *A World of Struggle: How Power, Law & Expertise Shape Global Political Economy* (Princeton, NJ: Princeton University Press, 2016)

'Challenging Expert Rule: The Politics of Global Governance' (2005) 27 *Sydney Law Review* 5–28

The Dark Side of Virtue (Princeton, NJ: Princeton University Press, 2005)

'The Mystery of Global Governance' (2008) 34 *Ohio Northern University Law Review* 827–60

Of War and Law (Princeton, NJ: Princeton University Press, 2006)

Kennedy, Duncan, 'Toward and Historical Understanding of Legal Consciousness: The Case of Classical Legal Thought in America, 1850–1940' (1980) 3 *Research in Law and Sociology* 3–24

Keohane, Robert O., 'International Relations and International Law: Two Optics' (1997) 38 *Harvard International Law Journal* 487–502

Keohane, Robert O. and David G. Victor, 'The Regime Complex for Climate Change' (2011) 9 *Perspectives on Politics* 7–23

Kingsbury, Benedict, 'International Courts: Uneven Judicialisation in Global Order', in James Crawford and Martti Koskenniemi (eds), *The Cambridge Companion to Interntional Law* (Cambridge: Cambridge University Press, 2012), pp. 203–27

Klabbers, Jan, 'The Bridge Crack'd: A Critical Look at Interdisciplinary Relations' (2009) 23 *International Relations* 119–25

'Of Round Pegs and Square Holes: International Law and the Private Sector', in Paulius Jurčys, Poul F. Kjaer and Ren Yatsunami (eds), *Regulatory Hybridization in the Transnational Sphere* (The Hague: Martinus Nijhoff, 2013)

'Two Concepts of International Organization' (2005) 2 *International Organizations Law Review* 277–94

'The Virtues of Expertise', in Monika Ambrus et al. (eds), *The Role of Experts in International and European Decision-Making Processes* (Cambridge: Cambridge University Press, 2014), 82–102

Klabbers, Jan, Anne Peters and Geir Ulfstein, *The Constitutionalization of International Law* (Oxford: Oxford University Press, 2009)

Klabbers, J. and T. Piiparinen (eds), *Normative Pluralism and International Law: Exploring Global Governance* (Cambridge: Cambridge University Press, 2013)

Klepp, Silja, 'Illegal Migration and Migrant Fatalities in Malta', paper presented at 'The Human Cost of Border Control in the Context of EU Maritime Migration Systems', Vrije Universiteit, Amsterdam, 25–27 October (2009)

Kneebone, Susan, 'The Bali Process and Global Refugee Policy in the Asia-Pacific Region' (2014) 27 *Journal of Refugee Studies* 596–618

Koh, Harold H., 'The "Haiti Paradigm" in United States Human Rights Policy' (1993–94) 103 *The Yale Law Journal* 103

'Why Do Nations Obey International Law?' (1996) 106 *Yale Law Journal* 2599–659

Koskenniemi, Martti, 'Breach of Treaty or Non-Compliance? Reflections on the Enforcement of the Montreal Protocol' (1992) 3 *Yearbook of International Environmental Law* 123–62

'Constitutionalism as Mindset: Reflections on Kantian Themes about International Law and Globalization' (2007) 8(1) *Theoretical Inquiries in Law* 9–36

'The Fate of Public International Law: Between Technique and Politics' (2007) 70 *Modern Law Review* 1–30

'Formalism, Fragmentation, Freedom: Kantian Themes in Today's International Law' (2007) 4 *No Foundations* 7–28

From Apology to Utopia: The Structure of International Legal Argument (1989; repr., Cambridge: Cambridge University Press, 2005)

'The Future of Statehood' (1991) 32 *Harvard International Law Journal* 397–410

'International Law and Hegemony: A Reconfiguration' (2004) 17 *Cambridge Review of International Affairs* 197–218

'International Legislation Today: Limits and Possibilities' (2005) 23 *Wisconsin International Law Journal* 61–92

'Law, Teleology and International Relations: An Essay in Counterdisciplinarity' (2012) 26 *International Relations* 3–34

'Miserable Comforters: International Relations as New Natural Law' (2009) 15 *European Journal of International Relations* 395–422

'The Politics of International Law' (1990) 1 *European Journal of International Law* 4–33

'The Politics of International Law – 20 Years Later' (2009) 20 *European Journal of International Law* 7–19

Koskenniemi, Martti and Päivi Leino, 'Fragmentation of International Law? Postmodern Anxieties' (2002) 15 *Leiden Journal of International Law* 553–79

Krasner, Stephen D. (ed.), *International Regimes* (Ithaca, NY: Cornell University Press, 1983)

Sovereignty: Organized Hypocrisy (Princeton, NJ: Princeton University Press, 1999)

Kratochwil, Friedrich, 'Making Sense of "International Practices"', in Emanuel Adler and Vincent Pouliot (eds), *International Practices* (Cambridge: Cambridge University Press, 2011), pp. 36–60

Rules, Norms and Decisions: On the Conditions of Practical and Legal Reasoning in International Relations and Domestic Affairs (Cambridge: Cambridge University Press, 1991)

The Status of Law in World Society: Meditations on the Role and Rule of Law (Cambridge: Cambridge University Press, 2014)

Krisch, Nico, *Beyond Constitutionalism: The Pluralist Structure of Postnational Law* (Oxford: Oxford University Press, 2010)

'International Law in Times of Hegemony: Unequal Power and the Shaping of the International Legal Order' (2005) 16 *European Journal of International Law* 369–408

Ku, Charlotte, 'Global Governance and the Changing Face of International Law', CUNS Keynote Paper (2001–2)

Kurtz, Jürgen, 'Australia's Rejection of Investor–State Arbitration: Causation, Omission and Implication' (2012) 27(1) *ICSID Review* 65–86

Lakoff, George and Mark Johnson (eds), *Metaphors We Live By*, 2nd edn (Chicago: University of Chicago Press, 2003)

Lander, Sir Stephen, 'International Intelligence Cooperation: An Inside Perspective' (2013) 17(3) *Cambridge Review of International Affairs*

Langford, Malcolm, 'Cosmopolitan Competition: The Case of International Investment', in Cecilia Bailliet and Katja Aas (eds), *Cosmpolitanism Justice and Its Discontents* (New York: Routledge, 2011), pp. 178–204

'The New Apologists: The International Court of Justice and Human Rights' (2015) 48(1) *Retfærd* 49–78

Langford, Malcolm and Daniel Behn, 'Managing Backlash: The Evolving Investment Treaty Arbitrator', (forthcoming) *European Journal of International Law*

Laudal, Tarald Berge and Øyvind Stiansen, 'Negotiating BITs with Models: The Power of Expertise', PluriCourts Research Paper No. 16–13 (2016)

Lausten, Martin Schwartz, *Jøder og kristne i Danmark: Fra middelalderen til nyere tid* (Copenhagen: Anis, 2012)

Lavopa, Federico, Lucas Barreiros and Victoria Bruno, 'How to Kill a BIT and Not Die Trying: Legal and Political Challenges of Denouncing or Renegotiating Bilateral Investment Treaties' (2013) 17 *Journal of International Economic Law* 869–91

Lawson, Rick, 'Life after Bankovic: On the Extraterritorial Application of the European Convention on Human Rights', in Fons Coomans and Menno T. Kamminga (eds), *Extraterritorial Application of Human Rights Treaties* (Antwerp: Intersentia, 2004), pp. 83–123

Leach, Philip, *Taking a Case to the European Court of Human Rights* (Oxford: Oxford University Press, 2011)

Leander, Anna, 'The Paradoxical Impunity of Private Military Companies: Authority and the Limits to Legal Accountability' (2010) 41 *Security Dialogue* 467–90

Leander, Anna and Tanja Aalberts, 'Introduction: The Co-Constitution of Legal Expertise and International Security (Symposium)' (2013) 26 *Leiden Journal of International Law* 783–92

Legomsky, Stephen H., 'Secondary Refugee Movements and the Return of Asylum Seekers to Third Countries: The Meaning of Effective Protection' (2003) 15 *International Journal of Refugee Law* 567–667

Liste, Philip, 'The Politics of (Legal) Intertextuality' (2010) 4 *International Political Sociology* 318–21

Lutterbeck, Derek, 'Migrants, Weapons and Oil: Europe and Libya after the Sanctions' (2009) 14 *Journal of North African Studies* 169–84

'Small Frontier Island: Malta and the Challenge of Irregular Migraiton' (2009) 20 *Mediterranean Quarterly* 119–41

Macneil, Ian, 'Contracts: Adjustment of Long-Term Economic Relations Under Classical, Neoclassical, and Relational Contract Law' (1977–78) 72(6) *Northwestern University Law Review* 805–902

Madsen, Mikael Rask, 'The Challenging Authority of the European Court of Human Rights' (2016) 79 *Law and Contemporary Problems* 141–78

Madsen, Mikael Rask, Henrik Palmer Olsen and Urska Sadl, 'Competing Supremacies and Clashing Institutional Rationalities: The Danish Supreme Court's Decision in the Ajos Case and the National Limits of Judicial Cooperation' (2017) 23(1–2) *European Law Journal* 140–150

Magner, Tara, 'The Less Than 'Pacific' Solution for Asylum Seekers in Australia' (2004) 16 *International Journal of Refugee Law* 53–90

Mann, Itamar, 'Dialectic of Transnationalism: Unauthorized Migration and Human Rights, 1993–2013' (2013) 54(2) *Harvard International Law Journal* 315–523

McDougal, Myres S., *Studies in World Public Order* (New Haven, CT: Yale University Press, 1960)

Meisenhelder, Thomas, 'Law as Symbolic Action: Kenneth Burke's Sociology of Law' (1981) 4 *Symbolic Interaction* 43–57.

Milanovic, Marko, *Extraterritorial Application of Human Right Treaties – Law, Principles, and Policy* (Cambridge: Cambridge University Press, 2011)

'Human Rights Treaties and Foreign Surveillance: Privacy in the Digital Age' (2015) 56(1) *Harvard International Law Journal* 81–146

Mishra, Pankaj, *Age of Anger: A History of the Present* (New York: Farrar, Straus, and Giroux, 2017)

Morano-Foadi, Sonia and Stelios Andreadakis, 'The Convergence of the European Legal System in the Treatment of Third Country Nationals in Europe: The ECJ and ECtHR Jurisprudence' (2011) 22 *European Journal of International Law* 1071–88

Moreno-Lax, Violeta and Efthymios Papastavridis (eds), *'Boat Refugees' and Migrants at Sea: A Comprehensive Approach: Integrating Maritime Security with Human Rights* (The Hague: Brill, 2016)

Morgenthau, Hans J., *Politics among Nations: The Struggle for Power and Peace*, 3rd edn (New York: Knoff, 1966)

Murphy, Cian C., 'The Dynamics of Transnational Counter-Terrorism Law: Towards a Methodology, Map, and Critique', in Federico Fabbrini and Vicki C. Jackson (eds), *Constitutionalism across Borders in the Struggle against Terrorism* (Cheltenham, UK: Edward Elgar, 2015)

Myjer, Egbert, 'Why Much of the Criticism of the European Court of Human Rights is Unfounded', in Spyridon Flogaitis, Tom Zwart and Julie Fraser (eds), *The European Court of Human Rights and Its Discontents: Turning Criticism into Strength* (Cheltenham, UK: Edward Elgar, 2013), pp. 37–53

Ninkovich, F., *The United States and Imperialism* (Malden, MA: Blackwell, 2001)

Noll, Gregor, 'The Politics of Saving Lives: Interception, Search and Rescue and the Question of Human Rights at Sea', paper presented at the Future of Asylum Policy in the European Union, Turku, 10 October (2006)

Nollkaemper, André, 'Inside or Out: Two Types of International Legal Pluralism', in Jan Klabbers and Touko Piiparinen (eds), *Normative Pluralism and*

International Law: Exploring Global Governance (Cambridge: Cambridge University Press, 2014), pp. 94–142

'The Process of Legalisation after 1989 and Its Contribution to the International Rule of Law', in James Crawford and Sarah Nouwen (eds), *Select Proceedings of the European Society of International Law* (Oxford: Hart, 2012), pp. 89–102

Obermaier, Andreas J., *The End of Territoriality? The Impact of ECJ Rulings ECJ Rulings on British, German and French Social Policy* (Aldershot, UK: Ashgate, 2009)

Onuf, Nicholas G., *World of Our Making: Rules and Rule in Social Theory and International Relations* (Columbia: University of South Carolina Press, 1989)

Oomen, Barbara M., 'A Serious Case of Strasbourg-Bashing? An Evaluation of the Debates on the Legitimacy of the European Court of Human Rights in the Netherlands' (2016) 20 *International Journal of Human Rights* 407–25

Palan, Ronen, 'Tax Havens and the Commercialization of State Sovereignty' (2002) 56 *International Organization* 151–76

Palan, Ronen, R. Murphy and C. Chavagneux, *Tax Havens – How Globalization Really Works* (Ithaca, NY: Cornell University Press, 2010)

Panke, Diana, 'Socil and Taxation Policies – Domaine Réservé Fields? Member States Non-Compliance with Sensitive European Secondary Law' (2009) 31 *European Integration* 489–509

Patterson, Dennis M., 'Law's Pragmatism: Law as Practice and Narrative', in Dennis M. Patterson (ed.), *Wittgenstein and Legal Theory* (Boulder, CO: Westview Press, 1992), pp. 85–121

Pauwelyn, Joost, 'The Rule of Law without the Rule of Lawyers? Why Investment Arbitrators Are from Mars, Trade Panelists Are from Venus' (2015) 109 *American Journal of International Law* 761–805

Peinhardt, Clint and Rachel Wellhausen, 'Withdrawing from Investment Treaties but Protecting Investment' (2016) 7(2) *Global Policy* 571–76

Phlogaitēs, Spyridōn I., Tom Zwart and Julie Fraser (eds), *The European Court of Human Rights and Its Discontents: Turning Criticism into Strength* (Cheltenham, UK: Edward Elgar, 2013)

Pierson, Paul, 'Increasing Returns, Path Dependence, and the Study of Politics' (2000) 94 *American Political Science Review* 251–67

Pitney, John J., Jr and John-Clark Levin, *Private Anti-Piracy Navies: Warships for Hire Are Changing Maritime Security* (Plymouth, UK: Lexington Books, 2013)

Posner, Eric A. and John C. Yoo, 'Judicial Independence in International Tribunals' (2005) 93 *California Law Review* 1–74

Poulsen, Lauge and Emma Aisbett, 'When the Claim Hits: Bilateral Investment Treaties and Bounded Rational Learning' (2013) 65(2) *World Politics* 273–313

Pugh, Michael, 'Drowning Not Waving: Boat People and Humanitarianism at Sea' (2004) 17 *Journal of Refugee Studies* 50–68

Purvis, Nigel, 'Critical Legal Studies in Public International Law' (1991) 32 *Harvard International Law Journal* 80–127

Rajkovic, Nikolas M., Tanja E. Aalberts and Thomas Gammeltoft-Hansen (eds), *The Power of Legality: Practices of International Law and Their Politics* (Cambridge: Cambridge University Press, 2016)

Ranganathan, Surabhi, *Strategically Created Treaty Conflicts and the Politics of International Law* (Cambridge: Cambridge University Press, 2015)

Raustiala, K., *Does the Constitution Follow the Flag? The Evolution of Territoriality in American Law* (Oxford: Oxford University Press, 2009)

Raustiala, Kal and David Victor, 'The Regime Complex for Plant Genetic Resources' (2004) 85 *International Organization* 277–309

Reus-Smit, Christian, 'Introduction', in Christian Reus-Smit (ed.), *The Politics of International Law* (Cambridge: Cambridge University Press, 2004), pp. 1–13

The Moral Purpose of the State: Culture, Social Identity, and Institutional Rationality in International Relations (Princeton, NJ: Princeton University Press, 1999)

'The Politics of International Law', in Christian Reus-Smit (ed.), *The Politics of International Law* (Cambridge: Cambridge University Press, 2004), pp. 14–44

(ed.), *The Politics of International Law* (Cambridge: Cambridge University Press, 2004)

Richardson, Jeffrey T., *The Ties That Bind: Intelligence Cooperation between the UK/USA Countries* (New York: HarperCollins, 1986)

Rijsdijk, Erna, 'The Politics of Hard Knowledge: Uncertainty, Intelligence Failures, and the "Last Minute Genocide" of Srebrenica' (2011) 37 *Review of International Studies* 2221–35

Rivers, Julian, 'Kant's Concept of International Law'(2010) 16 *Legal Theory* 229–57

Roberts, Anthea, 'Power and Persuasion in Investment Treaty Interpretation: The Dual Role of States' (2010) 104(2) *American Journal of International Law* 179–225

Rodriguez-Garavito, César, 'Beyond the Courtroom: The Impact of Judicial Activism on Socioeconomic Rights in Latin America' (2011) 89 *Texas Law Review* 1669–98

Romano, Cesare, 'International Justice and Developing Countries' (2002) 1 *The Law and Practice of International Courts and Tribunals* 539–611

Roxstrom, Erik, Mark Gibney and Terje Einarsen, 'The NATO Bombing Case (Bankovic et al. v. Belgium et al.) and the Limits of Western Human Rights Protection' (2005) 23 *Boston University International Law Journal* 56–136

Ryngaert, C., *Jurisdiction in International Law* (Oxford: Oxford University Press, 2008)

Sand, Peter H., 'Diego Garcia: British-American Legal Black Hole in the Indian Ocean?' (2009) 21 *Journal of Environmental Law* 113–37

'Whither CITES? The Evolution of a Treaty Regime in the Borderland of Trade and Environment' (1997) 8 *European Journal of International Law* 29–58

Sands, P., *Lawless World: America and the Making and Breaking of Global Rules* (London: Allen Lane, 2005)

Saroléa, Sylvie, 'From Protection of the Migrant to the Rights of the Migrant Person: Free the Migrant from His Legal Exile . . .', in Jean-Christophe Merle (ed.), *Spheres of Global Justice* (Dordrecht, Netherlands: Springer, 2013)

Sassen, Saskia, *Territory, Authority, Rights: From Medieval to Global Assemblages* (Princeton, NJ: Princeton University Press, 2006)

Schmidt, Susanne K., 'Judicial Europeanisation: The Case of Zambrano in Ireland' (2014) 37 *West European Politics* 769–85

Schneiderman, David, *Constitutionalizing Economic Globalization: Investment Rules and Democracy's Promise* (Cambridge: Cambridge University Press, 2008)

Schwebel, Stephen, 'Injunction of Arbitral Proceedings and Truncation of the Tribunal' (2003) 18(4) *International Arbitration Report* 33

Scobbie, Iain, 'Towards the Elimination of International Law: Some Radical Scepticism about Sceptical Radicalism' (1991) 61 *British Yearbook of International Law* 339–62

Scott, Shirley V., *International Law in World Politics: An Introduction* (Boulder, CO: Lynne Rienner, 2010)

Searle, John R., *The Construction of Social Reality* (New York: Free Press, 1995)

Shaffer, Gregory and Tom Ginsburg, 'The Empirical Turn in International Law' (2012) 106 *American Journal of International Law* 1–46

Shany, Yuval, *Assessing the Effectiveness of International Courts* (Oxford: Oxford University Press, 2014)

Shearer, Ivan Anthony, 'In Fear of International Law' (2005) 12 *Indiana Journal of Global Legal Studies* 345–78

Simmons, Beth, 'Bargaining over BITS, Arbitrating Awards: The Regime for Protection and Promotion of International Investment' (2014) 66 *World Politics* 12–46

Skogly, Sigrun and Mark Gibney, 'Transnational Human Rights Obligations' (2002) 24 *Human Rights Quarterly* 781–98

Slaughter, Anne-Marie, *A New World Order* (Princeton, NJ: Princeton University Press, 2004)

'Governing the Global Economy through Government Networks', in Michael Byers (ed.), *The Role of Law in International Politics: Essays in International Relations and International Law* (Oxford: Oxford University Press, 2000), pp. 177–205

Smith, Brian D., *State Responsibility and the Marine Environment: The Rules of Decision* (Oxford: Clarendon Press, 1988)

Sørensen, Georg, *Changes in Statehood: The Transformation of International Relations* (Houndmills, UK: Palgrave, 2001)

Spijkerboer, Thomas, 'Subsidiarity and "Arguability": The European Court of Human Rights' Case Law on Judicial Review in Asylum Cases' (2009) 21 *International Journal of Refugee Law* 48–74

Steiner, Henry, 'International Protection of Human Rights', in Malcolm D. Evans (ed.), *International Law*, 2nd edn (Oxford: Oxford University Press, 2006), pp. 753–82

Steyn, Johan, 'Guantanamo Bay: The Legal Black Hole' (2004) 53 *International and Comparative Law Quarterly* 1–15

Strauss, M., 'Cuba and State Responsibility for Human Rights at Guantanamo' (2013) 37 *Southern Illinois University Law Journal* 533–50

The Leasing of Guantanamo Bay (Westport, CT: Praeger, 2009)

Sullivan, Gavin and Marieke De Goede, 'Between Law and the Exception: The UN 1267 Ombudsperson as a Hybrid Model of Expertise' (2013) 26 *Leiden Journal of International Law* 833–54

Tanaka, Y., *The International Law of the Sea* (Cambridge: Cambridge University Press, 2012)

Thym, Daniel, 'Respect for Private and Family Fife under Article 8 ECHR in Immigration Cases: A Human Right to Regularize Illegal Stay?' (2008) 57 *International and Comparative Law Quarterly* 87–112

Tondini, Matteo, 'The Legality of Intercepting Boat People under Search and Rescue and Border Control Operations with Reference to Recent Italian Interventions in the Mediterranean Sea and the Ecthr Decision in the Hirsi Case' (2012) 18 *Journal of International Maritime Law* 59074

Trevisanut, Seline, 'Search and Rescue Operations in the Mediterranean: Factor of Cooperation or Conflict?' (2010) 25 *International Journal of Marine and Coastal Law* 523–42

Urry, J., *Offshoring* (Oxford: Polity, 2014)

Vagts, Detlev F., 'Hegemonic International Law' (2001) 95 *American Journal of International Law* 843–48

Veitch, Scott, *Law and Irresponsibility: On the Legitimation of Human Suffering* (Abingdon, UK: Routledge, 2007)

Vennesson, Pascal and Nikolas M. Rajkovic, 'The Transnational Politics of Warfare Accountability: Human Rights Watch versus the Israel Defense Forces' (2012) 26 *International Relations* 409–29

Venzke, Ingo, *How Interpretation Makes International Law: On Semantic Change and Normative Twists* (Oxford: Oxford University Press, 2013)

Verdirame, Guglielmo, 'A Normative Theory of Sovereignty Transfers' (2013) 49 *Stanford Journal of International Law* 371–426

The UN and Human Rights – Who Guards the Guardians? (Cambridge: Cambridge University Press, 2011)

Vicuna, Francisco Orrego, *The Changing International Law of High Seas Fisheries* (Cambridge: Cambridge University Press, 1999)

Vine, D., *Island of Shame: The Secret History of the U.S. Military Base on Diego Garcia* (Princeton, NJ: Princeton University Press, 2009)

Voon, Tanja, Andrew Mitchell and James Munro, 'Parting Ways: The Impact of Investor Rights on Mutual Termination of Investment Treaties' (2014) 29(2) *ICSID Review – Foreign Investment Law Journal* 451–73

Waelde, Thomas, '"Equality of Arms" in Investment Arbitration: Procedural Challenges', in Katia Yannaca-Small (ed.), *Arbitration under International Investment Agreements: A Guide to the Key Issues* (Oxford: Oxford University Press, 2008)

Waibel, Michael, Asha Kaushal, Kyo-Hwa Chung and Claire Balchin (eds), *The Backlash against Investment Arbitration: Perceptions and Reality* (The Hague: Kluwer Law, 2010)

Weiler, J. H. H. et al., 'Special Issue: Changing Paradigms in International Law' (2009) 20 *European Journal of International Law* 21–109

Welsh, Nancy, Andrea Kupfer Schneider and Kathryn Rimpfel, 'Using the Theories of Exit Voice, Loyalty, and Procedural Justice to Reconceptualize Brazil's Rejection of Bilateral Investment Treaties' (2014) 45 *Washington Universtity Journal of Law and Policy* 105–43

Wendt, Alexander, *A Social Theory of International Politics* (Cambridge: Cambridge University Press, 1999)

Werksman, Jacob, 'Compliance and Transition: Russia's Non-Compliance Tests the Ozone Regime' (1996) 56 *Zeitschrift für ausländisches öffentliches Recht und Völkerrecht* 750–73

Werner, Wouter G., 'State Sovereignty and International Legal Discourse', in Ige F. Dekker and Wouter G. Werner (eds), *Governance and International Legal Theory* (Leiden: Martinus Nijhoff, 2004), pp. 125–157

'The Curious Career of Lawfare' (2010) 43 *Case Western Reserve Journal of International Law* 61–72

'The Politics of Expertise: Applying Paradoxes of Scientific Expertise to International Law', in Monika Ambrus, Karin Arts, Ellen Hey and Helen Raulus (eds), *The Role of Experts in International and European Decision-Making Processes: Advisors, Decision Makers or Irrelevant Actors?* (Cambridge: Cambridge University Press, 2014), pp. 44–62

'The Use of Law in International Political Sociology' (2010) 4 *International Political Sociology* 304–7

Whiteside, Kerry H., *Precautionary Politics: Principle and Practice in Confronting Environmental Risk* (Cambridge, MA: MIT Press, 2006)

Wilde, Ralph, 'Legal "Black Hole"? Extraterritorial State Action and International Treaty Law on Civil and Political Rights' (2005) 26 *Michigan Journal of International Law* 739–806

Wittgenstein, Ludwig J. J., *Philosophical Investigations*, 3rd edn (London: Prentice Hall, 1958)

Young, Margaret A. (ed.), *Regime Interaction in International Law: Facing Fragmentation* (Cambridge: Cambridge University Press, 2012)

Zimmermann, W., *First Great Triumph: How Five Americans Made Their Country a World Power* (New York: Farrar, Straus and Giroux, 2002)

Zolberg, Aristide, 'Beyond the Crisis', in Peter M. Benda and Aristide Zolberg (eds), *Global Migrants, Global Refugees* (New York: Berghahn Books, 2001), pp. 1–19

'Matters of State', in Charles Hirschman, Philip Kasinitz and Josh DeWind (eds), *The Handbook on International Immigration* (New York: Russell Sage Foundation, 1999), pp. 71–93

INDEX

abandonment of sovereign territory, 49, 50–54, 69
Abbott, Kenneth, 161
absolute opponents, 75
accountability, 66
adjudication, 162, 163–64, 173–79
Aeroport Belbek LLC and Mr. Igor Valerievich Kolomoisky v. The Russian Federation, 87
Afghanistan Sigint Coalition (AFSC), 140
Agenda 21 (1992), 169
Agreement for the Establishment of the General Fisheries Commission for the Mediterranean, 172–73
Agreement on the Application of Sanitary and Phytosanitary Measures (SPS Agreement), 160, 162, 179–83
Agreement on Trade-Related Aspects of Intellectual Property Rights (TRIPS), 13
Al Jedda case, 67
Al Warraq v. Indonesia, 91–92
Albania, 60–61, 91
Albright, Madeline, 14, 19, 36
Algeria, 141
Al-Nashiri v. Poland, 61–63, 66
Al-Saadoon and Mufdhi v. United Kingdom, 65, 199
Al-Skeini and Others v. United Kingdom, 64, 65, 201
Amnesty International, 124
anticipatory measures, 104, 115–19
AQAP terrorist targets, 147
arbitral awards, 95–98
arbitrations. *See* investment treaty arbitrations (ITAs)
Argentina, 78, 80–81, 87, 96, 99
asylum seekers, 113, 118, 198, 203, 212
Australia, 84, 86, 99, 137, 202
Australian High Court, 203
Austria, 141
Austro-German Customs Union Case (Austria vs. Germany), 38

Bahaddar v. the Netherlands, 114
Bank Century, 91–92
Bankovic case, 201
Battle of the Sexes, 33
Becchetti, Francesco, 91
Behrami case, 66
Belgium, 141
Belgium-Luxembourg Economic Union, 80–81
Bevin, Ernest, 139
bilateral investment treaties (BITs)
  2004 model US BIT, 85
  expansion of, 2
  model, 101
  network of, 70
  renegotiation of, 83–84
  termination of, 78, 80–81
boat migrants, 188–89, 192–94, 198–200, 201, 202, 204, 205
Bolivia, 78, 80–81, 86, 90, 99
Border Timbers v. Zimbabwe and Von Pezold v. Zimbabwe, 89–90
Boumedienne v. Bush, 51
Bowker, D., 50
Bozbey v. Turkmenistan, 93
Brazil, 80–81, 86

Brexit, 3
British Government Code and Cipher School, 138
British Indian Ocean Territory, 55
British Indian Ocean Territory Order of 1965, 55
Brussel Court, 4
Bulgaria, 82, 86
Bundesnachrichtendienst, 142–45
Bush, George W., administration of, 42, 50, 139, 151

Canada, 80–81, 83, 85–86, 137, 178
Caratube v. Kazakhstan (Caratube I), 90–91
Caratube v. Kazakhstan (Caratube II), 90–91
carrier sanctions, 12–13, 18
categoriaal beschermingsbeleid, 118
Cat's Eye secret prison (Thailand), 59–60
Central Intelligence Agency (CIA), 148
  rendition program, 11
  secret prisons, 47, 59, 61–63, 64, 69
Chagos Agalega Ltd., 56–57
Chagos Archipelago, 49, 54–55
Changing Structure of International Law, The (Friedmann), 1
Chevron v. Ecuador (Chevron I), 95
Chevron v. Ecuador (Chevron II), 95
Chicken Game, 33
Chile, 80–81
China, 80–81, 82, 85–86
China-Lao PDR BIT, 94–95
Churchill Mining and Planet Mining v. Indonesia, 92
Clapper, James, 147
climate change, 175, 177
Climategate, 184
Clinton, Hillary, 132
Codex Alimentarius Commission, 183, 184–85
Colombia, 86
Colonial Boundaries Act 1895, 55
Commissioner of BIOT, 56, 58
compliance
  behavioural, 217
  costs of, 75
  in environmental regimes, 173–79
  with international law, 34
  measurement of, 33, 113
  non-compliance, 96
  semi-compliance, 41, 212
  short-term, 123–24
compliers, 75
Comprehensive Economic and Trade Agreement (CETA), 85–86
Concept of Law, The (Hart), 162
conceptual orientation, 209–10
Conference of the Parties, 172
constitutive rules, 38
constructivism, 104
Convention on Biological Diversity (CBD), 13
Convention on Future Multilateral Cooperation in North-East Atlantic Fisheries, 172–73
Convention on International Trade in Endangered Species (CITES), 172
Convention on the Conservation and Management of Fisheries Resources in the South East Atlantic Ocean, 172–73
Convention on the Conservation of Antarctic Marine Living Resources, 172–73
Convention on the High Seas (1958), 190
Cook, Robert, 14
Corfu Channel Case (United Kingdom/Albania), 28, 60–61, 167, 168, 174
counterterrorism, 151
Court of Justice of the EU (CJEU), 7, 104, 105–10, 116–17, 122
critical legal studies, 28–29, 36
Croatia, 141
Cuba, 51, 53, 80–81
Customs Union case, 38
Czech Republic, 81, 82, 84, 86, 99, 141

Danish Supreme Court, 8
De Renzis, Mauro, 91
Deeks, Ashley, 153

Denmark, 18, 80–81, 141
detention centers, 46
  Guantanamo Bay, 11, 45, 47, 50–51, 54, 69, 130–31
  Poland, 60, 61–63, 64, 69
  Thailand, 59–60
Detention Site Green (Thailand), 59–60
Diego Garcia island, 45, 47, 54–59, 69
disaggregated sovereignty, 151–52, 153–54
disembarkation, 192
Dispute Settlement Body (DSB), 180
domaine réservé, 106, 120
domestic accountability, 155
domestic supremacy, 26–27
Dominican Republic, 80–81
drug smuggling, 12
dual accountability model, 155
Dublin Regulation, 108
Dunoff, Jeffrey, 215
Dutch Aliens Law of 2000, 118

EC-Biotech, 180–81, 183
EC-Hormones, 163, 164, 181
Ecuador, 78, 80–81, 86, 99
Ecuador v. US, 95
Egypt, 82, 86, 124
Elgafaji v. Staatssecretaris van Justitie, 112, 118
El-Masri v. the Former Yugoslav Republic of Macedonia, 63–64
Emmerson, Ben, 136
empirical reorientation, 210–12
End of History (Fukuyama), 140–41
Energy Charter Treaty, 3
enforcement networks, 152
English school, 28–29
environmental law. *See* international environmental law
environmental regimes, 171–73. *See also* international environmental law
  adjudication, 173–79
  compliance, 173–79
  scientific expertise in, 171–73
  standard-setting bodies, 183–86
environmental summits, 169
equality of arms, 88, 92
Ethiopia, 141
EU Charter of Fundamental Rights, 105, 109, 111
EU Qualifications Directive, 118
European Commission (EC), 97
European Convention on Human Rights (ECHR), 4, 62, 103, 135
  Article 35, 113–14
  Article 37, 114
  Protocol 11 to, 106
European Court of Human Rights (ECtHR), 3, 7, 61–63, 64, 65, 66, 103, 104, 105–10, 113, 116, 122–23, 125, 199, 201
European new legal realism, 214, 217
European Union, 86
European Union (EU), 98
Everest Estate LLC and others v. The Russian Federation, 87
exceptionalism, 42
expertise
  beyond Judiciary's capacity, 16
  economic, 167
  in environmental regimes, 184–85
  extra-legal, 15–16, 158–59
  as legitimization and excuse, 161
  linguistic, 139
  politics of, 15
  sovereign, 171–73
  technical and scientific, 15, 152, 161, 167, 171–73, 180, 183, 184–85
external sovereignty, 26–27
extralegal deferral, 43, 163
extraterritorial zones, 45
  formation of, 47–48, 69, 212
    abandonment of sovereign territory, 49, 50–54, 69
    construction, 49, 54–59, 69
    denial, 49, 59–65, 69
  irresponsibility and, 67–69
  overview, 46–49
  responsibility of state partners in, 65–67
extraterritorialization, 47, 108

Finland, 80–81, 82, 141
Fischer-Locano, Andreas, 159–60
fisheries commissions, 172–73

Fisheries Jurisdiction Case (Spain/Canada), 174
Five Eyes framework, 137–38, 140, 149, 152
Foreign Affairs Directorate (FAD), 154
Foreign Intelligence Surveillance Act of 1978, 134
Foresti v. South Africa, 84
forum shopping, 163–64
Fourth Amendment, 149, 150
FRA (Sweden's sigint intelligence agency), 145
fragmentation, 163
France, 80–81, 140, 141
free trade, 163–64
free trade agreements (FTAs), 70
Free Trade Commission (FTC), 94
Friedmann, Wolfgang, 1, 208
Fukuyama, Francis, 140–41
Future We Want, The, 169

G-10 Privacy Law, 143
Gabcíkovo-Nagymaros Project Case, 174
game metaphor
  rational choice game theory, 32–34
  role of international law, 38–39
  Wittgensteinian notion of language games, 32, 34–37
game theory, 32
Gebremedhin v. France, 109, 116
Gehring, Thomas, 172
General Communications Headquarters (UK), 136–37, 142, 146, 154
Germany, 80–81, 82, 86, 101, 141, 143, 154
global mass surveillance, 129–36, 157
  aims of, 133–34
  bilateralism, 140–50
  collection of metadata in, 134
  definition of, 133
  disaggregated law of, 150–53
  international law and, 135–37
  "law against law," 129–31, 153–56
  leaked documents on, 130–31
  limitations on data use under US domestic law, 149
  of non-American citizens outside of US, 135
  NSA's bilateral partnership with, 142
    Germany, 142–45
    Israel, 148–50
    Saudi Arabia, 146–48
    Sweden, 145–46
  privacy violations, 133
  surveillance charter, 136–40
  threats and, 151
  US domestic law and, 134–35
globalization, 6
Goldsmith, Jack, 32, 33
Greece, 83, 125, 141
Grotius, Hugo, 3, 190–91
Grundgesetz, 143
Gruszczynski, Lucaz, 181–82
Guantanamo Bay, 47, 69
  abandonment of sovereign territory in, 50–54
  American national security policy and, 130–31
  commercialization of sovereignty in, 11
  history, 45, 51
  two identities of, 51
  US lease in, 51
Guatemala, 80–81, 86, 97
Gulf Cooperation Council (GCC), 147
Gulf War of 1991, 147

Hadley, Stephen, 151
Hart, H. L. A., 10–13, 35, 162
Hayden, Michael, 134
Helfer, Laurence R., 14
Henkin, Louis, 17
Herman, Michael, 141
high seas, 46, 190, 194
high-value detainees, 62
Hirsi Jamaa and Others v. Italy, 108, 110–14, 123–24, 125–26, 198–200, 202
Holmes, Oliver Wendell, 19
Honduras, 80–81
Hormones case, 163
Horn, Henrik, 181
Hourani, Devincci, 90–91
Howse, Robert, 181

human rights, 163–64, 191
human rights courts, 3
humint asset (human source), 147
Hungary, 141
Hurrell, Andrew, 218
Husayn (Abu Zubaydah) v. Poland, 48, 60–64, 66
Hussun and others v. Italy, 113–14
hybrid tactics, 81–84
Hydro v. Albania, 91

ICSID Convention (Washington Convention), 79–80
  Article 53, 96
  direct enforceability of awards under, 96
  termination of, 84–85
  withdrawal from, 78
IIAs. *See* international investment agreements (IIAs)
Ilascu and Others v. Moldova and Russia, 62, 63
Imran v. Minister van Buitenlandse Zaken, 117, 119
indeterminacy, 35, 36, 40, 68–69
India, 81, 85–86, 141
Indonesia, 81, 86, 91–92, 99, 202, 203–04
instrumentalism, 27, 32, 38, 40, 49, 54, 161
intelligence sharing, 152
Intergovernmental Panel on Climate Change (IPCC), 184–85
internal sovereignty, 26–27
International Centre for Settlement of Investment Disputes (ICSID), 97–98
International Convention for the Safety of Life at Sea, 191–92
International Convention on Maritime Search and Rescue, 191–92
International Corporation for Assigned Names and Numbers, 15
International Court of Justice (ICJ), 3, 18, 60–61, 137, 174
International Covenant on Civil and Political Rights (ICCPR), 135, 136
International Criminal Tribunal for Rwanda (ICTR), 3
International Criminal Tribunal for the Former Yugoslavia (ICTY), 3
international environmental law, 158–87
  adjudication and, 163–64
  delegation in, 163
  development of, 159–60, 211
  environmental regimes, 170–79
    adjudication, 173–79
    compliance, 173–79
    scientific expertise in, 171–73
  environmental summits, 169–70
  extra-legal deferral in, 164–66
  forum-shopping, 163–64
  fragmentation in, 163
  inefficiency and, 160
  legalization in, 161–63, 167, 179–83
  managerialism and, 159–60
  obligation in, 163
  overview, 158–61
  precision in, 163
  SPS Agreement, 184
  standard-setting bodies, 183–86
  state responsibility and, 167–69
  trajectory of, 166–70
international investment agreements (IIAs), 86, 101
  balanced, 84–85
  legitimacy concerns in, 100
  mandatory ISDS provisions in, 101
  as one-sided agreements, 83–84
  renewal of, 79
  rights granted to forein investors, 71, 72
  stickiness of, 80, 99, 100
  termination of, 79–80
  treaty protections fro foreign investors, 80
international investment law, 41, 70–102
  legitimacy crisis, 71
  reasserting sovereign control over, 72–73
  strategies and tactics by states, 73–76
    as both principals and litigants, 74

functions of, 75–76
as litigants, 75
as principals, 74–75, 76–86
scope and intensity of, 74
symbolic effects of, 76
international judicial institutions, 2–3
international law, 6–8
in twentieth century, 1
expansion of treaty law, 2
increasing role of international legal institutions, 4–5
international judicial institutions, 2–3
multiplication of actors/subjects, 1–2
political and judicial interdependence, 3–4
challenges to
gaps and inefficiencies, 6
increasing role of international legal institutions, 4–5
loss of internal coherence, 6–7
political backlash, 7–8
of co-existence to co-operation, 1
decentralised structure of, 6–7
implications of, 17–21
interdisciplinary agenda, 217
international relations and, 46
political-legal practices in, 9–16
extralegal deferral, 15–16
international cooperation to circumvent legal obligations, 11–12
interpretive framing, 14–15
judicial forum shopping, 14
jurisdiction shopping, 11
outsourcing of governmental functions to private actors, 12–13
regime or treaty shopping, 13–14
politics of, 36
post-Second World War, 1
practice of, 214–15
search and rescue as geopolitics of, 188–207
as social practice, 218
sovereignty game and, 37–41
International Law Commission (ILC), 167–69
international legal process, 28–29
international legal theory, 28–29, 35
international relations (IR), 208
compliance and, 34
interdisciplinary agenda, 217
language game metaphor and, 35
linguistic turn, 35
practice of, 214–15
vs. international law, 27
international spaces, 46
interpretative framing, 14–15, 18, 40, 110, 123
interterritoriality, 48
investment protection, 163–64
investment treaty arbitrations (ITAs), 72, 73
domestic judicial proceedings, 89
equality of arms, 88
renegotiation, 83
states as litigants in, 86–98
success ratios, 99–100
investor-state dispute settlement (ISDS), 72, 84, 85, 86, 100
Iran, 148
Iraq, 68–69
Iraq War of 2003, 19
irresponsibility, 39, 41, 68–69, 210
Island of Palmas Case (Netherlands/ United States), 38–39, 167, 168, 174
Israel, 141, 148–50
Issa and Others v. Turkey, 65, 68
Italba Corporation v. Oriental Republic of Uruguay, 92
Italy, 80–81, 86, 123–24, 141, 195, 199

Jaloud v. The Netherlands, 65–66, 68
Japan, 141
Johns, Fleur, 210
Jordan, 141
judicial activism, 7
judicial forum shopping, 14
jurisdiction shopping, 11, 47, 201–04

K and A case, 117
Kazakhstan, 83, 90–91, 97, 99

Kennedy, David, 5
Keohane, Robert, 161
Klabbers, Jan, 166
knowledge societies, 186
Korea, 83, 84, 141
Koskenniemi, Martti, 32, 34, 66–67, 68, 159–60
Kosovo, 14, 19, 36
Kratochwil, Friedrich, 32
Kwasniewski, Aleksander, 60
Kyoto Protocol, 175, 177–78
Kyrgyzstan, 96, 99

Lander, Stephen, 139
language game metaphor, 32, 34–37
law against law, 153–56
Law of the Sea, 15
legal intertextuality, 213
legal reasoning, 42
legalization, 28–29
  conceptual orientation, 209–10
  empirical reorientation, 210–12
  era of, 5
  interdisciplinary agenda, 216
  in international environmental law, 161–63, 167, 179–83
  methodological reorientation, 214–16
  politicization and, 209–10
  research agenda for, 212–14
  strategies, 213–14
Libya, 97, 199, 201, 203–04
López Burgos v. Uruguay, 65
Lustre, 140

Macau, 94–95
Macedonia, 141
Maduro, Miguel (Advocate General), 113
Malta, 195, 197
managerialism, 159–60
manoeuvrability, 10–13, 14, 15, 28, 38, 41–43, 104, 115, 119, 158–59, 161, 194, 200
Mare Liberum, 190–94, 205
Mare Nostrum, 124
marine protected areas (MPAs), 58
Maroni, Robert, 125
mass surveillance, 133–36
  aims of, 133–34
  bilateralism, 140–50
  collection of metadata in, 134
  definition of, 133
  international law and, 136–37
  "law against law," 129–31, 153–56
  leaked documents on, 130–31
  limitations on data use under U.S. domestic law, 149
  of non-American citizens outside of US, 135
  NSA's bilateral partnership with, 142
    Germany, 142–45
    Israel, 148–50
    Saudi Arabia, 146–48
    Sweden, 145–46
  surveillance charter, 136–40
  US domestic law and, 134–35
Mauritius, 55, 56, 57–58
Medvedyev and Others v. France, 65, 199
memorandums of understanding, 41, 141, 152, 211
Merkel, Angela, 144
metadata, collection of, 134
methodological reorientation, 214–16
Mexico, 85–86, 97
Micula v. Romania, 97–98
migrant rights, 103–28
  anticipatory measures, 115–19
  CJEU and, 105–10
  ECtHR and, 105–10
  international cooperation and, 119–23
  legal arguments, 110–15
  overview, 103–05
  peer mobilization and, 119–23
  post-judgment positioning, 123–26
migration, 12–13, 104, 106, 108, 198, 212
  boat migrants, 192–93, 194
  cases, 114, 121, 122–23, 212
  control of, 12–13, 108, 124, 194, 195, 196–97, 198, 199, 211
  law, 110
  laws, 107
  marketization of management of, 201–04

non-refoulement principle and, 193–94
policies on, 106
post-judgment positioning and, 123–26
privatization of governmental functions in, 12–13, 108
refugees and, 192–93
search and rescue operations, 196–97
Milanovic, Marko, 47
Minister van Buitenlandse Zaken v. K and A, 117
Minister voor Immigratie en Asiel v. X, Y, and Z, 111, 117–18
Montego Bay Convention, 199
Montréal Protocol on Substances, 174, 176
Moravcsik, Andrew, 161
Morgenthau, Hans, 27, 28, 208
Morocco, 82, 86
Mossad, 148
Moulinie & Co. Ltd., 56–57
MOX Plant Case, 174
M.S.S. v. Belgium and Greece, 108–09, 114, 120, 125
multilateral treaties, 2

N.A. v. the United Kingdom, 107, 112, 114
National Security Agency (NSA), 154
Bundesnachrichtendienst, partnership with, 142–45
GCHQ, partnership with, 142
leaked documents, 133
partnerships with foreign governments, 142, 154
Germany, 142–45
Israel, 148–50
Saudi Arabia, 146–48
Sweden, 145–46
surveillance program, 134–35, 136–37
Nationality Decrees in Tunis and Morocco (Britain v. France), 39
Nauru, 202
Netherlands, 80–81, 86, 141
networks of networks, 152
New Haven school, 28–29
New World Order, 151
New Zealand, 137
Nicaragua, 68, 80–81
non-refoulement principle, 107, 110, 112, 192, 193–94, 197–98
North American Free Trade Agreement (NAFTA), 3, 14, 94
North Atlantic Treaty Organization (NATO), 137
North-East Atlantic Fisheries Convention, 172–73
Northwest Atlantic Fisheries Convention, 172–73
Norway, 86, 141
N.S./M.E., 111, 112, 113, 121, 122
Nuclear Test Cases (Australia/France; New Zealand/France), 173–79

offshoring, 17, 50, 198, 203
outsourcing, 12–13, 17, 108, 149, 154

Pacific Solution, 202
Pad and Others v. Turkey, 201
Pakistan, 101, 141
Paposhvili v. Belgium, 115
Papua New Guinea, 202, 203
Paraguay, 80–81
Paris Agreement, 8, 158, 177
partial exit, 78–81
Passenger Act 1902 (United States), 18
peer mobilization, 104, 119–23, 212
Permanent Court of Arbitration (PCA), 3
Permanent Court of International Justice (PCIJ), 39
Peru, 80–81
Pillay, Navi, 135, 136–37, 154
Pinto de Albuquerque, Paulo, 115
PJSC CB PrivatBank and Finance Company Finilon LLC v. The Russian Federation, 87
Platt Amendnment, 53
Poland, 86, 141
CIA detention center in, 60, 61–63, 64, 69
political-legal strategies, 12–13, 15–16, 213–14

politics of international law, 9–16, 36, 41, 211, 218–19
  international cooperation to circumvent legal obligations, 11–12
  interpretive framing, 14–15
  jurisdiction shopping in, 11, 201–04
  outsourcing and, 12–13
  politics of interpretation and, 194–97
  regime or treaty shopping, 13–14
  regime shopping in, 197–201
  search and rescue in, 188–207
Posner, Eric, 32, 33
post-judgment positioning, 104, 118, 123–26
precautionary principle, 42
principled opponents, 75, 99
Prisoner's Dilemma, 33
Pulp Mills on the River Uruguay case, 164, 174

Quantum collection program, 146
Quiborax S.A. and Non-Metallic Minerals S.A. v. Plurinational State of Bolivia, 90

Ramzy v. the Netherlands, 120, 121–22
Rasul v. Bush, 51
rational choice game theory, 32–34, 100–01
recognition rules, 38, 162
Refugee Convention (1951), 4, 112, 193, 197–98, 203–04
regime complexity, 13–14
regime shopping, 13–14, 111, 112, 197–201
regime theory, 28–29
reluctant compliers, 75, 99
remedial rights, 72
Resolution 1441, 19
responsibility, 49, 60–61, 65
  enactment of, 62
  establishment of, 20
  evading, 65, 68–69
  extralegal, 15–16
  extraterritorial, 201
  freedom and, 38–39
  in the high seas, 194
  for human rights, 66, 200
  jurisdictional, 68–69
  minimum legal, 51
  over asylum seekers, 111
  over boat migrants, 198–200
  for prison atrocities, 65
  for search and rescue, 195–97
  sovereignity and, 39, 41, 47, 49, 68–69
  state, 12–13, 19, 63–64, 108, 160, 167–69
  territorial obligations and, 67
Responsibility to Protect paradigm, 39
Rice, Condoleezza, 54
Right to Privacy in the Digital Age, The (Pillay), 135
Rio + 20 (2012), 169
risk management, 26–27, 42, 171
Romania, 80–81, 82, 83, 86, 97–98, 141
Ruffing, Eva, 172
Russia, 86, 96, 99, 177
Russia-Ukraine BIT, 87

Safety of Life at Sea Convention (1974), 194–96, 204, 205
Salah Sheekh v. the Netherlands, 107, 114, 116
sanitary and phytosanitary (SPS) measures, 160, 162, 179–83
Sanum Investments v. Lao PDR, 94–95
Saudi Arabia, 141, 146–48
search and rescue, 188–207
  accountability mechanisms, 195
  of boat migrants, 198–200
  disembarkation and, 192
  division of responsibilities in, 195–96
  international agreement on, 197
  jurisdiction shopping in, 201–04
  law and politics of, 190–94, 204–06
  law of the sea and, 196–97, 198
  obligation of states in, 196
  overview, 188–89
  politics of interpretation in, 194–97
  refugee flows and, 192–93
  regime shopping in, 197–201
  return to country of origin, 192
  third-party profit motive in, 204
Search and Rescue Convention (1979), 194–96

secondary rules, 162
September 11 attacks (2001), 139
Sharpston, Eleanor (Advocate General), 113, 117
shipriders, 12
Shirley McCarthy v. Secretary of State for the Home Department, 111
Sigint National Unit (ISNU, Unit 8200) (Israel), 148–49
Sigint Seniors Europe (SSEUR), 140
Sigint Seniors Pacific (SSPAC), 140
signals intelligence (signit), 129, 137
Singapore, 94–95, 141
S.J. v. Belgium, 109, 114, 115, 119
Slaughter, Anne-Marie, 131–32, 151, 152–54, 155, 161
Slovakia, 82, 83, 86
Snidal, Duncan, 161
Snowden, Edward, 129, 133, 149, 154
soft law, 10–13, 14–15, 26–27, 41, 130–31, 137, 211
South Africa, 81, 84, 86, 99
South China Sea Arbitration, 164, 174
Southern Bluefin Tuna Cases, 174
sovereignty
  abandonment of sovereign territory, 49
  external, 26–27
  formal categories of, 47
  internal, 26–27
  international law and, 38
  rights of other states and, 38–39
sovereignty games, 30–32
  elements of, 38
  game metaphors, 32–37
    rational choice game theory, 32–34
    Wittgensteinian notion of language games, 32, 34–37
  international law and, 37–41
  meaning in use, 40
  moves, 31–32, 38
  players, 31, 38
  rules, 31, 38, 39
  strategies in, 40
Soviet Union, 177
Spain, 80–81, 141
Spanish-American War of 1898, 51
Special Operations division, 148
Special Rapporteur on the Right to Privacy, 136
SPS Agreement, 160, 162, 179–83
  Dispute Settlement Body, 180
  legal interpretations of, 182–83
  panels, 181–82
standard-setting bodies (SSBs), 183–86
Stare Kiejkuty village, Poland, 45, 47
states
  as both principals and litigants, 75
  as litigants, 75, 86–98
    criminal proceedings, 89–93
    dual role, 94–95
    refusing to enforce/satisfy arbitral awards, 95–98
  as the original masters of treaty, 103
  as principals, 74–75, 76–86
    hybrid tactics, 81–84
    partial exit, 78–81
    systemic voice, 84–86
  strategies and tactics by, 73–76
Stockholm Action Plan for the Human Environment (1972), 169
Stockholm Convention on Persistent Organic Pollutants, 171
Strasbourg Court, 4, 107, 114, 115
strategies
  in European courts, 110–15
  game metaphors and, 32–37
  in international environmental law
    engagement and avoidance, 161–63
    extra-legal deferral, 164–66
    forum shopping, 163–64
  in international investment law, 73–76
    abuse of dual role of states, 94–95
    as both principals and litigants, 74
    criminal proceedings, 89–93
    functions of, 75–76
    hybrid tactics, 81–84
    as litigants, 75
    non-enforcement of arbitral awards, 95–98
    partial exit, 78–81
    as principals, 74–75, 76–86
    scope and intensity of, 74

strategies (*cont.*)
symbolic effects of, 76
systemic voice, 84–86
in legalization, 213–14
political-legal, 12–13, 15–16, 191–92, 213–14, 218–19
international cooperation to circumvent legal obligations, 11–12
interpretative framing, 14–15, 18
judicial forum shopping, 14
jurisdiction shopping, 11
outsourcing of governmental functions, 12–13
regime or treaty shopping, 13–14
role of, 36–37
in sovereignty games, 40
treaty conflicts/rambling as, 213
Straw, Jack, 54
Sufi and Elmi v. the United Kingdom, 107, 112, 127
survival clauses, 80
Sweden, 80–81, 141, 145–46, 154
Switzerland, 80–81

Taiwan, 141
Tarakhel v. Switzerland, 109, 121, 123–24
Targeted Killings case, 16
tax breaks, 154
terrorism, 132–33
Terrorist Financing Targeting Center, 147
Teubner, Gunther, 159–60
Thailand, 96, 99, 141
CIA detention center in, 59–60
third-party interventions (TPIs), 121
threats, 151
Tier B countries, 141
Trail Smelter Arbitration (United States/Canada), 168
transnational accountability, 155
Trans-Pacific Partnership Agreement (TPPA), 8, 9
treaty law, expansion of, 2
Treaty of Amsterdam, 107
Treaty on the Functioning of European Union (TFEU), 106
treaty shopping, 111, 112, 213
Trump, Donald, 147
Tunisia, 124, 141, 200
Turkey, 83, 86, 141
Turkmenistan, 93

UKUSA Agreement, 137, 138–39, 151–52
United Arab Emirates, 141
United Kingdom, 86
Diego Garcia's sovereign-jurisdictional status and, 54–59
sanctions regime in Iraq, 68–69
United Nations Charter, 31, 137, 151–52
United Nations Conference on Trade and Development (UNCTAD), 101
United Nations Convention on the Law of the Sea (UNCLOS), 3, 191–92
United Nations Declaration on Territorial Asylum, 191
United Nations Human Rights Committee (UNHRC), 93
United Nations Human Rights Council, 136
United Nations Security Council, 42
United Nations Treaty Collection, 2
US, 80–81, 86
2004 model US BIT, 85
carrier sanctions, 18
detention centers, 46
Guantanamo Bay, 11, 45, 47, 50–51, 54, 69, 130–31
Poland, 60, 61–63, 64, 69
Thailand, 59–60
Diego Garcia military base, 47, 54–55, 57, 69
extraterritorial zones, 45
lease of British Indian Ocean Territory to, 49, 55, 57
mass surveillance. *See* mass surveillance
NSA. *See* National Security Agency (NSA)
withdrawal from TPPA, 8, 9
US Justice Department, 52
US Senate Intelligence Committee, 59

Uruguay, 80–81, 92
USA Freedom Act, 135
USA PATRIOT Act, 134

Veitch, Scott, 68–69, 218–19
Venezuela, 78, 80–81, 87, 96
Vienna Convention on the Law of Treaties (VCLT), 137
Vines, Vanee, 140
V.M. and others v. Belgium, 113–14

War Department, 138
war on terror, 139
Washington Convention. *See* ICSID Convention
Whaling in the Atlantic (Australia v. Japan), 174
Wittgenstein, Ludwig, 34
World Health Organization (WHO), 13
World Trade Organization (WTO), 3, 14, 160

X, Y, and Z, 111, 117–18
Xhavara and fifteen v. Italy and Albania, 199

Zambrano v. Office national de l'emploi (ONEm), 111, 113, 116, 122
Zimbabwe, 89–90, 96, 99
zoning, 46